PAPERS

of the

NEW WORLD ARCHAEOLOGICAL FOUNDATION

NUMBER FORTY

Mesoamerican Communication Routes and Cultural Contacts

Edited by

THOMAS A. LEE, JR., AND CARLOS NAVARRETE

T0338146

NEW WORLD ARCHAEOLOGICAL FOUNDATION

BRIGHAM YOUNG UNIVERSITY

PROVO, UTAH

1978

GARETH W. LOWE
DIRECTOR

SUSANNA M. EKHOLM
EDITOR

Printed by
BRIGHAM YOUNG UNIVERSITY PRINTING SERVICES
PROVO, UTAH

PREFACE

This report is the result of an idea born in the early-morning hours of one of many discussions between Carlos Navarrete and me in the fall of 1971. For several years prior to that date both of us had been interested in routes of communication in Chiapas and the thought occurred to us that perhaps it was time to organize our information and compare it to what was known for Mesoamerica in general. In order to carry this out we decided to organize a symposium for the 40th International Congress of Americanists to be held in Rome in September of 1972.

Since we desired a general coverage of Mesoamerica and since the number of symposium participants had to be limited to be practical and manageable, it was necessary to divide the area into several large geographical sub-divisions. We established nine sub-divisions partly arbitrarily and partly based on several other considerations, the most important of which was the presence of some integrating geographical or topographical features as well as some cultural unity. A not unimportant factor, however, was the availability of someone knowledgeable about a given area. The result was a higher representation for southern Mesoamerica than for northern Mesoamerica.

It was hoped that the areal papers would serve as a framework of routes and route systems from which we could discuss their role in the development of Mesoamerican cultural history.

Besides the papers on the nine geographical sub-divisions we thought that it would be profitable to invite other more specialized papers on topics involving specific aspects of Mesoamerican environment, culture, and history which generated or structured communications.

For a variety of reasons it was impossible for all individuals who prepared papers to attend the International Congress of Americanists. Ten did, however, participating in Symposium 4: Routes of Communication and Cultural Contact in Mesoamerica, which was well attended throughout the day. Those participating in Rome included Litvak King, Feldman, Lee, Edwards, Bittmann, Sullivan, Davies, Rathje, and Hammond. Barbara Price valiantly accepted my very late plea to serve as the Discussant of the symposium.

Due to time and publication space limitations it was impossible to present in Rome the complete versions of many papers. The shorter symposium-version of most of these papers will be published in the *Acts and Memoirs* of the Congress.

Since our original idea was to present a detailed view of as many Mesoamerican communication routes as possible, it was decided among members of the Symposium that we would try to publish a separate volume on the symposium theme, but which would include all symposium papers in their original form, all papers prepared for the symposium but which were not read there, and several new papers pertinent to the theme which came to our attention from discussion before, during, and after the symposium.

The contributions of Piña Chan and Navarrete have been translated from the Spanish.

The New World Archaeological Foundation, through the good offices of its Director, Gareth W. Lowe, has responded to a call for editorial and publishing funds and we are in his debt for accepting this volume in the Foundation's series.

I would also like to acknowledge the encouragement and support I received from Carlos Navarrete throughout the long planning of the symposium and final volume. Through circumstances beyond his control he was prevented from participating in the debut of many of his ideas in Rome.

Professor Ernesta Cerulli, President, Dr. Italo Signorini, Secretary General, and Dr. Gabriella Marucci, Secretary of the Organizing Committee, of the Rome Congress were very helpful in everything related to the Symposium. Their friendship and aid throughout the Congress will always be remembered, and I am happy to be able to acknowledge our debt to them here.

Last, but certainly not least, I wish to thank all of the contributors to this volume for their hard work and patience.

T.A.L.

CONTRIBUTORS

Richard E. W. Adams	University of Texas, San Antonio
Hugh G. Ball	University of Arizona
Frances Frei Berdan	California State College, San Bernardino
Bente Bittmann	Universidad de Chile
Donald L. Brockington	University of North Carolina
Nigel B. Davies	Instituto Nacional de Antropología e Historia, Mexico
Clinton R. Edwards	University of Wisconsin, Milwaukee
Lawrence H. Feldman	Museum of Anthropology, University of Missouri
David A. Gregory	University of Arizona
Norman Hammond	Cambridge University
Jaime Litvak King	Universidad Nacional Autónoma de México
Ulrich Köhler	Seminar für Völkerkunde, Wilhelms Universität
Thomas A. Lee, Jr.	New World Archaeological Foundation
Donald E. McVicker	North Central College, Illinois
Joseph B. Mountjoy	University of North Carolina, Greensboro
Carlos Navarrete	Universidad Nacional Autónoma de México
Román Piña Chan	Instituto Nacional de Antropología e Historia, Mexico
Barbara J. Price	Temple University
William L. Rathje	University of Arizona
Thelma D. Sullivan	Escuela Nacional de Antropología e Historia, Mexico
Frederick M. Wiseman	University of Arizona

CONTENTS

FIGURES

1. INTRODUCTION
by
Thomas A. Lee, Jr.

COMMUNICATIONS AND CULTURAL CONTACT

Similarities and differences between cultures have been of concern to anthropologists since the beginning of the discipline and are still of vital interest today. The presence of cultural similarities in different sectors of a given cultural area, such as Mesoamerica, are usually thought of as being historically related and are often used, particularly in archaeology, to establish relationships between widely separated areas. Much cultural similarity in Mesoamerica can be traced to cultural contact begun on the basis of trade and commercial intercourse.

An excellent example of a regional trade system is the modern market system in the Valley of Oaxaca (Malinowski and de la Fuente 1957) which interlocks the numerous individual town markets economically and is the primary mechanism through which different groups come in contact with and are influenced by one another. The market system is not an autonomous unit and has no fixed spacial limits (Malinowski and de la Fuente 1957: 34), but is connected to other towns and areas depending on the direction and product concerned.

Commerce between regional trade systems of ecologically different loci is the result of symbiotic stimulus and is widespread throughout Mesoamerica. Perhaps the most detailed modern study available on interregional commerce is that of McBryde (1947) on southwestern Guatemala, covering the cool temperate central highlands and the hot Pacific coastal lowlands. McBryde demonstrates how complex the commercial relations between the towns of these two general ecological provinces are and how closely they are conditioned by the natural environment. This report should serve as a general caution to archaeologists who more often than not see trade relations through a simplistic symbiotic model constructed of only a few commercial elements. However, Hammond (Paper 2) makes an attractive case for prehistoric exchange on the basis of only two items, obsidian and cacao, between eastern Guatemala and southern Belize. This would suggest that both simple and complex types of symbiotic trade systems were present in Mesoamerica, as must well have been the case. Due to the nature of their evidence, archaeologists will always be forced to present evidence of less complex systems than the ethnohistorian or the ethnologist. However, archaeological evidence offers the opportunity of viewing, if in a less detailed way, the change or lack of it in the systems over a much longer period of time.

There is ample archaeological evidence that the highly developed and complex commercial network alluded to by many early Spanish chroniclers during the conquest of Nueva España must have had roots which reach back, deep into the Precolumbian era. The *pochteca* organization (Bittman and Sullivan Paper 18) of the Aculhua Mexica is perhaps the best known example of this commercial activity. Many investigators are willing to push this advanced type of trading tradition back to at least the beginning of the Classic Period, if not considerably before (cf. Parsons and Price 1971; for a dissenting view see Chapman 1971).

The importance of trade in establishing intercultural relations and as the impetus for culture change can not be denied. Rathje (1971b: 275) has gone so far as to present a model "involving methods of procuring and distributing the resources necessary to the efficiency of an agricultural subsistence economy (which) explains the loci of Lowland Maya development and the order in which these loci developed." Rathje's paper as well as earlier studies of trade and commerce such as Blom (1932), Othón de Mendizábal (1946), Chapman (1957, 1959), Cardós de Méndez (1959), León-Portilla (1962), Thompson (1964) and Flannery (1968) are concerned with primarily the kinds of resources exchanged between symbiotic regions, and either not at all

1

or only slightly touch on the actual routes over which this culture contact was begun and maintained. Exceptions to this general statement are studies by Beals (1971), McBryde (1947), and Thompson (1929, 1970).

Commerce is not the only reason for establishing cultural contact. It may, however, be the principal mechanism through which contact was always first established. Chapman (1957) has argued that trade, the free interchange of goods, always precedes tribute, implying conquest prior to taxation. It would seem a foregone conclusion that there is little likelihood that any area would be actively sought out and brought under control without previous knowledge of the economic value of the area. There must be economic factors which make the costs of conquest worthwhile. Again the *pochteca*, with their group of merchant spies, *nahualoztomeca*, admirably demonstrated their utility as economic investigators prior to attempted domination and agents of surveillance after conquest when taxation had begun. This aspect of the *pochteca* activity was not their primary one, of course, but it demonstrates that the merchant, not the soldier, was the first to penetrate an alien territory.

Religion and commerce were recognized as interdependent factors of Mesoamerican society as early as the beginnings of the Spanish Conquest. The proximity of the *plaza* or marketplace and the ceremonial precinct has been remarked upon by many early chroniclers. The coincidence of an important religious sanctuary, the focal point of long pilgrimages, and trading ports (Chapman 1959) is frequently found throughout Mesoamerica, two of the best known being Xicalango and Chetumal in the Maya area.

Since one of the characteristics of Mesoamerica is its surprisingly uniform religion it might be expected that religion could have been important in the establishment and maintenance of communication and cultural contact throughout the area. Sanctuaries and the religious pilgrimages to them were just mentioned as important aspects of the religion of this area and may be significant mechanisms in maintaining cultural contact,

but could they have originally been the cause for establishing such a contact? This seems rather unlikely, in view of the fact that there is no ethnographic evidence, that I know, of native evangelical movements in Mesoamerica. Nor have significant archaeological manifestations been interpreted as such without commercial or tributary aspects also being causal.

Theoretically one can go any number of ways from one point to another, but practically speaking, local topography, navigability of rivers, climate, vegetation, cultural boundaries, economics, and many other factors will effect the selection and use of any given trail or other type of communication route. It can also be demonstrated, at least in Chiapas, and I suspect elsewhere, that the actual routes available can give a significant character to the contact established and the extent to which it is the impetus to culture change.

ROUTE DESCRIPTION

It was suggested that the original symposium, and therefore this volume, present the actual communication routes documentable throughout Mesoamerica in considerable detail in order to achieve two basic objectives.

First it is felt that there is a definite need to establish a compendium of the major routes used during the past in Mesoamerica. There has been a long-standing need for a Mesoamerican-wide compendium since archaeologists, historians, and ethnologists as well as other specialists have discussed contact, trade, acculturation, or "influences" between distinct ethnic groups and regions without taking into account the practical aspects of the communications established. Certainly part of the testing of a contact or trade model or hypothesis between two groups or regions would be investigations at intermediate points between the two. The first step in this investigation would be the careful study of all known routes used between the two groups or regions in order to select the area in which the highest probability of success lies.

This volume is far from being the all-encompassing route compendium which we would someday like to see available. Rather it is an attempt to show the need for such a research tool and the mere beginnings of such a work.

As much detail as known should be given about each route, such as the towns passed, distances between them, travel time on foot, overnight stopping places, types of terrain covered, etc. Of particular interest would be natural problem areas which tend to hamper free communications due to difficult relief, swamps or rivers and rapids since these would channel travel along certain optimum courses. Other physical aspects of the routes, or special features used to improve the utility or comfort of the route such as maintenance, garrisons or their lack, shelters at *ventas* or way-stations, bridges, wharves, piers, warehouses, canoes stationed at fords, and the like are important to note since they may well give some idea about the social relations and relationships between the route users and the inhabitants of the area through which the route passes.

The types of traffic which used each route should be given where known including foot, horseback, and canoe or raft, and as concerns the latter two, how they were propelled. The use of sails, oars, rudders, poles, ropes, and other related gear will be important to point out since their presence or absence may be decisive in the dating or indicative of the point of origin of a particular transport tradition. Furthermore, the type of traffic may give an indication as to the efficiency of a route. The better the route the bigger the load that can be carried along it or the faster the trip can be made and vice versa. Such factors as flat solid level land and navigable waters contribute to maximum route efficiency just as broken terrain, swamps, and non-navigable waters restrict efficiency.

Known examples of large or small pilgrimages and the routes to religious sanctuaries can add another facet to communications and cultural contact. An example from this century is the three annual pilgrimages the nahuatl people from Milpa Alta make to the shrine of the Lord of Calma about forty miles to the southwest of their village (Horcasitas 1972: 53–73). The cult of this particular saint, which is founded on the site and prehistoric tradition of *Oztoteotl*, God of the Cave (Martínez Marín 1972: 168), is widely observed by many different ethnic groups of which the Milpa Alta villagers are only one. Nevertheless the description of the Milpa Alta pilgrimage alone offers us new insights into the route use, pilgrimage organization, observances, and relationships to permanent residents along the route which are not otherwise available to us and are similar to other pilgrimage practices far away in Mesoamerica, but of no close historical connection. Other examples are the *floreros* of Chiapa de Corzo and their pilgrimage to the Chiapas Highlands (Lee 1970) and the old Zoque pilgrimage from Tuxtla Gutiérrez each year to the great shrine of the Lord of Esquipulas in Guatemala. Items in common are the presence of a leader and lesser officials, and the established, almost sacred, schedule for travel and places to eat and sleep, the initiation of novitiates, the maintenance of the "right" frame of mind to insure the successful outcome of the pilgrimage, the harmonious relationship with those who live along the route, and the cooperative spirit of the venture among all participants. In the Chalma pilgrimage there is a periodical use of the route by different communities at different times in what seems to be a definite interest in not "over-loading" the route, since many of the people start out without either food or money, expecting alms along the way to provide for them. This is a feature held in common with the Zoque Esquipulas pilgrimage, but not with the Chiapa de Corzo *floreros* who carry fresh and dried vegetables and money into the highlands to maintain themselves.

Certainly the social relations between route users and route "owners" are significantly different from those that would pertain if the users were merchants or conquering armies and not religious pilgrims. Pre-Hispanic pilgrimages were very common, but we have very little information on their nature; therefore any insights into their structure and everyday operation will be of interest to anyone concerned with cultural contact and communications in Mesoamerica.

Since religion permeated almost all aspects of Precolumbian Mesoamerican human activity, it will be most significant to point out cults dedicated to traders, trading societies, or trading deities such as the nahuatl *Yiacatecutli* or *Yacacoliuhqui* (Sahagún 1950: 17–20; Torquemada 1969, Vol. 2, p. 57) or the Maya *Ek Chuah* (Thompson 1970: 306–308), prayers and rituals observed prior to, during, or after trading expeditions, and any other supernatural observations related to trading trips and commercial activity.

Lists of finished goods, crops, and raw materials that were transported over the routes will contribute another aspect to our knowledge of routes and contact. Since almost any given commerce route has a complementary flow of the above items, the place of origin, the direction of flow, and the final destination is of upmost importance. This range of information may give us insights into the needs of different peoples, the items of necessity, and their desires, the exotic or luxury goods. Rathje's (1971b) hypothesis on the origin and development of Classic Maya civilization is based on just this thesis. We may be able to obtain some idea about the value of items from the relative quantities exchanged. The variation of goods or materials through time along a particular route may give us clues as to internal social change in the trading areas themselves. These are only a few of the contributions that cargo lists might provide.

It is an obvious fact that people with different reasons may use the same route, but the different social, political, religious or economic reasons of the route users may suggest why a particular route was used and the nature of the contact maintained. Questions that should be answered concerning groups of route users may include some of the following: What types of groups used the routes? How were these groups organized? Were routes controlled by specific groups? Were tolls or use-taxes paid by route users? Who owned the merchandise carried for commerce? Was merchandise staged and transferred or did the owner accompany his goods and materials from place of acquisition to the market?

Or were goods and materials continually bought and resold at the edge of social boundaries? Of considerable interest would also be information concerning the organization and operation of formal markets, ports-of-trade, and trading posts (Chapman 1959; Berdan, Paper 15).

The second basic objective of this volume is to delimit, where possible, the way in which the use of a specific route or the character of its users structured or affected the cultural contact established. As mentioned above, it is obvious that pilgrims using a route would not have the same effect on people and their culture surrounding the route as would another group that is forced to conquer an area in order to keep a vital commerce route open. In another hypothetical situation the navigability of a river between two regions may place in contact different human groups while the absence of the river would have severely reduced communications and probably altered significantly the quantity and type of goods exchanged and therefore reduced the effect of the contact established.

Certainly this second objective is the most difficult to realize since it requires going beyond the solid land of facts and into the exciting, if unnerving, quicksand swamp of interpretation. Nevertheless it is an objective well worth striving for, if a search for cultural constants which have a wider utility than explaining just the local cultural contact processes is a valid research goal, as I believe it is.

REFERENCES

Beals 1971
Blom 1932
Cardós de Méndez 1959
Chapman 1957, 1959, 1971
Flannery 1968
Horcasitas 1972
Lee 1970
León-Portilla 1962
McBryde 1947
Malinowski and de la Fuente 1957
Martínez Marín 1972
Othón de Mendizábal 1946
Parsons and Price 1971
Rathje 1971b
Sahagún 1950
Thompson 1929, 1964, 1970
Torquemada 1969

PART I
COMMUNICATION ROUTES

2. MOVING MERCHANDISE IN PROTOHISTORIC CENTRAL QUAUHTEMALLAN
by
Lawrence H. Feldman

THE SUBJECT

At the end of the pre-Hispanic period, in the fifteenth and sixteenth centuries, many different kinds of merchandise traveled along the trade routes of Mesoamerica. In the lands of Central Quauhtemallan (Fig. 1) more than fifty different items are cited in the different sources (cf. Feldman 1971). These items fall into one of two categories: *exotics*, items of high value per unit weight that preserve their value indefinitely in time, and *essentials*, items necessary to maintain the population at its current level of density. This paper is a study of the differing effects of these two categories of trade goods on the organization of commerce and routes of trade in early Quauhtemallan.

One part of Central Quauhtemallan is of special interest here; this is the area that ultimately became known as Verapaz (Fig. 2). Within it were the nesting grounds of the quetzal, whose highly valued plummage was exported to distant parts of Mesoamerica (Montero de Miranda 1954, Zúñiga 1608). Immediately to the south or east, were huge deposits of highly valued stone (obsidian, jade, and steatite, Anonymous 1965; flint, Fuentes y Guzmán 1932–1934). Verapaz was also the last portion of Quauhtemallan to be brought under the control of the Spanish crown. The means by which this control was established was unusual, a peaceful conquest that involved no soldiers; for both of these reasons, a late conquest and an unusual conquest, chroniclers have devoted more attention to Verapaz than other portions of Quauhtemallan. When to this is added a huge mass of colonial documents (i.e., native language dictionaries, land titles, local histories, census tallies, official inventories of local resources) an ample base is provided for examining Quauhtemallan from the vantage point of Verapaz. Accordingly this report takes as its basic starting point the economy of Verapaz, noting where significant, deviations from its commercial practices elsewhere in Quauhtemallan.

THE ESSENTIALS

Not all crops can be grown everywhere equally well nor are other resources, like pottery clay, found in all localities. This division of nature is followed by a cultural division. Thus maize growers search for the best soil to grow their crops and cacao plantations appear in the climates appropriate for their existence. Ultimately communities appear so highly specialized that they must import essential goods from other peoples. This can be seen in Verapaz, where the people of the town of San Cristóbal Cahcoh, who specialized in the manufacture of maguey and reed fiber products, were forced to import maize from Santa Cruz Munchu (Andonaigue 1936). Specializations of other Verapaz towns are noted in Figure 2. None of these towns can export their essential specialities to every town of Quauhtemallan. There is always a distance beyond which it does not pay to transport merchandise. Goods spoil or other centers of production become closer to the consumer beyond a given distance.

How far is this given distance? Antigua, the Spanish capital of Guatemala at the end of the sixteenth century, was served by means of transportation of essentials that had changed little from those of the pre-Hispanic era. Therefore, the trade of this town of perhaps 60,000 residents (Fuentes y Guzmán 1932–1934, Vol. 1, p. 151) can serve as a measuring rod for the trade of the previous period. The most important food, maize, was imported from within an area of 488 square kilometers of 48,800 hectares. Antigua, it can be seen from the tabulation of data, was surrounded by progressively more distant import zones (Table 1). The towns closest to Antigua supplied fruit and laborers. These settlements and the more distant towns provided maize, various kinds of fruit, and some fish. Peripher-

7

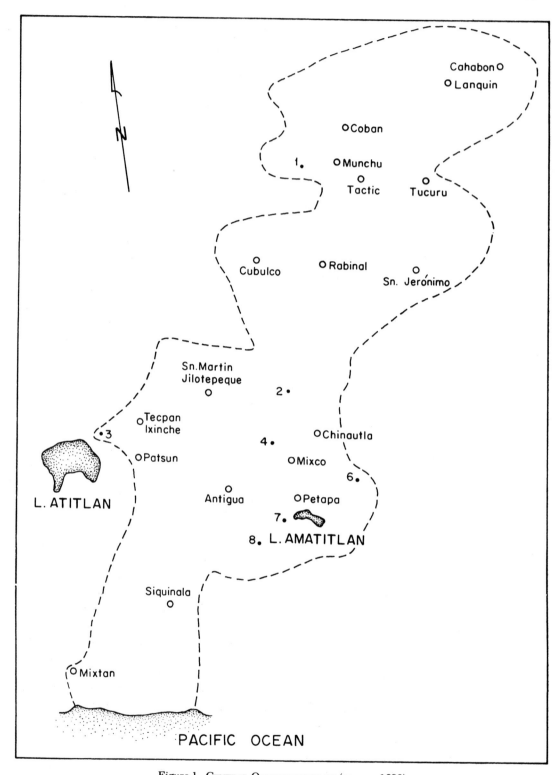

Figure 1. CENTRAL QUAUHTEMALLAN (ca. A.D. 1690)
Towns designated by numbers are: (1) San Cristóbal Cahcoh, (2) San Raimundo, (3) Semetabaj, (4) San Pedro Sacatepequez, (6) Pinula, (7) Amatitlan, (8) Palin. One centimeter equals ten kilometers.

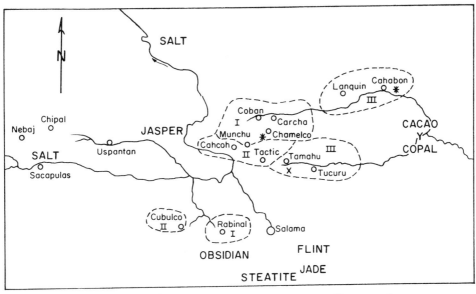

Figure 2. Verapaz Settlements, Specializations, and Resource Areas
Numbers on the map indicate (I) maize and bean surplus crops, (II) maguey and reed specialties, and (III) cotton and large game animal products. Information given is for about the year 1550 A.D. One centimeter equals ten kilometers.

al to the later towns were the suppliers of wood, most fish or ceramics, and some fruits.

Finally, at a really great distance were the sources of more exotic goods (e.g., balsam). All this movement was by means of land transportation. The reason for the lack of water transportation is that, with a few notable exceptions, the rivers flowed at right angles to the major routes of trade. They went from areas of little population to areas of almost none (e.g., the Río Michatoya which drained into the Pacific Ocean).

There are several ways of determining the routes between the different communities. Within Verapaz, there are the journeys of colonial travelers and modern traffic that follows colonial patterns (e.g., hand-carried pottery). Other indirect means allow one to infer a more complex network of lines of communication. A most fruitful technique comes from the study of native names. In Dialect Geography the plotting of word usage results ultimately in a map showing important dialect boundaries (cf. Hockett 1958: 471–84). By plotting the distribution of personal native names this same technique results in the formation of maps showing the lines of inter-

action between adjacent communities. This is because native names are symbols attached to particular social institutions (e.g., patrilineal clan, Carrasco 1964: 323–24). These symbols are passed on by marriage and marriage is a form of contact. Therefore if two towns have a high number of these symbols in common, it indicates that their inhabitants have had a high degree of interaction (Table 2).

In Figure 3 the explicit statements in the colonial sources have been combined with the implicit lines of communication derived from analysis of names to determine the trade routes of Verapaz in about the year A.D. 1600. These routes show a pattern that, as mentioned above, is unusual in Quauhtemallan. Routes seem to follow along rivers rather than cut across them (e.g., the route from Tamahu into the lowlands following the Río Polochic).

Most merchandise of Quauhtemallan, even during the period of the Spanish colony, traveled on the shoulders of the porter (cf. Fuentes y Guzmán 1932–1934, Vol. 1, p. 341). In the first part of the twentieth century goods were still hand carried, making it possible to determine the nonstop portage distance per day. The average estimated distance is 23

Table 1. SOME ANTIGUA IMPORT SOURCES (ca. A.D. 1750)*

Parramos: maize
Sumpango: maize, wood
Santa María Cauque: maize, wood
San Martín Jilotepeque: fish
Santa Catarina Barahona: maize, cloth
San Antonio Aguacalientes: maize
Ciudad Vieja: fish, fruit
Santa María de Jesús: maize, wood
San Pablo Laguna: fruit
Jocotenango: fruit, workers, maize
San Jaun Obispo: wood, maize
Santa Lucía Milpas Altas: maize, fruit
San Miguel Milpas Altas: fruit
San Cristóbal El Bajo: wood
San Cristóbal El Alto: fruit, wood

Mixco: pottery
Gueymoco: balsam
Pastores: maize
Amatitlan: fish
Petapa: fish
Alotenango: maize, wood
Xenacoj: maize
Patzun: maize
Patzicia: maize
Panajachel: fruit
Acasaguastlan: fruit
Tecpan: wood
Palin: wood
San Diego: wood

*The major references for this table are: Cerrato et al. 1549; Coronado 1953; Cortés y Larraz 1958; Fuentes y Guzmán 1932–1934; Juarros 1936; Pineda 1925; "Dos Religiosos" 1873; Vásquez 1937–1944, Vol. 1, pp. 33–36; Warner and Dixon 1969; and Checa y Quesada 1936.

Table 2. NAME INTERACTION SERIES*

Settlement	1	2	3	4	5	6	7	8	9	10
1. Cubulco	—	4.5	4.5	0	0	4.5	0	4.5	9	
2. Cahabon	4.5	—	23.8	22.2	0	15.6	3.8	24.	7.4	17.5
3. Cahcoh	4.5	23.8	—	27.7	16.6	18.7	0	28.5	22.2	
4. Tamahu	0	22.2	27.7	—	8.3	37.5	0	19.4	18.5	
5. Lanquin	0	0	16.6	8.3	—	0	0	8.3	25	
6. Tucuru	4.5	15.6	18.7	37.5	0	—	0	15.6	14.8	
7. Rabinal	0	3.8	0	0	0	0	—	0	0	
8. Coban	4.5	24	28.5	19.4	8.3	15.6	0	—	18.5	
9. Carcha	9	7.4	22.2	18.5	25	14.8	0	18.5	—	
10. Manche	4.3	17.5	0.8	0	6.1	0	6.1	0.8	0	—

*A difficult problem in obtaining a true comparison arose from differing sample sizes. The list from Rabinal was 198 items long and that from Lanquin had only 12 items; how could one compare both with a third sample of 50 names (i.e., of Coban)? If Rabinal had a higher degree of resemblance did that mean that its degree of relationship was closer or did it only reflect the greater possibility of finding resemblances because of the larger Rabinal sample? In order that there would be some adjustment of numerical inequality a scaling factor was calculated and subtracted from the number of shared items each set of towns had in common. The scaling factor is the difference between the two samples divided by ten. The adjusted number of shared items was converted into a percentage of sharing and tabulated above.

Reference citations are: Coban (Anonymous 1816a), Cahcoh (Anonymous 1821a, Cay 1785), Rabinal (Anonymous 1813b), Cubulco (Anonymous 1813a), Cahabon (Anonymous 1821b), Tamahu (Anonymous 1821c), Lanquin (Anonymous 1820), Tucuru (Anonymous 1821d), Carcha (Anonymous 1816b), and Manche (Hellmuth 1971). The Manche data are for the towns of San Philipe, San Miguel, San Jacinto, and San Pablo. Work is continuing on a more comprehensive study of Maya names and will be presented in another paper in the future.

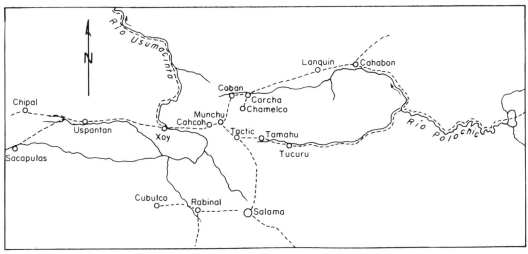

Figure 3. THE TRADE ROUTES OF VERAPAZ
Dotted lines mark trade routes. The period of the map is the sixteenth century. One centimeter equals ten kilometers.

kilometers, based upon data in Bunzel (1959). In reference to Verapaz trade this means that going from east to west (Cahabon to Cahcoh) the land portage time would be four days and from north to south (Coban to Rabinal) about three days. Carrying time between the various towns of, and adjacent to, this area are given in Table 3.

Who were the people involved in this traffic? What were the means by which goods were exchanged with those of other areas? Several kinds of merchants may be distinguished in Quauhtemallan. They were the Professional Trader, the Petty Trader and the Retailer. The Trader is today, when professional, primarily a wholesaler. He sells his goods to other merchants, not directly to the public. His trade involves the sending of agents to buy from manufacturers and sell to retailers; in other words his function is that of a jobber (cf. Bunzel 1959: 68-70, 73-74). In earlier times the Professional Trader, who dealt in relatively large sums of money, handled his transactions on a more personal basis.

The richest of these merchants, the Professional Traders, personally took part in long distance trading operations (Tovilla 1960: 72). Their numbers were highly limited; in all the Verapaz there were only six in the last half of the sixteenth century (Viana, Gallego, and Cadena 1955: 22). As in Yucatan, all these richer merchants of the Guatemala (and Chiapas) highlands seem to have been members of the upper class (Pineda 1925; Landa 1941: 39; Tovilla 1960: 72). The others, the Petty Traders, made generally only short trips within the local area. Concern with the movement of a single item that originated in a very limited territory (e.g., salt) was his specialty (cf. Viana, Gallego, and Cadena 1955: 22; Paez and Arboleda 1964). Frequently the Petty Trader was the Manufacturer of his single line of goods (e.g., wooden planks and beams, Vásquez 1937-1944).

Retailers (the *ajqaibali* of Coto 1608) were the most common of all merchants. Besides being a role that other kinds of merchants might assume, there was the Retailer or Retailer-Manufacturer who was the farmer who came to sell perishables and the craftsmen who made their goods in the market upon request (i.e., obsidian blades). If one reads the descriptions of early Mesoamerican markets, it is evident that many goods fell into this category and that most merchants were Retailers (see Cortés 1962; Díaz 1963; Sahagún 1959).

The Quauhtemallan protohistoric market (e.g., at Iximche or Rabinal García Pelaez 1968: 52, Las Casas 1909) was organized along certain standard lines. The Market had political authorities to judge the disputes, and in the more important Markets, to house the foreign merchants (Las Casas 1909, Tovilla 1960: 72). In the large towns (e.g., at Iximche) a plaza was set aside near the temples for permanent market usage (Herrera 1728, Las Casas 1909: 623–24). It was divided into different sections for the sale of meat (see *chaqubal* in Saenz 1940), *tortillas* (Cortés y Larraz 1958, Vol. 1, p. 38) and other perishables. As Benzoni (1970: 158) writes of the Guatemalan markets he visited in the 1540's, "they hold daily markets, most of their goods being eatables and drinkables, that is — salt, fish, fruits, calabashes, battate (sweet potatoes)...". Ceramics and other hardware manufactured by specialists in other towns were, nevertheless, carried in on a daily basis to the largest Markets (Fuentes y Guzmán 1932–1934, Vol. 1, p. 290). So much for the movement of essential goods. What about the *exotics*, the rare, the unusual merchandise?

THE EXOTICS

Produced in a limited, sometimes very limited, number of localities, they in them-selves, by their presence alone can mark out the routes of commerce. Therefore the artifacts of archaeology, as well as the records of ethnohistory, are of considerable value. Exotics are the goods of long distance trade and Verapaz was both a way station and a starting point for several major prehispanic routes. What did Verapaz have to offer?

One of the most valued articles of commerce in the prehispanic Mesoamerican world were the long green plumes of the quetzal bird. The feathers were fastened with glue to form feather "paintings" and they were tied with cord to make fans, feathered bracelets, devices born upon the back, skirts, etc. (Sahagún 1959: 96). The quetzal lived in the mountain cloud forests of Mesoamerica, but only in the Verapaz was the harvesting of the plumes so regulated as to prevent injury to the birds. Here the green feathers were regularly removed from the living birds who were caught by hand and then released to grow more (Tovilla 1960: 142). Killing of these birds was punished by death (Viana,

Table 3. PORTAGE TIME

Destination	Time	Distance	Intermediate Stations
		CHICHICASTENANGO*	
Solola	1 day	21 km.	
Mazatenango	3 days	65 km.	Los Encuentros, Santa Lucía, Santo Tomás la Unión Chocola
Guatemala	6 days	54 km.	Tecpan, Chimaltenango, Sumpango, Mixco
Coban	10 days	100 km.	Joyabaj (2 days), Cubulco (2 days), Rabinal (1½ days), Salama (2 days), Coban (3 days)
		COBAN	
Cahabon	3 days	47 km.	Carcha, Lanquin
Chamelco	1 day	11 km.	Carcha
Rabinal	3 days	64 km.	Munchu (10 km.), Tactic (8 km.)
Tucuru	2 days	36 km.	Munchu (8 km.), Tactic (8 km.), Tamahu (10 km.)
Cahcoh	1 day	15 km.	Munchu (10 km.)
		CAHCOH	
Sacapulas	4 days†	79 km.	Xoy (15 km.), Uspantan (30 km.), Cunen (23 km.), Sacapulas (11 km.)
		CAHABON	
Manche towns	3 days	50 km. (estimate)	

*Average estimated nonstop portage distance per day is 23 km., determined from the Chichicastenango data collected by Bunzel (1959).

†This time is confirmed by Viana, Gallego, and Cadena (1955: 21), who state that Sacapulas is four days "of road" from Verapaz.

Gallego, and Cadena 1955: 20; Las Casas 1909: 617). As a result, the harvest of this rare commodity was abundant and remained at a high level from year to year.

In the sixteenth century a large percentage of the annual feather harvest went into the western lands. This route, the West Road, began in the Valley of Oaxaca, the Coyolapan province of the Aztec Empire of the Triple Alliance (Fig. 4). Both the Imperial government and local subordinate governments levied taxes in green feathers (Barlow 1949). Unfortunately for the inhabitants, these birds did not occur naturally in this province. The feathers could be acquired by "going to the Isthmus (of Tehuantepec) and working six

months or a year there cultivating lands" (Barlow 1949: 124). The Tehuantepec merchants traded with Xoconochco for the feathers (Tezozomoc 1944: 370–71) or went directly to Verapaz for these valued goods (Anonymous 1664). Two alternative routes are indicated: (1) Coyolapan to Tehuantepec to Verapaz, and (2) Coyolapan to Tehuantepec to Xoconochco (the Pacific coast of Chiapas). The first of these routes was opened, but as we shall see, only for a few years, to the merchants of Central Mexico in the reign of Ahuitzotl of Tenochtitlan. Imperial outposts were established at Chiapa, Tzinacantlan, Huixtan, and Comitan in the Chiapas highlands (Barlow 1949, end map). Beyond Comi-

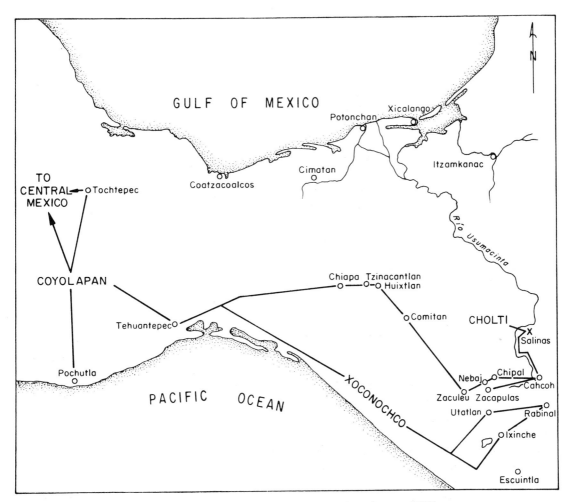

Figure 4. THE VERAPAZ-COYOLAPAN WEST ROAD (ca. A.D. 1500)
One centimeter equals approximately thirty-seven kilometers.

tan were the protohistoric towns, now archaeological sites, of Zaculeu, Nebaj, and Chipal. At these localities have been found Central Mexican turquoise (Foshag 1954: 24; Butler 1940: 265; Woodbury and Trik 1953, Vol. 1, p. 239), Oaxacan coast shell (*Patella mexicana* whose special habitat occurs closest near Pochutla, Oaxaca), and Oaxacan gold (Las Casas 1909: 623–24; Butler 1940; etc.). Close by was a source of Verapaz salt, Sacapulas, only four days from the Verapaz town of Cahcoh (Viana, Gallego, and Cadena 1955: 22, 27). To Cahcoh came "Oaxaca or Tehuantepec" shrimp (Zúñiga 1608). Finally, the Pokom language of Cahcoh had words for amber, which could only be imported from Chiapas (there are no other Mesoamerican sources), and a precious greenstone called *xit* (Zúñiga 1608). This last is clearly a loan from the Nahua of Central Mexico of the word *xihuitl* meaning turquoise.

What of the other routes from Coyolapan to Xoconochco? Again the route is marked by artifacts. The Imperial province of Xoconochco paid a tribute of 1,400 bunches of feathers of several colors as well as 800 handfuls of only quetzal feathers. The same province paid an annual tax of eight gold disks to the Imperial government. This is a very curious assessment since there were neither gold mines nor living quetzal birds in this province (Ponce de León 1961: 140; Alvarez del Toro 1961: 21–22). The mystery is compounded when one notes that members of the *pochteca*, an official trading organization of the Imperial government organized to deal with powers *outside* of the Empire, made regular trips to this province *of* the Empire. What was going on in Xoconochco?

A hint is provided by a statement of a Guatemalan author who writes that Central Mexican traders were massacred by the Lords of Quauhtemallan at the end of the reign of Ahuitzotl (Fuentes y Guzmán 1932–1934, Vol. 1, pp. 47–48). Trade in neighboring Quauhtemallan was not administered through official corporations or guilds. It took place by means of private individuals. Traders with the most capital often were members of the upper class (see above) but as traders they did not represent their government. Evidently governments feared the official trader and prohibited his activities. Thus the *pochteca* had no official bodies with whom they could enter into commercial interactions.

There was a mechanism, used in medieval Europe, that would allow for commercial interaction between the Central Mexican official trader and the private Guatemalan ones. This was the Fair. These were easily accessible places where, for a limited time each year, merchants coming from distant regions could enjoy special protection from the local authorities. "The latter usually exempted visitors to fairs from the ordinary restrictions placed upon foreigners and from some aspects of local legislation. At the same time, international fairs enabled the authority which organized them to attract, to tax, and to control more easily foreign traders and trade" (López and Raymond 1954: 77). The Fair was held on a date important in the ritual calendar and often coincided with an object of pilgrimage (cf. López and Raymond 1954).

This model answers many questions. It explains the presence of gold and feather tribute as taxes laid upon a biannual fair, the reason for biannual trips of the *pochteca* to this province. Fairs were by no means unknown elsewhere in prehispanic Mesoamerica (cf. Cortés 1962 for the one at Cholula). These had all the religious ritual of medieval Europe (Durán 1951, Vol. 2, pp. 215–24). As a mechanism necessary for the importation of goods from beyond the Empire, a Fair was both possible and plausible, and therefore it is felt was the goal of the *pochteca* when they traveled to this distant province of the Empire.

Less can be said of other routes out of Verapaz. Traffic went *down the Usumacintla river* into the lands of the Cholti Lacandon (Fig. 4), as witnessed by lowland terms for cultigens in Early Verapaz dictionaries (e.g., cotton and guayava fruit, Gongora 1725) and highland Verapaz words for manufactured goods in a Cholti dictionary (e.g., shift or *huipil*, Moran 1935). Inhabitants of both areas obtained salt from the same Usumacintla deposits and protohistoric natives of Cahcoh had lived for a time in the lowlands (Thompson 1970, Sapper 1904).

A *North Road* went from Cahabon to the Manche Chol towns (Fig. 5). Thompson (1970: 134) notes that the Manche Chol "made trading visits in the seventeenth and eighteenth centuries to Cajabon in the Alta Verapaz" and that the Indians of Cajabon "always used to enter and trade with them" (see also Ximénez 1929–1931, Vol. 2, pp. 382, 394, 402). Close relationship between the two areas is further documented by the many personal names shared between the Manche towns and Cahabon (Table 2). Cacao (Remesal, in Thompson 1970: 135), tree gourds (the Verapaz terms for tree gourd are typical lowland forms even though they are *not* found in Cholti), and perhaps copal incense (Montero de Miranda 1954) were imported from these lowlands. In return salt was much desired by the Manche Chol (Thompson 1970: 135). Other possible exports were cotton, a specialty of Cahabon (Viana, Gallego, and Cadena 1955: 25) and quetzal plumes (Pineda 1925: 358).

Las Casas (1909: 623–24) wrote that "gold and silver comes to Verapaz from Soconusco (Xoconochco) and goes from Verapaz to Nicaragua." The route to Verapaz, the "West Road," was noted earlier; what about the route from Verapaz to Nicaragua (Fig. 6)? Travel was common from Cahabon, or Tucuru, down into the lowlands of the Río Polochic. Orchards of the towns "toward the Gulf" yielded cacao (Viana, Gallego, and Cadena 1955: 27). Beyond the Gulfo Dulce (today the Lago de Izabal) was the port of Nito.

Nito was of considerable importance as a station on the route from Xicalanco on the Gulf of Mexico to Nicaragua, merchants of at least one town near Xicalanco (Itzamkanac) maintaining a permanent station at this settlement (Gómara 1954, Vol. 2, pp. 314, 322). Therefore when a source (Torquemada 1969, Vol. 1; p. 335) mentions Maya coming to Nicaragua by sea in canoes and bringing feathers to exchange for cacao, it seems very likely that the feathers came from Verapaz (traffic entering Nicaragua via the San Juan River, see Peralta 1883: 117).

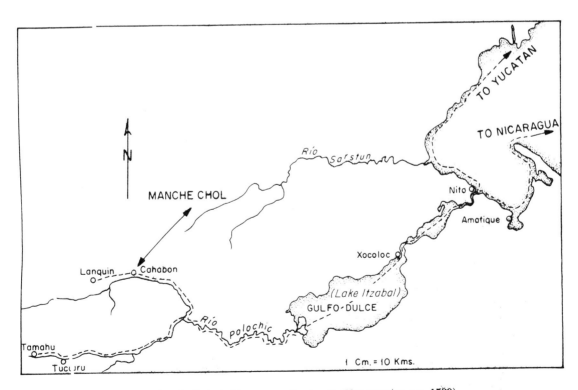

Figure 5. Routes North and East from Verapaz (ca. A.D. 1500)

With all the activity centered on the rivers draining into the Atlantic ocean and the northern coast of Mesoamerica, it would seem strange that sea-borne commerce would be absent from the shores of the Pacific. Yet this is precisely what the records say for the southern sea coast of Quauhtemallan. The Spaniards found no good harbours on this coast, and after the first years of conquest funneled all commerce through ports elsewhere (Palacio 1860; Rubio Sánchez 1956). Even minor coastal traffic is not mentioned in any early text (see Estrada and Niebla 1955: 80–81, who comment on its absence). In the absence of coastal usage the archaeological data tends to support the ethnohistoric records, at least to the extent of generally all highland sites of all periods lacking the remains of marine fauna of the Guatemalan Pacific coast, as most faunal remains labeled as from the Pacific Ocean are *not* native to *this* portion of its coastline (cf. Feldman n.d.).

Land traffic was also restricted in its scope. Alvarado (1924) notes that the Nahua-speaking inhabitants of Escuintla had little contact with the Maya further west or north. Analysis of names supports that statement of Escuintla's isolation, since few Escuintla names are found among Cakchiquel or Pokom speakers (studies in progress by the author). Nor does colonial or modern movement of exotics contradict the feeling that there is an economic barrier between Central and Eastern Quauhtemallan (Escuintla east into El Salvador). Thus Cahabon copal, Chinautla water jars, and Nahuala metates were often sent to the lands around Lake Atitlan, the Valley of Guatemala, and Verapaz; while Jocotan-Ataco copal, San Luis Jilotepeque water jars, and Jalapa metates were sent to Escuintla, Jutiapa, Chiquimula, Copan, and Sonsonate (cf. Feldman 1971). Eastern Quauhtemallan seems cut off economically, both by land and water routes, from Central Quauhtemallan. Its ties are not with northwestern lands and therefore its discussion is beyond the scope of this paper. Instead concern has been with the Verapaz of Central Quauhtemallan, the place of origin of a major article of prehispanic commerce, the locality where goods from places as distant as Central Mexico and Nicaragua in lower Central America were received and the region where at least four major routes met, truly one of the more im-

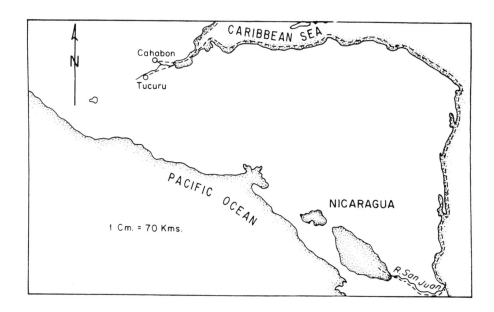

Figure 6. LAKE ITZABAL-NICARAGUA VIA THE CARIBBEAN COASTAL ROUTE

portant crossroads of trade in protohistoric Mesoamerica.

REFERENCES

Alvarado 1924
Alvarez del Toro 1961
Andonaigue 1936
Anonymous 1664, 1813a, 1813b, 1816a, 1816b, 1820, 1821a, 1821b, 1821c, 1821d, 1965
Barlow 1949
Benzoni 1970
Bunzel 1959
Butler 1940
Carrasco 1964
Cay 1785
Cerrato et al. 1549
Checa y Quesada 1936
Coronado 1953
Cortés 1962
Cortés y Larraz 1958
Coto 1608
Díaz 1963
"Dos Religiosos" 1873
Durán 1951
Estrada and Niebla 1955
Feldman 1971, n.d.
Foshag 1954
Fuentes y Guzmán 1932–1934
García Pelaez 1968
Gómara 1954
Gongora 1725
Hellmuth 1971
Herrera 1728
Hockett 1958
Juarros 1936
Landa 1941
Las Casas 1909
López and Raymond 1954
Montero de Miranda 1954
Morán 1935
Paez and Arboleda 1964
Palacio 1860
Peralta 1883
Pineda 1925
Ponce de León 1961
Rubio Sánchez 1956
Saenz 1940
Sahagún 1959
Sapper 1904
Scholes and Roys 1948
Tezozomoc 1944
Thompson 1970
Torquemada 1969
Tovilla 1960
Vásquez 1937–1944
Viana, Gallego, and Cadena 1955
Warner and Dixon 1969
Woodbury and Trik 1953
Ximénez 1929–1931
Zúñiga 1608

3. CACAO AND COBANEROS: AN OVERLAND TRADE ROUTE BETWEEN THE MAYA HIGHLANDS AND LOWLANDS

by

Norman Hammond

The question of trade between the highland and lowland zones of the Maya Area has been discussed extensively, both on the theoretical level of the advantages of symbiosis and the more practical one of the actual goods exchanged (Sanders and Price 1968; Thompson 1970). The presence of certain basic resources in the highlands and their absence in the central part of the Yucatan Peninsula has been used to generate a "core-buffer zone" model to explain both the rise and the collapse of Classic civilization in the lowlands (Rathje 1971, 1973; Molloy and Rathje 1972). Rathje has made much of the use of major rivers as bulk transport systems, and indeed such routes are both topographically and economically obvious lines of communication.

Overland routes have received less attention, partly because they are less obvious on a map and their feasibility must be tested in the field, not only from the point of view of topography but also that of the distribution of archaeological material. We need to examine the ethnographic, ethnohistoric and archaeological evidence for particular routes having been used, and for continuity or discontinuity in their operation. The purpose of this paper is to describe an overland route between the highland and lowland zones, the course of which is known in detail from recent ethnography and for which there is convincing ethnohistoric and archaeological evidence of use going back to the Late Classic period, the 8th–9th centuries A.D.

The route runs between the highlands around Coban in the Guatemalan department of Alta Verapaz, and the lowlands on the southeastern flanks of the Maya Mountains in the south Toledo District of Belize (Fig. 7). It is still used, in a form recently modified by road construction, by the *cobanero* peddlers who bring small manufactured goods down from Alta Verapaz (Fig. 8) and the detailed course of the route was documented some years ago by Don Owen-Lewis, then Kekchi Liaison Officer based on Crique Sarco, Toledo District. His journey was from Crique Sarco

to Coban, and the description of the northern part of the route, from Poite to San Miguel, is based on a journey made by myself and Charles Wright in 1970.

The northeastern end of the route and the furthest markets of the *cobaneros* are in the Kekchi villages of San Miguel and San Pedro Columbia which lie a short distance apart on the two main branches of the Río Grande (Fig. 9). These villages were settled in the last century by families moving down from Alta Verapaz to escape Guatemalan oppression, and clearly this route was a natural, perhaps a traditional one to follow. Both villages, together with the Mopan Maya settlement of San Antonio and other communities, lie in the rolling foothills of the Maya Mountains between 25 and 200 m. elevation on soils which Wright (1970) has recently classified as good quality for maize and prime quality for cacao cultivation with a neolithic technology. Near San Pedro are the notable Late Classic ruins of Lubaantun, which seems to have been the economic and political centre of the region in the eighth and ninth centuries A.D. and which is admirably situated to control both river and land traffic as well as to exploit the agricultural soils and the natural resources of the Río Grande and the coastal plain (Hammond 1972a).

From the Río Grande basin the route crosses the low watershed into the Moho River drainage and runs to San Antonio before turning southeast to round the end of the steep ridge that closes the San Antonio valley on the south. The whole route so far has remained below the 200 m. contour, in the rolling foothills formed by the dissection of the Toledo Beds, avoiding the steep high limestone foothills that run out eastward in several long ridges. In the Moho River basin proper, the route crosses the Blue Creek and Aguacate Creek tributaries by shallow fords near the villages of Blue Creek and Aguacate. From the latter village, where the modern jeep road ends, the trail leads over a spur of

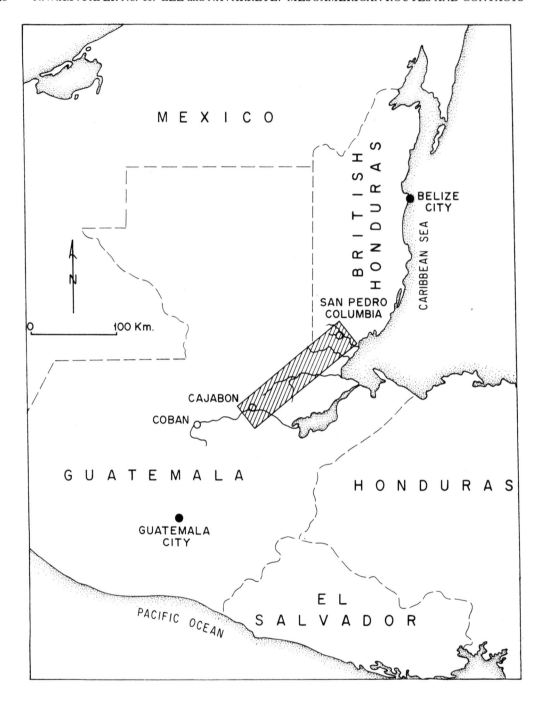

Figure 7. Map of Southern Mesoamerica

General location of the Cajabon-San Pedro de Columbia route section shown by shaded area. For details see
Figure 9.

steep but fairly low limestone hills into the Moho River valley; it runs along north of the river between flood-plain and hills before running down to the bank opposite the village of Poite.

This Kekchi settlement, recently established on the site of the Classic ceremonial centre of Pusilha (Joyce, Gann, Gruning, and Long 1928; Joyce 1929; Gruning 1930), lies between the two major branches of the Moho River, the northern Río Blanco and the Río Pusilha. It was settled by families moving northwards from Otoxha not many years ago.

The trail reaches the Río Blanco opposite a limestone bar which forms a low fall in the river; in the dry season this is mostly exposed,

and at all times except high flood is used as a crossing. After passing through the village the trail runs down to the Río Pusilha some 100 m. upstream of the massive abutments of the Classic bridge first reported by Thompson (1927). The river here is 20 m. wide, narrowing to 10 m. between the bridge abutments, and is too deep to wade; a number of dugout canoes are kept by the bank, and from the far side the trail to Otoxha runs off along the base of the steep limestone hills. The valley at this point lies at nearly 200 m. elevation, the crest of the hills at about 400 m. The range is penetrated by a number of long valleys from either side, and a short distance upstream from Poite the trail swings south into one of

Figure 8. Two COBANERO TRADERS AT SANTA CRUZ, BELIZE

these, crosses the divide and descends into the Temax basin, running almost due south to Otoxha, which lies by a small creek just north of the main river. From Otoxha the route lies across the creek and southeastward, more or less parallel to the Temax until the river is crossed as it bends northwards; the trail continues southeast until it meets the east–west route from Crique Sarco to Dolores which runs along the southern side of the Temax valley.

From Crique Sarco the route is that taken by Owen-Lewis; distances and populations are his estimates. On the map (Fig. 9) the overnight halts used on his journey are underlined, with those not indicated on the 1:250,000 scale map of Guatemala (1968) in brackets. This was however a return journey: Owen-Lewis notes (personal communication) that "cobaneros sleep at almost every village and used to take 3 weeks each way", while his journey took little over a week.

The route runs west from Crique Sarco, passing the junction with the Otoxha trail on the right, and after some 16 km. reaches Dolores, the last settlement in Belize. After checking with the police here the cobaneros continue due west across the border to Chacalte, a community of about 200 people some 11 km. from Dolores. Chacalte lies where the upper basins of the Temax and Sarstoon merge, and when the trail runs south out of the village it is into the latter drainage. The Sarstoon is divided in this area into two major streams, the Río San Pedro to the north and the Río Gracias a Diós, which separate around a block of hills and converge again some way to the east in Belize. The route descends a creek valley to the Río San Pedro, runs upstream for a distance and then crosses to the village of Carche (Secaache) on the south bank, some 16 km. from Chacalte and with a population of about 50. This was the first overnight halt: the day's journey had covered some 43 km., all below 200 m. elevation.

The next day's route ran upstream to the small village of Samaje, 9 km. from Carche and about the same size, lying on the south bank of the Río San Pedro just below the divergence from the Río Gracias a Diós. The route

crossed this latter stream near the divergence and followed the south bank of the single river upstream to the village of Gracias a Diós, also of about 50 persons and some 12 km. from Samaje. The trail again crosses the river, to the north bank, this time to avoid a stretch of swampy territory with many meanders. Above this is the confluence of the Río Chiyu and the Río Chahal, which together form the Río Gracias a Diós, and the route crosses here to the tongue of land between the rivers. Some 12 km. from Gracias a Diós, Owen-Lewis gives an overnight halt at a place called Pemech, a large village of some 400 people, which is probably that indicated on the 1:250,000 scale map as Las Conchas since this is the only settlement of any size in the relevant area. The second day's journey was of 34 km.

Las Conchas lies on the south bank of the Río Chiyu where several sets of rapids necessitate a transfer from canoe to land transport for some distance; the cobanero route runs out of the back of the village, southwestward towards the Río Chahal. It skirts a large block of hills that lies between the rivers, and keeping some way north of the Río Chahal itself climbs up to the town of Chahal, which lies on a broken plateau, a spur of the hills to the south, at between 200 and 300 m. elevation. This also was an overnight halt, the day's journey being of only 20 km. Chahal is a large settlement of some 1,000 persons, lying in a well-drained, well-ventilated and defensible position, with river valley, foothills and high hills all within a few km. radius. It is also the point of transition from highlands to lowlands. Northeast from here the entire route lies below 200 m. elevation, except for the brief climb over the hills between Poite and Otoxha. Southwest of Chahal the route runs always above 200 m., except for one brief stretch between Baúl and Chimuy, if the trail runs as far north as Figure 9 depicts. This combination of local advantages with the position as an important node on the highland-lowland route is one reason why Chahal is the largest settlement for some distance around.

Owen-Lewis's next overnight stop, and in fact the next halting-place on the route, is given as Baúl, approximately 32 km. from

Chahal. A further day's journey brings the traveller to Chimuy, 32 km. beyond Baúl. The former has a population of about 100, the latter of about 50, and neither is marked on the 1:250,000 scale map. There are two possible routes from Chahal towards Cajabon: one runs north of Cerro Tabol, a massif of nearly 1000 m. elevation, on the southern side of the upper basin of the Río Chiyu; the other runs east of Cerro Tabol through a pass into the upper valley of the Río Oxec, a tributary of the Río Cajabon. For several reasons the northern route is the more likely: the known trails are all on that side, and the stop beyond Chimuy, given by Owen-Lewis as Cala, would seem to be the village of Secala at the headwaters of the Río Chiaxon, a tributary of the Chiyu.

The section from Chahal to Secala has therefore been interpolated on the map as the most topographically likely route, following known trails. Since the airline distance from Chahal to Cajabon is only 32 km., and the total estimated ground distance given by Owen-Lewis is about 100 km., 72 km. of it between Chahal and (Se)cala, this stretch of the route remains problematical; a further foot-traverse is needed.

Secala is a small village of about fifty persons, from which the trail winds up to Rubelbalam, where there is a narrow pass at over 500 m. elevation through the Sierra de Chama into the basin of the Río Cajabon. The town of Cajabon, with a population which Owen-Lewis estimated at 2,000, lies in a broad upland valley where several streams converge at 200–300 m. elevation; it was the sixth overnight stop on the journey.

Beyond Cajabon a further day's journey of 32 km. brought the cobaneros to San Agustín, and the next morning they travelled by bus the 64 km. to San Pedro Carcha, stopping there before journeying also by bus the final 8 km. to Coban. The entire journey lies in the upper basin of the Río Cajabon and its tributary the Río Lanquin; the modern road, which now reaches down to Cajabon, runs high on the north side of the valley, but the precise path of the old foot-trail has not been recorded. Coban lies at an elevation of 1,330 m.

This, then, is the route travelled to within the last few years by the cobaneros. It was even then changing from the still recent past, as in the use of motor transport from San Agustín to Coban, and since the date of Owen-Lewis's journey further changes have occurred. The motor road now reaches Cajabon, as noted above, and from Chacalte the cobaneros now catch another bus north up the new trans-Peten road to San Luis before cutting due east across country to Pueblo Viejo in Belize. Roads have been built inland from Punta Gorda to San Miguel, San Pedro, San Antonio, Blue Creek, and Aguacate, and west from San Antonio to Santa Cruz, Río Blanco, and Pueblo Viejo; the cobaneros use these, but those I encountered at Santa Cruz in 1971 (Fig. 8) were about to take the old foot-trail to San José in spite of the existence of a motor road.

When they set out from Coban each man carries a load of about 45 kg., made up of small manufactured goods including skirts, blouses or huipils, blankets, hammocks, necklaces, cigars, sweets, patent medicines, catapults (slingshots) and other toys. They are supplied by traders in Coban, presumably on commission. By the time they reach San Antonio and San Pedro they are virtually sold out. They stock up for the return journey with cacao (Thompson 1970: 135) and also with goods that are either cheaper in Belize, (such as matches and soap) or which are illegal in Guatemala (such as shotguns) (Owen-Lewis, personal communication).

In the past other goods could have been shipped along this route. The lowlands lack obsidian sources, and the distribution pattern of obsidians from the El Chayal source near Guatemala City suggests that this route was used to bring the material down to southern Belize (Hammond 1972b); if the source reported by Blom near Coban exists (Thompson 1970: 143), then its products also may have been traded that way. Other Alta Verapaz goods would have included quetzal feathers, portrayed on many of the Lubaantun figurines (Joyce 1933), and possibly huipils as suggested by Thompson (1970: 135).

What seems so probable as to be a virtual certainty is that the lowland area at the northeastern end of the route, inhabited by the now-extinct Manche Chol, was producing and exporting cacao in exchange for these highland goods. The existence of contacts between the two areas in the 17th and 16th centuries is noted by Thompson (1970: 134–35), who quotes two colonial sources, Remesal (1932, Book 11, Chap. 18) and Villagutierre (1933, Book 9, Chap. 2), which record visits of the Manche Chol to Cajabon for the feast of the Nativity of the Blessed Virgin in 1596 and 1697. Remesal also records that the Manche Chol left bundles of cacao in trees near Cajabon to indicate their desire to make contact and presumably trade. Ximénez (1929–31, Book 5, Chap. 38) records that the people of Cajabon "always used to enter and trade" with the Manche Chol, which sounds very much like the modern *cobanero*. So we have evidence that the Manche Chol brought cacao to Cajabon, that they visited the town for a major festival (and presumably market) on two occasions a century apart, and that the highlanders also visited the Manche Chol territory. The 1596 and 1697 visits were presumably the only two recorded during a period of continuous contact, a supposition reinforced by the many personal names shared by the two areas (Feldman 1972b). That the recorded *cobanero* route was used at this time seems probable: certainly the route through the Rubelbalam pass, down the upper basin of the Sarstoon and along the flanks of the Maya Mountains is the most direct and efficient way of reaching the Manche Chol territory.

Before the colonial period we have only the evidence of archaeology, and it is, although scanty, suggestive. The northern part of the Alta Verapaz is generally recognized as coming within the cultural ambit of the Central Area, the southern lowlands, rather than the Southern Area of the Guatemalan highlands with which it belongs on topographic grounds, and this argues for close contact during the Classic period. The stimulus for contact is clearly that of reciprocal exchange between the two adjacent regions of contrasting environment and resources, and the advantages of this symbiosis great enough to enable contact to be maintained throughout the historic period in spite of the barriers erected by modern political boundaries, depopulation, and the like.

The specific evidence for Classic period contact between the Manche Chol around Lubaantun and the area of Coban rests mainly on the well-known Lubaantun-style figurines (Hammond, in preparation; Joyce 1933). The use of cacao at Lubaantun in the Late Classic is documented by a figurine found there in 1970 (Hammond 1972c, Fig. 24) of a musician wearing a cacao-pod pendant, and the likelihood is, therefore, that cacao was traded up to the Alta Verapaz at this date. The presence of El Chayal obsidian at a number of sites in the realm of Lubaantun (Hammond 1972b) suggests that the *cobanero* route or a similar one was used, and finally the presence of what seems to be a Lubaantun-made figurine in a highland context near Coban confirms the supposition. The figurine, depicting an old woman cradling a rat-like creature in her lap, is in the Dieseldorff collection (Dieseldorff 1926–1933, Vol. I, Pl. 10, No. 45), and is matched by one found by Joyce in 1927 (Joyce, Cooper Clark, and Thompson 1927, Pl. XIX, Fig. 1, lower right), and by at least one other example from the same mold, and by what seems to be the mold itself, both from the British Museum excavations of 1926–1927 at Lubaantun (Hammond, in preparation). Several other figurines illustrated by Dieseldorff are in the Lubaantun style, without precise parallels (but this latter point is not surprising when we consider that of the 1,000 or so figurines from Lubaantun itself only a handful are duplicated). Analysis of the clays of these would settle the question of their origin.

Our archaeological evidence therefore consists of one very probable and several probable figurines exported in the Late Classic from the Manche Chol site of Lubaantun to the area of Coban, and the demonstration from another figurine that cacao was grown at Lubaantun at that time and could have been exported to the highlands. Taken by itself this evidence is merely suggestive, but if it is considered together with the ethnohistoric and ethnographic data, the three classes of evidence being seen as successive transects through a processual continuum, it becomes compelling: all three transects demonstrate contact between the two areas, the two latter document the trade goods as well as the symbiotic stimulus, and ethnographic observation enables us to suggest the exact route followed.

ACKNOWLEDGMENTS

Don Owen-Lewis supplied the data on the modern *cobanero* route. Kate Pretty drew Figure 9. Eric Thompson was, as always, an invaluable consultant. The background against which this article is written was acquired partly with the aid of a grant from the Wenner-Gren Foundation, and during tenure of a Fellowship at the Centre of Latin American Studies at Cambridge University, England.

REFERENCES

Dieseldorff 1926–1933
Feldman 1972b
Gruning 1930
Hammond 1972a, 1972b, 1972c
Joyce 1929, 1933
Joyce, Cooper Clark, and Thompson 1927
Joyce, Gann, Gruning, and Long 1928
Molloy and Rathje 1972
Rathje 1971a, 1973
Remesal 1932
Sanders and Price 1968
Thompson 1927, 1970
Villagutierre y Soto-Mayor 1933
Wright 1970
Ximénez 1929–1931

4. ROUTES OF COMMUNICATION IN MESOAMERICA: THE NORTHERN GUATEMALAN HIGHLANDS AND THE PETEN

by

Richard E. W. Adams

Prehistoric major routes of access within the southern Maya Lowlands and the north Highlands can be defined from a number of sources of information. Historical accounts of early Spanish *entradas*, colonial routes, and recorded pre-Hispanic trail networks can often indicate those used in the still more ancient past. Ethnographic studies often contain information which provides analogues of means of communication to indigenous times. Lacking these data, one can turn to geographical constraints, looking on maps and on the ground for natural routes which would have given accessibility to specific areas. Finally, archaeological work which gives site distributions, and the pragmatic travel experience of archaeologists themselves can be used as data sources.

The areas assigned me are vast and diverse, and, although I have personal experience of some parts of both zones, it is clearly inadequate to provide complete and reliable data in general. The sources I have consulted are also incomplete in their coverage, although this may be a function of my own limitations in the historical literature. Therefore, I have taken the approach of attempting to define geographically the major routes of access within the northern highlands and southern lowlands, and between these two areas. Other routes are indicated by historical and ethnographic sources. The times and details of routes are often filled in from the travel accounts of such persons as S. G. Morley and A. L. Smith. These men traveled the zones, at least parts of their careers, in times when modern travel was not much different from that of the 16th century. Airlines and road networks have changed things greatly in the past twenty-five years, although some areas are still accessible only by foot, dugout, or mule. What follows, in other words, makes no pretense at completeness, but is more of a sampling approach to the problem.

Rates of Travel[1]

We can best approach the problem of zones which lack good ethnohistoric, historic, or ethnological evidence from the point of view of maximum travel rates. These we can derive from the sample zones discussed below. In the highlands of Guatemala, over difficult country involving crossing of mountain ranges, the rate of travel is about 2 km. per hour for modern pack trains. Men can travel considerably faster than mules or horses and therefore up to 3 km. per hour is an outside estimate for a group of porters (*tamemes*) really pushing along. This approaches the 3 km. per hour which is typical of an unladen person traveling alone and afoot.

In the lowlands there are two means of travel, overland and by water. Something between 2 and 3 km. per hour is typical of travel through the rain forest today. This is on unimproved trails, full of obstacles and with detours around fallen trees, etc. In ancient times, it is safe to assume that at least the main routes of travel were kept cleared, open, and bridged. Thirty-one to thirty-five km. can be covered in ten hours if one urges the party on. Morley's daily journeys often hit this pace, which is over the 3 km. per hour average. More than usually difficult country, with ridges, *bajos*, and fords brings this rate down to 2.2 km. per hour on some days, however.

River travel is more variable still, as seen from various journeys cited below. Generally, Morley counted on 3–4 km. per hour upstream, in a dugout being paddled by three or four men. He counted on some 9–10 km. per hour downstream. This accords well with the rates adjusted from the recent Pasión River expeditions in which 21- to 33-foot dugouts

[1]I wish to acknowledge discussions, both recent and past, with A. L. Smith and Ian Graham who have greatly aided me in understanding the constraints and possibilities of travel in the Maya area.

pushed by 18 hp. motors travel 14 km. per hour downstream and only slightly less coming against the current. The size of the craft, the heavier or lighter load in it, the number of paddlers used, the current in the stream traveled, and shoals or rapids can all bring this figure drastically down or slightly up.

MAJOR ROUTES OF ACCESS TO THE PETEN AND NORTH HIGHLANDS

A map study, using the recently completed series of 1:250,000 sheets from the National Geographic Institute of Guatemala, indicates several water or valley routes on north–south and east–west axes (Fig. 10).

North-South Lowland Routes

North–south routes are dominated by the large river systems of the Pasión and the Chixoy-Salinas, which eventually unite to form the Usumacinta.[2] Tributary streams from the northern sides of the Sierra de Chama in the Alta Verapaz and from the north of the Cuchumatanes Mountains of Quiche lead down to the tropical forest zones. Changes in elevations are from the 2,400 m. (7,700 ft.) passes just south of Nebaj to the 125 m. (410 ft.) level on the lower Pasión River. As an estimate of the amount of time necessary to get from the highlands to the main courses of the Pasión, Chixoy, and Usumacinta, a trip from Coban overland to Sebol on a tributary of the Pasión, and thence downstream to the mouth of the same river took just seven days in 1962 for a man carrying supplies for the Altar de Sacrificios Project. This trip was accomplished with outboard motors, trucks, and dugout canoes. However, adjustment can be made for modern improvements by reference to Morley's trips in which paddling and foot was the motive power. Morley (1938, Vol. 2, pp. 235–36) counted on 9–10 km. per hour downstream and 3 km. upstream in a lightly laden dugout. However, the 80 km. from Sayaxche to Altar required eighteen

hours, an average of only 4½ km. per hour downstream. The Altar project boat with an 18 hp. outboard motor, 21 ft. in length, and loaded lightly, consistently made the trip in 5½ hours, an average of 14 km. per hour downstream. Our heavily laden dugout of 33-ft. length, with an 18 hp. engine, made only 8 km. per hour, probably the average of the supply trip from Sebol. In other words, the likelihood is that paddling is about ½ as fast as an 18 hp. outboard engine on a relatively slow stream like the Pasión. Therefore, the time expended in 1962 for the trip should be doubled to arrive at paddling time. This means a travel time of fourteen days on the river to which must be added the travel time on foot overland from Coban to Sebol. Morley accomplished about this same journey in six days, covering 160 km. from Cahabon to within 20 km. of the site of Cancuen. Two days should be subtracted to allow for the fact that Cancuen is that much farther along the Pasión than Sebol. This means some eighteen days of travel from the Coban vicinity to the confluence of the Pasión and Chixoy-Salinas Rivers. Some confirmation of parts of this trip come from Sedat and Sharer's (1972: 29) comment that the trail from around Chamelco, which is near Coban, brings one to the Peten in less than a week. However, this would be only the extreme southern portion of the Maya Lowlands, and considerably more traveling would be required to reach the lower Pasión and still more to cross overland to sites such as Tikal, about 90 km. by trail (56 miles) north of the river.

It should be noted that the Coban zone seems to have been the highland area through which passed influences on lowland Maya cultures from the southern Maya Highlands. Certainly by the Protoclassic period contact is established. Sedat and Sharer (1972) claim a Preclassic date for such contact, but the issue is still in doubt.

The Nebaj-Cotzal zone, on the other hand, seems not to have been in close contact with the adjacent highland zones. Contact with the lowlands is established only in Protoclassic times, and then seemingly broken off after the Late Classic (R. E. W. Adams 1972). Pre-

---

[2]The Pasión was known as the Ayn and the Chixoy as the Dz'ununteilha in the 16th and 17th centuries (Villaguiterre y Soto-Mayor 1933 and Thompson 1970: 126).

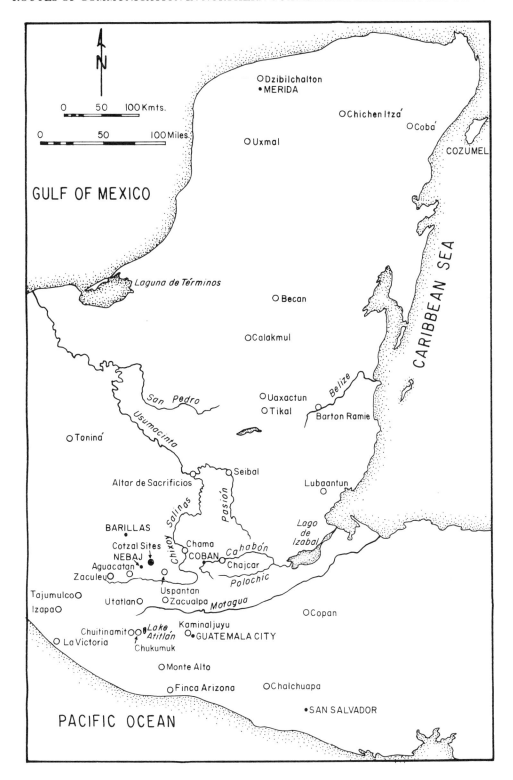

Figure 10. MAP OF THE MAYA AREA
Selected sites and major river systems in the Guatemala Highlands and the Peten are stressed.

sumably, the more rugged nature of the Cuchumatanes and the existence of relatively easier corridors of passage in the Coban zone account for this difference. Chamelco is only four days by foot, unladen, to Guatemala City, and therefore only about eleven days of travel separate Kaminaljuyu and the edge of the southern Maya Lowlands through the Coban zone (Sedat and Sharer 1972: 29). Another two days bring one to the Classic Period site on which the modern town of Sayaxche is built, and thence 90 km. more or less straight to Tikal, probably three to four days overland travel, for a total of fifteen or sixteen days from Kaminaljuyu to Tikal, traveling light. With cargo, the trip would likely require twice as much time.

The Chixoy-Salinas drainage is much more complex and a number of tributary streams (the Icbolay, Ixcan, and Xacbal) lead from the area which is now occupied by the Ixil, into the Lacantun or the Chixoy-Salinas. Both river systems feed into the Usumacinta only 19 km. from one another.

During archaeological work on the Cotzal River in 1965 and 1966, I gathered some information on travel modes and times from one place to another (Fig. 11, Table 4). The project was centered on the sites around the junction of the Cotzal and Chipal Rivers, just north of the Cuchumatanes, on Finca San Francisco. My informants were the workmen who had lived their lives on the finca and who were Ixil Indians. Table 4 summarizes this information. It is regretably incomplete, but gives some ideas of rates of travel in the highlands and the length of time needed to reach the lowlands. Traveling with pack trains, which, according to A. L. Smith (personal communication), are slower than trains of human porters, one can still make 25–30 km. per day over the rugged highland topography. More pertinent here is the travel time to the Río Ixcan, a river flowing into the Lacantun and thence into the Usumacinta: five days. Thence downstream at about 8 km. per hour in modern canoes works out to about ten days to reach the confluence of the Pasión and Chixoy. This was the rate of travel made by Sr. Jorge Brol in 1961 and 1966. Doubling

this to allow for paddling in aboriginal times, means about three weeks or more to go from Nebaj and Finca San Francisco to the site of Altar de Sacrificios at the confluence and two more days, or about twenty-eight days total, to reach the site at Sayaxche where one would begin the overland trek to Tikal if that were the destination. Four days to Tikal would total thirty-two days from Nebaj to Tikal, considerably more than from Kaminaljuyu to Tikal via the Coban route. Using the above figures, one could get to Yaxchilan in some twenty-seven days, although returning would require forty-eight days up the same streams. Use of another Lacantun tributary, the Xacbal, would perhaps save a few days, but not more than two or three. Thompson notes that the Ixil indeed did travel these areas in the 19th century, going to Tabasco to trade for cacao (Thompson 1970: 135).

Ethnographic confirmation of the uses of these routes are both through Ixil trade and nineteenth and twentieth century Kekchi migration. The latter have migrated both overland and down the Pasión River.

The only overland route from highlands to lowlands is indicated by the latter migration which has traditionally gone out through Chisec, heading for the great bend of the Pasión where it turns from a northward course to a westerly one (R. N. Adams 1965). A tentative confirmation of this route having been used earlier comes from an unpublished map of Thomas Gates' found in his papers deposited at Brigham Young University and kindly furnished to me by Thomas Lee. This map shows two trails from the highlands to the lowlands. One follows a straight line to Lake Petén from Coban and seems to make no allowance for topography. It is labeled the Chinaja trail and indeed does pass near the zone now called Chinaja in the southern lowlands. The new motor road from Coban to the Peten more or less follows this route (NGI 1965). The other trail leaves Cahabon and proceeds north to a place called Dolores in the Peten and keeps to the east of the Pasión, bending to a northwesterly course thereafter to arrive at Lake Peten. This is labeled the Dolores Trail and presumably this settlement

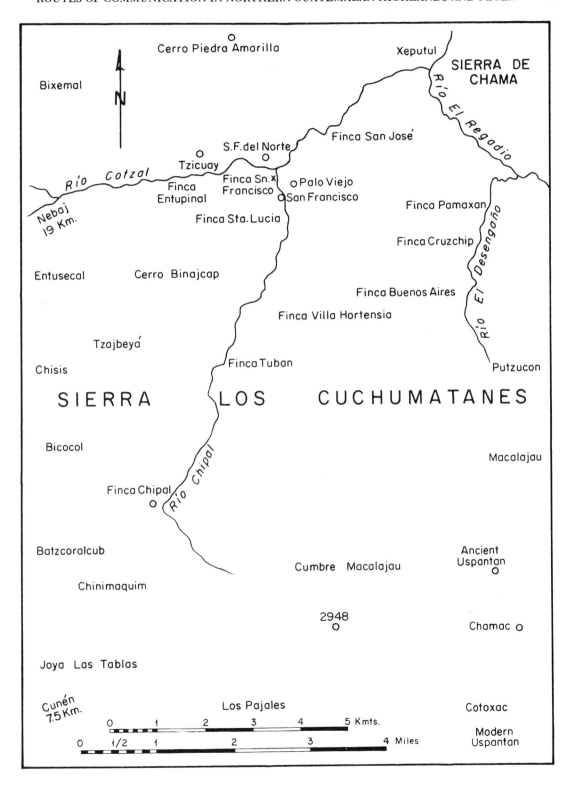

Figure 11. MAP OF THE COTZAL-CHIPAL RIVER AREA

is the same early 16th century settlement founded by the Spaniards among the Manche Chol. However, the map is suspect, since there are gross errors of several kinds: mis-location of linguistic groups, and the mis-placement of major archaeological sites (Yaxchilan is shown on the right bank of the Usumacinta instead of being correctly placed on the left bank). Nonetheless, the Chinaja trail closely corresponds to the Chisec route historically used by the Kekchi and seems to be an approximation of reality. It is note-worthy that the major overland route from highlands to lowlands is through the Alta Verapaz region and only one trail is noted from the Nebaj (Ixil) region. This seems to correspond with the general archaeological patterns that are showing up, indicating for the Ixil region mainly Early Classic contact with the lowlands. Late Classic contact be-tween the Coban region and Yaxchilan and Altar de Sacrificios is documented (R. E. W. Adams 1972).

Travel times overland are much easier to calculate, being that whether they are high-land or lowland they average about 31 to 36 km. per day. This rate can be reduced due to terrain, but considering the distance involved (about 140 km. from Coban to Sayaxche), it would seem that a trip of five to six days is not unreasonable for the journey for a person on foot, alone, and with no goods.

Sixteenth and seventeenth century pene-tration of the Lacandon zones on the Lacan-tun and around Lake Petha followed the waterways: for example, the *entrada* of Al-cayaga in 1696 to Nuestra Señora de los Dolores, a Lacandon village (Morley 1938, Vol. 1, p. 411).

Finally, the Polochic-Izabal route should be mentioned as one which ties in the north-eastern Highlands (Coban and Cahabon) with the trade route around the peninsula. Canoes from the coastal trade could come directly up to near the present El Estor and thence easily by two days' (60 km.) travel to the Cahabon region. It seems possible that this was a route used for highland-lowland contact, since it gives access to the coastal region of the penin-sula. Whether it was actually much used is a problem that awaits archaeological investiga-tion. Certainly one could have gone from Coban or Cahabon to Izabal, thence to the Belize River, and then inland to Naranjo or Tikal. Such a trip would take a minimum of twenty-eight days: two days from Cahabon to El Estor, three days on the lake (90 km.), and ten days to the mouth of the Belize River (310 km.), nine days to Xunantunich (255 km.), and then four days to Tikal.

Another possible route is from the western highlands of Chiapas to the Tabasco and Chiapas lowlands. Tonina and Chinkultic, both highland sites, are definitely lowland in cultural cast as noted by Thompson (1970: 126) and others. The Alcayaga expedition to the Lancandon country noted above started from Sta. María Ixtatan on the northern edge of the Western highlands. About the only useful observation to be made here is that this

Table 4: SUMMARY OF TRAVEL TIMES AROUND THE MIDDLE COTZAL VALLEY, GUATEMALAN HIGHLANDS

	alone on foot	alone on horse	with pack train
Finca San Francisco to Cunen (18 air km.) 9000 ft. pass	6 hr. (5–11 a.m.)	7 hr. (5 a.m.–12 noon)	10 hr. (5 a.m.–3 p.m.)
Finca San Francisco to Uspantan (12 air km.)			6 hr.
Finca San Francisco to Chajul via S. J. Cotzal (8 leagues; 32 km.)		7 hr.	8 hr.
Finca San Francisco to Putul (1½ leagues; 6 km.)	1½ hr.		
Finca San Francisco to Río Ixcan			5 days
Sacapulas to Cunen (9 leagues; 36 km.)		9 hr.	

area is even more difficult than the Ixil zone to traverse, and thus seems unlikely as a transmission route from other parts of the highlands to lowlands or vice versa. However, the northern edges were certainly in contact with the lowlands, although this contact was probably intermittent, difficult, and by means of small groups.

East-West Lowland Routes

Again, based on a map study, there is a possible route into the Maya Lowlands from the West using the Jatate-Lacantun-Pasión pattern of waterways. One can journey to the headwaters of the Sarstoon or the Moho River from the Pasión River overland and complete the journey from the Gulf of Mexico to the Caribbean Sea. This route is onerous, difficult, and at least in the sixteenth century, was avoided, as is documented below. Thompson and others have argued that to get to Honduras from Tabasco ports such as Xicalango it was preferable to go around the peninsula by canoe.

This southern, east-west (west-east?) route is full of portages and rapids on the Jatate as can be best seen from the admirable map that Blom prepared in 1953 (Blom and Duby 1957).

An alternative is to use the Usumacinta, and thence the Pasión and go overland to the Sarstoon. However, this is a trip that involves a long overland segment around a gorge and rapids on the Usumacinta (above Tenosique and below the site of Piedras Negras). A trip was made by Morley (1938, Vol. 2, pp. 349–50) from Isla Carmen to Yaxchilan and required six and one-half days. However, Morley covered 336 km. in a river boat *the first day* and this must be stretched out to allow for paddling. At the maximum of 40 km. a day on the lower Usumacinta, this would mean at least eight and one-half days and thus a total of fourteen days of which five would be overland. Another four days to the mouth (Boca) of the Pasión and thence three more days to the Great Bend of the Pasión, three days to the Sarstoon, and two days to the Caribbean Sea total twenty-six days without allowing for rest, probably thirty days in all in aborigi-

nal times. The comparative time for canoes traveling from Isla Carmen around the Yucatan Peninsula to the mouth of the Sarstoon is unknown, but even if it totaled the same thirty days, the travel would be greatly eased and less complicated due to the lack of overland trips.

Similarly the route taken by Cortés in his march to Honduras in 1525 was a famously difficult one even without a rest stop. The trip from the Acalan capital of Itzamkanac (El Tigre archaeological site) to Lake Peten required five days. Thirty leagues was the distance and if one uses the 4 km. average for a league then a day's journey was about 24 km. Using 3 km. per league yields around eighteen km. per day. Since Cortés was moving a great number of people (over 3,000) and armies are notorious for straggling, the lower figure may well be correct. In addition, the trip was through unfamiliar country, although the Acalan people had provided Cortés with a map of the Cehache country which he would have to cross.[3] In any case, Cortés' trip would seem to have been slower than necessary although certainly arduous enough even for a single man. The point here is that the east–west passage over the peninsula was, by the 16th century, certainly not the preferred route.

The Río Acalan, now known as the Candelaria, is a stream evidently with about the speed of current of the Pasión. Paxbolon and Bravo covered 110 km. in thirty-four or thirty-six hours which is an average of 3.3 or 3.1 km. per hour (Scholes and Roys 1948: 422–23).

The other river that could be used to penetrate the Peten from the west is the San Pedro, between the Candelaria on the north and the Usumacinta system to the south. I understand that river conditions are again similar to those on the Pasión, with low-speed current, numerous shoals, and seasonal rise and flow which greatly affects the speed

---

[3]For a more thorough and lengthy discussion of this journey and others made in the 16th and 17th centuries in the Acalan region, see Scholes and Roys 1948. Average speeds, time, and modes of travel are all considered.

of travel (Ian Graham, personal communication).

The Belize River is the major avenue to the central Peten from the east and brings one into the very heartland of Maya Classic culture ending at the major site of Xunantunich and within 10 km. of the even larger center of Naranjo. The early Carnegie expeditions used this river as an access to the Peten. Two hundred fifty-five km. is the distance from the mouth of the Belize River to El Cayo (Xunantunich), yielding a paddling travel time of eight and one-half days at 3 km. per hour and ten-hour days. Thence it would be only one half day to Naranjo and three more to Tikal. Conceivably, it was easier to go to Tikal from Tabasco by using a route around the Yucatan Peninsula and then up the Belize River and overland. This assumes that trails were blocked and no facilities were available in the eastern reaches of the Peten, that is, that conditions in the Classic period approximated conditions of travel in the sixteenth century and later. This is patently not the case, but political hostilities could also have intervened.

Travel on the lakes in the central Peten was by canoe. Canek met Cortés, accompanied by 500 men carried in 80 canoes, an average capacity of 64 men per canoe. These traveled the three leagues to Tayasal in four and one-half hours or at about 3½ km. per hour on the lake which has no appreciable current. Two things are noteworthy here. Speed does not seem to increase with the size of the canoe; one must simply have more paddlers to push more deadweight at an average speed. The other point is that there were much larger canoes in the sixteenth and seventeenth centuries than those seen today of two to three or seven to eight man capacity. A native from Lake Peten, sub-chief Quixan, informed the Spaniards that the Itza had forty-man canoes (Morley 1938, Vol. 1, pp. 44, 52). Wind, not usually a factor on rivers, might affect lake travel.

Overland travel in the Peten in ancient times no doubt more closely approximated present-day off-the-road conditions. A. L. Smith notes that it took four days to get to Uaxactun from El Cayo, an average of about 32 km. per day. Smith comments that this was with a pack train and that porters would have been faster than mules. Porters or *tamemes* can negotiate tough going such as is found in the dry or wet *bajos* much better. Morley (1938 Vol. 2, p. 234) gives an average pack load of around 25 kg. per man as optimum. However, much heavier loads could have been carried for shorter distances.

Mud can slow down men and mules, and a trip of 19 km. from Uaxactun was made in a miserable rain by the author in seven hours, less than 3 km. per hour.

The sixteenth century Peten was certainly a difficult place in which to move any distance, as is indicated by the fact that it took twenty days for the Itza to strike at the southern Lacandon going overland from Tayasal to Lake Petha and returning (Scholes and Roys 1948: 44).

SUMMARY AND DISCUSSION

Overland travel for small trains of porters in either highlands or lowlands would seem to have been about the same regardless of topography, unless a pass were being negotiated or a direct uphill journey was being made. Otherwise, average travel time is about 31–35 km. per day. These are trail distances and not air distances. Smaller parties move faster than large ones as seems to be demonstrated by the contrast between the usual archaeological party's travel time and that of Cortés' army.

As far as water travel goes, the Alta Verapaz seems to be much more accessible to the Peten than the Ixil zone. Even so, the Sebol River is full of rapids down to the juncture with the Pasión and a trip along it is no picnic.

A zone of "easy" access along the rivers of the lowlands might be delimited with 30 km. limits as the reasonable distance one might travel away from the river.

The hypothesis also might be advanced that long distance peaceful communication was likely limited in ancient times to small groups of persons. This would also explain the apparent elite class nature of trade and contact within the lowlands. Only where access was had to the inland waterways of the coast could large bulk cargoes such as salt be shipped easily. Cost of commodities such as salt must have been high when transport was by means of porters.

Based on examination of possible routes outlined above, it seems that only the Coban zone was one of frequently used access to the lowlands. Even this route was not an easy one, and anyone planning on penetrating to the central Peten had to plan on a one way trip of weeks whichever way he went. Likewise, anyone traveling any distance within the lowlands or highlands probably could plan on more than a week's journey of some difficulty.

In attempting to draw parallels between either Africa with the large Congolese canoes,

or the Pacific with equally impressive and well propelled craft, one must refer back to the observed rates of canoe travel in the Peten which usually do not exceed 3 or 3.5 km. per hour. Given these parameters, it is easier to understand why Maya Classic cultures were so regionalized even though contact may have been maintained at the upper levels of society.

REFERENCES

Adams, R. N. 1965
Adams, R. E. W. 1972
Blom and Duby 1957
Morley 1938
National Geographic Institute of Guatemala (NGI) 1965
Scholes and Roys 1948
Sedat and Sharer 1972
Thompson 1970
Villaguiterre y Soto-Mayor 1933

5. COMMERCE IN THE YUCATAN PENINSULA: THE CONQUEST AND COLONIAL PERIOD
by
Román Piña Chan

THE REGION AND ITS JURISDICTIONS

Commerce among the pre-Hispanic Maya is a subject that has interested numerous investigators. It embraces different cultural periods and generally has been treated from the point of view of the historical sources. As I see the use of historical sources, they are only applicable to the earliest times of the Spanish conquest and colonialization, that is to say, the period between A.D. 1550 and 1600. However, knowledge from this period might apply to the previous century or back to 1400 of the Christian era.

For this reason, I will consider anew here the period of the historical sources with the object of obtaining a general view of the problem and a basic knowledge which will permit the study of earlier periods. I will also limit myself to Yucatan, Campeche, Quintana Roo, and part of Belize since other investigators will consider the rest of the Maya region (Fig. 12).

The territory embraced in this study is located in the so-called north and central Maya regions. The first can be thought of as a low limestone plain with low forest, the second, an alluvial plain of high forest trenched by many rivers, even though several ecological zones can be observed throughout, such as the Atlantic and Caribbean Coasts, with low-lying, frequently swampy, dry or wet, semiarid or rainy tropical lands.

The northern region is a low dry and somewhat arid forest and savanna with small areas of forest, without rivers and rarely, with lakes. The same applies to the Puuc hills that branch off toward Campeche and Chetumal. The Chenes area lies to the southeast and consists of *milpa* lands and savanna with deciduous forest or rainier low or medium cover.

The southern region of rivers and lagoons consists of an intricate aquatic network that crosses hot and humid alluvial plains and swampy lands covered with a forest of medium to high trees. The high tropical forest, composed of perceptible elevations and known as *La Montaña* adjoins the Peten provenience, low tropical lands and high rainy forests that rise toward the south to constitute the Highlands of Chiapas and Guatemala.

According to the studies of Roys (1957) and Scholes and Roys (1948) this territory was divided into jurisdictions with more or less known limits: Ah Canul, Chakan, Cehpech, Mani, Canpech, Chanputun, Acalan, etc. Some of these regions had *cabeceras* or important capitals that dominated a series of towns and neighboring villages.

The jurisdication or territorial division (*cuchcabal*) was governed by a *Halach uinic* who resided in a regional center, such as in Cehpech, Mani, and Sotuta, or by various *batabes* or village chiefs who were independent and grouped as a confederation, as happened at Ah Canul, or by a *batab* who dominated the rest as in the case of Cupul. Sometimes several towns of one jurisdiction incorporated themselves within a better organized neighbor as happened in the case of Chakan and Chikinchel.

Within the jurisdictions families of great lineages governed: the Canules, Peches, Cocomes, Xius, Cheles, etc. A large part of the population was dispersed in large and small towns and villages. The large towns could have *barrios* with certain autonomy. Even though the land belonged to the towns there were certain plantations of cacao, fruit trees, and edible plants that were considered the private property of the nobles or upper class.

According to the *Lista de Tributos y Encomiendas* of 1549 the territory was well populated and many jurisdictions were composed of numerous towns. The names of the majority of these towns last until today. Since Roys (1957) estimated a population of 256,200 inhabitants without counting the jurisdictions of Uaymil, Chetumal, Cehache, Acalan, and the territory of Belize it is possible that the total for the territory could have reached a half a million people during those times.

In about 1549 the jurisdiction of Ah Canul extended from Point Kopte to the Homtun River, not far from Campeche. It was an ample coastal strip with little agriculture but rich in salt works and fish. Through there one traveled from Campeche to Mérida touching several important towns. This was the route that Montejo *el hijo* followed in 1541 when he marched to the conquest of Tiho (Mérida). In Calkine the tribute was gathered which was given to Montejo; this consisted of corn, turkeys, honey, and cotton. The towns of the jurisdiction gave tribute to the Spanish in the form of salt, fish, cotton, and perhaps hennequen. Besides the route or road which went from Becal to the rich salt works at La Desconocida, one left from Becal for Maxcanu and Mérida, and a thrid passed by the Aguada Yiba, near Uxmal, in the direction of Mani.

The jurisdiction of Chakan seems to have been constituted of several independent towns predominantly in savannas that were apt for henequen cultivation. Those towns gave tribute to the *encomenderos* of salt and fish perhaps obtained directly from the coast or through intermediaries.

The jurisdiction of Cehpech occupied an arid, dry zone near the coast. It had important towns ruled by a *Halach uinic*. The principal tribute consisted of salt and fish. The capital was Motul, which also gave as tribute cotton mantles.

The jurisdiction of Hocaba was ruled by a *Halach uinic* of the lineage Iuit; the capital was Hocaba. It is said that the jurisdiction was constantly at war with its neighbors, taking them prisoners, and perhaps selling them as slaves.

The jurisdiction of Mani was governed by a *Halach uinic* of the Xiu lineage and bordered the low Puuc Hills which perhaps produced flint. It maintained rivalry wtih the people of Sotuta. It possessed good lands for agriculture and fruit trees. There was a road from Xul to Oxkutzcab over which corn was carried. The capital, Mani, was an important religious center where annual feasts were celebrated in honor of Kukulcan.

The jurisdiction of Ah Kin Chel had a high rainfall and therefore there were some cedar forests. Along the northern coast was an important exploitation of salt. It was also rich in fishing. A road is mentioned which went from Izamal to Ake, the former reputed to be a great religious center. The people of the town of Cansahcab sold salt to other towns that needed it. Those of the town of Buctzotz captured people for slavery and produced cedar lumber. At Dzidzantun green stones arrived through commerce.

The jurisdiction of Sotuta was governed by a *Halach uinic* of the Cocom lineage and maintained rivalries with the people of Mani.

The jurisdiction of Chikinchel or Chauaca was a region of forests with access to the coast, rich in salt works; it also produced fish and great quantities of copal that were exported to other places. The capital was Chauaca. There were other important towns, such as Sinsimato, which had a monopoly on copal.

For its part, the jurisdiction of Tases was composed of a group of towns and was the smallest. It had some cedar and zapote forests, although the land was mostly flat and rocky. The capital was Chancenote and it is said that from here a road went to Conil, another important commercial center.

The Cupul jurisdiction possessed lands adequate for agriculture and had numerous cenotes. It is possible that there were some cacao plantations there. The jurisdiction was governed by *Batabes* of the lineage Cupul. The town of Sodzil paid a tribute of red beads, green stones, corn, and wild turkeys to the lord Naobon Cupul who resided at Chichen Itza.

The Cochuah jurisdiction seems to have controlled the region of Bahía de la Ascención, since in the town of Ichmul there were temples where the lords of Chichen Itza made sacrifices when they embarked on or returned from a commerce trip to Honduras. At the same time Ichmul had cacao orchards. It maintained relations and had communication with Bahía de la Ascención. The *Halach uinic* who governed the jurisdiction lived in Tihosuco and was of the Cochuah lineage, the same family which had commercial agents in the Ulua River of Honduras.

The Ecab jurisdiction was governed by a *Halach uinic* whose residence was in the capital, the commercially important town of Ecab. In this jurisdiction were the ports of Conil and Pole as well as the town of Cachi, another commercial center. The *encomenderos* received as tribute from this jurisdiction salt, fish, corn, and ornaments that came from other places. Isla de Mujeres produced corn and salt, while Cozumel was a center of pilgrimage which produced honey and wax and at the same time paid tribute in salt and fish. There was communication by sea to the islands or along the coast to Pole, Tulum, and Chetumal.

The Uaymil jurisdiction had forests of mahogany, cedar, *Palo de Campeche*, and copal. Perhaps cacao and wild cotton were also harvested. There were roads from Cochuah and from Ichmul to Bacalar. The latter place was a port of embarcation for merchandise, especially cacao, toward the interior of the Yucatan Peninsula. Thus it is said that Mani went in search of cacao to Bacalar, passing through the town of Ucum.

The jurisdiction of Chetumal exported honey, corn, and cacao and maintained relations directly with Bacalar. It is said that Nachan Can, Lord of Chetumal, had a commercial agent on the Ulua River of Honduras.

The Campech jurisdiction had good lands for the cultivation of corn and fruit trees. It produced much cotton and maize, as well as honey and wax. Salt and fish were the tribute given to the Spanish.

Large quantities of fish were also produced by the Chanputun jurisdiction which was ruled by a *Halach uinic* of the Couah lineage. Commerce was conducted with the interior of the jurisdiction via the Río Champoton. The town of Tixchel produced objects made of turtle shell and feather fans.

A *Halach uinic* of the Chontal lineage governed the Acalan jurisdiction from its capital of Itzamkanac, located in the bend of the Río Candelaria (see Lee, Paper 10). The Acalan merchants dominated the course of this river

which emptied into the Laguna de Términos and they maintained commercial relations with Xicalango and Tabasco, as well as with the Peten Itza and Cimatan. The Acalan merchants occupied a *barrio* in the town of Nito near the mouth of the Río Dulce in Guatemala. Hernán Cortes, on his trip to Las Hibueras (Honduras) in 1525 entered the jurisdiction of Acalan at a point between Petenecte and Tenosique, following a road known by the merchants, even though the easiest route was by canoe along the Usumacinta to Palizada and into the Laguna de Términos and from there by the Candelaria to the capital.

The little-known jurisdiction of Cehache or Mazatlan had forests, lakes, and swampy land. Relations were maintained via its several rivers with Uaymil, Chetumal, and perhaps Belize. From it one reached the jurisdiction of Peten Itza, whose capital was Tayasal.

At the same time the jurisdiction of Cimatan extended almost to the Gulf Coast maintaining relations with Tabasco, especially along the course of the Río Grijalva and its tributaries. From the town of Tatalapa amber was carried to Tabasco.

Other historical sources proportion some more data on the subject that concerns us here. Bartolomé Colón (1947?) mentions that while he was in Guanja in 1502 there arrived "a vessel loaded with merchandise, which was said to come from a certain province called Maian (Maya), of Yucatan ... (and that) it had in the center a cover made of palm leaves, no different from those that the gondolas of Venice have, which protected whatever was below it ... the children, the women, and all the baggage and the merchandise." The canoe was as large as a galley and eight feet wide, made from a single tree trunk, and crewed by twenty-five men. The canoe came, perhaps, from Honduras.

Cortés (1960) entered the province of Acalan in 1525 and he said of it that it was "a great thing, because there are in it many towns and many people ... there are in it many merchants and people who trade with many places ... it is surrounded by estuaries (rivers) and all of them empty into the bay or port that is called Términos, through which they have a great commerce by canoe with Xicalango and Tabasco."

Montejo (19) in 1528 penetrated the Ecab jurisdiction, finding important centers such as Cachi, Chauaca, Sinsimato, etc., that had markets, temples, houses, and much merchandise. Continuing on from there, Montejo went to Chichen Itza and Ake by known roads.

According to Oviedo y Valdés (1851–55), "the town of Champoton is where the government of Yucatan communicates through the area on its west with New Spain. The people of this town carry on commerce with those of another center which is called Xicalango, consisting entirely of merchants, on the coast of the Río Grijalva . . . and it is something to see that every day more than two thousand canoes ordinarily leave from that city to fish in the ocean along the coast, returning each night." Landa (1938) mentions "that the Indians put signals in the trees in order to show the way coming or going by water from Tabasco to Yucatan."

Landa also mentions that "25 leagues from Ichmul is Bahía de la Ascención . . . a very good and great port . . . it is more than 30 leagues of dry road from the city of Valladolid . . . (where they leave with) merchandise which they carry across from Bacalar with great work and risk in spite of the distance, swamps, and lakes." At the same time "*el padre comisario* (Fray Alonso Ponce) left Ichmul . . . and traveling four leagues on good road arrived at . . . Tizolop" (Tiholop) (Noyers 1932).

LOCAL AND FOREIGN MERCHANDISE

Taking into account the tribute that was paid to the *encomenderos* in 1549 which indicates a certain abundance of some products in the jurisdictions mentioned above, as well as the information from other historical sources, we see that the territory under study here had the following:

Salt. In the Ah Canul jurisdiction salt works were exploited from Desconocida to Celestun with people from the coastal towns and perhaps Humucma, Sihunchen, Yabucu, Tetis, Kinchil, etc. Similar work was carried

on in the jurisdictions of Chakan, Ah Kin Chel, and Chikinchel, and the same in Cozumel, which was rich in salt works. In this regard "there is a swamp in Yucatan . . . it is all salt. It begins at the coast of Ecab that is near Isla Mujeres and continues very close to the sea coast, between the coast itself and the forests until near to Campeche" (Landa 1938). "Along most of the coast to the north much salt was taken from the salt works . . . much salt from this land is taken to Mexico, to Tabasco, to Honduras, and to other parts (*Relación de Yucatan* 1872).

Fish. Fisheries existed north of the town of Chauaca and on Cozumel. The lord Ah Canul had canoes for fishing in Hinal or Jaina. Fish could be carried from the coast to the interior for 20 to 30 leagues in the roasted form. It could also be preserved salted and dried in the sun. Certain jurisdictions had a monopoly on some products among which figured salt and fish. For example "the Chel that was on the coast did not want to give either salt or fish to Cocom, making him go very far for them and the Cocom did not let Chel hunt or gather fruits (from his area)" (Landa 1938).

Honey and Wax. These products were produced on Cozumel, in Bacalar, and in Chetumal. The people from Acalan traded much honey also. In the town of Tiquibalon, Yucatan "there were storehouses of wax and honey" (Landa 1938). The town of Calkini, in 1541, gathered "50 large jars of honey" to give as tribute to Montejo (*Códice de Calkini*, Barrera Vásquez 1957). In Campeche there was "an abundance of wax and honey which the Indians paid in tribute to the Spanish without any cup or measure . . ." (Ximénez (1929).

Cotton. It could be found in various jurisdictions as a raw material and in manufactured articles, as in Uaymil, Campeche, and Acalan. In Yucatan "they had their inherited lands planted in 'wine trees' and they planted cotton" (Landa 1938). In Calkini tribute given to Montejo was "20 baskets of cotton and white cotton thread" (*Códice de Calkini*, Barrera Vásquez 1957). In Campeche "Hernández de Córdoba bartered for cotton cloths" (Torquemada 1723) and it is said of

Campeche that "there is much cotton, but they (who raise it) cannot enjoy it because cloths are made for tribute to the Christians and if there is any left over they sell it to buy chickens for tribute" (Ximénez 1929). Motul also gave cotton cloths in tribute.

Corn. In general all the jurisdictions planted corn for the consumption of the inhabitants, although special mention is made that Montejo received "100 *cargas* of corn" (*Códice de Calkini*, Barrera Vásquez 1957). The town of Sodzil gave corn in tribute to Chichen Itza. The town of Xul took corn to Mani. Cortés received corn as a staple on his trip through Acalan.

Turkeys. There are very few citations which refer to turkeys and it is not specified whether the turkeys are wild or of some other type. It is said that Montejo received as tribute in Calkini "100 turkeys" (*Códice Calkini*, Barrera Vásquez 1957) and that the town of Sodzil paid a tribute of turkeys to Chichen Itza. In Campeche chickens are mentioned (native "chickens" could be wild turkeys).

Henequén. While it is presumed that henequén was exploited in northern Yucatan, only Landa (1938) mentions that "there is a type of tree which the Indians call *qui* and the Spanish *maguey* . . . from this tree there is a great profit . . . because it serves instead of hemp, because from the leaves threads are obtained by scraping them with a stick."

Slaves. In Xicalango and Acalan men were traded or sold to slavery. Mention is also made that the towns of Buctzotz and Hocaba made war in order to capture slaves.

Wood. It was utilized as prime material and in some manufactured objects commonly in the jurisdictions mentioned, especially Buctzotz, Uaymil, and Bacalar, taking advantage of the cedar, mahogany, pine, and zapote. In Acalan it is said that they traded in pine splinters for light and for Bacalar it is mentioned that "this town provided canoes to all the Indians of the surrounding area for their fleets and from this they make a living" (Oviedo y Valdés 1851–55). It is probable that Belize produced the *palo de Campeche* and mahogany. In Yucatan there were carpenters who made idols of wood.

Cacao. The little cacao that was produced in Yucatan was property of the nobles. Perhaps Bacalar and Chetumal controlled the cacao production and that which came from Honduras; it is said that Mani went in search of cacao in Bacalar.

Copal. There was much copal in the jurisdiction of Chikinchel or Chauaca where the town of Sinsimato had a monopoly on that product. It also occurred at places in Quintana Roo and Belize and in Tixchel "much copal grows, which is the incense of this land" (Ciudad Real 1873).

Feathers. In Yucatan "a certain breed of large white mallard, which I think came to them from Peru, is raised for feathers . . . and they want these feathers to decorate their clothes" (Landa 1938). The people of Tixchel made "very fine fans or fly-swatters" of feathers (Ciudad Real 1873). Hernández de Córdoba bartered for feathers in Campeche (Torquemada 1723) and in the same place "everything the Indians wear and put on their feet is handsomely worked with feathers of diverse colors and with red and yellow cotton" (Ximénez 1929).

Cochineal. In Tiquibalon and in other parts of Yucatan "cochineal is collected and it is said that it was the best in the Indies because it comes from a dry area. The Indians still collect it a little in some parts" (Landa 1938).

Palms. Palm is mentioned most often in the form of manufactured articles. "There are other trees . . . from which ropes are made . . . they have many different types of long willows in the field and forests . . . from which they make all kinds of baskets" (Landa 1938). In Xicalango "we slept on some mats that the Indians make with rushes; some are very handsome with red and black designs of the same leaf" (Ximénez 1929).

Dyes. The *palo de Campeche* or *ek* and the *palo de Brasil* or *chacte* were possibly used as dye, the same as *achiote*. "There is another tree dark orange in color from which staffs are made; it is very strong and I believe it is called Brazil" (Landa 1938). Acalan traded in "colors for dying (and) certain other types of ink with which they dye their bodies in order to protect themselves from the heat and the cold" (Cortés 1960).

Flint. It is presumed that flint could have been utilized to make tools or weapons, especially in towns located in the hills or Puuc area. Landa (1938) informs us that "since they lacked metals, God provided them with a hill of flint next to the mountain that I said crossed the land."

Pottery. There are no specific mentions of pottery, but "the trades of the Indians were as potters and carpenters. They earned a lot for making idols of clay and wood with much fasting and ritual practices" (Landa 1938).

Among the foreign merchandise that can be mentioned are the following:

Rabbit fur. "From New Spain is brought a class of merchandise that is called *tuchumitl,* which is a wool thread dyed different colors" (*Relación de Motul* in *Relación de Yucatan* 1872), that is, rabbit fur (*tochomitl*) dyed different colors for decoration of clothes; this was carried to Xicalango by the Mexican merchants.

Obsidian. "Earspools and knives of *iztli* were taken by the *pochteca* to Xicalango for sale" (Sahagún 1946). With the knives they shaved their heads and cut.

Brass. Brass was taken from Tabasco to Yucatan. As mentioned by Landa (1938) "they had a certain soft brass, some with a little gold mixed in it ... (that) those from Tabasco brought to exchange for their things".

Cacao. Cacao came principally from Tabasco and Honduras for "they use a great quantity of cacao which is brought from the provinces of Tabasco and Honduras, because they make their beverages from it ... and it serves them as money" (*Relación de Mérida* in *Relación de Yucatan* 1872). "Along the Río Grijalva there were many towns that were rich in cacao, that is the money of the Indians (Ximénez 1929).

Some other facts are found as generalities in some sources. The canoe found by Bartolomé Colón in 1502 carried cotton cloths and sleeveless shifts worked and painted in different colors and designs, breechcloths, wooden swords with flint edges, copper axes

to cut wood, copper bells, metal medallions and melting-pots to smelt them, tubers (manihot or sweet potato), corn and cacao.

The people of the province of Acalan dealt or traded in "cacao, cotton clothes, colors for dying, certain other classes of dye with which they dyed their bodies ... pitchy splints for light, pine rosin for the incense burners of their idols, slaves, and red snail beads, of which they have many used to ornament themselves. In their fiestas and markets they trade in some gold, although all is mixed with copper and other mixtures (Cortés 1960).

In Yucatan "their principal products for exportation were wax, honey, *cochinilla,* cacao, *achiote,* indigo, cotton and others," similarly "cotton from which they weave their clothes and other specialties that they export to other provinces" (Vásquez de Espinosa 1948). At the same time in all Tabasco "no salt is gathered and so it is provided from the provinces of Yucatán" (*Relación de Yucatan* 1872). To Cocom were sent "birds, honey, salt, fish, game, clothes, and other things" (Landa 1938).

The Tixchel people had "very good knives, boxes, rings, (ear?)spools and other curious things made of turtle carapace (Cuidad Real 1873). Hernández de Córdoba bartered in Campeche for some "snails set in silver and gold" (Torquemada 1723). The Mexica took to Xicalango woven cloth, ornaments, gold, copper, obsidian, rabbit fur, slaves, large worked green stones, rock crystal, etc., and obtained cacao, jaguar skins, turtle shells, precious stones, jade, etc. (Sahagún 1946). According to Alonso López (19) in Tabasco they had "medallions, thin as gold paper, ornaments in the form of butterflies, masks, earplugs or earrings and necklaces with beads in the form of turtles, all in gold."

Possibly they had other food products such as beans, squash, and chile that were common in the jurisdictions. In Yucatan there was "a grain that the Spanish called *frisoles* (beans) and the Indians *bul,* that are like beans. There are Spanish squash and there is another ... that the Indians call *kun* ... they eat them roasted and boiled. There is a large quantity of chile, that in Spain is called "pepper of the Indians" (*Relación de Yucatan* 1872).

MARKETS AND THEIR ORGANIZATION

In general, the capitals of the jurisdictions were commercial centers or markets, the same as other strategically located towns. This was the case of Xicalango, Itzumkanac, Tayasal, Nito, Naco, Cozumel, Pole, Bahía de la Ascención, Bacalar, Chetumal, Champoton, Ecab, Conil, Cachi, etc.

Thus, the lord of Acalan "had in many market towns, like Nito, an agent and a neighborhood populated with his subjects and trading servants" (López de Gómara 1943). In Ichmul and the Bahía de la Asención "there were temples that the lords of Chichén Itzá had erected to their gods in order to render them offerings and sacrifice on the way to Honduras in their commercial trips" (Noyers 1932).

Chauaca "had a thousands residents... (a) town with masonry stone houses covered with straw, where they congregate and make their markets" (*Relación de Yucatan* 1872). Cachi "had a great market or *plaza* with many traders and much merchandise, many staples and things to eat, as of all the others things that are bought, sold, and traded there among the natives" (Oviedo 1851–55).

"Ecab was a town on the beach and so large that our people called it Cairo... and there were fairs and commerce there" (Mártyr de Anglería 1892).

Cozumel was "level and had very fertile soil; it has gold, but of foreign origin and carried (there) from other places [with which] ... it has ... commerce" (Mártyr de Anglería 1892). From Tulum it is said that the sailors that come from Honduras by sea see the hills of the port of Zama, that appear to be a fort" (Raygosa 19).

In Mayapan there was a kind of house of commerce and trade to which the merchants repair with their merchandise in order that the steward of the *Halach uinic* can acquire what his lord needs. This steward, called Caluac, "had the accounts of the towns and of those that ruled them and to them notice was given of what was needed in the house of the

lord... (which) was provided rapidly, because his house was like an office of his lord" (Landa 1938).

In the commercial center of Cachi "there were their inspectors of weights and measures and judges in a house near one end of the plaza, like a town hall, where all the litigations were settled in a few words... giving to each one what was justly his" (Oviedo 1851–55). In Ecab there were "houses with towers, magnificent temples, orderly streets, and plazas" (Mártyr de Anglería 1892). Cozumel had "economy and order like those of Yucatan in its houses, temples, and roads (Mártyr de Anglería 1892, 1912).

UNITS OF TRADE

"The money that they used was small bells and jingle bells of copper that had a value according to their size (López de Cogolludo 1957, Chí 1946). "They had other money made from certain red shells" (Landa 1938); red stones that they call *Kan*, with which they buy what they need" (*Relación de Yucatan* 1872); shells that not only served as money, as in Xicalango there were "certain red spools and rings" (Sahagún 1946); and in Yucatan there were "red shells brought from outside the province with which they made strings like rosaries" (Chí 1941).

"In their commerce they use... precious stones and small copper axes that have been brought (from New Spain), almost T-shaped ... and were thin small plates" (Chí 1941, Torquemada 1723). "The business to which they were most inclined was trade, taking salt, clothes, and slaves to the land of Ulua and Tabasco, exchanging all for cacao and stone beads, which were their money" (Landa 1938). The Cupules "had orchards... where they cultivated the cacao that is the gold of this country and that serves as money in the plaza and market of this city" (Sánchez de Aguilar 1937). In Yucatan "there are cacao trees in holes, the cacao that is the money used among them (*Relación de Valladolid*, in *Relación de Yucatan* 1872).

With respect to the value of cacao, which was the most important money, it is said that "200 seeds were worth a *real* among the

Indians, and is the money which among them and the Spanish ordinarily was exchanged for small items" (Herrera y Tordesillas 1934–36). Cortés obtained cacao as tribute from the *caciques* and from their lands that produced it, with which he always paid his soldiers (Mártyr de Anglería 1892, 1912). Cacao was counted in *contles* (400 seeds), *xiquipiles* (1,800 seeds), and *cargas* (24,000 seeds). This was so because "the counting system is by fives to twenty, and by twenties to one hundred, and by hundreds to four hundred, and by four hundreds to eight thousand. This counting system aided them greatly for the cacao business" (Landa 1938).

THE MERCHANTS

The professional merchant is called *ppolom* and the traveling merchant, *ah ppolom-yoc*.

They knew very well the roads and routes that they frequented; to Cortés "they told him they were merchants and understanding his intent they showed him a canvas, woven of cotton, (where) the road to Naco and Nito in Honduras and even to Nicaragua was painted" (Herrera y Tordesillas 1934–36).

There were lodgings on the roads where the merchants passed, for "they had to pay for their lodging and the rest of the services, and this custom many *caciques* have preserved" (Chí 1941). "An official-innkeeper was in charge of the local lodging and took care of providing food and forage to those who could only stay a day and a night in each town" (Roys 1957).

The lords of the jurisdictions were the richest merchants. "In this land of Acalan, they used to make the wealthiest merchant the lord, and thus it was Apoxpalon who had great trade . . . (and) agents in many towns where fairs were held" (Herrera y Tordesillas 1934–36). Meanwhile in Chauaca "the population was composed of noble citizens of higher classes and merchants" (Oviedo 1851–55).

In their transactions, the merchants gave credit, lended, and paid courteously and without interest" (Landa 1938). They had as a patron or titular god *Ek Chuah*, to which they made celebrations in the month of *Muan*. "The travelers carried incense and a little plate in which to burn it on his trips" (Landa 1938) so that he would return well from his trips. The polar star or *Xaman Ek* was the merchants' guide.

Commerce was the motive of enmity. "Among the three houses of the principal lords who were Cocomes, Xius, and Cheles there were great factions and hatreds . . . a Cocom escaped death by being absent in his commercial dealings in the lands of Ulua, which is beyond the town de Salamanca (Bucalar) . . . the Chel that were on the coast did not want to give salt or fish to the Cocom . . . and the Cocom did not let the Chel take out wild game or fruit" (Landa 1938). The natives of Hibueras and Honduras "ate small loaves of corn cooked with ashes and some salt, when they were able to get some previously with great effort, as merchants who carried it to sell were killed on the road (Herrera y Tordesillas 1934–36).

SUMMARY

As can be seen in the map (Fig. 12), we have located the ecological provinces, the jurisdictions and towns that form them, the capitals or *cabeceras* of some of them, the products mentioned, and the roads and communications that are pointed out in the sources, and relationships that must have existed between the jurisdictions through their governors. With all the information given before we can pass on to a summary and conclusions such as can be perceived for the period of 1400 to 1600 of the Christian era.

Yucatan, Campeche, Quintana Roo, and perhaps Belize constituted an ample territory that was divided into jurisdictions with more or less known limits. The jurisdictions could be governed by a *Halach uinic* who resided in the *cabecera* or capital, by *Batabes* or chiefs of confederated towns, or by a *Batab* that dominated the rest.

In the social and political organization of those times one can see the persistence of nobles or a hereditary aristocracy that monopolized the authority or power (lords, *caciques*, nobles, priests, merchants, warriors), of the plebeians or commoners who were craftsmen and free working men and of the slaves who were the servants and common men, generally obtained in war and who could be sold.

The *Halach uinic*, the true or real man, was the governor and lord *par exelence* who exacted a moderate tribute from all towns in his jurisdiction. He had a large lineage or many relations. His position was hereditary and he could be the richest merchant.

The *Batab*es were the chiefs of the towns, as much of the capitals as of those of the rest of the jurisdiction. They generally belonged to the same lineage as the governor. They had executive, judicial, and military functions. They were supported by the town and had a *parcela* or piece of property for their benefit.

The *Nacom* helped the *Batab* in war, training the army and they conducted the military enterprises. The *Ah Kulel*es were those who saw to it that the orders of the *Batab* were carried out. The *Ah Cuch Cobes* were the neighborhood administrators in large towns. The *Caluac* was like a supplier of all that was needed by the principal lord. The *Holpap* was perhaps a *Batab*, a family patriarch, a head of the town lineage.

In the jurisdictions reigned families of great lineage, such as the Canuls, Peches, Cocoms, Xius, Chels, Chens, Couohs, etc. Some managed their jurisdictions with a good political strategy, maintaining peaceful relationships. Others were more drawn to military enterprises and commerce. In the towns there could be lands and cultivation of private property of the nobles and lords. The *barrio* (neighborhood) was the smallest political unit of the town; it possessed certain autonomy since it could exercise a veto in the Consejo. Sometimes the *barrios* were fortified in order to defend themselves from one another, as in the town of Tiac (Roys 1957).

The jurisdictions, by way of their various nearby towns, communicated by land routes and by the river courses, (which) constituted routes frequented by merchants traveling by land or water coming and going through the ample territory combining the two forms of transport. Thus it is seen that:

(1) There existed a great maritime route that followed the coast of the Gulf of Mexico, from Tabasco to the northern coast of the Yucatan Peninsula, passing by Xicalango, Champoton, Campeche, Jaina, Celestun, Sisal, Conil, and Ecab, which could be traversed by sections in both directions.

(2) There was another maritime route that went down the northern coast of the Peninsula, by the Caribbean, to Honduras, touching Isla Mujeres, Cozumel, Pole, Tulum, Bahía de la Ascensión, Chetumul, etc. This was also usable completely, or in sections, and in both directions.

(3) Another water route, run in canoes, was that of the Río Candelaria, from Itzamkanac to the Laguna de Términos and from there to Atasta and Xicalango. This was frequented by the merchants of Acalan, who took one day going and three in returning due to the falls and rapids in the river.

(4) From Xicalango and Atasta the merchants entered by the Río Palizada that connected with the Ríos San Antonio, Usumacinta, Chacamax, etc., via which they could reach several river towns such as Emiliano Zapata, Balancan, Tenosique, Palenque, and others of the Peten.

(5) The Ríos San Pedro and San Pablo could also be traversed in the same way as the Río Grijalva and its tributaries to connect the jurisdiction of Cimatan with Tabasco.

(6) There was water communication by way of the Arroyo Caribe, Arroyo Esperanza, Río Paixban, etc., that together with foot trails could reach the Peten Itza and Cehache. In the same manner one could reach Bacalar and Chetumal by the Ríos Azul and Hondo.

(7) From the Usumacinta to the Río San Pedro Mártir one could reach the Peten Itza. Also from the Usumacinta to the Río de La Pasión, via the Ríos Cancuen and Sarstoon one could come out at the Bay of Amatique and the mouth of the Río Dulce.

(8) With all probability the Río Champoton connected various towns of the jurisdiction, while by the Río Mamantel one could arrive at the jurisdiction of Cehache.

(9) There was a land route from Campeche to Mérida which touched important towns like Becal, Maxcanu, etc.

(10) A land route from Chichén Itzá to the Bahía de la Ascención and Bacalar touched Tihosuco, Ichmul, etc.

(11) Another land route or perhaps a water and land route went from Itzam Kanac to Tayasal, Nito, and Naco.

(12) There were numerous communication roads between towns on the coasts and the interior, between important capitals, between towns and recognized religious sanctuaries, etc., like those from Ecab to Conil and Chancenote; from Sodzil to Chichen Itza; from Chichen Itza to Yaxuna, Coba, and Pole; from Becal to Uxmal and Mani; from Izamal to Ake and to Merida; from Tiholop to Ichmul and to Bacalar; from Mani to Oxkutzcab and Xul; from Dzonotake to Pole; from Mani to Ucum and Bacalar; from Chable to Bahía de la Ascención, etc.

The merchandise, in prime materials or worked, traveled over these routes and roads of intercommunication. Foods, utensils, and luxury goods did likewise. The merchandise could be local, regional, or foreign, taken and brought by individuals or groups of merchants.

Local merchandise included salt, fish, honey, wax, cotton, corn, turkeys, henequén, lumber, *copal*, feathers, *cochinilla*, palms, dyes, pottery, flint, turtle shells, slaves, and marine shells. In the same group were chiles, beans, squash, achiote, and perhaps other items not mentioned in the historical sources.

Merchandise foreign to the territory under study was: cacao, rabbit fur, obsidian, brass, green stones, amber, rock crystal, metals, volcanic rock, and perhaps tobacco, alum, turquoise, red ochre, and other items.

Cotton could be transformed into cloth, *huipiles*, loin-cloths, thread, shirts, etc. Henequen was made into cords or ropes. The woods could have been made into benches, canoes, oars, lance throwers, idols, and clubs with obsidian edges. The feathers were used in colorful headdresses, clothes, fans, and insignia. The palm went into baskets, mats, and fire fans. Among the dyes were indigo, *añil*, the *palo de Campeche*, and *palo de Brasil*. From flint were made knives and dart points. The pottery could be used as utensils or in rituals. The marine shells served to make ornaments and musical instruments. As for the turtle carapaces, they served as vessels, for ornaments, and perhaps were used as drums.

The rabbit fur served for adorning clothing. Obsidian was transformed into knives, blades, and perhaps ornaments. The green stones came as beads for necklaces and other ornaments. Rock crystal, turquoise, and other precious materials served as jewelry the same as did amber and metals, especially copper in the form of bells, small axes, rings, and other ornaments.

Cacao could be produced on a limited scale and it was imported principally from Tabasco and Honduras. The feathers could be local, or, as in the case of the quetzal, brought from Chiapas and Guatemala. Animal skins likewise came from several regions. Pottery could be brought from the Peten Itza, metals from Honduras and Central America or Oaxaca and the Central Mexican Highland. Amber came from Chiapas. Obsidian could have come from central Mexico, Guatemala, or Belize. Also imported were tobacco, liquid amber, alabaster, etc. but they are not mentioned directly in the historical sources.

All these prime materials, food products, and worked goods were traded or bought and sold in large and small markets, or from town to town, perhaps by intermediate merchants. In the historical sources are mentioned principally localized markets in or near the coasts, possibly because the maritime commerce was the most important. Thus we have mentioned Ecab, Conil, Cachi, Chauaca, Pole, Bahía de la Ascensión, Bacalar, Chetumal, Champoton, Xicalango, Itzamkanac, Tayasal, Nito, Naco, Cozumel, and perhaps Chichen Itza, Mayapan, Mani, Ichmul, Atasta, and others.

In the large markets there were special constructions and a type of mercantile court or judge located in one of the corners of the plaza, with the object of knowing and deciding about all the problems involved in the exchange of commercial articles made there.

In the commercial interchange some products reached the level of money, such as small bells and tinklers of copper, red shells, red stones and other precious stones, small copper axes, stone discs or beads, quetzal feathers, and, principally, cacao seeds (Cardós de Méndez 1959).

The merchants knew very well the roads and routes that they frequented. They took human porters and sometimes military escorts. They lodged in special lodgings for which they paid. They had agents in the *barrios* of the most important towns. The richest merchants were generally the lords of the jurisdictions. The merchants gave credit, lent, and paid courteously without interest. They had a titular god to which they made offerings and celebrations. Commerce was the motive for enmity among the lords dedicated to this profession.

CONCLUSIONS

Even though the territory occupied by the Maya of Yucatan, Campeche, Quintana Roo, and Belize had certain adverse ecological factors like the aridity of the northern lands, great forests in the mountains, a hydrographic network of rivers and lakes, or a low marshy coast, these were not obstacles to it being well populated during the conquest and colonialization times and a little before, thanks to the exploitation of the natural resources and the contacts between the groups and the commerce.

Commerce came to occupy an important role in the economy since it maintained an equilibrium among certain scarce prime materials and products. It maintained the craft production and was a source of personal enrichment. It was also a vehicle of social cohesion, in that it congregated in the markets people from several towns and was a unifying force between the great center or capital and the towns of the jurisdiction.

The commercial points were situated strategically, many times in the capitals of the jurisdictions, where the governors resided; at those points were the markets. Those points constituted a commercial chain and were the richest. The traffic could be direct or broken by intermediaries. The population was concentrated at the extreme ends of the commercial chain, but other sites along the route also proliferated, where there could be retailers, redistributing the merchandise to other nearby places.

The lords and governors were also the richest merchants. They maintained monopolies on certain merchandise which created rivalries among them. Through supply and demand there were few products that increased in value. A money economy was created in order to buy instead of exchange goods, with certain products that played the role of money.

Commerce connected the towns of a jurisdiction by means of ambulatory merchants and professional traders who went on foot or in canoes by land routes or by sea or in the river courses and their tributaries. They knew the roads and routes, the products in most demand, their value, and the areas in which they were produced. They could enter regions not frequently entered in search of prime materials and objects. They also knew the wealth of the areas, their population, and the possibility of extending commerce and even colonization.

Commerce was facilitated by the similarity of the language, since all of the territory was a cultural unity, but foreign ideas and people also infiltrated and modified the existing culture, as was the case of the Mexica who introduced new traits to the prevailing pattern such as sacrifices, gods, weapons, etc.

The merchants could be organized in the important towns and constituted an important economic and social class. They had as a god *Ek Chuah* and they made offerings and ceremonies to him. Perhaps their clothing was in accord with their rank, since the majority of them were lords of the lineage. They traveled land and maritime routes accompanied by porters and escorts to defend them. The important markets were duly organized and controlled.

Commerce strengthened internal and external relations. It was an index of the natural resources and the artisan production. It influenced the social organization of the society. The merchants inhabited special neighborhoods and they took to and brought from the markets numerous products for their activities of exchange and sale.

REFERENCES

Academia de Geografía e Historia de Costa Rica 1952
Archivo General de Indias 1541–45
Barrera Vásquez 1957
Cardós de Méndez 1959
Chí 1941
Ciudad Real 1873
Colón 1947
Cortés 1960
Herrera y Tordesillas 1934–36

Landa 1938
López de Cogolludo 1957
López de Gómara 1943
Mártyr de Anglería 1892, 1912
Noyers 1932
Oviedo y Valdés 1951–55
Piña Chán 1970
Relaciones de Yucatán 1872
Roys 1957
Sahagún 1946
Sánchez de Aguilar 1937
Scholes and Roys 1948
Torquemada 1723
Vázquez de Espinosa 1948
Ximénez 1929

6. THE HISTORICAL ROUTES OF TABASCO AND NORTHERN CHIAPAS AND THEIR RELATIONSHIP TO EARLY CULTURAL DEVELOPMENTS IN CENTRAL CHIAPAS

by

THOMAS A. LEE, JR.

INTRODUCTION

As mentioned in the call for collaboration in this series of papers, the primary factor limiting inter-regional social interaction is apt to be the physical environment. Topography and climate are the particular aspects of environment which most seriously determine the ease or difficulty of inter-regional communication. Human contact and interaction is obviously limited and channeled by the presence of impassable marshes or of high mountains with swift rivers, and uncrossable or impenetrable canyons, just as it is aided by navigable rivers and level coastal plains. Nevertheless, under some circumstances differences in regional climate and topography may provide an impetus to social intercourse between regions. Regional environmental differences may be responsible for differences in available natural resources, which differences often are compensated for by trade. It is between two such different and usually adjacent regions that a symbiotic trade relationship may develop. Symbiosis of this sort is probably a primary reason for prolonged contact between culturally disparate regions. This relationship has been discussed by numerous investigators (for example, Sanders 1965, Flannery 1968, Sanders and Price 1968, Rathje 1971b) and it seems applicable to the situation existing at times between lowland Tabasco and the neighboring Highlands and Central Depression of Chiapas to the south.

The importance of the physical environment in limiting cultural contact is, of course, on a scale which decreases in the direction of societies which have the ability to control or change the physical world around them. Pre-Columbian societies, lacking draft animals and durable metal tools, were particularly limited and hampered by their physical surroundings, especially with regard to inter-regional overland transport. They often made good use of waterways and developed numerous foot trails over the most convenient mountain passes. A review of the principal communication routes known since the Conquest in Tabasco and northern Chiapas may shed some light on the direction of early pre-Hispanic diffusion processes.

The Natural Regions of Tabasco and Northern Chiapas

The environment of Tabasco and northern Chiapas has received considerable study and is widely published (Echeagaray Bablot 1957, West 1964).

Briefly, the Tabasco region may be characterized topographically as a low-lying coastal plain dissected transversely by many navigable rivers and interrupted intermittently along most of the coast by large bays, lagoons, and estuaries. The major river systems which empty into the Gulf of Mexico along the more than 300 km. of shoreline, from east to west, are the Candelaria, Usumacinta, Grijalva, Tonala, and Coatzacoalcos. All of these principal river systems except the Coatzacoalcos are interconnected by rivers or sheltered lagoons and estuaries, constituting in all over 2,900 km. of navigable waters, with many accesses to the sea as well (see Table 5).

Navigability is a relative quality which requires some discussion. A very conservative recent figure of 1,350 km. of navigable waters for Tabasco has been published (Echeagaray Bablot 1957: 311), but the figures were based on boats of deeper draft than were used by the original inhabitants. Navigability involves water velocity, natural impediments such as rapids and falls, and the draft depth of the craft used. Water velocity on traveled rivers throughout the two regions under consideration is not often a limiting factor; due to the flat nature of the terrain even the navigable

Table 5. Navigable Inland Waters of the Tabasco Riverine Market Complex

Name of Water	Kilometers navigable	Connections
Río Coatzacoalcos	170	Gulf of Mexico
Río Chiquito	30	Río Coatzacoalcos
Río Coachapan	15	Río Coatzacoalcos
Río Uzpanapa	130	Río Coatzacoalcos
Río Nanchital	10	Río Coatzacoalcos
Río Tonala	50	Gulf of Mexico
Río Pedregal	20	Río Tonala
Río Zanapa	70	Río Tonala
Río Blasillo	10	Río Tonala
Río Tancochapa	50	Río Tonala
Río Chico Zapote and Laguna Palmas	30	Río Tonala and Lagunas del Carmen and Machona
Lagunas del Carmen and Machona	40	Gulf of Mexico
Río San Felipe	20	Laguna del Carmen
Río Naranjeño	20	Laguna del Carmen
Río Santa Ana	30	Laguna Machona
Laguna Tupilco	16	Gulf of Mexico
Río Tortuguero	25	Laguna Tupilco
Arroyo Tula	12	Laguna Tupilco
Río Cocohita	25	Laguna Tupilco
Laguna Tres Palmas	2	Lagunas Tupilco and Arrastradero
Laguna Arrastradero	4	Laguna Las Palmas and Canal del Jobo
Canal del Jobo	3	Lower Río Seco and Laguna Arrastradero
Río Seco	60*	Río Grijalva and Gulf of Mexico
Río Seco	18	Gulf of Mexico
Laguna Mecoacan	11	Río Seco and Gulf of Mexico
Río Cuscuchapa	40	Laguna Mecoacan
Laguna Tinaja	5	Río González and probably Laguna Mecoacan
Río González	55	Gulf of Mexico
Río Nacajuca	15	Río González
Río Mecoacan	10	Río Nacajuca
Río Chacalapa	22	Río Nacajuca
Río Cuaduacan	22	Río Chacalapa
Río La Piedra	15	Río Chacalapa
Río Zumpano	25	Río González
Río Tula	15	Río Zumpano
Arroyo Aguacero	10	Río Zumpano
Río Cedro	11	Río Zumpano
Río Cañas	15	Río Tula and Arroyo Aguacero
Río Samaria	16	Ríos Grijalva and Cañas
Río Carrizal	39	Ríos Grijalva and González
No name Dead end between Ríos Cañas and Carrizal	41	Río Carrizal
Río Pigua	3	Ríos Grijalva and González
Arroyo Boca Grande	20	Río González
Río Medellín	20	Río González oxbow

Table 5, Continued

Name of Water	Kilometers navigable	Connections
Río Grijalva	270	Gulf of Mexico, Ríos Pigua, Samaria, and González
Arroyo Coco	8	Río Grijalva
Río San Pedrito	15	Ríos Grijalva and Usumacinta
Arroyo Pantaje	20	Ríos Grijalva and Usumacinta
Laguna del Viento	7	Río Grijalva and Lagunas
Laguna Conconada	10	Laguna del Viento and Río Hormiguero
Río Hormiguero	15	Río Chichicaste and Laguna Conconada
Río Chichicaste	21	Río Usumacinta and Hormiguero
Laguna Chichicaste	6	Río Chichicaste, Arroyo Chichicastillo
Arroyo Chichicastillo	5	Laguna Chichicaste and Arroyo Sauz
Arroyo Sauz	7	Río Usumacinta, Arroyo Chichicastillo and Laguna Sauzal
Laguna Sauzal	5	Arroyos Sauz and Lechugal
Arroyo Lechugal	5	Lagunas Chichicaste and Lechugal
Laguna Lechugal	2	Laguna Sauzal and Arroyo Lechugal
Río del Maluco	60	Río Macuspana and Laguna Lechugal
Río del Maluco Oxbow and Laguna de la Pitaya	15	Río del Maluco
Río Chilapa	75	Río Grijalva
Río Tepetlitan	35	Ríos Chilapa and Macuspana
Río Macuspana	65	Ríos del Maluco and Tepetlitan
Río Pomna	20	Río Macuspana
Río Puxcaton	10	Río Macuspana
Río de la Sierra	45	Río Grijalva
Río Tacotalpa	30	Río de la Sierra
Río Teapa	35	Río de la Sierra
Río Puyacatengo	25	Río de Teapa
Río Pichucalco	52	Río Grijalva
Río Campoapan	15	Río Grijalva
Río Platanar	5	Río Grijalva
Río Sayula	10	Río Grijalva
Río Yomono	3	Río Grijalva
Río Totopac	1	Río Grijalva
Río San Pedro y San Pablo	65	Gulf of Mexico
Río Chico	30	Río San Pedro y San Pablo
Río San Antonio	18	Río San Pedro y San Pablo
Río Usumacinta	360	Ríos San Pedro y San Pablo, Chico, San Antonio, and Palizada
Río San Pedro Mártir	100+	Río Usumacinta
Río Palizada	20	Laguna de Términos and Río Usumacinta
Laguna de Términos	50	Gulf of Mexico
Río de los Pinos	5	Laguna de Términos
Río del Este	10	Laguna de Términos
Río Chumpan	20	Laguna de Términos
Río Candelaria	50	Laguna de Términos
Río Mamantel	10	Laguna de Términos
Río Sabancuy	10	Laguna de Términos

Total 2,906 Km.

*Not added in total.

part of the Grijalva River, which is not limited to the coastal plain but extends well into the mountains, has less than a 200 m. fall in its 270 km. course. The usual unloaded draft ranges from 10 to 25 cm. for most native canoes in the area which are carved from a single tree trunk. When loaded even a large canoe will seldom draw more than double this amount.

In their unequalled ethnohistorical study which includes the Chontalpa Indians of Tabasco, Scholes and Roys (1948) place great importance on the many water routes used for commerce and communication. The large river courses of this area, however, as in many other delta zones, are not static, since huge volumes of alluvium may build up the river bottoms until they are higher than the surrounding area and the river is forced to seek a new course. The zones of such diverted rivers are locally known as *rompidos* and they may cause great damage. Such changes in river courses are often extreme, perhaps leaving large areas suddenly miles from navigable waters and consequently off the mainstream of commerce and easy communication, and at the same time giving a new area the advantages lost by another.

The Tabasco lowlands are hot and humid, receiving from 1,500 to 2,000 mm. of rainfall annually, with an annual temperature minimum of 10° C., a maximum of 44° C. and an annual mean of from 26° to 27° C. (Echeagaray Bablot 1957, Figs. 7, 8; Falcón de Gyves 1965: 11–12). Under the Koeppen system of climate classification the area is Afwg, characterized by a monsoon or tropical forest climate with fall rains and the maximum temperature peak prior to the summer solstice on June 21 (Echeagaray Bablot 1957, Fig. 11).

The highlands of Chiapas are the dominant topographical feature in the two adjacent regions and are the controlling factor for the climate and vegetation in both. This deeply trenched mountain massif reaches a height of over 2,700 m. and receives a high annual rainfall on its northern slopes; the rainfall increases progressively as the elevation rises from the Tabasco plain southward, to reach a maximum of 4,000 mm. at the peaks of the

mountains. The great river systems of the two regions are the dramatic result of this highland mass and its extension, the Cuchumatanes range in Guatemala to the east. The Sierra Madre mountains of Chiapas, bordering the Pacific Coast, also contribute a great flow of water to Tabasco via tributaries of the Grijalva and La Venta Rivers.

The climate of much of northern Chiapas is similar to that of the Gulf Coast, but many valley ridges are pine clad and cooler. The higher reaches change significantly to a temperate climate, with the temperature of the hottest month lower than 22° C.

Principal Travel Routes
(See Figure 13)

I can only discuss very briefly here the major routes crossing Tabasco and some interregional routes which linked the Gulf Coast lowlands to northern and central Chiapas. Some of the local routes were parts of larger Mesoamerican routes and where this is known, connecting points will be mentioned. The full importance of some regional routes is appreciated only when it is understood that they are parts of larger systems, and this is particularly true of the east–west routes crossing Tabasco. The routes leading south from Tabasco had to compete with the major trans-Isthmian route to and from Central America, and apparently were more important for an overseas-oriented post-Conquest elite populace in Chiapas than they were for most of the pre-Hispanic occupations.

THE TABASCO ROUTES

The principal routes of the Tabasco plain ran east–west and were part of the Culhua-Mexica *pochteca* route, one of the longest lines of communication known in Mesoamerica prior to the Spanish conquest and of considerable importance later. They were perhaps one of the most important commercial sections of this great trade route. One author has pointed out the importance of the Tabasco and southeastern Veracruz coastal plain as a huge port of exchange with five groups of principal ports: (1) those at the mouth of the Coatzacoalcos river, (2) the towns inland from Cimatan, (3) those of the Chontalpa, (4) the town of Potonchan at the mouth of the Grijalva River, and (5) Xicalango at the west end of the Laguna de Términos (Chapman 1959: 45–54). The *pochteca* route was clearly established and maintained in order to participate in this great market area.

The *pochteca* route originated, of course, in the Valley of Mexico and proceeded to Tuxtepec on the Papaloapan River via Cuautla, Izúcar de Matamoros, and Tehuacan (based on Wallrath 1967: 14, quoting Brasseur de Bourbourg 1858, Vol. 3, pp. 242–43). At Tuxtepec the route divided into two principal roads, one which led to Anahuac Ayotlan on the Pacific Coast via the Isthmus of Tehuantepec and the other to Anahuac Xicalango in Tabasco (Dibble and Anderson 1959: 17), over 200 leagues from the point of origin. While these specified routes ended at already distant posts on the coasts of the Gulf of Mexico and the Pacific Ocean, in each instance they connected with other routes which extended beyond by land and/or sea to Guatemala, Honduras, and even deeper into Central America (see Feldman, Paper 2).

The Tabasco Coastal Route

The Tabasco coastal route was that used by Cortés on his way to Honduras in 1524, leaving from Espíritu Santo and passing in turn Tonala, Ahualulco, and the Chontalpa (Cortés 1960, 1963, Quinta Carta; Díaz del Castillo 1964, Chap. 174). Cortés is the earliest description of this route. Cortés relates, "I began my trip by the coast to a province that is called Cupilcon (after the village Cupilco, but better known as the province of Chontalpa) which is from the village of Espíritu Santo 35 leagues" (Cortés 1963: 245).

Whether Cortés took the Tabasco coastal route because it was the main overland way through the Ahualulcos or because it was a drier and firmer route for his large expedition which included many horses, notoriously inefficient in swampy terrain, is not known. The route was well known to the settlers in Espíritu Santo (near Coatzacoalcos) many of whom had *encomiendas* in the Ahualulcos and Chontalpa provinces. Bernal Díaz del

Castillo had been over this route to the Río Seco and through the Cimatan villages at least twice prior to his participation with Cortés (Díaz del Castillo 1964: 395–96, 410). As if this were not enough, Cortés also had the aid of a map drawn on cloth by Indians he had called from Tabasco and Xicalango (Scholes and Roys 1948: 430–31; Cortés 1960: 188).

The account by Bernal Díaz del Castillo is more informative of the first part of the journey through Tabasco than is Cortés' despite the fact that Díaz did not accompany the main party but instead had been sent on ahead with 3,000 Mexican warriors and 30 Spanish captains to put down a Cimatan uprising (Díaz del Castillo 1964: 426). This may have been a pretext in order to quarter this great army in someone else's backyard while the rest of the party passed through this nearby, relatively safe, region. Following then primarily Bernal Díaz's account very briefly, from Espíritu Santo it was 8 or 9 leagues to the Tonala River where a crossing in canoes was necessary. Ahualulco lay 9 leagues further along the coast and was located at the Santa Ana bar, an estuary exit to the sea of the del Carmen lagoon. Here I agree with Scholes and Roys (1948: 95, Map 3) who question the identity of Ahualulco with an archaeological site of that name further east on the south side of the Machona lagoon which connects with Carmen. Reasons for this are Cortés' statement that they went along the coast and that the Santa Ana bar is about the distance both give from Tonala, since the archaeological site called Ahualulco is some 7 or 8 leagues farther on.

Leaving Ahualulco the route probably kept close to the lagoon shore rather than the coast, if we can judge by the location of villages and colonies, and the trails which connect them, as seen on a map (Falcón de Gyves 1965, Map 6) which probably dates to the first part of the seventeenth century or just before. Tupilco bar was reached 7 leagues later and here the party built its first of more than fifty bridges, about a half a league from the sea. This tremendous construction Cortés said was 934 paces long (Cortés 1963: 245). Cortés' need for a bridge here was due to the horses which could not swim so far through the current. Apparently Díaz del Castillo did not have problems crossing here earlier.

The next crossing was of the mighty Mazapa (Río Seco or Río de Dos Bocas) which the expedition passed in many canoes tied together by twos. Iquinuapa was the next town they passed and here Díaz del Castillo rejoined the expedition, coming down from the Cimatan area. Iquinuapa was probably located not far from the southwest side of Laguna Mecoacan and here the group turned away from the coast to push inland. Before arriving at Cupilco, the first town in the Chontalpa province, the group crossed a river where a bridge was built and then finally crossed an estuary. The term estuary was often interchanged with river and since nothing special was noted in the estuary crossing we may assume that it was a river. One of the streams crossed must have been the Cuscuchuapa River, as Cupilco lies just to the east of it. This was the boundary of the Chontalpa zone and the often-cited westernmost boundary of the Maya country (*Relaciones de Yucatán* 1898–1900, Vol. 11, p. 360).

At Nacajujuyca or Anaxuxuca (Nacajuca) the next town they reached, Cortés said, "according to the figure (map) that those of Tabasco and Xacalango gave me, I must go to another (town) called Zagoatan, and as they (the Indians) did not go except by water, they did not know the way that I had to take by land.... thus I was forced from there on to send ... some Spaniards and Indians to discover the way, and once known, open it so that we could pass" (Cortés 1963: 245). This demonstrates that he had come to the end of the overland trail. From here on Cortés went mainly perpendicular to the principal communications routes in use at the time, the rivers which flowed from the mountains to the sea in a northerly direction. He was going against topography and had a truly difficult time. Later even when he went parallel to the rivers, cutting upstream for many leagues, he arrived at a town where the Indians told him "that they did not go by land, but by the rivers and estuaries in their canoes and ... further than that on the water ... they knew the way but not by land" (Cortés 1960: 188).

For our purposes here there is no need to continue the Cortés trek farther than Nacajuca since beyond here he obviously had left any established route of communication and failed to utilize the rivers of interest to us. The rivers and estuaries of Tabasco form a unique transportation system about which at present not much new can be said but it is necessary to summarize what is known.

Fluvial Routes of the
Tabasco Riverine Market Complex

By the time Cortés reached Nacajuca he had already crossed the Río de Dos Bocas and several smaller feeder rivers which connect with the lower Grijalva and the multitude of lagoons and estuaries that parallel the Gulf Coast. He was well out into an area traditionally communicable by water transport.

Near Nacajuca the "overland" section of the *pochteca* trade route must have ended and the water-borne portion begun for those who would go on to visit the Chontalpa, Potochan, and Xicalango trading exchanges. One can easily visualize a weary Oztomeca resting quietly with his cargo in a slowly rocking canoe as it is poled carefully along the edge of a river or lagoon by its Chontal owner on their way to the Xicalango fair. Even the "overland" portion through western coastal Tabasco was intermittently by water for the normal traveller, as canoes would have been used to cross those channels and swampy areas where Cortés found it necessary to construct bridges for his horses: "More than fifty bridges were constructed over a distance of about 20 leagues" between the Río Copilco and Nacajuca (Scholes and Roys 1948: 96).

Leading away from the Tabasco market area there were other partly overland trails, the most famous being those to Nito, Guatemala, and to Naco, Honduras, from the Acalan-Tixchel capital of Itzamkanak, at the eastern edge of the zone. Native merchants from the latter place related to Cortés (1963: 265) their trade of salt for clothing in Mazatlan to the east, but the approach from Tabasco to this point of departure was entirely by water up the Candelaria River. A land route or routes leading away from the Acalan-Tixchel area to the interior of the Yucatan Peninsula must also have been important.

Almost all of the major communication networks in southeastern Mesoamerica were combinations of water and overland routes.

For example, located directly on the Lower Usumacinta, Trinidad was in more constant contact with the southern Lowland Maya culture during the Classic period than was Palenque not far away to the southwest but distant from the Usumacinta River (Rands 1969: 10); Rands proposes that rivers provided easier communication between Trinidad and the Maya core area, which, when combined with some sort of social or cultural frontiers, accounts for the difference seen in the ceramics between the two sites. Thompson (1970: 25–47) has made an excellent case for the expansion of the Putun Maya into the upper Usumacinta and Pasión drainages from centers along the lower courses of these same rivers. Nevertheless, since the Usumacinta River is not navigable beginning a few kilometers above Tenosique to Desempeño, a distance by river of about 50 km., the route of contact between the wet alluvial plain and the upper Usumacinta and Pasión drainages probably followed the well-known overland trail through the hills from Tenosique to Desempeño. Once above Desempeño almost 800 km. of navigable rivers are available for transportation in the Usumacinta, Lacantun, Salinas, and Pasión Rivers (González 1946: 36, 110), with only short portages here and there during low water. Even within the riverine market complex in lowland Tabasco there were numerous short portages around rapids or shallows or from one nearby drainage to another, but practically never were there long, well organized overland roads as Blom (1932: 547–48) has previously commented. The Alfaro map demonstrates this situation admirably (Scholes and Roys 1948, Map 2).

Perhaps not all of the over 2,900 km. of navigable waters charted in Tabasco, northern Chiapas, and Campeche was intercommunicable, but a close look at hydrographic maps of the area will lead one to believe that very little of it was not. There is no need to describe here the connections with the sea;

seaborne traffic close to shore was an established fact in the pre-Columbian period, and must have been combined with interior waterways. Two other papers here deal with this theme.

Waterways. In Table 5 I have listed in a west-to-east order the navigable waters in the area between the Coatzacoalcos River on the west and the Estuary of Sabancuy (on which Tixchel is located) at the eastern end of Laguna de Términos. Some isolated navigable lagoons were not included if they had no other navigable water connecting to them, and some very small rivers may have been missed. River tributaries are listed proceeding upriver, those on the left bank first, then those on the right. River connections are limited to those immediately downstream only unless they connect with major lagoons or other lateral drainages.

Some of the figures for kilometers of navigable water in Table 5 were obtained from a report of the Secretaría de Recursos Hidráulicos (Echeagaray Bablot 1957: 311–12), and other distances were obtained by measuring directly from an excellent state map of Tabasco prepared with the collaboration of the Instituto de Geografía of the Universidad Nacional Autónoma de México (Falcón de Gyves 1965, Map 1). The kilometer figures are minimum, as not all curves in the rivers could be taken into account. Nevertheless, my map-derived figures in those thirteen instances which could be checked never varied more than a few kilometers from those given by Echaegaray Bablot. Lagoons and estuaries were measured only along their longest dimension.

Table 5 demonstrates the great amount of navigable water in the central Tabasco area and emphasizes the numerous inter-connections which provided extraordinary mobility for cargo and personnel by boat across an area truly formidable for foot or horse traffic.

Commerce. One of the aspects important to the early development of the large coastal lowland area tied together by water transport, as I suggested earlier, was the huge and largely mountainous sustaining area from which the river systems emerge. Not only was the upland area culturally diverse by a very early date, but differences in climate, altitude, vegetation, soils, etc., all contributed to produce a diversity of prime raw materials and finished goods which found an outlet at times in the lowland central Tabasco market system. At other times, the movement of goods from or through the lowlands into the highlands was of equal or greater importance, especially in the colonial and modern periods. Thompson (1964) had discussed at length the trade relations between the Maya Highlands and Lowlands; while he does not include much of Chiapas in his detailed discusssion, Thompson does point out the uniquely important market role of the Chontalpa and of the Acalan Chontals who seem to have controlled much of the water traffic in and around the Maya area.

In Table 6 are listed a wide range of raw materials and finished goods which entered into what I have called the Tabasco Riverine Market Complex. This list provides only a brief survey of the most common items and of the regions from which they originated. It is clear from this list that by the time of the Culhua-Mexica domination in Mesoamerica the Tabasco market was supplied with raw materials for the most part by the areas surrounding it, and that the Mexica were the suppliers of finished goods many of which must have been made from materials obtained in the same market. This particular arrangement may have a very long history, but it is one that may be difficult to test archaeologically.

The Tabasco Riverine Market Complex involved more than just huge fairs, as López de Gómara (1941: 119) called the exchange at Xicalango. He himself stated that both Xicalango and Acuzamil (Cozumel) were great religious sanctuaries for their respective areas (López de Gómara 1941: 118). Each town had temples or altars where the people worshipped, and among them were found many crosses of wood and *latón* (sheet metal), the latter surely having arrived by commerce.

The combination of markets and religious centers is, of course, common to Mesoamerica and much of the world, but which was more important probably depends on the case at hand. I have simply emphasized the commercial aspect here. Blom (1932: 545) has pointed out the importance of holy places as significant factors in trade.

One interesting native religious shrine in the Laguna de Términos area as observed by Grijalva and his men is worth mentioning, however, inasmuch as its possible position in the water suggests that it was related to the water-borne transportation system:

> When leaving by water they found among some trees an idol of gold and many of clay, two wooden men mounted one on the other as though they were from Sodom and another of fired clay with both hands on his (member), which was circumcised as are almost all Indians of Yucatan. This find along with the bodies of sacrificed men did not please the Spanish. (López de Gómara 1941: 110, translation mine).

One would expect from this description some sort of wooden platform built in the trees to be necessary to support the artifacts and the human bodies found. It would appear that the trees were in the water, so that the shrine may have been part of a religious system related to the canoe transport complex. Signs were also placed in trees to direct traffic through the maze of waterways in Tabasco deltas, according to Landa (cited and discussed by Thompson 1964: 17; see below, page 61).

Tabasco Inland Route

This route left from the general Espíritu Santo and Acayucan area, in southeastern Veracruz (the specific point of departure depending on the period involved) and passed overland to the general Comalcalco-Huimanguillo area on the Río Seco.

The Tabasco Inland Route was well documented as early as 1599 by José de Solís who compiled a large file now in the Archivo General de la Nación (Mexico) as the result of a study of the Ahualulco area of Southern Veracruz and Western Tabasco prior to an attempted Spanish population concentration (de Solís 1945). This file contains among other items nine maps of the areas surrounding eleven towns of the region. These maps depict roads, trails, rivers, fords, canoe crossings, townsites, cacao orchards, and other natural and cultural features which allow us to reconstruct more than 40 leagues of the *Camino Real* through the Ahualulco region from Espíritu Santo to the Tabasco village of Pichucalco near the Río Seco or Río de Dos Bocas. Apart from the important ethnohistorical and linguistic data which this file provides, it also helps identify the original sites of at least eleven Ahualulco towns as they were prior to the 17th century upheaval and relocation caused by repeated English and French pirate attacks on these towns so near the coast (Scholes and Roys 1948: 95; García de León 1970: 29–30).

The route left the Espíritu Santo area and crossed the Tonala River just below the Blasillo River but above the Arroyo Cangrejero, not very far from the archaeological site of La Venta. It passed in turn the towns of Chocacan, Cosliacac, Ocoapa, San Miguel Tnepantlaothi, Mecatepec, Ostitlan, and Pichucalco, and probably continued on to Comalcalco. This last link in the route is not definitely established, since the 1599 file has no villages mapped beyond Pichucalco. Pichucalco during this period was undoubtedly at its original site on the headwaters of the Tortuguero River; the present village of Pichucalco is on the Cunduacan River east of the Río Seco.

Another file in the Mexican Nacional Archives, but dating to the nineteenth century, contains a map which shows the Tabasco Inland Route much further inland than in 1599, connecting Acayucan and Huimanguillo in almost a straight line (Archivo General de la Nación, *Ramo de Infidencias*, Vol. 100, and Vol. 1816, Fol. 15). The only intermediate town shown is Ocoapan, near Huimanguillo, but certainly others existed since many of the towns mentioned in the 1599 file are now relocated precisely between these terminal points of this route. It will be recalled that the English and French pirate raids of the seventeenth century forced the relocation of most of the towns along the coast to sites further inland (Scholes and Roys 1948: 95; García de León 1969: 17–19; 1970: 29–31).

Another version of the Tabasco Inland Route, with some antiquity, reports it as part of a route to Guatemala starting near Acayucan and the Coatzacoalcos River at Cosoleacaque (relocation of the sixteenth century Ahualulco town of Cosliacac), from where it can be traced step by step through Ixhuatan, Moloacan, Zanape, Tecominaocan, Mecatepec, Ocoapan, and probably Huimanguillo (García de León 1969: 166, footnote). This account is based on modern ethnographic sources but it coincides with the documents presented above from the nineteenth century.

The modern highway from Coatzacoalcos to Villahermosa runs between the cited colonial and modern versions of the Tabasco Inland Route.

A logical question at this point is did the Tabasco Inland Route function in the pre-Columbian period? I suggest that it probably did, but whether it was important as an inter-regional communications route is debatable. Despite Scholes and Roys' (1948: 31) point that the three Cimatan towns of Cimatan, Cunduacan, and Cuaquilteupa were in a "strategic position commercially, for they were the first Tabasco towns encountered by the merchants from the Valley of Mexico" it seems strange that a more direct route to them such as the 1599 Ahualulco maps contain would not have been used by Díaz del Castillo on his trip through this area. There is no indication that either Díaz del Castillo or Cortés, who followed him, ever went any other way through the Ahualulco region except near the sea. Nevertheless, the evidence is not conclusive and the question of the antiquity of the Tabasco Inland Route must remain open.

We can be almost certain that the more recent Tabasco Inland Route connected with a riverine communication system at Huimanguillo and that probably the colonial route did also, somewhere not far east of Comalcalco. Prior to the *Rompido* of 1675 (Echeagaray Bablot 1957, Fig. 24) which reduced the Río de Dos Bocas, the then main course of the Grijalva River to the sea, to an insignificant small stream known later as the Río Seco, the point of embarkation on the Tabasco fluvial system may have been further north near Comalcalco.

Table 6. Towns or Areas and their Contribution to the Tabasco Riverine Market Complex

Place	Period	Raw Materials or Finished Goods	Source
Chontalpa			
Cimatan- Ahualulco- Xicalango- Coatzacoalcos	PC	Cacao Salt Jade and jadeite all colors, shapes, and qualities	de Solís 1945; Blom 1932: 538 Blom 1932: 536, 546; Sahagún 1959: 18–19
		Turquoise mosaic shields	Sahagún 1959: 18–19
		Stone (discs?) with green mosaic of pyrites	Sahagún 1959: 18–19
		Large red sea shells	Sahagún 1959: 18–19
		Red coral-colored shells	Sahagún 1959: 18–19
		Tortoise shell cups	Sahagún 1959: 18–19
		Feathers of red spoonbill, troupial, blue honeycreeper, yellow parrot	Sahagún 1959: 18–19
		Crude petroleum	Scholes and Roys 1948, Map 2
		Rubber, crude	Blom 1932: 540
		Rubber balls	Blom 1932: 540
	PC, M	Gold, rare, but there are modern mines near Pichucalco	
		Precious woods, cedar, brazil	
		Canoes	Cardós de Méndez 1959: 28
		Henequén, ixtle (pita) etc.	de Solís 1945
		Azofar (latón or brass)	Landa (Tozzer 1941)
		Basalt for sculptures	Coe 1968: 102
		Serpentine	Coe 1968: 102
Chiapas			
Zinacantan	PC	Cacao	
		Amber (probably from Simojovel; see Navarrete and Lee 1969)	Sahagún 1959: 21
		Quetzal feathers	Sahagún 1959: 21
		Blue cotingas feathers	Sahagún 1959: 21
		Blue honeycreeper	Sahagún 1959: 21
		Skins of wild animals of all kinds	Sahagún 1959: 21
Ixtapa and Salinas		Salt	Ximénez (Cardós de Méndez 1959: 41)
		Toldillos, white cloth	Cardós de Méndez 1959: 69
		Zoque-made cotton cloth	Scholes and Roys 1948: 38–39, 319 Ximénez 1929
Via Quechula	M	*Anil* from Tonalá, Pacific Coast	Castañón Gamboa 1951: 78
	M	Agricultural products	Castañón Gamboa 1951: 78

Tapalapa	PC	Amber may refer to the amber from
		    Simojovel (see Navarrete and
		    Lee 1969)
			Vásquez de Espinosa 1948: 196–97

Peninsula of Yucatan	PC	Salt	Cardós de Méndez 1959: 41
		Palo de Campeche, stain	Cardós de Méndez 1959: 30

Table 6. Continued

Place	Period	Raw Materials or Finished Goods	Source
Peten			
Salinas	PC	Salt	Blom 1932: 536
Acolhua-Mexica	PC	Royal gifts to local leaders: ropes, skirts, shifts	Sahagún 1959: 17–18
		Royal Merchandise: rulers' capes and loincloths	Sahagún 1959: 17–18
		Precious skirts embroidered in designs of squared stones, and embroidered shifts	Sahagún 1959: 17–18
		Pochteca merchandise for local leaders: gold crowns, forehead rosettes, golden tooth necklaces and plaited golden necklaces	Sahagún 1959: 17–18
		For local princesses: golden bowls for spindles, earplugs of gold and rock crystal	Sahagún 1959: 17–18
		For commoners: obsidian earplugs, copper earplugs, obsidian razors with leather handles, pointed obisdian blades	Sahagún 1959: 17–18
		Shells	Sahagún 1959: 17–18
		Needles	Sahagún 1959: 17–18
		Cochineal	Sahagún 1959: 17–18
		Red ochre	Sahagún 1959: 22
		Alum	Sahagún 1959: 17
		Rabbit fur	Sahagún 1959: 17
		Medicinal plants	Sahagún 1959: 17
		Salt	Sahagún 1959: 17
		Slave Traders: men, women and children	Cardós de Méndez 1959: 41
Oaxaca		Gold	Blom 1932: 542
Nito	PC	Cacao	Cortés 1960: 199
		Cotton cloth	Cortés 1960: 199
		Colors for dyeing and body stain	Cortés 1960: 199
		Tar	Cortés 1960: 199
		Resin for incense	Cortés 1960: 199
		Slaves	Cortés 1960: 199
		Red shell beads	Cortés 1960: 199
		Gold-copper alloys	Cortés 1960: 199

Period

PC = Precolumbian

M = Modern

Another important route utilized the Grijalva River, usually beginning at Huimanguillo or some point further north, which went to or from Chiapas points to the south. This is our next route for discussion.

TABASCO TO CHIAPAS ROUTES

The Grijalva River to the Chiapas Central Depression Route

This route, probably the most important connecting Northern Chiapas and Tabasco, has been used at least since 1523 when Luis Marín made the first known Spanish *entrada* into Chiapas in a plan to bring it under control (Díaz del Castillo 1964: 387–89). The Marín expedition apparently crossed overland through forests and swamps from Espíritu Santo and came out at Tepuzuntlan, probably somewhere on the Grijalva River above Huimanguillo since he said that up until that time they could get there only by going in canoe (Díaz del Castillo 1964: 387). From Tepuzuntlan they went up into the mountains to Quechula where they obtained Zoque Indians to aid them in opening the trail across the mountains into the Central Depression of Chiapas; the trail was said to be blocked off with trees felled across it to keep the Chiapanecas from penetrating the Quechula area.

Carlos Navarrete (1966b: 9–11) following Trens (1957) and others has interpreted the last section of this route as having crossed the Grijalva River at Quechula and then proceeding upriver at first parallel to its left margin and then moving away from it toward San Fernando and thence down into the Río Sabinal drainage and, passing Tuxtla, on to Chiapa de Corzo and up into the Chiapas Highlands.

The Quechula-San Fernando-Tuxtla Gutiérrez trail was until 1965 a most important route of access into the Central Depression from Quechula, though little used in late years. A slightly varied route, perhaps more important, took advantage of a pass with lesser elevation entering the Central Depression at Ocozocoautla. The latter route has assumed a greater role with the construction of an all-weather road from Ocozocoautla to the edge of the recently created Mal Paso lake which

has flooded portions of both the Grijalva and the La Venta Rivers for a combined length of over 100 km. including the old pre-Hispanic and Colonial town of Quechula.

While participating in the archaeological salvage of the Mal Paso lake basin in 1966, I collected ethnographic data including some regarding the canoe transportation system which functioned up until the mid-1920's (Navarrete and Lee, in preparation). River trips which I had taken down the Grijalva River prior to 1965 from Caguare above the formidable Sumidero Canyon (Lee 1966) down to the dam site, some 104 km. by river, amply demonstrated to me the well-recognized non-navigable nature of this section of the river. Nor indeed did travel along the broken margins of the river canyon country above Quechula appear practical. In contrast, it is a relatively easy trip by river from Quechula on down to Huimanguillo, with only a few sections of rough water.

The upper portion of the Quechula-Huimanguillo route on the Grijalva River was considered very dangerous during the Colonial period, as is demonstrated by an edict in which the Spanish government in Guatemala ordered the Grijalva river route blocked in order to prevent, they claimed, a great loss of boatmen's lives in the rapids below Quechula (Castañón Gamboa 1951: 78–79). The cargo was said to have been portaged around the rapids. After having personally been over the worst part of this route, and even though several motor boats were lost to the rapids in recent years, I would suggest that the Guatemalan Capitanía order was not to save lives, which I doubt were in any more danger than on many sections of other navigable rivers; more probably the directive was aimed at stopping the flow of merchandise through a distant route, in the westernmost part of their authority, over which they had no control and which therefore represented a threatened loss of potential taxes on goods transported over it. Nevertheless, Spanish authorities have shown elsewhere the same concern for the welfare of the Indian canoemen (see below, page 62).

The Huimanguillo-Quechula route is mentioned in an oral tradition of Southern Veracruz which claims that Guatemalan *nahuales* used it to reach Pajapan on the south slopes of the Los Tuxtlas mountains (García de León 1969: 166 footnote). That this route was said to go on to Tecpatan, Tuxtla Gutiérrez, Soconusco, and Guatemala demonstrates that the Pajapanecos understood the trajectory of this very long line of communication. Tecpatan was another important Zoque center during the Colonial period (García de Bargas y Rivera, Ms., 1774). Tecpatan could be reached either via Quechula or more directly from lower down on the Grijalva River.

Tecpatan Shortcut Route

The northern and western mountain flanks of Chiapas occupied by the Zoque were controlled by Cimatan on the Tabasco plain (Scholes and Roys 1948: 32, 39), so that as early as we have a written record this area was tied to the lowlands of Tabasco. Scholes and Roys (1948: 39) suggest that Zoque products were marketable in Tabasco because most people in that area dedicated their time to the production of cacao, and to this we could add commerce. There must have been many routes out of the mountainous area and several of these led to the Grijalva upon which cargo transport was greatly facilitated. Not all travel utilized the river, however. One of the most important trails, according to some early 19th century documents, was from Huimanguillo to Tecpatan along the left bank of the Grijalva, crossing in canoe the Chicoacan and Lamacoite arroyos to arrive at La Peña, where the Grijalva was crossed in canoe just below and opposite the junction of the Madgalena or Sayula River which was followed along its right bank through Hustoacan (Ostuacan) and Magdalena (Francisco León) and then on to Tecpatan over the mountains. We know from other sources that this trail went on from Tecpatan through Copainalá and Chicoasen to Soyalo and Ixtapa (the modern all-weather road through the same towns is maintained over essentially this old route) or more directly over and down to Chiapa de Corzo, and the Central Depression.

I have called the Huimanguillo to Tecpatan trail the "shortcut" route in reference to its connections with the Central Depression because like most shortcuts its advantages may be more apparent than real. The extremely high and broken relief between Tecpatan and Ixtapa or Chiapa de Corzo is the reason that this part of the route seems to have been used mainly for local traffic. On the other hand, this route avoided the shoals and boating problems on the Middle Grijalva which were intensified during the dry season. There were no easy trails crossing the mountain divide.

Moving slightly eastward along the mountainous northern flank of Chiapas we come to the last and possibly the most important inter-regional communication route connecting Tabasco and Chiapas.

Tacotalpa-Chiapas Highlands Route

This route was described in 1545 by Fray Tomás de la Torre (1944–1945) who accompanied Bishop de Las Casas and the first group of Dominican missionaries who followed him to the Highlands of Chiapas to begin their spiritual conquest of that region. The group had landed on this continent at Campeche and from there proceeded down the coast by boat to Laguna de Términos. What followed from there provides an enlightening account of travel on the combined Tabasco fluvial routes and the overland highland trails.

At Laguna de Términos the Dominican group divided, Las Casas and four others going on by boat along the coast and arriving at night under a strong wind off the mouth of the Grijalva River into which they were guided by a fire on shore (de la Torre 1944–45: 143). Further use of navigational aids in the form of signs placed in trees to guide traffic through the maze of waterways is reported by Landa in the same area (Tozzer 1941: 5), as we have noted above.

The Dominicans remaining behind at Laguna de Términos left the island of El Carmen and landed on the mainland where they were guided by Indians on foot to Xicalango. Leaving Xicalango the group went by canoe westward across a large open body of water. The canoes were tied up in pairs for stability in crossing this open stretch of water, much to the relief of the priests. Night overtook them in the crossing and since the area was shallow the Indians stuck long poles down into the lagoon bottom, tied up the boats to them and slept until morning (de la Torre 1944–45: 159). In continuing their journey, the canoes were untied from one another, as the open water soon gave way to narrow winding waterways often not much wider than the canoes and for extended stretches were completely covered over by the surrounding forest.

For some 6 km. just before arriving at the San Pedro and San Pablo River the Dominicans' route became very shallow, requiring the Indians to get out and pull the canoes through the low water and deep mud. Turning upstream into the San Pedro and San Pablo they traveled all day and into the night. Late at night the group turned again downstream into another branch of the lower Usumacinta, arriving near midday at the junction of the Grijalva and Usumacinta Rivers. By nightfall they had reached the village of Tabasco near where the rivers empty into the Gulf. The route from Tabasco to Chiapa Real (San Cristóbal) was from 60 to 70 leguas (180–210 miles), according to the account, half of which was by canoe (de la Torre 1944–45: 161). Keeping to the Lower Grijalva the route went upstream past Villahermosa and then into the Teapa and Tacotalpa Rivers to the village of the latter name where the transportation by canoe ended.

As an aside, the Tacotalpa River was navigable for at least another 30 km. upriver, as is demonstrated by an order given in 1591 by the Viceroy in Mexico to the Alcalde Mayor of the Villa de Tabasco advising that the native canoes and canoemen in the villages of Cauathan (Jahuacapa?), Aztapa, Tapijulapa, and Oxolotan were not to be forced against their will to carry Spanish merchants and merchandise upriver, that the Indians should not be forced to row 24 hours a day, that they should not be held liable for the cargo, and that they be paid a fair wage for their services (Archivo General de la Nación, *Ramo de Indias*, Vol. 5, Exp. 942–43). To continue the Dominican account, the trail overland from the village of Tacotalpa to Teapa is four leagues long with one ford midway, across the fast but not deep Puyacatengo. Here the *frailes* crossed on the backs of the Indians, arriving at last at Teapa.

One of the sick priests was sent on ahead of the group at Teapa in a net hammock hung from a long pole which was carried on the shoulders of two men walking in single file (de la Torre 1944–45: 175). De la Torre remarks that it was the common form of transport for native leaders and that the Spanish women who traveled in this area were carried in the same manner just as were Spanish men when the trails were too bad to go on horseback!

At Teapa, the group divided into two parts, one to leave a day ahead of the others, as a necessary measure in order to not work a hardship on the Indians who carried their baggage, and upon others along the way who would be expected to give food and shelter. Outside of Teapa the large deep river of the same name had to be forded and this time it was chest deep and very cold. Each *fraile* crossed with the aid of two or three Indians around him in order not to be swept off his feet. Only two leagues were covered the first day through water and mud and across steep ridges, arriving at Ixtapangoya.

Solosuchiapa is about three leagues (9 m.) from Ixtapangoya but since the main trail crossed the Teapa river four times and because the river was up the group took a mountain trail, much more difficult and trying, arriving, as de la Torre says, more dead than alive late in the afternoon.

Leaving Solosuchiapa the Teapa was again forded waist deep. The trail was only one foot wide, and like the rest, was covered completely by trees, with small arroyos being crossed frequently. On very steep hills wooden handrails were found in places to help in getting down the slopes. The group stopped at the Río de las Minas and passed the night with a Spanish *encomendero*. The next day the Dominicans arrived at Ixtuatan, a sugar plantation with a large native population nearby. The great climb up to Tapilula began soon after leaving Ixtuatan the next day. The group passed by Tapilula and stayed overnight in a small hut on the trail in the forest, probably between Rayón and Pueblo Nuevo. After a day's rest, the missionaries continued their trip, staying in the forest a second night in a similar hut as before, possibly between Jitotol and Amatan. The following day saw the group in Amatan and the next day they left the Zoque-speaking area and spent the night in a Tzotzil village. Nistlan was the next overnight stop. Leaving here the trail passed through Larrainzar and on to Muztenango for the night. The following day saw the Dominican group in San Cristóbal after passing by San Juan Chamula, crossing the Río Amarillo, and entering through the Mexican *barrio*, 40 days after leaving the island of Términos, some 500 km. away.

It is of interest to note that between Amatan and the first Tzotzil village, the frontier zone between Zoques and Tzotziles, at the top of one of the highest hills over which the trail crossed was a fortification built by the Indians for defense (de la Torre 1944–45: 136).

The same route from San Juan Chamula to Tapilula had been used twenty years earlier by Luis Marín when returning to Coatzacoalcos from his conquest of Chiapas, when he had been accompanied by Díaz del Castillo (1964: 396). They undoubtedly followed the same trail down to Teapa, but Díaz only mentions villages well out in the center of the coastal plain after passing Teapa, in order of their appearance Cimatan, Talatupan, Huimango, Acaxuyxuyca (Nacajuca), Teotitán Copilco, Ulapa, the Ahualulco River, the Tonala River, and finally into Coatzacoalcos. The lowland part of their trip apparently joined the Tabasco Coastal route at Nacajuca where they returned on it to Coatzacoalcos.

Díaz del Castillo (1946: 396) mentions that they were attacked by Indians near Talatupan and Cimatan from fortified palisades with holes, built in the edge of the forest surrounding *ciénagas* in park-like areas through which the trail passed (see also Scholes and Roys 1948: 32).

EARLY CULTURE CONTACT BETWEEN TABASCO AND CHIAPAS

The most important known inter-regional communication routes of the historical period connecting central Tabasco and west and south were (1) the Tabasco Coastal Route, (2) the Tabasco Inland Route, (3) the Grijalva River to Chiapas Central Depression Route, (4) the Tacotalpa to Chiapas Highlands Route, and (5) the integrating system for all of them, called the Fluvial Route of the Tabasco Riverine Market Complex. Opposed to these northern routes into Chiapas were other routes from the west and south which came across the Isthmus from Central Mexico avoiding the wet Gulf Coastal plain entirely. Our problem here is to determine the role of the northern routes only.

How did the northern communication routes affect early pre-Hispanic cultural contact between Tabasco and Chiapas? This, of course, is dangerous ground since much work remains to be done before we can properly trace the movement of either Formative or Classic period traits into or out of Chiapas. We must first assume that the topography and environment in general have been relatively stable for the last 3,000 and more years. We have some documented changes in river courses caused by the *rompidos* in Tabasco, but in general I believe that we can consider the natural environment to have changed little, as Sisson (1970: 44) has suggested previously.

The earliest evidence for man in either Chiapas or Tabasco is at the Santa Marta shelter cave site near Ocozocoautla in the Central Depression of Chiapas (MacNeish and Peterson 1962). The Santa Marta phase, the earliest occupation found, has been dated by radio carbon in round figures to between 7000 and 3500 B.C. This occupation, on the basis of its tool assemblage, was characterized by "mainly food gathering, some hunting or trapping, with possible incipient seed agriculture" and the absence of corn (MacNeish and Peterson 1962: 12). Despite the present lack of equally early evidence of man in Tabasco, such may be found in the future. Early migrations through Mexico and further south may logically have passed through or utilized the Ahualulcos area and other parts of the Chontalpa and northern Chiapas. A safe hypothesis would seem to be that early peoples followed rivers and valleys to their mountain sources or ocean exits, as the case might be, crossing divides and dropping down into any new drainage basins encountered. It may be significant that the earliest discovered human occupation in the Central Depression of Chiapas rests neatly at the end of the most practical route into this interior upland basin. This route follows the Grijalva River from the Tabasco plain into the Chiapas mountains, and over low passes into the Central Depression. The Santa Marta data, nevertheless, are available to us as the result of unusual preservation, but equally early occupations are apparently present across the Chiapas interior, as the burin found at Teopisca by Lorenzo (1961) and the San Pablo cave lithics on the lower Usumacinta River (Lee 1965) indicate.

It must also be pointed out that the early non-ceramic shell middens of the central Pacific Coast to date remain poorly studied, in spite of their relatively early recognition (Drucker 1948: 165–66; Lorenzo 1955) and may represent a southern source of early human populating of the Chiapas highlands. As elsewhere in Mexico, there seems no doubt that by at least 1500 B.C., throughout western Tabasco and Central and Southern Chiapas, there were settled communities with ceramic and agricultural systems in most of the coastal and riverine environments (Rands 1969: 18; Lowe 1971, Fig 1). The earliest ceramic-using communities are generally attributed to the Ocós horizon cultures which occupied both coasts of the general Isthmus area. Once this point was reached, cultural development accelerated and not many centuries passed before the first great art style appeared, blossomed and quickly burst into full splendor.

At San Lorenzo, on the Coatzacoalcos River, Coe (1970: 26) has placed the beginning of the Olmec development during the Chicharras phase dating to between 1250 and 1150 B.C. During the ensuing centuries, up until about 600 or 500 B.C., the Olmec art style climaxed and further evolved. The evolution and chronology of the monumental stone art is still being unravelled, and the developmental history of ceramic styles is slowly becoming understood. Some diagnostic ceramic attributes common to Early Olmec culture are differential firing, or the smudged or "smothered" black-and-white and often white-rim black tradition. Particularly distinctive of this period are the carved and incised designs, the incised red slips, the figurine styles, and the flat bottom bowl and *tecomate* or neckless jar shapes. The distribution of Olmec culture outside of the Metropolitan Olmec area in southeastern Veracruz and western Tabasco (Bernal 1969) is best known from the appearance of these ceramic modes and attributes, as major complex constituents. Perhaps significantly, monumental Olmec stone art has a slightly different or more sparse distribution pattern. The most consistent Olmec occupation area, in terms of both monuments and ceramics, includes portions of Veracruz and Tabasco and the Pacific Coast of Chiapas and part of Guatemala (with an apparent extension into El Salvador at Chalchuapa). In terms of ceramics we have to add the Isthmus section of Oaxaca, and western and central Chiapas. In the latter regions of Chiapas we have strikingly close Olmec ceramic complexes and some Olmec ceremonial patterns, but only a single Olmec monument, located at Padre Piedra (Navarrete 1960, Fig. 11; Bernal 1969, Fig. 33). In northeastern Chiapas, one clearly Olmec rock carving is known, at Xoc (Bernal 1969, Fig. 34; Ekholm-Miller 1973). Portable stone objects in the Olmec style appear infrequently throughout Chiapas. Olmec celts found in the vicinity of Simojovel, in northern Chiapas, as well as the Xoc carving, may represent an early movement from Veracruz and/or Tabasco south and east over the route from Tacotalpa which is about 100 km. due north of Simojovel.

A particularly significant Olmec style occupation was discovered at San Isidro on the Grijalva River, a short distance downstream from Quechula, where both early Olmec ceramics and later Olmec mosaic celt offerings were common (Lowe 1969). San Isidro undoubtedly was a way station and perhaps anciently, the chief terminal on the route from Tabasco to the Chiapas Central Depression. Olmec figurines of both stone and clay have been found in the adjacent western portion of the Central Depression at Mirador, Miramar, Piedra Parada, Ocozocoautla, Chiapa de Corzo, and elsewhere. Four portable Olmec stone carvings — figurines and scepters of unusual merit — were recently published from Piedra Parada and Ocozocoautla (Navarrete 1971: 69–71). These occurrences again seem favorable to our argument, inasmuch as this zone is a recognized terminal point of the Río Grijalva route into the Central Depression from Tabasco.

Evidences supporting a southward Olmec movement into Central Chiapas continue to come to light. One of the most striking duplications known of the San Lorenzo Olmec (ca. 1100 B.C.) ceramic complex was uncovered in 1970 at Mirador (Agrinier in preparation). Mirador is on the upper Río La Venta, the major tributary of the Middle Grijalva River and another logical entry point of Grijalva-based routes into the Central Depression. The possibility exists, of course, that some Olmec travel was from the Río Tonala near the La Venta ceremonial center on the Tabasco coast, and up its main tributary, the Río Playas to Pueblo Viejo, Veracruz. Pueblo Viejo is only a short distance to the Río La Venta (unnavigable) or to the nearby navigable Río Grijalva. An even wider abundance of similar San Lorenzo phase ceramics at San Isidro, however, indicates that the Middle Grijalva was an important part of the Olmec route into Chiapas.

On the basis of present evidence, it cannot be decided whether the rather strong Olmec cultural manifestations on the Pacific Coast (Green and Lowe 1967: 63–68, 74; Navarrete 1969, 1971) arrived there via the Central Depression and the natural routes from Tabasco or by other routes which connected the Pacific Coast to Veracruz centers by way of the Isthmus. Both portable and monumental Olmec art objects have been found at Tzutzuculi near Tonala (McDonald n.d.), Pijijiapan (Navarrete 1969), Ojo de Agua (Navarrete 1971), Cacahoatan, and further south in Guatemala (Parsons and Jensen 1965, Navarrete 1971). Viewing the complete absence of Olmec monuments in the southern or Oaxacan half of the Isthmus of Tehuantepec, it is tempting to suppose that the Olmecs who were responsible for the few known monuments farther east in Chiapa did indeed come into this area, all the way to the Pacific Coast, via the riverine routes leading south out of Tabasco. An early ethnic pattern resembling the known ethnohistorical positioning of the Zapotec peoples in the Tehuantepec-to-Juchitan zone and the Mixe-Zoque occupation from the Gulf to Pacific coasts through Tabasco and Chiapas could explain this postulate, based as it is upon the remarkable lack of more clearly Olmec elements in the Tehuantepec region (Lee, Lowe, and Navarrete, in preparation). Better knowledge of the Southern Isthmus may modify this picture, of course.

The transitional evolution of Olmec ceramics in the Metropolitan area during the Middle and Late Preclassic periods appears (from collections and poorly published samples) to be closely related in varied degrees to similar developmental histories at San Isidro, Mirador, Chiapa de Corzo, and many other sites in Central Chiapas. These developments, which precede and parallel the Mamom Ceramic Sphere in the Maya area, may well have had a strong base in Veracruz, as Warren (1964: 294–95) has argued. Directions of movement cannot be determined until more adequate investigations are made and published, but active participation of San Isidro and other sites on the Middle Grijalva indicates that the river routes continued to be important (Lee, Lowe, and Navarrete, in preparation).

During the Protoclassic and Classic periods in central-western Chiapas there was a return in emphasis to the smudged black-and-white tradition in ceramics which shows even more important relationships to southern Veracruz and western Tabasco. Ample presence of this class of non-Maya pottery at San Isidro again demonstrates that the Grijalva River continued as a main route for transmitting ceramic ideas, if indeed, not of actual peoples. The routes farther to the east, meanwhile, served to bring in items from the western Maya regions during periods of accentuated regional development.

In summary, the ecological diversity of the Tabasco lowlands and the Chiapa highlands provided a very early and continuing potential for the development of inter-regional symbiotic relationships. The large market complexes so important and characteristic at the time of the Conquest were formed where navigable waters aided the concentration of population and merchandise. To these centers southward-reaching rivers provided ready-made supply or migration routes from highland areas of Chiapas and these seem to have been utilized from earliest times. The precise role of particular routes was subject to numerous historical factors through the course of time. It is one task of the archaeologist to determine what these factors were, and in this difficult assignment he can be guided somewhat by analogies drawn from historical accounts.

ACKNOWLEDGMENTS

Miguel Medina provided me with the copies of the papers by Antonio García de León (1969, 1970) for which I am truly grateful. I wish to thank Gareth W. Lowe for his aid in reading and criticizing the rough draft of this paper. His editorial aid on the final copy is also greatly appreciated.

REFERENCES

Archivo General de la Nación 1591, 1816
Bernal 1969
Blom 1932
Brasseur de Bourbourg 1858
Cardós de Méndez 1959
Castañón Gamboa 1951
Chapman 1959
Coe 1968, 1970
Cortés 1960, 1963
Díaz del Castillo 1964
Dibble and Anderson 1959
Drucker 1948
Echeagaray Bablot 1957
Ekholm-Miller 1973
Falcón de Gyves 1965
Flannery 1968
García de Bargas y Rivera 1774
García de León 1969, 1970
González 1946
Green and Lowe 1967
Lee 1965, 1966
López de Gómara 1941
Lorenzo 1955, 1961
Lowe 1969, 1971
McDonald n.d.
MacNeish and Peterson 1962
Navarrete 1960, 1966b, 1969, 1971
Navarrete and Lee 1969
Parsons and Jenson 1965
Rands 1969
Rathje 1971b
Relaciones de Yucatán 1889–1900
Sahagún 1959
Sanders 1965
Sanders and Price 1968
Scholes and Roys 1948
Sisson 1970
de Solís 1945
Thompson 1964, 1970
de la Torre 1944–45
Tozzer 1941
Trens 1957
Vázquez de Espinoza 1948
Wallrath 1967
Warren 1964
West 1964
Ximénez 1929–1931

7. REFLECTIONS ON ZINACANTAN'S ROLE IN AZTEC TRADE WITH SOCONUSCO

by

Ulrich Köhler

In late pre-Columbian times Zinacantan seems to have been the major commercial center of the *Serranía Central de Chiapas,* then, as now, inhabited by various tribes of the linguistic groups that have come to be known as Tzotzil and Tzeltal. Prior to its being subdued the *pochteca,* the Aztec long distance traders, reached Zinacantan disguised as natives of that province and traded obsidian knives, awls, needles, bells, cochineal, alum, ochre, and rabbit hair for amber, the skins of wild animals, and different kinds of feathers, particularly those of the quetzal (Sahagún 1952: 192f.). Although the *Codex Florentinus* version (Sahagún 1969, Vol. 3, p. 30f.) contains no specific reference to the reign of Ahuitzotl (1486–1503), the *Codex Matritense,* the primary source cited above, relates this description of Zinacantan as a market where the disguised *pochteca* traded within territory hostile specifically to his reign, a clear indication of the independence of the area at this time. For a detailed comment on the items of exchange between Aztec and Zinacantec see Blom (1959).

Contrasted with this description of early commercial relations between Aztec and Zinacantec, Chapman's (1959: 54) conclusion that Zinacantan did in fact later become an Aztec stronghold on their long distance trade route to Soconusco lacks solid documentation. To clarify whether this role may be ascribed to Zinacantan, when this may have occurred, and along which route trading may have taken place, we first have to touch upon the controversial question of whether the Chiapanec — then occupying an extended lowland area to the west and south of Zinacantan — were indeed ever conquered by the Aztec.

In analyzing the possibility of the conquest of Chiapa in the present State of Chiapas by the Aztec, we must distinguish two historical events: 1) the conquest of a town called Chiapa during the early reign of Ahuitzotl, as reported in lists of conquests and by various historians; and 2) the conquest of a Teochiapan or Teochiyappa by Motecuçoma Xocoyotzin, as reported in the *Codex Mendoza* and the *Historia de los Reynos de Colhuacan y de México (Anales de Cuauhtitlan).* Concerning the first event, Tschohl's (1964: 30–42, 181) detailed critical analysis convincingly demonstrates that all reports of the conquest of a Chiapa between 1482 and 1490 refer to an Otomi town to the northwest of Tenochtitlan, and that the reports of Ahuitzotl's conquest of a town of the name of Comitlan do not refer to Comitan in Chiapas but that it is very probable that these refer to the present Comitancillo near Tehuantepec (Tschohl 1964: 170f.). After a lengthy discussion of the possible location of Teochiapan, and taking into account the fact that the prefixes Teo-, Huey-, Hui-, Uei-, and Guey- are interchangeable, he strongly suggests that the proper identity of this town is Huichiapa (Huichiapan) in the present State of Hidalgo (Tschohl 1964: 183, 185). Turning our attention to the relevant list in the *Codex Mendoza* (1925: 15f.), Tschohl's probability becomes certainty: Teochiapan is listed together with Tecozauhtla — a town neighbouring Huichiapan in the State of Hidalgo. For its location see Soustelle (1937, Map 5) or any current road map. We may thus conclude that none of the towns by the name of Chiapa or a similar word which are listed in Aztec lists of conquest are identical with the Chiapanec capital to the east of the Isthmus of Tehuantepec. Thus there is no direct evidence of its subjection. On the contrary Díaz del Castillo (1947: 224f.) and Herrera (1934–1936, Dec. IV, Lib. X, Cap. XI), report, independently of one another that the Chiapanec were enemies of the Aztec and they never lost their independence.

In considering the problem of an Aztec conquest of Zinacantan and its eventual conversion to a stronghold on a trade route to Soconusco we must take into account two constants: 1) the obstacle presented by the high mountain chain of the Sierra Madre del Sur which runs parallel to the Pacific Coast, and 2) the unbroken bulwark of the Chiapanec nation in the Central Depression of Chiapas. The latter reduces all attempts to reconstruct proto-historic Aztec trade routes from Tehuantepec via Chiapa, Zinacantan, and Comitan to Guatemala or Soconusco (cf., for example, Barlow 1949, map; Feldman, paper in this volume) to a mere fiction.

The conquest of a Zinacantlan by Mote-cuçoma Xocoyotzin is reported in both the *Codex Mendoza* (1925, Fol. 15f) and the *Historia de los Reynos de Colhuacan y de*

México (Lehmann 1938: 318) (Fig. 14). In each case Zinacantlan is listed together with a town by the name of Huitztlan. The fact that a town in the neighbourhood of Zinacantan bore that name favours the interpretation that the list of conquests describes an advance into the Highlands of Chiapas. Furthermore, Sahagún (1952: 190f.) mentions the subdual of a Tzinacantlan. He gives no further information as to the time and circumstances, but from his description it is clear that the town implied was Zinacantan in Chiapas. Herrera even reports an Aztec garrison in Zinacantan which was involved in warfare with the Chiapanec (loc. cit.), a passage which was

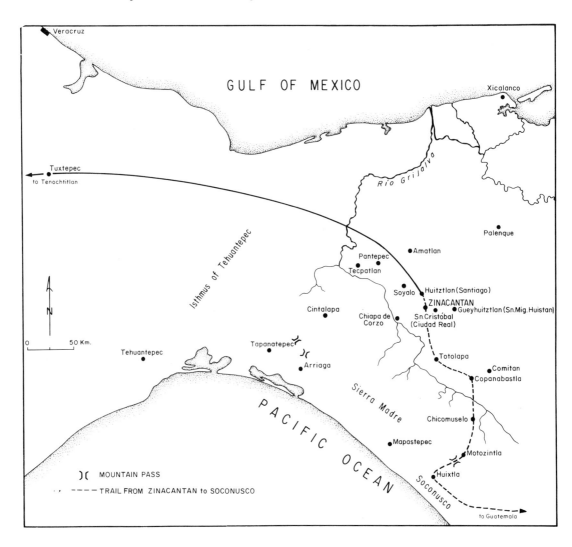

Figure 14. The Greater Isthmus Area showing Zinacantan and its Relationship to One Version of the Soconusco-to-Tenochtitlan Route

later copied by Remesal (1932, Vol. 1, p. 378). From these various sources we may conclude that the Aztec did indeed extend their power to Zinacantan. The fact that Díaz del Castillo and Godoy do not mention an Aztec garrison is scarcely a serious argument to the contrary, for they first reached Chiapas three years after the collapse of Tenochtitlan and it would have been rather astonishing to discover Aztec overlordship still present in 1524. It should be added that Aztec military penetration into this area was of recent origin and may not have occurred earlier than two decades before the *Conquista*. We may assume, therefore, that their garrison in Zinacantan was a provisional outpost rather than an established center of regional domination.

We have no direct information as to the route along which the Aztec conquerors entered Zinacantan. A conquest from Tehuantepec via hostile Chiapanec territory cannot be entirely excluded but is highly improbable. Tschohl (1964: 171) believes that the conquest of Zinacantan and Huistan occurred from the stable province of Soconusco and served primarily to assure a continual flow of desired products. On the other hand he tries to suggest that the region around Chicomuselo was not subdued by the Aztec (Tschohl 1964: 190). Such an interpretation ignores the topography of southern Chiapas. Since early historical times only three passes cross the high mountain chain of the Sierra Madre: Tapanatepec–Cintalapa and Arriaga–Cintalapa in the northwest, and Huixtla–Motozintla in the extreme southeast. According to Waibel (1933: 148) the small trails across the mountains between Huixtla and Arriaga are of recent origin and were innovated after the railroad along the Pacific coast was built early this century. Tschohl's (1964: 172) assertion that the traditional post-Columbian pass through the Sierra Madre began at Mapachtepec must be a typographical error! The reports of the early and more recent travellers quoted by him contradict his statement; Mapachtepec should be read as Tapanatepec.

A conquest of Zinacantan via one of the two passes in the northwest would have met with the same problem as the one from Tehuantepec previously discussed. A penetration from Soconusco via Motozintla would make a route through Chicomuselo a necessity. We cannot exclude such a penetration from Soconusco although no evidence supporting this hypothesis of Tschohl can be found. However, the alleged transport of goods from Zinacantan to Soconusco, then along the Pacific coastline via Tehuantepec to Tenochtitlan seems quite absurd. It is even less probable, since we know from Sahagún (1952: 187ff.) that the disguised *pochteca* who entered Zinacantan from Tuxtepec were one group of the traders whose main goal was Xicalanco and other markets near the Atlantic coast. The same author also informs us a few pages later that one of the other duties of these *pochteca* was to explore the routes of unknown territories in order to be able to lead the troops on their way to new conquests (Sahagún 1952: 196f.). Thus, the available data strongly suggest a route of trade and conquest through the northern Zoque area.

This interpretation is further supported by the *Codex Mendoza* (1925, Fol. 15f.), which lists under the items 21 to 24 the following towns as having been conquered by Motecuçoma Xocoyotzin: Tecpatlan, Amatlan, Caltepec, Pantepec. With the exception of Caltepec these seem to be the Zoque towns of identical names in northwestern Chiapas. For some reason Tschohl (1964: 148ff.) disliked the location of these towns in Chiapas and he therefore searched for alternatives all over Mexico, each in another direction, without, however, coming to conclusive results. Although we have no direct evidence of the location of the above-mentioned towns, their identification as those of the Zoque seems plausible in the general context of intensified Aztec activities in the southeast during the reign of Motecuçoma Xocoyotzin.

Even if we discard the whole problem of a conquest of Tecpatlan, Amatlan, and Pantepec we reach the following conclusions: 1.) There is no direct information as to the route of conquest to Zinacantan but a penetration from Tuxtepec is, however, far more probable than one from Tehuantepec via hostile Chiapanec territory or from distant Soconusco via Motozintla; 2.) As for the trade route from

Tenochtitlan to Zinacantan, we have no reason to assume that the Aztec, after having conquered Zinacantan, abandoned the traditional route of the *pochteca* from Tuxtepec through the northern Zoque area for a geographically and politically more difficult one.

A few words must be said concerning the location of Huiztlan, which is reported to have been conquered together with Zinacantlan. At present there is a community to the east of San Cristóbal by the name of San Miguel Huistan. During the early sixteenth century there existed two communities with similar names in the Serranía Central de Chiapas: one Vistlan (Viztlan) and one Gueyhuiztlan (Gueyguistitlan, Huegueztean). The latter is mentioned in the reports of Díaz del Castillo (1947: 227ff.) and Godoy (1852: 465ff.) as a rebellious town which offered resistance during the expedition of 1524. The other is reported as Vistlan by the Dominican Fray Tomás de la Torre in 1545. His original chronical is probably lost but this information is included in Remesal (1932, Vol. 1, p. 377) and Ximénez (1929-1931, Vol. 1, p. 333). There Vistlan is referred to as the first town of the *quelenos* (Tzotzil) reached by the Dominicans on their way from Tabasco to Ciudad Real. It is at present known as Santiago although its official name is El Pinar. Most scholars have identified Gueyhuiztlan as the present San Miguel Huistan; recently, however, Adams (1961: 357) related the name to Santiago. This interpretation also appears in Vol. 2, Pt. 1 of the *Handbook of Middle American Indians* (map on p. 196). It is incorrect. In a document dating from 1547 in the archives of Guatemala and quoted by Calnek (1970: 123), a witness in a quarrel over *encomiendas*, identifies Hueihuistan with San Miguel Huistan. Furthermore, the distance of Gueyhuiztlan from the site of Ciudad Real and the description of the route to it as reported by Díaz del Castillo and Godoy far better fit Huistan than Santiago.

In deciding on the question of which of these two towns was the Huiztlan conquered by Motecuçoma Xocoyotzin, I am inclined to assume that it was most probably the town which was identified as Vistlan in the early

sixteenth century and not the one known at that time as Gueyhuiztlan, that is, Santiago el Pinar and not San Miguel Huistan. Furthermore, Santiago is located on an ancient trade route — known since earliest colonial times — which descends from the central plateau area of San Cristóbal and Zinacantan via Jitotol and Tapilula to the northern Zoque lowlands. From this region only two routes lead to the *cabecera* of Zinacantan, one via Ixtapa, the other via Santiago. It may well have been in the interest of the Aztec to subdue this particular Huistlan — that is, Santiago — but as there is no evidence to this effect, it must remain a matter of speculative judgment.

After these necessarily extended preliminaries we may return to the problem of whether Zinacantan did become a stronghold defending Aztec trade with Soconusco. Two main questions remain to be answered: did the trade route from Tuxtepec via the northern Zoque region to Zinacantan extend further into Soconusco, and if so, which path did it follow? Having no direct evidence of an Aztec trade route from Zinacantan to Soconusco I should like to begin with a discussion of the second problem. The topography suggests only one possible line: across the upper Grijalva Valley and over the mountain pass between Motozintla and Huixtla. This mountain pass is located very close to a straight line drawn between Zinacantan and Soconusco. This route did constitute the link between the Serranía Central de Chiapas and Soconusco in colonial times, and even early this century the Indian seasonal workers from the area around San Cristóbal used it on their way to the coffee plantations of Soconusco (Waibel 1933: 145). For the Aztec this route to the east of Chiapanec territory would have been of approximately the same length as the one following the Pacific Coast via Tehuantepec. There is evidence that the authority of Zinacantan extended as far as, and probably beyond, Totolapa, at the time of the Conquista (Vogt 1969: 25, 386, 473), thus controlling the whole mountain area to the northeast of Chiapanec territory, which then extended as far as Ostuta in the Grijalva Valley (Navarrete 1966a: 16(. Since Gopanaustlan (Copanabastla), the next large town on the route to Chicomuselo and Motozintla, was also on hostile terms with the Chiapanec (Díaz del Castillo 1947: 227), trading in relative security from their attacks may have been possible.

It seems necessary to speak of relative security, because Bernal Díaz del Castillo (1947: 227) observed that the Chiapanec held prisoners from Tehuantepec and other Zapotec towns, as well as Quilenes (Tzotzil) and inhabitants of Soconusco who had been captured on the roads. This would indicate a general insecurity caused by Chiapanec movements through a vast zone to the east and south of Tehuantepec. The successful Chiapanec raids in the Tehuantepec area — solidly documented by the enforced relocation of at least one of their towns in about 1512 (Díaz del Castillo 1947: 225ff.) — suggest anything but secure Aztec trading and the safe transport of the collected tribute along the southern Isthmus and the Pacific coast. Apart from being exposed to the threat of Chiapanec attacks and from being almost impassible during the rainy season (cf. Ponce 1873, Vol. 1, pp. 291f, 294), this route to Soconusco was burdened with the additional disadvantage of the politically unstable situation in Tehuantepec, which never had been effectively subdued.

These facts suggest the conclusion that the Aztec acutely needed another route for tribute and merchandise from Soconusco during the reign of Motecuçoma Xocoyotzin — the very period during which Zinacantan was conquered. Against the route behind Chiapanec lines via Chicomuselo and Motozintla suggested here it might be argued that these towns do not appear in any report as having been conquered by the Aztec. But this cannot be regarded as countering the argument, for other routes, such as, for example, the well documented one from Tuxtepec to Xicalanco (Sahagún 1952: 186ff.), also include long passages through populated territory in which no conquered towns are mentioned. Comparing the probable military strength of Chicomuselo, Motozintla, and other smaller towns along the route with that of Tehuantepec, other Zapotec towns and the Chia-

panec, an Aztec breakthrough via the upper Grijalva Valley would seem the easier task. Furthermore, it is not necessary to assume that the Aztec themselves undertook trading between Zinacantan and Soconusco. It is quite possible that they left it to the Zinacantec and their vassals to close the gap between Zinacantan and Soconusco. We know from Díaz del Castillo (1947: 228) and Ximénez (1929–1931, Vol. 1, p. 360) that the Zinacantec were important traders at the time of Spanish conquest, as they are still today, and, in the early nineteenth century, they are reported to have been heavily engaged in long distance trade — including the transport of cacao to the Central Highlands from Soconusco (Vogt 1969: 25).

Let us summarize: we have no definite evidence that trade and the collection of tributes from Soconusco followed a route via the Motozintla pass and Zinacantan. The same lack of documentation also holds, however, for the alleged route along the Pacific coast via Tehuantepec. It is most probable, however, that the latter was used for a period after the initial conquest of Soconusco by Ahuitzotl. The sequence of towns conquered as contained in Aztec lists indicates a military expedition along the coast into the province of Soconusco. We may therefore assume that the initial transport of tribute and trade to Tenochtitlan followed the same line. Later, during the reign of Motecuçoma Xocoyotzin, this route was increasingly jeopardized by threats of Chiapanecan and Zapotecan attack. It was, therefore, in the interest of the Aztec to provide another outlet for the products of Soconusco. The suggested route via Motozintla and Zinacantan did not offer greater geographical difficulties and seems to have offered considerably fewer political and military obstacles than the one along the coast. If indeed this route to the east of Chiapanec territory was used by the Aztec during the reign of Motecuçoma Xocoyotzin, we may assume that merchandise from Guatemala, arriving in Soconusco, was forwarded to Tenochtitlan along the same line.

This tentative reconstruction of an Aztec trade route from the lowlands of the Gulf

Coast via the western fringe of the Serranía Central de Chiapas, through the upper Grijalva Valley, traversing the Sierra Madre near Motozintla and finally reaching the flat coastal strip on the Pacific in Soconusco is also of more general interest, for linguistic, archaeological, and historical data suggest that it may have been a major route of communication and migration at various prehistoric time levels.

In Soyalo — close to the northwestern border of Zinacantan, and in the neighbouring village of San Gabriel — Nahuatl was still spoken early in this century. Santibáñez (1908: 67) believed these minorities to be remnants of the auxiliary troops who accompanied the Spanish conquerors. Van Zantwijk's (1963: 179ff.) analysis of the language of informants from Soyalo and the nearby town of Bochil, however, shows that they did not speak Nahuatl, but rather Nahuat or Pipil, which suggests the arrival of the ancestors of these "Mexicans" during an earlier migration. This hypothesis is supported by Ximénez's (1929–1931, Vol. 2, p. 295) statement that the inhabitants of Totolapa spoke a "Mexican" dialect different from the Nahuatl spoken by the descendants of the Aztec and Tlaxcaltec who had accompanied the Spanish conquerors and who had settled permanently in the valley of Ciudad Real. These linguistic data from four communities along the western fringe of the Serranía Central de Chiapas suggest that at least one branch of the Pipil or Toltec migrations into Central America passed through this area. Yokes and *palmas* — closely related in style to those of northern Veracruz — which were found in the Late Classic site of Moxviquil above San Cristóbal (presently in Museum of Na-Bolom) tend to confirm even earlier contacts. While communication with central Mexico can definitely be proven we have less solid data as to a route of contact and migration leading into Central America. The easiest path from the Serranía Central to the coastal strip bordering the Pacific where the Pipil finally settled, is over the mountain pass near Motozintla. Is it mere coincidence that the Mayan language of Cotoque, closely related to Huastec in the far north (Zimmermann

1955, McQuown 1964), was spoken in Chicomuselo, on the route linking the Serranía Central with the pass across the Sierra Madre?

Our data tend to confirm Waibel's (1933: 95) conviction that the mountain pass between Huixtla and Motozintla was the scene of important population movements in the past, of which he specifically mentions the Chiapanec. Without entering here into a discussion of whether the Chiapanec originally migrated from Nicaragua, whether they dropped off to settle along an alleged migration route of the Mangue from northwestern to southeastern Mesoamerica, or whether they hived off from the Mangue in Nicaragua and remigrated into Chiapas, it should be noted that topographical conditions do in fact favour Waibel's interpretation of where the Chiapanec and/or Mangue crossed the Sierra Madre. Considering the possible pre-Columbian importance of the mountain pass near Motozintla it is not without interest that during the eighteenth century the principal trade route between the Laguna del Carmen (the site of ancient Xicalanco) and Guatemala passed through Palenque, Comitan and Soconusco (cf. Trens 1957: 147; Morelet 1872: 60f.). Only after the opening of a large port in the Gulf of Honduras was trade between Guatemala and Spain diverted along the shorter route. Although the mountain pass between Motozintla and Huixtla is not specifically mentioned in the reports referred to, it is evident that it was the scene of trade between Guatemala and its principal port on the Atlantic. There is no other mountain pass between Comitan and Soconusco. The fact that the trade route passed through Soconusco, not using a possible shortcut via Huehuetenango, may be indicative of pre-Columbian preferences, for goods were carried principally by Indian bearers, technology still having scarcely changed.

Though far from allowing definitive conclusions our data suggest considerable communication between central Mexico and the Atlantic coast via central Chiapas to Soconusco and further on into Central America. It would be wrong to assume the existence of a simple unchanging route. The route probably varied according to the contigencies of the given political and military situation, passing during certain periods through the mountains of the Serranía Central, during others along the Grijalva Valley. Our conclusion implies that in prehistoric times the flat coastal strip between Tehuantepec and Soconusco was of less importance for communication, trade, and migration than has usually been assumed. This is not surprising if we consider the fact that the plain in no way constituted an outstanding topographical advantage for cultures possessing a technological level lacking not only trains, cars, and oxcarts, but even pack animals.

Our conclusions may be summarized as follows: 1) we reject the postulate of a protohistoric Aztec trade route from Tehuantepec via Chiapa, Zinacantan, and Comitan into Guatemala or Soconusco; we are able to prove 2) the existence of an Aztec trade route via Tuxtepec and the northern Zoque area to Zinacantan since the reign of Ahuitzotl; we suggest 3) a probable prolongation of this route via Motozintla to Soconusco at some time after the conquest of Zinacantan by Motecuçoma Xocoyotzin, and 4) moving from the particular to the general, we conclude that a number of prehistoric migrations took place along the same route.

REFERENCES

Adams 1961
Barlow 1949
Blom 1959
Calnek 1970
Chapman 1959
Colección de (Codex) Mendoza o Códice Mendocino 1925
Díaz del Castillo 1947
Godoy 1852
Handbook of Middle American Indians 1965
Herrera 1934–1936
Lehmann 1938
McQuown 1964
Morelet 1872
Navarrete 1966a
Ponce 1873
Remesal 1932
Sahagún 1952, 1969
Santibáñez 1908
Soustelle 1937
Trens 1957
Tschohl 1964
Vogt 1969
Waibel 1933
Ximénez 1929–1931
van Zantwijk 1963
Zimmermann 1955

8. THE PRE-HISPANIC SYSTEM OF COMMUNICATIONS BETWEEN CHIAPAS AND TABASCO[1]

(Preliminary Report)

by
CARLOS NAVARRETE

In 1965, when the first season of archaeological investigations was initiated on the coast of Chiapas, and later, when I began a reconnaissance of the Sierra Madre, Central Depression, and the Comitan Valley in Chiapas, I became aware of the possibilities offered by the study of ancient commerce routes if all the historic information could be gathered together and augmented by ethnographic data from muleteers, canoemen, and merchants, Indian as well as *mestizo,* who had traveled by routes now abandoned and by others that still exist.

My interest became active investigation a few years later when I began to recheck my interviews with informants, the data found in publications of diverse content, and my personal experience in following trails, canals, and rivers, as well as the observations made during flights over the territory of Chiapas and Tabasco. Nevertheless, it was not until 1968, when the archaeological salvage was carried out in the lands inundated by the construction of the Mal Paso Dam on the Río Grijalva, that I could learn what this waterway represented, not only as a direct route, but also for the hundreds of trails that came down to its shores and formed a true network via incredible passes that tied together towns, places of religious pilgrimages, markets, centers of craft production, regions with differing climate and cultivation, and an enormous range of activities and languages.

This work, then, constitutes a first attempt at synthesis, a sort of guide to what has been investigated and to what remains to be done. For this reason it will be noted that more emphasis is placed on certain regions, or a simple reference is given to some work in preparation where particular aspects will be treated more amply.

I must also mention the method followed for the presentation of the data. First, I use what can be called "axis-systems," that consists of the following of those routes that have not varied from the pre-Hispanic era to today because they are bound by natural passes such as the coast of Chiapas, the middle and upper Río Grijalva, and the corridors to the Gulf Coast. After the description of these three systems I present the secondary ones, and, finally, the possibility of defining others about which there exists very little information.

Second, I recognize that most of our present-day roads were constructed over the old roads of the last century and of the colonial era which in turn followed the routes imposed by the conquerors; they always looked for the shortest, most expedient, and natural routes that the indigenous merchants followed. With today's economic development of our area of study that is manifest in the construction of a modern communications network, our work then becomes a sort of salvage of the ancient road charts before modern technology makes invalid our postulate concerning the "accumulation" of routes through time.

I must explain also that only in some cases this work will mention regional production, techniques employed and the social organization of work in the construction of the roads and their maintenance, the inter-ethnic and linguistic connections that were established with the communication routes, the merchants' schedules and rate of travel, the rest stations, and other economic and cultural aspects that will be treated in more ample studies and those which we will refer to throughout this article. Finally, I must make another clarification: the map in Figure 15 does not pretend to show all the roads and towns that are men-

---

[1]This is a translation of "El sistema prehispánico de comunicaciones entre Chiapas y Tabasco (informe preliminar)," *Anales de Antropología,* Vol. 10, pp. 32–92, Universidad Nacional Autónoma de México, Mexico.

tioned in this work; it is simply a schematic projection of the topography of one part of the area studied and the principal routes that cross it.

THE OVERLAND ROUTES ON THE COAST OF CHIAPAS

The first route parallel to the coast is indicated by the list of Aztec tributary towns that appears in the *Codex Mendocino* (Kingsborough 1831, Vol. I), where the following are mentioned: Xoconochco (Soconusco, a town whose ruins we have identified near Acacoyagua), Ayotla (Ayutla, the first Guatemalan town on the Río Suchiate), Coyoacan (not identified), Mapachtepec (Mapaztepec), Macatlan (Mazatan), Huiztlan (Huixtla), Acapetlantlan (Acapetagua), and Huehuetlan (Huehuetan). For our purposes it is important to point out that among the products in the tribute figure items not native to the coast such as amber in the shape of "a clear amber lip-plug with gold mounting" and "two pieces of clear amber the size of a brick." This indicates a relation between the coastal zone, conquered by the Aztecs in 1498, and the area of Simojovel, into which the Aztecs never penetrated [Ed.: see Lee 1973 and this volume for further reference to this amber source controlled by Zinacantan] and where the only amber deposits in all Mesoamerica are found (Navarrete and Lee 1969: 13–19). We will refer to this at greater length below.

The first direct account of this road is from the conqueror Pedro de Alvarado himself, who crossed the Soconusco in order to go to Guatemala and conquer Utatlan, the Quiche capital. He wrote from Utatlan on the 11th of April, 1524, to Hernán Cortés telling him what had happened (Alvarado 1934: 271–75). In this *Relación* he begins by saying that "from Soconusco I wrote to Your Grace all that had happened to me up to there," that is to say, there was another earlier letter, unfortunately lost, where he would have told all the details of the conquest route on the coast of Chiapas.

According to Alvarado (1934: 271), from Soconusco he went to Zapotitlan after a three-day walk through uninhabited forest; he says that before arriving at Zapotitlan "I found all the roads open and very wide, the main one as well as the ones that cross it, and the roads

that join the principal streets blocked." For two days he "crossed the land;" on the third he passed "two very bad rivers with sheer cliffs" and went up one estuary six leagues long in the middle of which he spent the night. On the fourth day he continued his trip on a rough road, fighting continually against the Indians until he encountered some plains and afterwards a spring, where he slept. On the fifth day he arrived at Quetzaltenango.

In the notes of Francis Gall on some documents of the sixteenth century relative to the conquest of Guatemala (Gall 1963: 8) it is made clear that the first battle of Pedro de Alvarado against the Quiches was in Xetulul or Zapotitlan, near the present-day municipal capital of San Francisco Zapotitlan, and that in his journey to Quetzaltenango he followed the road that goes by the hillside of Santa María de Jesús, a natural pass already used by the Indians of the western highlands in their trips to the coast before the arrival of the Spaniards.

Bernal Díaz del Castillo (1960, Vol. II, pp. 121–28) probably knew these letters of Alvarado to Cortés, for he repeats the above-mentioned route without adding a single fact more. Although it is not my purpose to discuss these roads, I have outlined them for the connection that is established between the Chiapas coast and the western highlands of other Central American regions.

This coastal route is the one that Fray Alonso Ponce followed on his trip between New Spain and the Audiencia de los Confines when he passed through Chiapas in 1586 (Ponce 1875, Vol. I, pp. 482 89). Coming from Oaxaca he stayed at Venta de la Gironda, a cattle ranch where the roads divide into the one that goes to Chiapa de los Indios and the one that follows the coast. He would pass by this same place months later on his return from Guatemala. The places visited in the first part of the trip, their distance from one another and some observations made by the cronicler, with some clarifications of ours, are presented below.

1. Tliltepec (Tiltepec, today a ranch near Tonala). Three leagues from Venta de la Gironda. Good road. In an earlier work (Navarrete 1968a: 368–73) I confused this route

by thinking that from Gironda he had gone down to the coast, when in reality from Tehuantepec on he never abandoned the coast. As Ponce says, he left the road to Chiapa and took the right fork to Soconusco, passing through some large plains and marshes; it seems to me that he followed approximately the present-day highway between Tapanatepec and Tonala.

2. Tonala. One league from Tiltepec. He crossed a creek and some dry marshes.

3. Quetzalapa. One league from Tonala. He crossed a river. Route uninhabited. Although he only makes this one mention of it, it is possible that he is referring to the famous "*despoblado del Soconusco*" as the area between Tonala and Pijijiapan was called. Today this area continues to be sparsely populated.

4. Marín Farm. Four leagues from Quetzalapa. He crossed three arroyos.

5. Maldonado Farm. Two leagues from the Marín Farm. He crossed one river.

6. Arroyo Farm. Three leagues from the Maldonado Farm. He crossed one river with many stones and two or three creeks.

7. Don Domingo's Farm. One league from Arroyo Farm. He crossed one river.

8. Pixixiapan (Pijijiapan). Two leagues from Don Domingo's Farm.

9. Coronado Farm. Four leagues from Pijijiapan. He crossed two creeks, one marsh, and much high, dense forest.

10. Mapaxtepec (Mapastepec). Four leagues from Coronado Farm. He crossed one river and two arroyos.

11. Alonso Pérez's small farm. Two leagues from Mapastepec. He crossed one river.

12. Cacalutla (Cacaluta). Two leagues from Alonso Pérez's farm.

13. Xoconusco (as I mentioned, we have identified it near the present town of Acacoyagua). One league and a half from Cacaluta. He says also that between Mapastepec and Soconusco there were six leagues.

14. Matzapetlahuac (probably Acapetagua; Becerra [1930: 189] is of the opinion that it is a town that has disappeared). Six "long" leagues from Soconusco. He crossed four rivers and much very thick forest between many hillsides covered with rocks and cliffs.

15. Vistlan (Huixtla). Three leagues from Matzapetlahuac. He passed through a high forest along a flat road and crossed four rivers.

16. Vevetlan (Huehuetan, which during that period began to substitute as a capital of Soconusco Province). Three leagues from Huixtla. He crossed four rivers and some slopes.

17. Copulco (according to oral tradition it was very near Tapachula). Becerra (1930: 69) says that it is a settlement in ruins on the shores of the Río Pumpuapa.

Three leagues and a half from Huehuetan. He crossed a large river on a ford filled with rocks and afterwards many hills and dense forests and another three rivers.

18. Chiltepec (town not identified, near Tapachula. According to Becerra [1930: 114–15] it was a town that had disappeared with references made to it between 1584 and 1611. He locates it between Huehuetan and Ayutla. In the description of the trip of Bernabé Cobo in 1630 Chilatepec is mentioned between Ayutla and Tapachula [Cobo 1944: 195–206]). Three and a half leagues from Copulco, passed three rivers.

19. Ayutla. Four leagues from Chiltepec. A good road that crosses four rivers, the first that is at the exit from Chiltepec is big (probably the Río Cahuacan), but larger and more dangerous is the fourth and last that flows past Ayutla (the Río Suchiate, present-day border between Mexico and Guatemala).

The trip between Tiltepec and Ayutla took ten days. Without stopping along the way as Father Ponce did, the trip took four or five days.

Another document, which I consider to date to the end of the sixteenth century or the beginning of the seventeenth if the type of handwriting and the connection that is made between Soconusco and Huehuetan are taken into account, is a fragment of a map that remained in the archives of the Tuxtla Chico church until 1956 (Fig. 16). At the present only a copy (that we publish here) remains in the hands of the historian Alberto Culebro. The heading reads: "This is the painting of the lands belonging to Huehuetlan and the lands that form the town and the surrounding area they take in, also all of the other towns

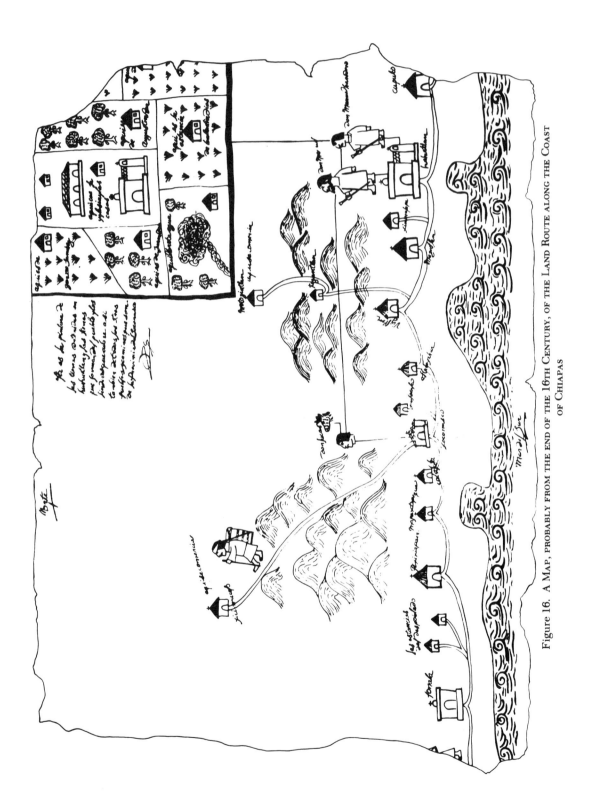

Figure 16. A Map, probably from the end of the 16th Century, of the Land Route along the Coast of Chiapas

and roads that are in the Province of Soco-nusco." The interpretation of the historical part of the map will be published in a special study of the archaeology and history of the coast.

Along the route the following towns are shown: Tonala; the farms of the Despoblado, where two short roads end that lead from the principal route; Pixixiapan; Mapaxtepeque; Cacaluta; Xoconusco; and Xolocalco, a town that has disappeared, whose ruins, known as Osolocalco, we have found opposite the present-day municipal capital of Acacoyagua; Atlacoyagua (Acacoyagua); Vixtlan (Huixtla); Mazatlan (Mazatan); Xiumulapa (present hamlet of Chamulapa); Huehuetlan; and Cupulco. The map probably ended with Ayutla. It is difficult to know what route was indicated for the Tonala side, where part of an individual is distinguishable going to the left, thereby indicating a commercial route.

In this manner the map shows a long road that goes from Soconusco to Xicimucelo (the present Chicomuselo), where above a porter we read "commerce is conducted here." The same legend is shown over the town of Motozintlan (Motozintla), where a route that starts at Huixtla and passes through the intermediate town of Tuzantlan (Tuzantan) finally ends. Both roads are still traveled by the merchants who go from the coast toward the center of the state; the first is in the form of a trail across the Sierra Madre, and the second corresponds to the modern highway that connects Huixtla and Motozintla. Below we will discuss these roads again.

The towns of Tonala, Pijijiapan, Mapastepec, Soconusco, Escuintla, Acapetagua, Huixtla, Huehuetan, and Tuxtla (Tuxtla Chico) appear on the route followed by Fray Tomás Torres described in his *Relación* of his visit to various towns and convents in the Province of Chiapas (Anonymous, *Relación de la visita ...*) in 1595; one is informed that the indigenous people kept the route clear and in a good state of repair because "over it they take out their products, of which the principal is cacao; for this reason Moctezuma maintained a good vigilance in the passes and towns of the coast of the Southern Ocean."

A late reference to this route, but important for the connection with west and central Guatemala, is that of the above-mentioned P. Jesuita Bernabé Cobo, who told of his journey in 1630 from the capital of Guatemala (today Antigua Guatemala) to Mexico. The part of the route that interests us is the following: Guatemala–Izapa (San Andrés Izapa, near Chimaltenango)–Pasasia (Patzicia)–Pason (Patzun)–Toliman (San Lucas Toliman, where he indicates that halfway from the previous town the road divides into two roads, one going through the mountains toward Chiapa and another one, that he followed, to the coast, which I think can be the present road from Atitlan to Chicacao)–Atitlan–San Bartolomé (very close to the city of Suchitepequez). In his description he notes that San Bartolomé is the first town in hot country, at which he arrived by "coming down the mountain to the hot country, by a bad road, which was all made of wood laid crosswise and together like a corduroy road, for fear of the mires and marshes." After San Bartolomé came San Julio de Nagualapa–San Antonio (San Antonio Suchitepeques, which he says was the capital of the province and a large town)–San Bernardino–Mazatenango–Cuyotenango–San Martí(?)–San Sebastián–Santa Catalina ("Here are two towns close together divided by a street, each with its own language;" so, on one side Quiche is spoken and on the other, Mam)–Cuyamesunga (?)–Tilapa ("This town is on the edge of a very large river which I forded with great fear; this river divides the jurisdictions and (here) begins the government of Soconusco")–Ayutla–Chilatepec–Tapachula–Huehuetlan (Huehuetan)–Huistla–Mazapetagua (Mazatan)–Escuincla (Escuintla)–Cacoyagua (Acacoyagua, next to Escuintla)–Amapastepec (Mapastepec; "Here begins the Despoblado, not because it is unpopulated, but because there are not as many towns as in the mountains")–"large farm" (he clarifies this as a large cattle range)–Pigigiapa (Pijijiapan)–the Chacalapa River–Tonala River–Las Arenas River ("This river is the line that divides the jurisdictions of the Audiencia of Guatemala from that of New Spain and the Diocese of Chiapa, that begins in Soconusco, from that of Guajaca").

THE COASTAL ROUTE THROUGH
ESTUARIES AND LAKES

The above-mentioned Fray Tomás Torres (Anonymous, *Relación de la visita*...) was the first to make a brief report on this communication system, which connects, by way of artificial and natural canals, the estuaries, lakes, entrances from the sea, and the lower courses of the rivers which run down from the Sierra Madre to empty into the Pacific Ocean: "The natives of these towns communicate with one another by means of drains and canals that they open in the marshes to make such a network that one could get lost in it if he should attempt to navigate them without a knowledgeable native. As this *Relación* has remained unpublished, the route has likewise sunk into oblivion and is unknown to investigators.

Even though many anthropologists passed near this route and recently two of them, Drucker (1948: 151–69) and Lorenzo (1955: 41–50), were forced to cross a section of the estuaries and to navigate a stretch of the canals, their determination to arrive directly at an archaeological site within the lakes prevented them from becoming aware of the route over which they travelled. That I can define the overall system I owe principally to my contact with fishermen and boatmen who still frequent it; for over three years I also was ignorant of it for the same reason as that mentioned above.

In 1965, while working on the sand bar of San Simón, I mentioned to some old canoemen Padre Ponce's trip.

"This Padre must have travelled in the dry season," they told me, "because if he had tried to do it in the rainy season he would not have been able to. The rivers grow and flow down from the mountains with force; for this reason the people who lived here before there was the train came by the canals."

From this moment on I began to examine the canals and collect information.

I found out that before the railroad line was inaugurated in 1908 the people who wanted to go from one town to another first went to the embarcation point that each town had on the closest navigable estuary or lake; within the canoes they placed some type of quilted seat and somewhat comfortably travelled to their destination. I learned also, through some old merchants, that in the holiday or harvest season they made convoys of up to forty canoes, whose boatmen had the obligation to sing a hymn at midday when they were travelling and the "captain" of the boatmen to announce them with three calls on the trumpet-shell before arriving at a port.

At that time the principal products that were transported the entire length of the coast were: cacao, which was concentrated in Tonala, with its port of departure at the present-day *colonia* of Cabeza de Toro where many of the products of the Soconusco were received; another important product was Guatemalan and Oaxacan pottery, whose transport by animals was very risky due to the fragile nature of the pottery; they also took out caiman and crocodile hides, large quantities of dried shrimp, salted fish, and live and smoked iguanas that were later carried into the center of Chiapas. Apart from this was another series of minor products: wax, alcohol, medicines, string, and other modern provisions necessary for daily life in the isolated hamlets of the estuaries.

Concerning this commerce system I know of only one other unpublished and anonymous report, probably written at the end of the eighteenth century:

The Province of Soconusco, which is forty leagues long on the South Coast, and six, seven, and ten wide in different areas, is bounded on the east by the Alcaldía Mayor of Suchitepeques, Guatemala, and on the west by that of Teguantepeque in the Intendencia of Oaxaca. It is divided into two Subdelegations, that of Tapachula and that of Tonala.

The products of this Province can be carried by the estuaries on the one hand to the Alcaldía Mayor of Escuintla, that is near Goatemala, and on the other hand to Teguantepeque (Anonymous, *Noticia topográfica*...).

I have personally traversed the complete route from Tonala (Cabeza de Toro, near Puerto Arista) to the Suchiate River, and according to reports in the last century a traveler could still go to the Port of San José in the center of the Guatemalan coast and continue on to very near to the Republic of El Salvador by way of the Chiquimulilla canal, which in some parts is still navigable.

One problem that always intrigued me was the way the canals were opened in order to connect one estuary with another and the way they were kept clean, given the lack of metal tools of sufficient hardness to fell the trees, principally the mangrove that grows very densely and is extremely hard. In some places where collective maintenance work is still done, I observed that there is no need to cut the problem vegetation, but only the large trees. On the trunk near the roots they cut a ring that impedes the sap that rises through the center of the tree from going down again through the bark. In a year the trees begin to rot and soon begin to fall over by themselves. The work of moving them to one side or burning them and freeing the canal or "drain" is thus much easier.

Then too it must be remembered that they were not made all at once; the collective work was carried out over many generations, as is demonstrated by the remains we have found of human habitation from the preceramic era (still not dated, but located on shell middens) to our times. Though with less certainty I believe that during our century no new canals were opened and even that the abandonment began that is closing them. In the summer it is practically impossible to travel directly from Cabeza de Toro to the Guatemalan border because of the lack of interest in maintenance. To this we must add the lowering of runoff into the rivers that come down from the Sierra Madre, where the deforestation is greater with each passing day. The founding of new agrarian colonies and the tremendous cultivation of cotton that needs flat lands is converting the coast of Chiapas into a treeless plain.

The trip in canoe from Cabeza de Toro to the Suchiate River used to be made in ten or twelve days including the time employed in receiving and turning over the cargo. Of course there is variability in the trip schedules and I only refer to the average for a normal canoe trip that took a direct course without entering the secondary canals and lakes. The travelling day on this type of trip would be of ten to twelve hours, beginning at four in the morning and lasting until five or six in the afternoon, with a long intermediate stop during the hottest hours as well as short rests during the morning and afternoon.

However, for trips by the canals and interior lakes the tidal schedule, which is variable, has to be taken into account; when the water level goes down there are lakes that become what the fishermen call "pampas" — great expanses of mud where one cannot travel on foot but must wait for the high tide in order to cross by canoe.

The reason for the abandonment of the system is also due to an economic reason. The present-day fisheries are interested in maintaining navigable waterways only in their working areas. Since the modern coastal highway was inaugurated in 1964, the towns which previously were reached by railroad, with a rigid, fixed schedule, are now connected with the ports of the waterways by wide roads, some of which are all-weather, and over which a bus transportation line operates. Over these roads the catch is brought out and no longer is it of interest to maintain intercommunication by water between the areas of the fishing groups.

THE ROUTES TOWARD THE CENTRAL DEPRESSION OF CHIAPAS

There exist four principal routes for travel to the center of Chiapas. The first connects Tonala with the Cintalapa Valley and more or less must have followed parts of the route of the modern highway that goes from Tonala to Arriaga and climbs the slope of the mountain, La Sepultura, which must be the one to which Fray Tomás Torres refers in his report: "the road that goes down to the Province of Xoconusco is a steep and dangerous descent with very bad passes and canyons and falling rocks that make the journey worrysome" (*Relación de la visita . . .*).

The road continued approximately to the point known as Las Cruces, where one branch went toward Tehuantepec and one continued to Cintalapa, Jiquipilas, Ocozocoautla, and Tuxtla. In the *Relación* it says of this last town:

> From this town roads go out to Chiapa, from which one goes to Eztapa (Ixtapa), and others to Tehuantepeque that is eight days' travel away; this is the most travelled, and by following one part of this road and then descending one goes to the province of Soconusco that is four or more days' travel away according to how far one wants to go since it is a long province . . . (Navarrete 1968a: 371).

On the return trip of Fray Alonso Ponce (1875: 482–89), in order to go from the center of Chiapas to Oaxaca he passed Tuxtla and Xiquipilas el Grande and although Ocozocoautla does not appear, it was a necessary way point and this will be discussed later. He says that he descended a mountainside that was "long and steep along a trail that did not seem for other than deer or goats" in order to arrive at a farm pertaining to the Bishopric of Guatemala and continue toward Tapanatepec in the Bishopric of Oaxaca.

A similar route was the one followed in 1783 by the Alcalde Mayor of Tuxtla in his trip to Oaxaca (Castañón Gamboa 1953: 77–81); the principal towns that he passed were Tuxtla, Ocozocoautla, Xiquipilas, Cintalapa, and Macuilapa, where he wrote that "in this ranch there are two roads, one that goes through the Gineta and the other that goes by Chilillo," the latter of which he took. After four leagues of bad road, all downhill, that led to Tapanatepec, he entered the lands of the Alcaldía of Tehuantepec. The ancient route by the Gineta pass corresponds to the Tehuantepec–Tuxtla section of the modern Panamerican Highway. The road mentioned that passes Chilillo is unknown to me and I have no information to give about it.

It seems to me that this trail, with its branches to Oaxaca, was the principal route down to the coast and the one by which influences from Soconusco and from Tehuantepec

reached the center of Chiapas, as I have reported elsewhere (Navarrete 1968b: 31–48).

The second route began at a place near Tonala called Tzutzuculi and went toward the region known as the Frailesca, today the municipalities of Villa Flores and Villa Corzo. I lack information on this road.

Of the third corridor through the Sierra Madre I only know one part, that which follows the present Villa Flores–Villa Corzo–Colonia Monterrey–Las Isabeles–El Parián road; the last is well up in the mountains. For the next section, El Parián–Estación Tres Picos, with the latter on the coast, I have no data, but it could have been the route by which some archaeological materials that were found in my survey of the Frailesca were carried (Navarrete 1960; 1966a: 26, 91–98).

I also have no data on the fourth road except those of an informant who traded in about 1930 between Mapastepec and the center of the state and then went up into the Highlands to make final sales in Comitan. The complete trip lasted eighteen days with a three-day rest for the pack animals and the men in either Tuxtla or Chiapa. The day's journey was from two until nine in the morning in order to take advantage of the freshness of the early morning and, in the case of merchants, to take advantage of the possibility of exchange or sale of products at the rest points during the day: the ranches known as Novillero (near Mapastepec), Liquidambar, La Suiza, Monte Grande, and Prusia; then the road led down to Chicomuselo, which is in a lateral valley of the Central Depression. It is important to point out that the father and even the grandfather of my informant had worked this route since the last century.

The last road through the Sierra Madre goes from Huixtla to Motozintla, a town that must have been an important point for the commerce that was carried on through these places; the present-day situation seems to repeat the early one. Waibel (1946: 216) was the first to mention the importance of this route that:

> takes advantage, on the Atlantic side, of the Motozintla River that penetrates far into the interior and that widens notably

in the river's upper course. It crosses the continental divide by the pass called la Cruz at an altitude of 1,970 meters. On the Pacific side the route takes advantage of the valley of the Huixtla River, descending until it reaches the town of Huixtla. A branch of this road goes from Motozintla, by a shorter and more rugged route, toward the southeast to the continental divide, reaching it at the border town of Niquivil (2,725 meters); it follows the divide for some kilometers to Pinavete (2,470 meters), and then descends to the Huehuetán River valley in order to pass through the ancient town of Cuilco Viejo, today the coffee plantation of Argovia, and to end in Huehuetan and Tapachula.

In the days when Waibel made his study the Huixtla-Motozintla highway, which partly follows the old indigenous road, had not yet been constructed. For this reason it seems interesting to reproduce here the observations he makes on the type of traffic it carried (Waibel 1946: 216-17):

All the traffic on this road is . . . very antiquated. Foot travelers, trains of heavily loaded mules and horses, as well as riders — men, women, and children — dominate the panorama. Those afoot as well as the pack animals and the mounted riders travel seven to eight leagues daily or about thirty kilometers. Since the road passes through valleys with few inhabitants and since the traffic does not earn enough to permit the carrying of forage and provisions, settlements have sprung up at eight-kilometer or so intervals to feed the men and animals; their aspect and function are determined completely by the traffic. These serve for resting and staying overnight. After an abundant breakfast, the travelers do not leave until nine or ten in the morning, then riding without interruption during the hottest part of the day in order to reach lodging as early as possible. They arrive at the next stop at four or five in the afternoon and take advantage of the remainder of the day to rest, care for the animals, make small repairs on the saddles, etc.

The departure from the Motozintla Valley to the Central Depression is: Motozintla-Mazapa de Díaz-Amatenango-La Nueva. As already indicated by reference to Waibel the road runs parallel to the Motozintla River. In Mazapa it joins the Talcanac River and in Amatenango, the Cuilco; both rivers come from Guatemala and along them are trails to the settlements of the other side of the border.

This relationship of the Motozintla Valley with Guatemala is evident when we see that in about 1770, Motozintla, Mazapa, and Amatenango were towns belonging to the Cuilco parish with the following distances between them and the capital (Cortés y Larraz 1958, Vol. II, pp. 135–40):

		Leagues
1.	The town of San Andrés Cuilco, Capital	
2.	The town of Santa María Magdalena Techtitlan at	11
3.	The town of Nuestra Señora de la Asumpción Tacana at	15
4.	The town of Santiago Amatenango at	13
5.	The town of San Martín Mazapa at	17
6.	The town of San Francisco de Motozintla at	20
7.	The ranch of Jalapa at	4

Of course Cortés y Larraz says that the roads are

very bad and the rivers are very high, which is the reason that very few families live in the towns and almost all live in the sparsely populated areas and in the corn fields; this conforms with the inclination of the Indians, who prefer to live alone in the forests . . .; the roads for the administration of this zone are almost untransitable because of the roughness of the mountains and the multitude of rivers that have to be crossed.

One 88-year-old informant, an old tumpline porter and later a muleteer, who for many years travelled the complete route, offered me one more possible route of communication. He used to go from the Highlands looking for the Grijalva River in order to continue to Motozintla and arrive at Huixtla. His route was the following: Tepancuapan Ranch (near the ruins of Chinkultic at the lakes of Montebello)–Zapaluta (today La Trinitaria, a settlement where porters were secured)–Potrerillo-Zapotal (resting place)–Altamira–Anonal (resting place)–Río Blanco (where the Río Grande or Grijalva River was crossed on a suspension or hammock bridge)– El Mango–Amatenango de la Frontera (resting place)–Valle Obregón-Mazapa–Motozintla (resting place)–Niquivil (resting place) – Pinabeto (resting place) – Guadalupe (resting place)–a series of coffee plantations, and, finally, Huixtla. In total eight days were spent on the road after leaving Zapaluta.

Someone who followed part of this road in search of archaeological sites was Gareth W. Lowe (1959: 56–68); he took the modern Panamerican Highway from Comitan down to the Santo Domingo River and its tributaries (which join with the San Miguel River to form the Grijalva), looking for a point of entrance to Motozintla. Near Ciudad Cuauhtemoc, at El Jocote, he turned aside to Comalapa de la Frontera and followed the other great affluent of the Grijalva, the San Miguel River, passing San Juan Chamique, Tapizala, El Mango, and Amatenango, and ending up at Motozintla (see map of the Central Depression that Lowe [1959, Fig. 64] includes in his paper).

Waibel (1946: 220) also mentions other routes (see map of the Sierra Madre, 1:400,000, prepared by that author) that cross the mountains transversely, pointing out that they have almost no economic importance because they pass through uninhabited forests and because they were constructed in recent times due to the stimulus of the railroad that passes at the base of the mountains. These roads which start out on the coast are: Escuintla to San Isidro (I personally have travelled it as far as the Colonia El Triunfo); Mapastepec to Monte Cristo (probably a branch of the road mentioned above that goes from Mapastepec to Chicomuselo); the Colonia Las Margaritas to Nuestra Señora); Pijijiapan to the ranch Mercedes; and San Pedro to Villa Flores. Waibel does not specify on his map where San Pedro is located, but I suppose that it could correspond to the road from Tonala to Villa Flores

or the one from the latter to Estación Tres Picos.

If Waibel believes that these routes are modern, something that should be well investigated, he categorically denies antiquity to a fifth road. This is a horse trail from the coffee plantations Liquidambar and Prusia to Mapastepec "constructed by these two German plantations in order to transport their coffee." This is the road which we have already discussed with traditions that begin in the last century.

I prefer to cite Waibel, whose observations agree in large part with my own experience, in reference to the form of covering the miles among the travellers he observed:

> The appearance of these horse trails is very characteristic in spite of diverse topographic areas of the Sierra. In the flat and open land of the plains the trails are narrow, marked with the tracks of the men and beasts that travel up to four and more abreast. But they also travel in a straight line in the Sierra, that is to say, they do not follow the valleys nor do they climb the steep slopes in great loops, but they try to continue in a straight direction without avoiding the slopes, except very steep ones. By preference they go along the narrow hill crests (Waibel 1946: 221).

This is what is known in common terms taking a "shortcut" or cutting the trail to eliminate the curves and go in a straight line.

On long trips, when the group of merchants is large, it is customary that one of them "sacrifice" himself by carrying only the provisions of the "company," which generally consist of rations of salted meat in strips, dried fish, beans, and coffee; every three days they buy stacks of tortillas in certain places. At the end of the trip the "boss" of the "company" divides proportionately among them all the profits of the transactions.

Another high road leaves from Motozintla and connects on one side with Chimalapa and El Porvenir (from where it is possible to go to Siltepec, Chicomuselo, and Angel Albino Corzo [before Jaltenango]), and on the other side (going around the Cerro Male, which is the principal eminence in the area), with the colonies Chimale, Miravalle, and the municipal capital Bejucal de Ocampo. From Bejucal de Ocampo, overlooking Amatenango de la Frontera, it is possible to make a very rapid descent which lasts between three and four hours due to the pronounced slope. In this manner one joins anew the Motozintla-Mazapa-Amatenango route. I must warn that in spite of having retraced part of these roads I still have much to investigate and I must return again to the region to complete a map to make comprehensible the indeterminable network established between colonies, towns, and isolated ranches; from Bejucal de Ocampo as well as from El Porvenir it is possible to reach the towns of Grandeza and Bella Vista and to arrive at Frontera Comalapa through which the doors of the Grijalva are open to the inhabitants of this part of the highlands. Some of these routes were pointed out also by Helbig (1964, Map 2), who retraced a great section of the Sierra Madre and its interior slope toward the Grijalva.

THE GRIJALVA SYSTEM

The first notice of the importance of Chiapa de Corzo as a river port and of a road parallel to the Grijalva River is by Juan de Pineda (1952: 57), who wrote in 1594:

> The town of Chiapa de los Indios is a little more than ten leagues from the town of Chiapa de los Españoles [San Cristóbal de Las Casas] and from the city of Guatemala it would be a little more than seventy leagues of rough and hilly road. This town is founded on a high plain, a hot and healthy land. Next to it passes a large river [Grijalva] that they cross all year round in canoes because it has no ford. In this river fish are taken in abundance during the rainy season. The foot-travellers and pack trains that depart from Guatemala for Mexico City come through this town because of the many swamps that there are in the road through the province of Soconusco to this city, and, in the same manner, those that depart from this city for Guatemala go by this same road.

He also mentions the road's relationship to the coast when describing the importance of the manufacture of cloth in the town [of Chiapa de Corzo]:

> ... the pious men of Santo Domingo who administer to them the sacraments, make large quantities of these cloths, and sent by them some of the principal *maceguales* take these blankets by porters and on horseback and go to sell them in the provinces of Soconusco and the coast of Zapotitlan and to Guatemala and the village of Trynidad ....

The important source by Fray Tomás Torres (*Relación de la visita...*) also emphasizes the importance that Chiapa de Corzo had in the control of regional commerce:

> These Indians are industrious and like to do business and as the merchants who go to the other Chiapa upon the hill must pass by Chiapa de Corzo, one always sees movement of people entering and leaving by the roads that go along the edge of the river. There is a good wharf and Chiapa is the final point for those who come down-river, since from Chiapa on down the river goes dashing between very close hills, but from here it goes down to the coast and it goes by the towns of the *quelenes* [Tzotzil] Indians and one can continue to wherever he wants to because the town is founded in the center of the province.

It seems that another town founded up-river that also served as a port was Acala; here they must have picked up part of the passengers and cargo that came from the San Miguel and San Gregorio Rivers and other tributaries of the Grijalva, especially in the rainy season.

This possibility is manifested in a trial for idolatry carried out in Chiapa de los Indios in 1605 (Anonymous, *Juicio levantado...*) when two presumed witches were interrogated. They said that they dedicated themselves to canoe work with those who travelled from Acala, of which they were natives, "up river" and to Chiapa.

The San Miguel and San Gregorio Rivers rise in the Cuchumatanes Mountains, in Guatemala. At their confluence the Grijalva acquires a width of twenty-six meters and a depth in the center of the current of up to five meters which make it navigable, or made it navigable, since the water has been retreating with the cutting down of the trees along the banks and in the mountains where the principal currents that feed it rise. Toward the northwest it receives from its left side the waters of the Jaltenango River; some kilometers further down and on the same side the La Concordia River joins it that comes from the extensive Custepeques valleys. A short distance away it receives on its right side the Río Blanco; afterwards it flows through the valley of San José, Paso de Canoas, Tamazulapa, and Chalchi. A little lower down it receives the waters of the San Pedro Buenavista [Dorado and Brillante] formed by the tributaries that flow south-to-north through the Custepeques valleys.

The river is enclosed in the narrow canyon of La Angostura. After joining the Río La Angostura and the Río Chiapilla it flows past Acala, receiving farther down the waters of the Suchiapa River joined with the Santo Domingo River. These drain the Suchiapa and Frailesca valleys. It later passes by Chiapa de Corzo and then enters the Sumidero Canyon.

Near these rivers run roads that parallel the river banks. They leave the shore only at those points where the topography does not permit the river and the road to run along together and this is what Fray Tomás Torres referred to:

> It must be said that many other rivers, some small and others large, enter the Río Grande [Grijalva]. Canoe traffic here is common with the good sailors that the Indians from these parts are. Where the canoes cannot pass the people go on foot, since there are many roads and ports that they maintain next to them.

The last road described at the end of this work is precisely the route from Guatemala to Chiapa that paralleled part of the course of the Grijalva River.

In a work on the Late Postclassic in the basin of the Middle Grijalva (the Mal Paso Dam region, Navarrete and Lee, in preparation) we are doing a study of Quechula, a Zoque settlement similar to Chiapa in that it is a main river port. There river navigation recommenced that had been suspended due to the Sumidero Canyon, which is impossible to traverse.

I only want to summarize some of the data from this forthcoming work about the way in which this starting point functioned in the communication with the Gulf Coast.

In the first place we have the testimony of the chronicler Bernal Díaz del Castillo (1960, Vol. 2, pp. 131–35) who in 1523 went up to Quechula from Coatzacoalcos for the purpose of pacifying Chiapa. He says that he passed a place called Tepunzuntlan, unfortunately not identified, to which they went up in canoes; afterwards he mentions the arrival at Quechula. It is a pity that the chronicler, who describes with so much detail many of the episodes of the Conquest, did not leave us more precise information about the route. He only indicates that they went upriver opening new roads, which is logical since they brought horses, and which makes me think that the communication down to the coast was made directly by river.

Fray Tomás Torres is more explicit and relates how important Quechula was as a river port, indicating that the Indians are good canoemen and that they carry cargo by river to the province of Tabasco "with much danger because of the bad currents there are below Quechula."

We also have a manuscript from 1607 (Anonymous, *Sobre el estado...*) where it says that because the settlement (Quechula) is on the banks of a navigable river, the Indians know how to take advantage of it to carry cargo down to the coast of Tabasco where they sell it. Better information is that given by Bishop Manuel García de Bargas y Rivera from 1769 to 1774 as he describes the river (*Relación de los pueblos...*):

> ... it is for canoes and from this town one can float down it to the port of Campeche, for it is the one which carries the most force and join to it all the rivers of this

province. The ones of Tabasco and Zendales which come out by the rivers of the Usumacinta as it is called, where, as the principal river, it gathers the others and flows out at the Laguna de Términos at the stated port of Campeche.

That is, on the Gulf Coast there is a situation similar to that described for the Soconusco, with the addition that in Tabasco not only did they take advantage of the estuaries and lakes, but also the long rivers — navigable for the most part — that form a much more ample network than that of the Chiapas coast, where the rivers are short and fast flowing due to the proximity of the Sierra Madre where they rise.

THE COMMUNICATIONS SYSTEM IN THE ZOQUE AREA AND THE WAY DOWN TO THE GULF COAST

I have given the name "Zoque System" to a series of roads that meet in the Central Depression and others that go up into the Chiapas Highlands and then down to the Gulf Coast, precisely because they connect some of the principal towns that speak the Zoque tongue, although these routes do not always terminate in regions of that affiliation.

The first point in Ocozocoautla, mentioned above in the discussion of the route taken by Fray Alonso Ponce from Chiapa to Oaxaca. In the *Relación de Ocozocoautla* one reads (Navarrete 1968a: 371):

... another road is the one that goes to Cachula (Quechula). Midway along it a road takes off for Chicuasentepe (Chicoasen), a long and hard march, and from Cachula and Chicuasentepe leave other roads to Copaynala (Copainala) and Tepatan (Tecpatan) that are another march over bad roads. From Cachula the route leaves by water (on the same river that passes through Chiapa and Chicuasentepe) for the province of Tabasco, a two day march with bad passes, and then goes to Guasacualco (Coatzacoalcos) and Campeche.

This last part sums up our information concerning the importance of Quechula as a river port for commerce with Tabasco.

I know of no other ancient reference to these roads which connect Ocozocoautla with Quechula, Copainala, and Tecpatan, except that which the Alcalde Mayor of Tuxtla followed in 1783 in his visit to these towns (Castañón Gamboa 1953: 81–85). This person left Tuxtla for what is now the town of San Fernando and he continued to Chicoasen and Copainala; afterwards he went to Tecpatan, and he descending finally to Quechula. Walking by the cliff overlooking the river he arrived again at Chicoasen, he returned to Tecpatan, and he followed the main road to Istacomitan, from which he visited Magdalena and Chapultenango. He continued to Ocotepec, Coapilla, again to Chicoasen, and ended his trip in Tuxtla (Navarrete and Lee, in preparation; we shall treat this visit in more detail).

Since I think that this very recent route necessarily had to follow the old trails (the *Relación de Ocozocoautla* already mentions the principal ones), we see that all of the west-central part of the state was kept in close communication. At the same time it was connected with the Tehuantepec-Chiapa-Ciudad Real road and the Campeche-Ciudad Real route which I will treat below.

Before continuing I wish to refer to a problem presented by the conquest route followed by Bernal Díaz (1960: 133–40), who says that they departed from Quechula in the direction of Chiapa. In transit they stopped at Eztapa (Ixtapa), where they won their first battle against the Chiapanecs. On the following day they fought two more fierce battles, at the close of which they arrived at the shore of the river that separated them from the city. They spent the night in a nearby town and the following day crossed the river, which, according to the route given, should have been from the right bank to the left.

It does not make sense to someone who knows the territory and topography that from Quechula they passed directly to Ixtapa, since necessarily they would have had to pass settlements such as Tecpatan or Copainala, Chicoasen, and possible Soyalo that during that period were important; however, they are not mentioned by the chronicler. For another reason, it is not logical that if they had fought first at Ixtapa, situated in the Highlands, and which never belonged to the Chiapanec, they would then go down to the Río Grande and again climb up to subdue Chamula. My opinion is that Bernal confused his route — he himself says that he does not remember well the exact years of the conquest. The geographically possible road by which one would not pass through the Zoque towns that I have mentioned went from Quechula toward what is today the town of San Fernando, passed by the small town of Tuxtla, crossed the Río Grande, and ended at Chiapa on the right bank where we have proved through excavations that the Chiapanec capital stood (Navarrete 1966a: 9–11).

The road which we consider correct we were able to traverse during the archaeological work in the Mal Paso basin when we located the routes from Quechula to Ocozocoautla, San Fernando, Tecpatan, and Copainala (Navarrete 1966b: 36–40).

References to the primary important route to the Gulf of Mexico are given by the conquistadores Bernal Díaz and Diego Godoy when they give us the details of the conquest of the Chiapas Highlands and the towns along the descent to Tabasco.

The former (Bernal Díaz 1960: 142–48) left from Chiapa de los Indios in the direction of Zinacantlan (Zinacantan) where the Indians lived who were "reasonable people and many are merchants and he (Luis Marín) told them that they should bring us 200 Indians to carry our baggage and that we were going to their town because from there was the road to Chamula". They left Chiapa one morning and went to sleep at some salt works (undoubtedly Ixtapa), continuing the following day to Zinacantan. From here they went to lay siege to the fortified town of Chamula.

After a hard battle, which they won, they returned to Zinacantan, three leagues distant. They went afterwards to reside temporarily next to a river "where the town of Ciudad Real now is, which is called by another name, Chiapa de los Españoles". From this camp they went out to put down the uprising of three small towns situated four leagues distant, to which Bernal refers by the name of Gueguiztlan (it could be the present Huixtan

[Ed.: see Köhler, p. 70, for clarification]), where they found the roads closed with timbers and cut trees.

Finished with this area they decided to depart for the faraway Province of Zimatan in Tabasco, always pacifying militarily,

> going to towns called Tapelola (Tapilula), and before arriving at them, there were some bad mountains and passes, on the climb up as well as in the descent so that it was a very difficult thing to pass through that part, and Luis Marín sent to beg the chiefs of those towns to fix up the road in such a manner that we could use it and they did so and the horses passed with much effort.

They continued then through Silo, Suchiapa (in reality it is a single town, Solosuchiapa), Coyumelapa, Panaguaxoya (Ixtapangajoya), Tecomayate (?), and Teapan (Teapa), which Bernal describes as a large and important town, where they had to fight anew against the natives. From Teapa they left for Zimatan and "other towns that are called Talatupan (?)" where they fought and then rested for two days. From here they went to Guazacualco (Coatzacoalcos) via the Chontalpa region via the towns of Guimango (Huimanguillo) and afterwards Acaxuyxuyca (it could be Acayucan, Veracruz, and Bernal would have been wrong in mentioning it among the towns of the Tabascan Chontalpa [Ed.: see Lee, p. 57, for clarification]), Teotitlan Copilco (Cupilco?), some towns without importance, Ulapa, the Agualulco River, the Tonala River, and finally, Coatzacoalcos.

The second source is Diego Godoy (Vedia 1946, Vol. 1, pp. 466–70), who was part of the same expedition reported by Bernal. He tries to give the impression that he was captain of the expedition, a political move typical of the competition among the conquerors and which we are not able to discuss here. Thanks to him, however, we have better information about the state of the road from the Highlands to the Gulf Coast.

In the first place he presents his own version of events at Chamula, from where he left for Zinacantan via a road that linked up five small villages "within sight of one another;

three leagues of very bad road, very little of which we could traverse on horseback."

After the battle of Chamula they left for Huegueyztean,

> and the road to within sight of this (town), head of this province, is all very good and flat, with good stands of pine and open forests; before reaching this province there is a big downhill slope and the town is on another hillside.

Information from the described topography assures us that it is Huixtan, which has similar characteristics.

After finishing the subjugation of this province they returned again to Zinacantan to depart, as Bernal Díaz says, toward the province of Cimatan, but first in some ranches where they slept, they received the gift-bearing representatives of some towns that were going to subject themselves: Anapanasclan (probably Copanaguastla, with a little gold they brought "a basket with points for arrows which they said that the Spaniard who is in Socomisco [Soconusco] had ordered them to make for Pedro de Albarado"; so that this would establish a double relationship between the Highlands, from where Godoy writes, with the low country where Copanagaastla was and the distant coast of Chiapas), Michampa (?), Hueyteupan (Huitiupan, near Simojovel) and Tesistebeque (?).

They continued for another three leagues on a good road in order to sleep in other ranches, from where they left for Clatipilula (Tapilula),

> which must have been up to three leagues away, and is the worst road which has ever been seen in New Spain; so much so that if the Indians had not had it well cleared it would have been impossible to go forward, and certainly there we would have remained, because it is all very high and very rough mountains, the descent of one and a half leagues, so steep that it could not be more dangerous, because in one place there was a deep valley with some cliffs, so rough that there was no place for the horses to put their feet; they

> had it well cleared, with many stakes driven into the hillside and very strong logs well tied to them (upon) which was thrown much earth, and the banks were hollowed out (on the uphill side) as much as possible, even in parts of the same little ravine; an infinite number of trees had been cut in order to open the road, among which there were trees that measured nine palms thick through the middle and others very thick, and it seemed to have been done with good will and the people must have worked hard to do it; truly even though Spaniards had worked with the Indians many days in its making it would not have been better done.

In this town they received the visit of some Zapotec Indians who had gone from Chiapa to live in Quechula "because it is near this town" (in reality, more than close, we would say connected, by the network that is established between the Zoque towns by the Quechula-Tecpatan system).

Later they traveled two leagues to reach Silusinchiapa (Solosuchiapa) with two intermediate towns by bad road where it occurred that,

> the same night that we arrived . . . it never did another thing except rain a very large quantity of water; as luck would have it the river rose in such a way and since the town is between the mountains and the river goes following where the road goes and as it was very violent we could not go backwards or forwards; during this time, the Indians of this town all left; not one returned or appeared; I don't know why they could have done it, since we were received so well and because they worked so much in preparing the trail.

They continued on to a town subject to the province of Cimatan called Estapanguajoya (Ixtapangajoya),

> and all of this trail is along the same river for most of the way and the river is crossed many times; upon crossing we worked very hard, and some Spaniards

were exposed to great danger; the trail is all cliffs and the rocks in the river are very large and it flows very fast; the truth is that I do not believe that horses have gone over a worse trail anywhere in the world.

Here ends the concern for roads and towns. The rest of the *relación* is complaints about the dividing up of the *encomiendas* and is not pertinent here.

About this same route, but more about Campeche, is the important *Diario del Viaje* written in 1545 by Fray Tomás de la Torre (1944–1945, principally Chapters XI through XVII, with notes and appendices by Frans Blom), who accompanied the Bishop Bartoloné de Las Casas and a group of forty-six Dominican frailes who left Salamanca, Spain, in order to come to Chiapas and Guatemala for the conversion of the Indians. His route is what Blom calls "the Royal Road of that time," since it was the entrance route for Chiapas and Guatemala for fifty years, "but was abandoned in favor of the trail of *Puerto Caballos* according to Melchor Alfaro in his 'relación de Tabasco' written in 1579 (page 19).

Although a first group of frailes left Campeche on the 18th of January, 1545, the misfortunes they suffered do not interest us greatly, since the author of the diary remained in Campeche until the 27th, on which he begins to write about his own experiences. About the first group it is important to bring out the discussion prior to the trip, with regard to whether they made it in a boat or in Indian canoes, because it shows us the aboriginal way of moving along the coast before going out to sea.

This first group ran aground on the island of Términos, where some of the ship-wrecked frailes crossed it lengthwise in order to get on the right road to Champotón in search of aid.

The larger (second) group left on the 27th for the island on which they remained until the 4th of February when they crossed the mouth of the Laguna de Términos, where they were obligated to cross some of their equipment in canoes toward the famous town of Xicalango, where they arrived on foot; be-

fore this they were in a small village whose name is not given.

On the 11th they left Xicalango in canoes tied together two by two; crossing the lake they took advantage of the shallow part and tied them up and passed the night in the canoes. The next day they untied them, and "after a little ways they entered, with the canoes, a passage so narrow that the canoe barely entered." After a league and a half of traveling they arrived at another lake "that was three crossbow-shots wide," afterwards

they entered by a tree-covered way so dense that they could not see the sun and they barely saw the sky. There was little water for the canoes to float in; it was mainly mud, and in those places the Indians hauled the canoes with much work and groaning (de la Torre 1944–45: 159–60).

After two leagues they passed a wide river called San Pedro y San Pablo.

They continued upriver to a branch "that leaves this river" (the Usumacinta proper) on which they traveled downriver to arrive on the 13th at the juncture with the Grijalva, and to continue on to the town of Tabasco (Villahermosa) [Ed.: Santa María de la Victoria]. The 18th of February they embarked in canoes and navigated up the Grijalva: "There are in that river upstream some small towns, but because the land is unhealthy due to all the lakes and swamps, the only way to travel is by water" (de la Torre 1944–45: 170).

In this part the chronicler makes a change in the description of the trip and returns to tell us of the vicissitudes of the other group that had stayed in Xicalango, who in general terms has a similar journey to that we have been describing. For that reason we will continue with the navigation of the Grijalva River upstream until they left its course and penetrated the Teapa River, something that is very unclear in the diary:

The canoe that Cordoba gave to his guests began to lag behind and even though we waited three, six and eight hours it did not come. Francisco Gil led us to understand that one of the rivers that had been seen to enter that river goes to the town from where the Indian oarsmen came and only God could make them go without passing by their town, and that afterwards all had to pass by it and there we would find those Padres and thus we did not worry about them and following the road arrived at a place called Toacotalpa (Tacotalpa) that was the end of that navigation (de la Torre 1944–45: 171).

According to Blom (de la Torre 1944–45: 208) it is possible that one group could have gone upstream directly by the Teapa River to this town in order to save themselves the walk between Tacotalpa and Teapa.

The group that arrived at Tacotalpa continued on foot and:

that day they began to experience the roads of these lands that are such that they cannot be believed without being seen.... We said that the devils had made those roads to trap men and that those who walked over them should not be called men.

They walked nearly four leagues and after passing a very swift river (surely the Puyacatengo) they arrived at Teapa and Tecomixiaca (Texomaxioca). Further on they crossed a very cold river (possibly the same Teapa River), a little town, and arrived at Ystapangajoya (Ixtapangajoya) where they rested. It is interesting to note some of the forms of human transport that are described in parts of the trip (de la Torre 1944–45: 172):

Fray Domingo de Medinillas did not know how to do anything because he had never dealt with Indians; he knew nothing of them just as we knew nothing having recently arrived, and if Fray Luis had not come in time, our baggage would have stayed there, but upon arriving he looked for Indians to carry it and they did so with good will, because they had no other beasts to serve them except their own bodies and upon the arrival of the Spanish they had been well used in that work. We pitied them and we made the packs small and as they were things of the fathers they already knew what they were to carry and seeing that it did not

weigh much they carried it with great joy and pleasure. Fray Luis without understanding them made them do it with even more pleasure with his good manner, telling them, "God, God, fathers, fathers," and showing them the Heaven and telling them in common Spanish that they were the children to whom we came and soon we will pay them for the work they will do for us.

And further along (de la Torre 1944–45: 173):

We came to a very swift river although not very deep, but it was the first that some of us had crossed in our lives. Fray Domingo de Medinillas was carried across by the Indians which seemed to the rest (as if they saw the devil) a greatly cruel thing, but now that we have seen the condition of the Indians and the love with which they do that and how they make merry doing it and how it is an honor for them that the father accepts that service, we did not hold it to be so important.

Another form was the following (de la Torre 1944–45: 175).

Fray Tomás de San Juan was very sick during the travels and thus it was agreed to send him ahead in a hammock. A hammock is a well made net of thin cords which without seeing it cannot be well described, and they tie the ends to a stout pole whose ends are carried on the shoulders of the men; in this one goes seated. It is a pleasant thing to travel that way, although some become seasick. In these hammocks the Indians commonly sleep, the men, that is. These people use them to carry their lords and principal persons and the sick and it is in them that the women of Castile travel on trips and even the Spanish men are themselves carried in them when they go to their towns, especially when the road is bad and they cannot go on horseback.

The 28th of February they left Ixtapangajoya, where they were proportioned *tamemes* or burden-bearers and food, and they followed a road where they endured hardships that the chronicler describes at great length. The same day they arrived in Xiloxuchiapa (Solosuchiapa).

They continued that difficult trip some days more during which they found small groups of Indians and a sugar mill which Blom believes is Ixhuatán, until the 5th of March when they began the hardest part of the trail, the climb to the top of the hill of Tapilula:

"In leaving the inn we began to climb that frightful hill sometimes upright and sometimes crawling on all fours where all, especially the sick, were forced to work greatly." The days that followed were not much less painful, since the hills and obstacles continued and during two nights they had to improvise a place to sleep in the open forest; on the 8th of March they arrived at a little place called Amatlcan (?), where they rested and asked for help from the Indians, who, with a very practical sense answered "that the great father has passed and they had given him a feast and that we were little fathers," referring to the Bishop Las Casas who had been in the same place a few days before, as he had gone ahead of the group.

They passed then some places which Blom supposes were the Highlands, the land of the Chamulas, where the christianity of the Indians, as was common in the 16th century, was made clear to the frailes:

as the Indians were alone with Fray Pedro Calvo they told him, "Rogue, you are good and fat, go on foot, and throwing him down on the ground, and the poor man's stomach was so tied up in knots that he could not move until they raised him up (de la Torre 1944–45: 185).

The trip continued until they arrived at an ancient indigenous fortress where they were attended to, since the Tzotziles showed themselves very obliging, and apart from that, here began the flat road. The following towns were Nistan (Santiago Huixtlan, distinct from San Miguel Huixtan on the road to Ocosingo. Becerra [1930: 114] situates it near Larrain-

zar noting that now it is only known by its Christian name. García de Bargas says that from here to Ciudad Real there are three leagues, so that if the friars first reached Huixtlan and afterwards Larrainzar, there must be some error, either in the route given by de la Torre or in the leagues given by García de Bargas.), Ixtacustuc (according to Becerra [1930: 150] the correct name is Istacostote, another name for San Andrés, today San Andrés Larrianzar. García de Bargas says that there are five leagues from this place to Ciudad Real), and Mustenango (?).

Finally on March 12, 1545, they made their entrance into Cuidad Real. From Salamanca, Spain, they had made it in 424 days, of which 53 were required in the section from Campeche [to San Cristóbal de Las Casas]. In the calculations of Fray Tomás de la Torre they covered approximately 120 leagues of indigenous road.

About the dangers of the ascent above Tapilula and the difficulty of the climb, Blom added to the diary of Fray Tomás de la Torre an appendix with his own experiences in 1944 (de la Torre 1944–45: 191–98). In 1956 I passed over it in a jeep on the improved road, but even then I understood the fear and fatigue suffered by all who left a testimony of the trip. Today this section is abandoned and the modern paved highway runs to one side of the Río Teapa.

Some of these towns were visited in the route to Tabasco which the Alcalde Mayor of Tuxtla followed in his trip to Habava (Castañón Gamboa 1953: 85–89): Tuxtla–Chiapa–Ixtapa – Zinacantan – Ciudad Real – Huixtan–Oxchuc – Cancuc – Guaguitepec – Sitala – Chilon – Yajalon – Tumbala – Palenque – El Rosario–San Jose–las Animas, en Playas de Catazaja (from which he went by canoe down river)–Palizada–Isla del Carmen–Campeche (where he arrived by sea in a sloop from Isla del Carmen). The trip lasted from October 20th to November 9th, 1787.

In a report of 1821, written by the Sociedad Económica de Amigos del País (Castañón Gamboa 1956: 131–58) about the importance that the region of Ocosingo would have if a new road was opened between Bachajon and Palenque, with the establishment of a warehouse at Playas de Catazaja, some rivers are mentioned where the use of canoes is absolutely necessary, which is indicative of their navigability. Separately emphasis is made of the transport situation toward Palenque which is on the backs of Indians by the Tumbala road. The canoe embarcation points mentioned are Tulija and Baccan.

This last road is marked by a chain of 16th century churches founded by the Dominicans to serve in the missionization of the Tzeltal, Tzotzil, and Chol Indians. They were also to attend to the warlike Lacandon. I refer to the towns that Bishop de Bargas y Rivera mentions (in the *Relación* we have been utilizing) strung out along the modern highway: San Cristóbal–Huixtan–Oxchuc–Abasolo, Ocosingo–Bachajon (from here a side road goes to Sitala and Guaquitepec)–Chilon–Yajalon (where another road takes off to Tumbala–Petalcingo and Tila). Let us summarize the bishop's information:

At one quarter of a league by level road, although muddy in the rainy season, one arrives at San Felipe (now almost a *barrio* of San Cristóbal de Las Casas); at ten leagues by bad road to the north, the town of Santo Domingo Oxchuc; to the west [east?] at six bad leagues is San Ildefonso Tenexapa (Tenejapa); to the south, at four rocky leagues San Miguel Guistan (Huixtan); to the east at six [leagues] of hills and rocks, San Martin (possibly Abasolo San Martín).

From Oxchuc to Cancuc there are six leagues of very bad road and from the latter to its annex Tenango there are four. Five leagues in front of Cancuc is Guaquitepeque (Guaquitepe, municipality of Sitala); two leagues forward, toward the north by a rough road, one arrives at Citala (Sitala). At "the back of those two towns" is the parish of Ocosingo, whose annex, Zibaca, is still a league of good road further on. Returning to the west and following "the mountain which goes down to the north," after eight leagues of bad road one arrives at Chilum (Chilon).

At three good leagues is Bachajon and at three from Chilon one goes to Yaxalum (Yajalon); at seven [leagues] by bad road is the parish of San Mateo of Tila, which at two

[leagues] further on has its annex called Patalcingo.

Seven hard leagues from this last place is Tumbala, where one can leave for Palenque, thirty-four leagues of "dangerous and painful" trail away.

It is suitable to mention here that this route also had a religious importance from the 16th century on, because it is the one pilgrims use to go to Tila to render devotion to the Black Christ that is venerated in that place. This cult always was important for the Tabasco towns, but with the amplification of the old road the devotion and commerce has been extended to the Highlands.

In order to understand the series of connections between the different indigenous towns of the Highlands with the Zoque region and the road down to Tabasco, it is worth continuing to cite Bargas y Rivera, because it seems to me, that between the 16th century and the last third of the 18th century the communications panorama did not vary much, to judge by the insistence on the terrible state of the roads, as we will see in the following summary:

From San Juan Chamula it is twenty-one leagues to Nuestra Señora Asunción Guytucpan from which one goes to the east to Santa Catarina and then "returning along the road and traveling the mountain down to the north one league of rough road" one arrives at San Pedro Gueyteupan (Becerra 1930: 141, says that the correct name should be Hueiteupan and that there were three: Santa Catarina, San Pedro, and Oluta Guiteupan of which only one continues with the name of Asunción Hueiteupan. It is the present Huitiupan near Simojovel, that I have visited).

At two leagues is Simojovel; in the *Relación* of Fray Tomás Torres it says that from the road that goes from Ciudad Real to Chiapa, another takes off that "cut off to the Zoque towns that fall on the side of the Tabasco province and by another (it must be another branch) makes a bad road to Simojovel, which is an industrious little town of Quelenes Indians." What the friar did not mention is that from Simojovel came all the amber that was used in Mesoamerica and that formed part of the tribute demanded by the Aztecs from the towns in the Soconusco. This implies by necessity a contact between Simojovel and the Chiapas coast that had to occur precisely by this "bad road" [see Köhler, Paper 7]. Fourteen leagues from Huitiupan, by a "very painful" road is the town of Moyos (municipality of Sabanilla). The description says that "there are many muddy hills and deep mires, full of rocks and with many different small streams, broken places, and rivers and one very large river which is crossed by canoe". Returning from this town "taking off towards the north and by the same road from Guyteupan, then south at about one league from that town is the hamlet called Sabanilla (present municipality head).

Ten leagues from Huitiupan, by bad road with rivers "unwadeable" during the rainy season, is found the town of Plátanos (municipality of Bosque), at a distance of three leagues from Santiago (El Pinar, municipality of Larrainzar). Three leagues from Huitiupan and again by the accustomed bad road one arrives at Amatan (present municipality head).

Twenty-nine leagues back along the road that we have covered and six from the town of Plátanos is Xitotol (Jitotol), from which

> traveling to the west for three leagues of rough road of palisaded hills, rocks and mires with two rivers that are on the said road, one at a distance of one and one half leagues from Xitotol and the other at two and one half leagues, is the town of San Dionisio that they call Pueblo Nuevo (Pueblo Nuevo Solistahuacan).

Three leagues to the south of Jitotol is found the hacienda of San Pedro Mártir Bochil.

Eleven leagues from Jitotol is Tapilula, from where four "arduous" roads leave, one for Pantepeuque (Pantepec), another for Pueblo Nuevo, another for Isgustan (Ixhuatán), and the last for Comistaguacan (according to Becerra [1930: 63] it is called San Bartolomé Comistlahuacan).

Nine leagues from Tapilula "traveling along the mountains by very arduous road because all is of stone, up hills and down, with

a large river that is crossed eight times, is Zulisuchiapa (Solosuchiapa). From here there are four leagues to Istacomitan (Ixtacomitan) from where one can continue to Pichucalco that is a "new town" [see Lee, p. 57, this volume], Istapangajoya, Chapultenango, and Nicapa (municipality of Pichucalco), with four leagues between each one. Three leagues from the last one and seven from Ixtacomitan one arrives at Sunuapa (municipality center) "because the towns follow one after another through a chain of mountains."

At ten leagues distance is found Tapalapa; at three from this town again there is a connection with Pantepec. From the same Tapalapa one arrives after four leagues of "very bad" road at Xocoltepeque (according to Becerra [1930: 298], there was a Socoaltepeque, partially disappeared annex of Sibaca in the district of Chilon). I believe there is a possibility that this could refer to another place with the same name due to the distance from Chilon y Sibaca). From here it is six leagues to Chapultenango. From Tapalapa leaves another road of the same distance to Coapilla (municipality center) "by a muddy, rocky and miry road; in order to travel on it it is necessary to build thick corduroy roads."

Six leagues from Ocotepec is Magdalena (Magdalenas Coaltipan, municipality center today called Francisco León). Becerra [1930: 59] says, citing the *Colección de Documentos Inéditos de la Iglesia de Chiapas* of Francisco Orozco y Jiménez, that Magdalena Chica was situated one league from Magdalena Grande, "all downhill," and that the neighbors left the place going up to Magdalena Grande, which presents a problem as to the location of the towns). There are five leagues from here to Ystuacan (Ostuacan, municipality center), and by the same road to Sayula (probably next to the river of the same name although I have not been able to locate it). Becerra (1930: 286) affirms that it is a town and municipality of the Pichucalco district, or, in other words, corresponds to this region. Paniagua (1876: 77) says "it is situated with an advantage for navigation because it is found on the right bank of the Grijalva and on the left of the Santa Mónica, a short distance from their confluence."

Twelve leagues from Magdalena is Tecpatan with a corduroy road made of thick trees and poles in order to avoid mud holes. From here one goes down five leagues to Quechula and one quarter of a league further on is Chicoacan (Chicoasen; in the trip of the Alcalde Mayor of Tuxtla we have seen that traveling by the river's edge he passed from one town to another. Such a short distance between the two towns as given by Bargas y Rivera seems exaggerated to me.

From Tecpatan one arrives at Copainala and after six leagues more to Chicoasen. An important note is that here one goes up to a ranch called Soteapa (municipality of San Fernando) after three leagues of uphill trail, at the end of which there are seven more to Tuxtla and nine to Ocozocoautla. Actually, there is a trail near Quechula, much used before the construction of the Mal Paso Dam, which divided into several branches to go to the towns of San Fernando and Ocozocoautla (Navarrete 1966b: 36–38). Two leagues from Chicoasen one arrives at the town of Osumacinta.

Because a source from the end of the 18th century, as is that of Bargas y Rivera, shows us how intricate the communications in this zone were, I leave for last the mention of a document from the 16th century (Castañón Gamboa 1957: 9–17) which is related to the depredations committed in 1528 by a resident of Coatzacoalcos in the towns of Quechula and Zinacantan, from where they come out at Tesompata(?), Tila, Ostuacan, Tapalapa, and Solistahuacan, which are relatively distant one from the other, but which, as we have seen, maintain perfect communication among themselves.

Complementary to the general description of these routes can be the map reproduced in Figure 17, made in 1813, in which is shown the distribution of the principal roads of the last century and where some of the towns mentioned can be seen, as well as their intercommunication. The reproduction is a schematic copy of a color map (Anonymous, *Mapa correspondiente . . .*).

Summarizing in terms of the modern highways the earlier routes, we can say that the axes over which all the mentioned trails cross are the equivalents of present-day highways: (1) San Cristóbal – Ixtapa – Soyalo – Bochil – Jitotol – Pueblo Neuvo Solistahuacan – Ixtacomitan – Pichucalco; (2) San Cristóbal – Huixtan – Oxchuc – Abasolo – Ocosingo – Bachajon – Chilon – Yajalon; (3) Ixtapa – Soyalo – Chicoasen–Copainala–Tecpatan.

THE ROUTES TO THE LACANDON FOREST

This is one of the most difficult aspects to study, first because of the immense published and documentary bibliography that exists (Hellmuth 1970), and second, because we have only a few studies of archaeological reconnaissance and excavations that help to understand the temporal sequence of the towns that were inhabited in the region, except some visits and appreciations concerning the monumental centers of the Classic Maya period.

For that reason, I will refer only to the principal roads that have been defined in the study of the "entradas" in the reduction of the Lacandon Indians during the Colonial period, with the addition of some modern information.

The oldest data we have were discussed by Doris Z. Stone (1932: 230–35) who describes, according to the version of Gonzalo Fernández de Oviedo, the expedition of Captains Alonso Dávila and Alonso de Luján. In the interpretation of Stone the point of departure is Teapa, from which they went to the city of Chiapa, covering thirty leagues. A problem the author discusses is which Chiapa is referred to, the present-day Chiapa de Corzo or Ciudad Real, which in that time was called Chiapa de los Españoles. It seems to me that if the expedition had passed through the first it would have had to mention the other, which by geographical situation is closer to any of the entrances to the jungle; besides, from Chiapa de Corzo it is impossible to leave directly for the Lacandon zone. Blom (1956: 4–6), who places the expedition in 1529–1530 does not even put it in doubt: they left from Ciudad Real.

In other words the route must have been the same one that Bernal Díaz and Godoy followed in their trip to Tabasco and by which the Dominicans entered from Campeche.

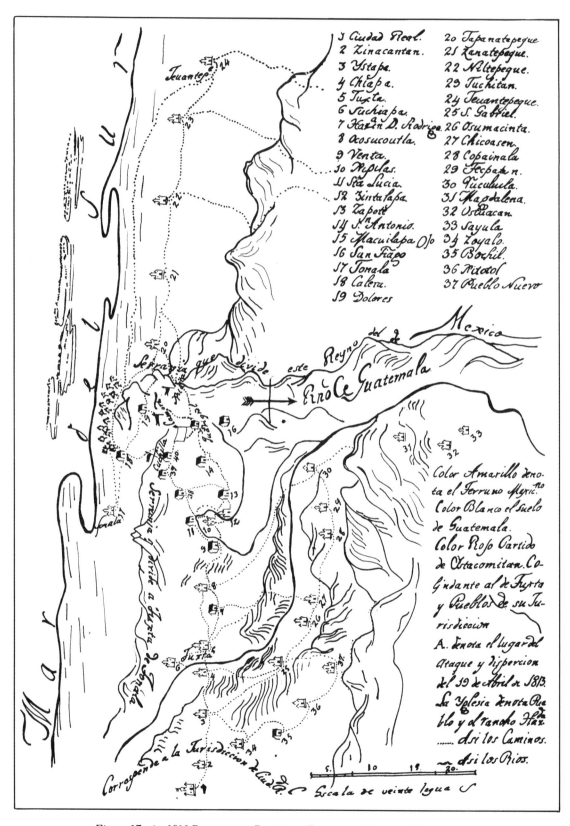

Figure 17. An 1813 Plan of the Principal Towns and Roads of Chiapas

According to Stone, from the *"cuidad de Chiapa"* the expedition traveled thirty leagues until they arrived at a lake with an inhabited island in the middle which she identifies as Lake Petha, between the Jatate and Usumacinta Rivers. Blom (1956: 4), in his work, reinterprets the route and says that after leaving Ciudad Real and traveling thirty leagues, "the guides" of the group returned saying that they had arrived at a town where another language was spoken, for which Blom notes "there are 30 leagues between Ciudad Real, where Tzotzil is spoken, and Comitan, where Tojolabal is spoken. The topography favors this route."

Blom makes another reinterpretation with respect to the name of the lake at which they arrived after having traveled thirty leagues. His version is based on the visit that he made in 1950, when he found a lake with the characteristics mentioned by the Spaniards: ten to twelve leagues in circumference (40 km.) and the remains of ancient occupation on an island. The name of the lake is Miramar or Lacandon Lake. On the map of the Lacandon Forest drawn by Blom (Blom and Duby 1957: Vol. 2) it appears situated between the Jatate and Azul Rivers.

Following the description of Stone (1932: 231), the expedition continued another thirty leagues (which to Blom and to me seems exaggerated) until they found a river which the author identifies as the Usumacinta. According to Blom the place where they struck the river's edge is known as Santa Margarita. In canoes they went downriver to join, near Tenosique, a section of Cortés' route to the Hibueras.

Concerning Comitan as the intermediate place in the expedition I must return to cite Fray Tomás Torres (*Relación de la visita . . .*)

From this town (Comitan) one goes down to the hot country that has very bad water and flies, the worst roads that run between swamps and dense forest where no one wants to pass because of the great fear that they have of the Indians who live in this wilderness and are called acandon, by which one can arrive at an exit of the river that goes to join with the same one from Chiapa; this exit is called Tenochec (Tenosique).

Blom notes other entrances to the jungle during the 16th century, but I prefer to refer directly to the chronicle of Villagutierre (1933: 46–57) from which he took his data. According to this chronicler the first entrance was in 1555 when the friars Domingo de Vico and Andrés López left from the city of Coban in the Guatemalan region of Alta Verapaz, to go to the Lacandon lands in an evangelical mission; they did not return from this trip as they were killed by Indians.

This resulted, the following year, in the initiation of preparations for a punitive expedition that could not be realized until the beginnings of 1559, headed up by the Governor of Guatemala himself, Pedro Ramírez de Quiñones, who solicited the help of six hundred Indians from Chiapa and two hundred from Zinacantan. It should be mentioned that this contingent was taken all the way to Guatemala City in order to participate in a pompous parade, from where they returned to concentrate themselves in Comitan before leaving for the jungle. The efficiency of the Indians became clear on "making the road, because the land was very densely forested and entangled, for the little or no experience they have in making them." I do not believe that the road was opened completely anew, but that it was made larger in order to give free passage to an army of such magnitude over simple Lacandon trails.

The expedition arrived at the Lacandon town next to the lake with a "fort" site in the middle, and it is important to note that the Lacandons fled in canoes by the river that flows out to Yucatan (Unimacinta). The expedition left for Totiltepeque (not located) and afterwards to Pochutla. In this unidentified town on the edge of a lake it was necessary to make rafts in order to lay siege to it and good swimmers from Chiapa towed them. From here, without being able to complete their mission totally they returned again to Comitan (Villagutierre 1933: 55–65).

Even though there were other entrances in the same century, not one gives us better information than that realized a century later in 1695 (Stone 1932: 272–77; Villagutierre

1933: 177–226). This was headed by the President of Guatemala, Don Jacinto de Barrios, having left January 17 for Jocotenango and Pazon (Patzun. These two towns are badly located on the map of Stone). From here they passed Gueguetenango (Huehuetenango) traveling twenty-one leagues to Santa Eulalia and continued to San Mateo Ixtatan. After eight leagues they slept on some plains and after two days continuously on the road on which they covered seventeen leagues they arrived at Comitan.

As they decided that the entrance would be better from Ocosingo they traveled the twenty-four leagues that separated the two towns. Here they made all the preparations for the final assault on the jungle and the army divided into three groups; one would enter from Ocosingo commanded by President Barrios himself, the second from Huehuetenango under the command of Melchor Rodríguez Mazariegos and Friar Pedro de la Concepción, and the last from the town of Cahabon in the Verapaz. Separately, from Yucatan, would come Governor Martín Urzúa opening up the road. Since only the first two came in direct contact with the Lacandons I will refer only to them.

The Huehuetenango group left on the last day of February for San Mateo Ixtatan, from which they traveled five leagues and encountered some ancient ruins; they continued two leagues to the stream called Chiup, eight more to a place called Labconob, and after several nights of sleeping in the open they arrived on the sixth day at other ruins. They climbed to the top of the mountain and went down to a large river and a place they called San Ramón on the 13th of March. They baptized the river with this name and followed its edge for several days until they found another they called San José and then they came to the junction of two other rivers. Up to this point they had traveled fifty-one leagues in thirty days. In the middle of Holy Week they arrived at the river that comes from Ocosingo (Jatate) and on Food Friday they arrived exhausted at the Lacandon town, which they called Dolores del Lacandon in honor of the date.

The Ocosingo group also left on the last

day of February, initially to El Próspero, from where they continued until the 12th of March, when they halted in a place they called San Juan de Diós. The 30th of March they were crossing a medium-sized river in order to arrive on Tuesday of Holy Week at a lake that they went around; after walking six leagues they arrived on the 18th of April at another site that they named San Perfecto Mártir; they crossed another river and on the 19th of the same month the meeting took place with Captain Melchor Rodríguez who had gone out from Dolores to look for them.

Even though in the narration of the two expeditions it is insisted that the Indian axe men went opening the path and they underline the continuous difficulties of the very bad state of the trail, the difficult crossings and the fatigue of clearing, the significant detail that they took Indian guides makes me think that in those places there was traffic on the part of the Indians of the region. Besides, the first group was following the course of the rivers which join the Lacantun, the same as the Jatate that joins the Lacantun, which always offers a route orientation.

Also, the information they received in Dolores indicates that there existed relations between towns that inhabited the jungle, above all with the Petén (possibly with the Itzaes), as they indicated to President Barrios (Villagutierre 1933: 223):

> And that the Petenca (Peten) had many Indians, who are very warlike and were the enemies of these Lacandons, because they had gone to kill and do ill, entering at night into their towns and catching them asleep, and for this reason they do not communicate with them.

More important still is what they added: "that in order to go to their places it had to be in the dry season, for in order to arrive there twenty days of travel were necessary downriver, and at the present one could not go because the rain, thunder, and lightning were approaching." In other words, that in the dry season traffic was possible even to the towns founded by the same Lacandons in the Partenote (?) and Tenosique Rivers that were thirty-five days of travel down the large river (Usumacinta).

Besides, communication on secondary rivers is suggested whenever they say that they have no canoes because the Indians of Petenca have stolen them, canoes which the thieves would not have transported overland to their homes. In the narration of the Lacandons is also included a relative time of travel: "that there would be a fifteen-day trip from there to Coban traveling in canoe upriver," and that by land "it would be an eight- to ten-day trip, and that the Indians of Coban were accustomed to come and talk with the Lacandons."

After making some disappointing exploratory incursions the expedition returned to Ocosingo.

A large part of these roads was retraveled by Blom (Blom and Duby 1957) who, in the majority of his trips, entered through Ocosingo. In truth, about this town and its possible exits to Tabasco and Campeche via the navigable tributaries of the Usumacinta we have reports dating from the beginning of the last century, where examples of the advantage of making the river route free from impediments and of the advantages it would bring to the region are given (Castañón Gamboa 1953: 73–120).

From Ocosingo the excellent explorer and "woodsman" Juan Ballinas also set out, perhaps as the first in the modern period to travel all of the jungle course of the Jataté River; he left his written memoirs and drew a map where he indicated his trip through the jungle until he came out at the Flores Lake in the Guatemalan Peten (Ballinas 1951).

I have personally collected information from old merchants and *chicleros* of Ocosingo who went into the jungle via the so-called "Fincas Route": San José Reforma-Sabintela and Caribal, where the trails forked, one going to Tenosique and Santa Margarita, the point where Blom (1956) believed Captains Dávila and Luján to have embarked in order to follow the course of the Usumacinta downriver.

THE SYSTEM OF THE CHIAPAS HIGHLANDS

It is in part parallel to that of the Central Depression and comprises, besides, a section of this region in the eastern climb up into the Highlands. We know this route principally from the trip of Friar Alonso Ponce (1875: 467–89) on his return from Guatemala to Oaxaca. I present below in a schematic form the stages of the journey from what is today San Antonio Huista in the Department of Huehuetenango, Guatemala:

Place visited, the distance from the previous town, and comments.

1. Vistlan (Huistan); 2 leagues; he crossed four streams and one full river which he had to ford using some planks.

2. Río de la Canoa (he says it is the same as the Chiapa River); 2 leagues; he passed one swamp and the Río de la Canoa.

3. Aquetzpala (Aquespala; he is now on the Mexican side of the border); ¼ league.

4. Izcumtenango (Escuintenango, a site located recently by Lowe [1959: 62, Fig. 58, *b*; also see Becerra 1930: 130]); 1½ leagues; flat road, full of water and mud.

5. Coapa (Becerra [1930: 58] thinks that the "bad swamps" correspond to the swamp of Shocmul and the site to any one of the Tepancoapan: hamlet, hacienda, or ranch that are found in Comitan, Zapaluta, and Margaritas) [Ed.: The actual location is given by Lee 1974 and is near the old ranch of Corral de Piedra in hot country]; 6 leagues; he crossed the Grijalva by canoe, now much deeper because two rivers join upstream; "They say each one is as large as it and even bigger." They must be the Santo Domingo and the San Gregorio. [Ed.: Lagartero and Selegua, not Santo Domingo, since the latter is downriver from Esquintenango]. He traveled through bad swamps and five streams.

6. Comitlan (Comitan, where he arrived after passing some ranches); 8 leagues in total; "and leaving the road that goes straight to Chiapa de los Indios he took the one that goes to Chiapa de los Españoles." He crossed one river and four streams and traveled uphill, or, in other words, he left the Depression in order to direct himself into the Highlands. The road that went to Chiapa will be discussed at the end of this study.

7. San Francisco Amatenango; 9 leagues in total; he passed through a narrow valley

between hills by rocky road and bad crossings; a little fountain with good water, some ranches that were military camps against the Lacandons and two streams. The "little water fountain" could be a spring called Yerba Buena, six leagues from Teopisca, as Bargas y Rivera reports.

8. Teopixca (Teopisca); ½ league; he crossed a very bad swamp, six or seven drains with wooden bridges, and another stream with bridge.

9. Ciudad Real de Chiapa (San Cristóbal de Las Casas); 5 leagues; road very bad with mud, marshes and rocks, a long and bad climb and a river with bridge.

10. Tzinacantan (Bargas y Rivera says that it is 2 leagues from Ciudad Real); 1½ leagues; road full of water and mud, a river with its bridge and five streams.

11. Iztapa (Bargas y Rivera places it 6 leagues from Ciudad Real by a bad road with hills and ravines passing through the sites of El Próspero, Burrero, and Río Hondo). I have passed over this old road that runs to the left of the modern Panamerican highway and it is still known as the Burrero road. Woolrich (1948: 184), when describing the Burrero River, says that it is formed by several springs that join at the finca named El Próspero. The river passes the fincas El Próspero and Tierra Colorada, of the municipality of Zinacantan; upon passing Ixtapa it is called Río Hondo; 5½ leagues (7 from Ciudad Real); he crossed five streams and three times a river: "the six leagues of the above mentioned seven are very bad road, with very high and stony hills and very difficult ascents and descents even though one is always going downhill, and such difficult and dangerous steep declivities that it was a miracle we did not fall many times that morning; among these was one descent where near the river's edge there was much swamp and partially dried clay in which the beasts of burden sank up to their bellies ... and passing the river we began to go up another, much higher, hill and it was so steep that the road went by the narrow ridge top, twisting and turning. There had been poles put up in different parts of the road so that the animals would not fall over the cliffs into the deep ravines that were on

all sides . . . ." This tiring journey was caused by "an Indian who guided us whose fault it was that the Father Comisario suffered on those two hills, because he guided us by that road which was so bad that it was no longer used nor did anyone ever go along it . . . ."

12. Chiapa de los Indios (Chiapa de Corzo); 4 leagues; he crossed a great ravine with a stream, some slight declines, another stream which joins with the first, other ravines, two streams and a small river with a rock bridge, and down "finally another very long and very painful hill." Possibly they passed the same arroyo several times which bears the name of El Escopetazo and which is known in Chiapa as Río Chiquito. The final slope is the descent into the Central Depression.

13. Tuchtla (Tuxtla); 2 leagues; he crossed a small river (Río Chiquito), the Río Grande (Grijalva) and then four streams. About the second he says "the river was in flood stage and was a large quarter of a league wide and in order to come out by canoe at the landing on the other side they took it a great stretch upriver and afterwards the furious current passed it across".

14. Xiquipila la Chica. Becerra (1930: 345) says that perhaps it was near the present Espinal de Morelos or Ocozocoautla. I also think that it could be this last town, which is not mentioned in the trip and was an important point in the 16th century. In my notes on the *Relación de Ocozocoautla* I did not mention this possibility; 5 leagues; he passed one league of flat road filled with puddles, mud and swamps, two streams and two rivers with wooden bridges. The ancient road in this section to Jiquipilas is not exactly the one that the Panamerican highway follows, but that one which from Tuxtla turns left (at Teran) through the part known as the Chivería and comes out in front of Berriozabal.

15. Xiquipila la Grande (I believe that this is the present-day Jiquipilas); 6 leagues in total; he passed a little river with a wooden bridge, some swamps, a high hill and a stream and finally a river called Xiquipilas that he crossed in canoe, and afterwards he continued by good road. Between Ocozocoautla and Jiquipilas there is a pronounced

descent that ends at the La Venta River that could be the large one mentioned.

16. Ranch of Vazquiañez or of Redondo; 3½ leagues; he crossed the Xiquipilas River again and five streams.

17. Another ranch with the same name as the preceding one; 2 short leagues; he crossed a river.

18. Macuilapa Ranch (present-day ranch); 2 long leagues; he crossed two streams.

19. Ranch of Potrero (now in the Diocese of Guatemala; 6 leagues in total; he crossed the Xiquipilas River eleven times, six streams tributary to it, and on the top of a pine-covered hill the Diocese of Chiapa ended. He descended a very difficult hill "by a road that did not seem to be for anything but deer and goats." He then crossed six streams and arrived "at a crossing where there was a cross and two roads, one on the right-hand side that goes to a ranch called Burrero and the other on the left-hand side that goes to another ranch called Potrero ... he did not take the road to Burrero because it is one league long and very bad road; continuing his trip by the other . . . ." He crossed another river two times and streams and a final river.

20. La Venta de Gironda; 2 leagues; he crossed two little rivers, two or three streams "which form a good river," and two leagues of flat road.

21. Amézquita Ranch in the same Diocese of Guatemala; 3½ leagues; he crossed one stream, many swamps, some bad crossings, another stream, and one river. The trip through these places was from the 3rd to the 15th of September, 1586.

In 1624 the Dominican friar Tomas Gage (1946: 127–32) traveled the same road and also suffered the penalties of the broken and difficult terrain. So much so that near Tepana-tepec and in view of the mountains where the trail goes up to Chiapas he had certain doubts about which route to follow [Ed.: taken from the 1946 English edition]:

> The sight of the rocks and mountains did terrify us, and the report of them did much offright us; so that in all this way we did confer which way to take, whether the road way to Guatemala which lieth under those mountains along the coast by the country of Soconusco, from whence (though out of our way) we might have turned to Chiapa, or whether we should steer our right course to Chiapa over those mountains, which we had been informed we might safely pass over if the winds did not blow too boisterously. We resolved that when we came to Tapanatepec we would choose our way according as the winds did favour or threaten us, but however to Chiapa we would go.

Finally it was resolved to go by the normal route, and between Tapanatepec and the peak of Macuilapa he had such a bad time that he wrote this about the translation of the name that had been given to the site (Gage 1946: 131–36) [Ed.: taken from 1946 English edition]):

> But when we came upon the very top of Maquilapa (which signifies in that tongue, head without hair) we perceived truly the danger so much talked of, and wished ourselves again with our green lemons in the way of Tapanatepec, for we found it indeed a head without hair, a top without a tree or branch to shelter a fearful traveler; the passage that lieth open to the sea may be no more than a quarter of a mile, but the height and narrowness of it stupifieth, for if we look on the one side, there is the wide and spacious South Sea lying so deep and low under it that it dazzles the eyes to behold it; if we look on the other side, there are rocks of at least six or seven miles depth, whose sight doth make the stoutest and hardest heart (though like themselves) to quake and quiver; so that here the sea expects to swallow, there the rocks threaten to tear with a downfall, and in the midst of those dangers in some places the passage is not above an ell broad. We needed better cordials for that quarter of a mile than feeding three days upon green lemons and water, and durst not man ourselves so much as to go through it upon our mules; we lighted, and gave the Indians our mules to lead, and we followed them one by one not doing with looking on either side, but lowering our bodies we crept upon our hands and feet

as near unto the tracks which beasts and travelers had made as we could without hindering our going. And when we had got to the end of that passage, and where the mountain was broader, and the trees promised relief, we then looked back boldly and accused of folly both ourselves and all other travellers that sought no other way though ten miles about, to avoid that danger both for man and beast.

This difficult hill is presently known as the Gineta; it is still dangerous and is on the modern Panamerican highway.

The complete route that Gage followed afterwards was: Hacienda de Juan Toledo, where they rested two days from the earlier fatigues; the town of Acapala, and without going into details he mentions immediately the two Chiapas: that of los Indios and that of los Españoles. Becerra (1930: 13) says that there are no traditional nor architectural vestiges conforming to Acapala and that it is probable that Gage "arrived at Acala by a road that did not touch Tuxtla, that existed in another time" and later went down to Chiapa. Becerra continues:

A Chiapas author, don Jesús B. Sánchez (1915) took as certain the data of Gage and says that when Mazariegos came he camped in Acapala, according to the author, it was where today stands the Yuquis ranch, near Tuxtla ... but I have not found any basis for such an affirmation, since we already saw that Gage places the town "on the edge of the same river that passes by Chiapa."

Personally I have found out that next to the small ranch called Cahuare, situated to one side of the Belisario Domínguez Bridge which crosses the Grijalva at the entrance to the Sumidero, there existed toward the beginning of this century a ranch called Acapala. Could this be the point touched by Gage?

Farther along Gage (1946: 159–71) describes his trip toward Guatemala, for which he left from Chiapa de los Españoles, he continued to Teopisca, and then Comitan, from where he visited Copanaguastla; he continued to Escuintenango, a town near "the great river that passes by Chiapa de los Indios" [Ed.: the following taken from 1946 English edition]:

No man nor beast travelling to Guatemala can go into it, or from Guatemala can go out of it, but by ferrying over. And the road being much used and beaten by travellers, and by such as they call *requas* of mules (every *requa* consisting of fifty or threescore mules) this ferry is day and night employed and yields much treasure to the town at the year's end; the Indians of the town besides the ferry boat, have made many other little boats, or canoes to go up and down the river.

From Escuintenango he continued on to a small town called San Martín, which the translator of Gage's work (1946: 162), thinks is San Martín Cuchumatan, in the Department of Huehuetenango, Guatemala. He also is of the opinion (p. 160) that Gage's route after leaving Comitan followed a road that descended to the south and is lost before the San Gregorio River, near Escuintenango, that he crossed the Grijalva and entered Guatemalan territory by the valley of the Huistla River.

THE SECONDARY ROADS

I call by this name the minor routes that turn off from some of those already described, or that form small independent systems.

The first is a short route that connects Navenchauc (Tzotzil town situated next to the Panamerican Highway in the Chiapa-San Cristóbal section) with Chiapa de Corzo. It is an indigenous merchants' road that descends from the Highlands to the Depression. It is also frequented by the Chiapa de Corzo pilgrims who annually take it on the pilgrimage of the "Niño Florero" when they go up to collect a certain species of flower in the hills neighboring Navenchauc with which they adorn the Cristmas altars (Lee 1970). The time occupied by the "floreros" in coming down to Chiapa is two and a half days, spending the nights at the hamlets of Mortajoc and Nache Grande.

In the same Highlands we have what is the equivalent of a second road, according to the information of Bargas y Rivera. This leaves Ciudad Real for Larrainzar and goes on to Santiago Huixtlan (see the last stage of the Dominican travels from Campeche to Ciudad Real). From here it goes to Santa Marta Solotepeque (Yolotepec), to Santa María Magdalena Tenezcatlan (Tenescaltan or Tenacatlan), and to San Pedro Chenelo (Chenalho); at three leagues is San Pablo (San Pablo Chalchihuitan) and to San Miguel Mitontic.

The third road I have taken from the *Relación* of Frair Tomás Torres and it begins in Teopisca going toward Venustiano Carranza (formerly San Bartolomé de los Llanos) where the road forks, one going to Soyatitan, which is important for its proximity to the ruins of what was Copanaguastla, and the "other to Chiapa, heading toward the big river where there was an embarcation point." Also from Teopisca, merchants departed for the Custepeques plains, the neighboring region to the Frailesca. This indicates an ancient communication route with what are today the municipalities of La Concordia (where the salt springs of Portatenco are, which Lowe [1959: 49] is of the opinion were important for the prehispanic settlement), Villa Corzo, and Villa Flores. Last, he indicates that Pinola (today Villa las Rosas) belonged to San Bartolomé de los Llanos by "two leagues of well-cared-for road."

There are still other connections: from Teopisca leave four roads: to Ciudad Real, to Comitan, to San Bartolomé (as mentioned above, it is Venustiano Carranza), and to Huixtan. The distance from Amatenango (Amatenango del Valle) is one league and from Aguacatenango, three.

About a fourth nucleus of routes Bargas y Rivera indicates that from Comitan one leaves for Amatenango, in the direction of Ciudad Real, passing by Teopisca at thirteen leagues distance; another goes to Zocoltenango via six leagues of rocky downhill road; a third goes to Ocosingo, via twenty-four leagues of flat road; and the fourth goes to Zapaluta (present-day La Trinitaria) at four leagues distance following the road to Guatemala. Via thirteen leagues of flat road is Escuintenango [Ed.: Bargas and Rivera apparently forgot

about the 1000-m. drop one must make to go from Trinitaria to Escuintenango as one leaves the Highlands to descend into the Central Depression. Friar Ponce is more precise in this section, as he speaks of several leagues of ascent returning over this same section of the route, see p. 99] where in the same way that the chronicler Father Ponce did, he informs us that two rivers must be crossed besides the Grande. Here we return to connect with the land route parallel to the Grijalva that comes from Guatemala and which takes one from Escuintenango to Chicomuselo by ten leagues of flat road, with one league more in order to reach Yayaguita. Becerra (1930: 346) mentions El Carmen Yayaguita in the municipality of Chicomuselo.

From Chicomuselo, returning to the south, one arrives at Comalapa (Frontera Comalapa, which I mentioned as the door to the Grijalva for some of the towns in the Sierra Madre) by four leagues of flat road. Continuing on the other side toward the north, after eighteen leagues of rocky road one reaches Socoltenango, from which four roads depart: the first to Pinola (Villa las Rosas) two leagues away in the direction of Ciudad Real; the second to Soyatitán, "Camino Real of this New Spain", two leagues away over good road; the third that returns to Esquintenango, "Camino Real to Guatemala", fourteen leagues of bad road away; and the last to Chicomuselo by the route has been serving as a base here.

Two leagues from Socoltenango is Zoyaltitan (Soyatitan); by two leagues of good road one arrives at Pinola, from where it goes to San Bartolomé after four good leagues "and the rest is plains with three little short hills that are in it and two deep rivers, one called the Borracho River and the other the Blanco River." Here there are "four exits and entrances" with three royal roads: the first is toward the town of Chiapilla which is at eight leagues distance by bad roads, "this road goes to the New Spain"; the second is toward Soyatitan on the route to Guatemala; the third is toward Teopisca, toward Ciudad Real, via nine leagues of bad road; and the fourth is toward the Custepeques.

Continuing the San Bartolomé route there are another eight leagues, six corresponding to the Camino Real of New Spain and the others of bad road; by it one arrives at Totolapa where in turn there are four "entrances": to Chiapilla, after covering three leagues of bad road; to San Bartolomé, following the route to Guatemala; another to Ciudad Real; and to San Lucas over three leagues of broken road (El Zapotal, presently municipality center). This road crosses "a deep river of brackish water". Woolrich (1948: 246) mentions a Salado River in the region which joins the Río Frío in the lands of the Finca San Pedro, municipality of Acala, and afterwards joins with the Grijalva.

From this place one arrives at Acala after four leagues of bad road, after which follow nine similar leagues in order to reach Chiapa, whose connections we have seen amply throughout this work.

For the importance that this route signifies I give below a summary of it which the Alcalde Mayor of Tuxtla followed from Guatemala (Castañón Gamboa 1953: 71–77): Guatemala – Mixco – Santiago – Sumpango – San Sebastián – Chimaltenango – Patzicia – Patzun – San Andrés – Concepción – Carrascosa – El Rancho Despoblado – Totonicapan – San Francisco el Alto – Aguas Calientes – San Ramón – Mazatenango – Huehuetenango – Chiantla – El Rosario – Todos Santos Chuchumatan – San Martín – Petatan – San Antonio Huista (where Gage entered Guatemala – Escuintenango – El Corral de Piedras – Socoltenango – Soyatitan – San Bartolomé de los Llanos – El Rosario – Chiapilla – Acala – Chiapa. The trip was made from the 28th of January to the 29th of February of 1783.

In synthesis, the land route parallel to the Grijalva River that connected some of the towns of the Central Depression touched the following points after leaving Escuintenango: Chicomuselo – Socoltenango – Soyatitan – Pinola – San Bartolomé – Chiapilla – San Lucas – Acala – Chiapa.

FINAL CONSIDERATIONS

Rather than a discussion of formal conclusions, upon rereading this attempt to situate the principal prehispanic routes between the coasts of Chiapas and Tabasco, with their

internal and external branches — the route of Xicalango on the Gulf and the Anahuac-Ayotla on the south (Chapman 1959: 45–55) — the tangled accumulation of data, figures, and names that I have presented, suggests to me more of a basis for reflection. Or for reflections.

To attempt to demonstrate, among other things, that there is an accumulation of routes throughout time, will necessitate analysis from a series of points of view which range from questioning of the validity of the sources used to meditation about the conditions of the "archaeological role" that should pertain in this type of investigation.

About the first aspect there must be an insistence on the first-hand observations at the moment of the conquest and the direct experience of the friars who wrote during the process of evangelization, when new ideas and customs began to penetrate over the native routes. However, we must recognize the validity of reports of later centuries, because if we project ourselves back from the present time we will see that many examples of the term "to construct" a modern highway are the same as "to amplify" from the last century in order to give passage to the coaches and carts, and "to open" of the colonial period when one thought in terms of animal transport.

For this reason it seems perfectly valid when we lack ancient documentation, to utilize the data that ethnography gives us, principally when dealing with routes traveled by foot or horse trails, whose material condition is similar to the path, trail, track, "bad pass" or difficult road that the old chronicles mention.

With this criterion it is important to confront the most varied aspects, from ecological observations — without falling into some deterministic viewpoint — to the establishment of centers of artisan production and regions of indigenous cultivations, even those of *mestizos*, which maintain a traditional form of distribution, without forgetting the susceptibility to change: new means of transport, amplification of markets, substitution of merchandise, etc.

We must put our hands on any resource that can be managed. We must study the foundation of the primitive convents and their geographic distribution; the routes of indigenous rebellions, and the group of towns in revolt, since some kind of information can be inferred from them; the roads by which the republican wars took place and situate the movements of armies in the revolutionary epoch, because they can give us some data, even though it be simply topographic. And something is told by the routes and schedules of the coaches and mule trains, the establishments of post offices, the distribution of inns and points of change of beasts and drivers; the regional economic reports that consist of the amplification of roads and the convenience of cleaning canals and rivers and of establishing warehouses and ports of embarcation.

The narrative literature can also throw light on some special aspect; the memorable case of B. Traven comes to mind in his *Rebelión de los Colgados,* where that horrible route through the jungle that for many years was known as the *"Camino de Zendales,"* where hundreds of deceived Indians went to die terrible deaths in the lumber camps. From this we can derive the need to know the distribution of the lumber businesses, whose workmen always looked for the best sites next to the navigable rivers and the points closest to the rude trails that crossed the jungle.

The study of ethnographic aspects which seem simple and lacking in importance can lead us to derive conclusions of a cultural character. I prefer to give an example: Until the beginnings of this century there arrived in Comitán "troops" of indigenous *mecapaleros* (tumpline burden-bearers) coming from Guatemala with an average of thirty to forty men. During the trip through the mountains and the ascent from the Grijalva they walked "Indian file" and generally barefooted. Before entering a town they washed their feet, put on sandals, put on clean clothes, and formed two lines in perfect order, taking the two outer edges of the road. At the front marched the captain or boss of the company, flanked by the drummer and the flute player.

The leader carried a baton of command and only carried in his tumpline (*cacaxtli*) the image of the patron saint in the form of a statue and the objects which served to render him adoration at the end of each day's journey and upon arriving at the market: copal, cloths for the altar that was improvised, and incense burners, apart from his personal clothes and things. The musicians also served as "sufferers" or in other words, they did not carry more than the food and personal things of the group.

Upon arriving at the center of the town the church was visited or a small ceremony was made in front of the market altar. Soon they dispersed to offer the merchandise. There exists one photograph of 1916 where a group of burden bearers are marching as a "troop" through the streets of Santa Cruz del Quiché, Guatemala (Lothrop 1961: 1–13, Fig. 5).

Forgetting for the moment the purely anecdotal side of this, we see that all this implies an internal organization of the group, a "guild," we could say. Customs of strictly a religious nature in association with commerce are suggested and if we were to find out what class of products they carried we could define, perhaps, the regions from which they came, the extent of the distribution and the commercial elements of interchange. Apart from the study of the customs and life of the merchants, the knowledge of the cultural aspects that go beyond the sphere of pure economics would be many.

How many valuable data we will obtain the day that the problems of depopulation of towns and entire areas and their cause is studied; the location of ancient communities, the changes in names, the displacement of population nucleations from one area to another, since in this is always manifested the aspect of communications.

The typological definition of archaeological materials should go beyond the simple quantification and the simple descriptive exercise. For this it is obvious that the dynamic utilization of new techniques of dating and analysis can contribute in resolving old questions, such as the provenience and supply of prime materials, the location of workshops, what elements pass from one region to another, and what is the mechanism of interchange. In that way we integrate the archaeology that has been called "old style," with the advanced techniques and the focus of the "new," forgetting once and for all the generational "bad-mouthings."

But this can only be accomplished if the archaeologists adopt a scientific humanistic position, or return in other words to anthropology in its full meaning from which we have been separated by a pragmatic criterion, superspecialized, where the application of techniques and experimental methods is worth more than the true reconstruction of the past, and have forgotten in this that, even as in our times, it is the human being who forms and models society.

There is where it seems to me that the archaeologist should apply his capacity and his technical rigor, his role or experience and his analytical sense without forgetting that the living together as human beings and the product of that is in the long run more important.

In this study of the ancient routes, I think that it is not simply a matter of placing areal photographs on a drawing board and analyzing them with steroscopic glasses but the taking off from this point to observe directly what nature has to offer and what man takes or adapts from it. In the end what travels the trails the archaeologist puts on a plan and sums up in graphs are not statistical numbers nor abstract theories, but men, whose commercial impulse or simple spirit of adventure must be captured with the desire to share a little of their desires and the means that encompass their passion.

I would say that what is contemplated and analyzed with the mind must be felt and seen by the feet.

REFERENCES

Alvarado 1934
Anonymous *Noticia topográfica* . . .
    Jucio levantado . . .
    Sobre el estado . . .
    Mapa correspondiente . . .
    Relación de la visita . . .
Ballinas 1951
Becerra 1930
Blom 1956
Blom and Duby 1957
Castañón Gamboa 1953, 1954, 1956, 1957
Chapman 1959
Cobo 1944
Cortés y Larraz 1958
Díaz del Castillo 1960
Drucker 1948
Gage 1946
Gall 1963
García de Bargas y Rivera 1774
Helbig 1964
Hellmuth 1970
Kingsborough 1831
Lee 1970
Lorenzo 1955
Lothrop 1961
Lowe 1959
Navarrete 1960, 1966a, 1966b, 1968a, 1968b
Navarrete and Lee 1969
Paniagua 1876
Pineda 1952
Ponce 1875
Sánchez 1915
Stone 1932
de la Torre 1944–45
Vedia 1946
Villagutierre y Soto-Mayor 1933
Waibel 1946
Woolrich 1948

9. TRADE AND TRAVEL IN PREHISPANIC OAXACA
by
Hugh G. Ball and Donald L. Brockington

Trade is considered by many to have played an important role in the development of Mesoamerican civilization and yet little attention has been paid to the basic elements of this aspect of the Mesoamerican continuum. The nature of the goods traded, how they were moved, where they moved to and from, and the routes over which they moved have not been given the deserved attention. We shall consider the nature of these variables and then consider possibilities for future research. First, we define *trade* as: the movement of goods (and services) between people and over space. This allows consideration of the institution of tribute as trade, something we find especially desirable because of the quantity of data available and because it places no restriction on the use of those data.

Second, routes are considered pathways between two points in space over which goods were moving from one to the other or in both directions. Determination of the points is done on the basis of documented statements but for the most part we shall not consider locations of disputed places or points. Actual routes are inferred by study of maps such as the tactical pilotage charts published by the U.S. government in 1936 and 1967 (Anonymous 1936, 1967). These show networks of footpaths that cross the area. As Sauer (1932: 1) has pointed out, the footpaths that cross any area today go ". . . as direct as the terrain, the need of food and drink in route, and reasonable security permitted, and were fixed by long experience as the best way of traversing a particular stretch of country." This appears to be particularly true of areas where penetration of modern roads and railroads has not been great. Borah (1954: 26) in this regard also noted that in many cases the Spaniards used pre-existing trails for their roads, making changes only where it was impossible for wheeled vehicles to follow paths designed for use by foot traffic and improving trails by widening and strengthening them and bridging rivers when necessary. Thus, colonial roads, where observable, in many cases are good approximations of indigenous routes. Also, in some cases distances between points or places are given in terms of leagues in some geographical descriptions collected by the Crown in the sixteenth century.

Third, conditioning variables play a very large role in the understanding of the nature of Mesoamerican trade. First and foremost, the lack of domesticated beasts of burden and wheeled transport placed a primary constraint on the movement of goods in inland areas. Because of these factors movement of goods in Mesoamerica depended on human bearers who were decidedly limited as to the amount they could be required to carry. This also limited the speed with which goods could be moved. Much controversy surrounds the question of the quantities of things that could be carried and how far a merchant caravan could travel in one day. Our studies have not produced any definitive answer, but some trends do show. Most sources relating to the conquest and life before the advent of the Spaniards indicate that definite limits were placed on what an individual bearer was required to carry. It usually is stated that the load was two *arrobas*, or about fifty pounds (Díaz del Castillo 1956: 89; Borah and Cook 1958: 11), but that varied with the product being carried. For example, cacao was supposed to be carried in loads of 24,000 beans which would have weighed 67.83 pounds, if it can be assumed that a cacao bean would average the same weight then as now (Millon 1955: 142). There also appear to have been some spacial variations, in particular between the Yucatan-Guatemala area and the Mexican part of Mesoamerica. Luis Aguilar, Cortés's translator, when captured by Maya slavers after being shipwrecked, was required to carry a load heavy enough to make him sick after traveling four kilometers (Roys 1943: 35). More or less contemporary reports from that area describe loads of one hundred and one hundred and fifty pounds (McBride 1947: 73;

Gann 1918: 7). Because various testimonies and documents for the Mexican part of Mesoamerica indicate that there was a definite limit to what might be carried by an individual and that in a caravan loads should be more or less equal (Zorita 1942; Sahagún 1969: 26; Scholes and Adams 1957; Torquemada 1723: 225; Acosta 1940), we feel that the weight carried by a bearer ranged from fifty to seventy-five pounds.

Water transportation, where it was possible, would have circumvented the above problem to some extent but it presents one nearly insurmountable problem to the investigator: the near total silence on this subject by the Spanish chroniclers. On the basis of physical geography, one would expect transportation by boat to have been more important on the Veracruz coastal plain and in areas drained by the Candalaria, Grijalva, and Pasión rivers than on the Pacific coast of Oaxaca where the rivers are unsuitable for such use. This is borne out by Cortés (1971: 334–47). Sea transportation probably was important on both coasts. While evidence for this concerns mainly the Gulf and Caribbean areas, it is difficult to believe that the kinds of canoes described by Columbus' son did not exist on the Pacific coast as well, especially since such are in use at present (María Jorrín, personal communication) and are illustrated in the reverse of the *Codex Nuttall* (p. 75). Dalgren de Jordan concludes that the lip-canoe of the Maya also was present on the Oaxaca coast (1954: 240–41).

The last consideration is the kind of evidence to be used in building a picture of trade routes in Oaxaca before the arrival of the Spaniards. Because of their interest in trade and travel, the Spaniards wrote much about it, but the sources are subject to differing interpretations and so must be used critically. By comparing several sources which describe different aspects of the same event, one usually can derive a reasonably accurate picture of the nature of the event in question. We shall assume that exchange patterns during the first thirty years after Spanish contact customarily reflect the older Mesoamerican patterns. This assumption may be less valid for the Aztec exchange sphere, which collapsed more

rapidly than interaction spheres less affected by the catastrophe of the Conquest. For example, most of Oaxaca accepted the Spanish presence without major opposition. Hence, Mixtec, Mazatec, and Zapotec institutions exhibited considerable continuity during the early Spanish contact period (Taylor 1972). Of necessity, our view will be primarily synchronic; we are unable to deal with anything earlier than the late Postclassic, except when there are some bits of archaeological evidence.

At the time of the Conquest there were three major exchange systems operating in Oaxaca: 1) the Aztec tribute-trade collection network organized around imperial military and paramilitary-Pochteca coercive collection, carriage, and distribution; 2) an alternative northwest-southeast Pacific coastal exchange system organized around a growing metal and luxury goods economy and politically integrated by a loose alliance of powerful nationstates; and, 3) a symbiotic interaction between two ecotomes, the highlands to an intermediate region and the coastal lowlands. Besides facilitating the highland-lowland symbiosis, this system served to interdigitate systems 1 and 2. For each system we shall look first at principal routes and the political-military-diplomatic ties that map such routes and then will briefly discuss principal goods and services that flowed along routes of each interaction system.

The Aztec Interaction Sphere

Brundage has provided an excellent discussion of the term "Aztec" (1972: 1–19). We use the term here in an emic and etic sense. That is, emically there were several groups operating out of the Meseta Central who laid claim to being Aztecs. Ethnically the term describes a cluster of Nahuatl speaking, highly organized communities settled after the fall of the Toltec empire. The Aztec combine grew slowly over a period of about seventy-five years from A.D. 1375 to 1450. The principal actors during this period of growth were Atzcapotzalco, Tlacopan, Texcoco, Tlateloco, and Tenochtitlan. Texcoco and Tlateloco opened the way for the penetration by groups from the Valley of Mexico into the Puebla-Oaxaca mountain states. Tlateloco took the critical town Quautinchan in 1438 and Texcoco, acting as the dominant partner of the Triple Alliance, led the way in making the critical conquests of Tepeanac, Coixtlahuaca, Tehuacan, and Tuxtepec. This opened a route along the edge of the Meseta Central in the second ecotome for access to the coastal plains on both sides of Mesoamerica (Gibson 1971: 384–85). The towns along this route, generally glossed as Nonohualca, had been under Nonohualca-Toltec and Cuautinchan-Chichimec domination and were among the most populous and highly developed trading powers in early late Postclassic Mesoamerica. Generally they were located just off the southern edge of the central plateau. These towns had served as integration centers for dependencies situated on the principal trade routes to southern Mesoamerica.

To define these routes we give consideration to three basic factors. First, there were "ties of emnity." That is, there were communities, Aztec or otherwise, that were opposed to the Triple Alliance and not conquered by it, such as Huexotzingo, Tlaxcala, and Cholula, situated across other possible trade routes and effectively barring Triple Alliance polities from using such routes. Second, using the Aztec tribute lists we consider the location of towns in a tribute province with regard to the ease of access to the central town of each province or the desired destination. Third, corroboration for hypothesized routes is sought in the nature of the tribute exacted from specific towns along the routes.

In beginning a venture from the Valley of Mexico the Aztec states were obliged to avoid certain areas that might have been chosen in preference over the ones actually used because enemies, the Huexotzinca and Tlaxcalans, effectively blocked their use. This forced the Triple Alliance to use the route through Chalco and Morelos to Izúcar de Matamoros. According to the map published by Barlow (1949), the parts of the Culhua-Mexica empire that fell within the area under consideration are (listed by the name of the collection center or garrison town as established by the Empire) Tuxtepec, Tlaxiaco, lished by the Empire) Tuxtepec, Tlaxiaco,

Coixtlahuaca, Cuilapan, and parts of Tepeacac. In the middle of these "provinces" (see Barlow [1949: 2] for a discussion of this term) and in apparent cooperation with the Empire, was the Lordship of Teotitlan del Camino which was not paying tribute to the Empire. It appears to have participated in the *pochteca* complex of ritual observances (compare Paso y Troncoso 1905, Vol. 4, p. 219 with Sahagún 1969, Vol. 3, pp. 43–45), particularly the slave trade, the mark of the highest *pochteca* group.

Two major long distance routes connect Tenochtitlan with these "provinces." Both begin with the Chalco-Amecameca-Cuautla-Izúcar de Matamoros road out of the Valley of Mexico. At Matamoros the road becomes problematical because there are no direct statements about it. However, if one consults the list of towns included in the province of Tepeacac, two very clear tendencies can be noted. First, there are towns strung along the border that served as a frontier line with the Tlaxcalteca who were at constant war with both the Tepeaca and Culhua-Mexica as well as the rest of the Triple Alliance. Second, the first feasible route below this border, according to maps consulted, is marked by a string of towns on the list of member towns in the province. These are Izucan, Necoxtla, Epatlan, Teopantlan (changed to Totolepec since 1936?), Huehuetlan, Tecali, and Tepeaca. This list is a compilation with actual routes taken from the 1936 chart which shows footpaths; Mexican maps only show dirt roads.

After Tepeaca was conquered by the Culhua-Mexica, part of its required tribute was food and housing for merchants passing through its area and service as a "free port" maket for trade between the coastal plain and highland zone around the town.

From Tepeaca the road goes through Tecamachalco and Tetzoyocan in the Tepeaca province and Tehuacan, Ajalpan, Zinacatepec, Coxcatlan, and Nanahuatipan and reaches Teotitlan del Camino without encountering major barriers. The road then turns north and east into the Mazatec mountains, some of the most rugged terrain in the area, and onto the Veracruz coastal plain ending at Tuxtepec on the Santo Domingo River shortly before it joins with the Tonto River to form the Papaloapan River.

There is little specific information about how traders proceeded until leaving the bounds of the Kingdom of Teotitlan but the subsequent route probably was through towns in the province of Tochtepec (present day Tuxtepec). Only one town, Ojitlan, which is on the plain and near the Santo Domingo, appears on the tribute list. Today, because of terrain, there is only one major route through the Mazateca. It goes through Teotitlan, Huautla de Jiménez, San Miguel Huatla, Coatzapan, Ayautla, Jalapa de Díaz, Ojitlan and, finally, Tuxtepec.

From Tuxtepec Aztec merchants took two roads, one to Xicalango and the other to Xoconusco, both through territories of peoples hostile to the Triple Alliance. Those peoples occasionally decided that goods carried by merchants were worth expropriating in spite of the merchants' objections. Sahagún's description of this part of the journey dwells on the dangers. The trip to Xicalango is described by Sahagún in the sketchiest of terms and, though evidence is inconclusive, we suggest the possibility that the rest of the trip to Xicalango was by boat rather than overland. Tuxtepec is located on the edge of a major river that empties into the Gulf of Mexico and Xicalango was located in an ideal place for sea trade in which it was heavily involved. According to Gillmor (1964), the Aztecs held Coatzacoalcos, the logical coastal provisioning station between the Papaloapan River and Anahuac Sicalango. Also, the Aztec *barrio* in Xicalanco was sending shiploads of goods around the peninsula of Yucatan to Naco and probably beyond (Stone 1972; Scholes and Roys 1968). A quick look at the problems faced by Cortés will give the reader some idea of the problems of foot travel by the overland route (Cortés 1971: 342–63). The other fork of the road crossed the Isthmus to Tehuantepec and then continued to points beyond. For a discussion of these in relation to the communities in Oaxaca, see below.

The second route from Izúcar de Matamoros is that connecting Tenochitlan with the Mixteca and Valley of Oaxaca. The first town conquered by the Aztecs in this area was Coaxtlahuaca which can be reached via Izúcar along a route which closely approximates the path of the Panamerican highway. Towns along the route are Izúcar, Tonala (listed by Barlow 1949 as being on the route where it crosses the Atoyac River but is not on the maps we consulted), Acatlan, Petlaltzingo, Chila, Icxitlan (Ixtlan), Tamazulapan, Tejupan, and Coixtlahuaca. Tonala and Acatlan were in the province of Yoaltepec. Tonala did not pay tribute and may have been only required to help merchants on their way and to allow tribute collectors to pass unhindered, as Petlaltzingo was. To reach Tlachquiauco (Tlaxiaco), today one follows the above route to Tamazulapan where the road turns south passing through Tamazulapan, Yolomecatl, Huamelupan, and Tlaxiaco. This is the shortest visible route from the above road to Tlaxiaco but because of paucity of other towns in the tribute lists, there is no good pattern and our argument is weak.

Attempts to determine the route to the Cuilapan province are not satisfactory. While other routes may have existed, the most probable follows the path taken by the Mexico City-Oaxaca rail line for most of its way. The route follows the described road from Izúcar to Teotitlan del Camino and then proceeds down the Mixteca Cañada to Tecomavaca, Quiotepec, Cuicatlan, Tomellin (here leaving the valley of the Quiotepec River), Dominquillo, Nacaltepec, Sedas (at the edge of the Valley of Oaxaca), Telixtlahuaca, Huitzo, Etla, San Jose Mogote and Oaxaca (where there was a Culhua-Mexica garrison), Xoxocotlan, and Cuilapan.

The other route into the Valley of Oaxaca area would follow the road to Coixtlahuaca and Tejupan and then go by way of Teposcolula, Yanhuitlan, Nochixtlan, Sosola (which had an Aztec garrison), and into the Valley of Oaxaca at Sedas. Evidence for this route is somewhat better than for the others. Of the towns listed on the route from Izúcar to Chilapan, five in a row—Tonala, Acatlan, Petlaltzingo, Chila, and Icxitlan—gave as tribute only food and weapons to "armies" passing through their territories. Three towns are listed as being garrisoned — Coixtlahuaca, Sosola, and Oaxaca. Since the *pochteca* were accorded the status and privileges of knights of the army (Sahagún 1969, Vol. 2; Gillmor 1964), it may be that merchants were taking advantage of this resource to ease their trips through the region.

At the ends of the three roads already described — roads to Tuxtepec, Coixtlahuaca and Cuilapa — lie other paths to the Soconusco and the Chiapas-Guatemala highlands. The possibilities of reaching Chiapas-Guatemala and Soconusco via tribute towns (which are listed by Barlow [1949] and said not to be paying actual tribute but only required not to molest Culhua-Mexica traders operating in their areas) will only be mentioned here because the destinations fall outside the scope of this paper. The tribute towns in Chiapas all are close to the Grijalva River which would allow most of the trip to be made by boat, at least to Tecpatan. One could then proceed along the river course for a way before crossing central Chiapas into Soconusco, an admittedly difficult route.

Tehuantepec may be reached either via the Tuxtepec route or through the Valley of Oaxaca. From the Tuxtepec region the first part of the trip could be accomplished by traveling down the Papaloapan River to the Gulf and then going up the Coatzalcoalcos River; in the same manner Cortés used to bring shipbuilding materials to Tehuantepec and Huatulco (Moorhead 1949). An alternative would be to travel overland to Jaltepec. There are two Jaltepecs on consulted maps, both on rivers easily reached by way of the Papaloapan and Coatzalcoalcos Rivers. Jaltepec Candayo is on the tip of the Jaltepec River, a tributary of the Coatzacoalcos, and therefore is less likely. Jaltepec is on the Trinidad River, a tributary of the Papaloapan. This town not only is easier to reach than Jaltepec Candayo but closer to the next towns listed by Barlow — Quetzaltepec, Itzcuintepec (in the Mixe mountains) and Jalapa del Marquís in the Tehuantepec River valley. From this last point, travelers may have passed down the river valley to Tehuantepec,

then to Juchitan and along the Pacific coast to Soconusco. The distance from Tuxtepec to Jaltepec or Jaltepec Candayo is great and with so much overland travel one would expect the Culhua-Mexica to have conquered some towns along the way and possibly to have garrisoned them as had been done elsewhere. Again, the evidence is suggestive but inconclusive.

The other route for reaching Tehuantepec is from the Valley of Oaxaca through the Mixería to Nejalpa on the Tehuantepec River and then on down the valley to Jalapa and on to Tehuantepec. It is a moot question whether or not the Culhua-Mexica had conquered Tehuantepec. They say they did and the Tehuantepecanos say they did not. Regardless, the mentioned routes are the "best ways" of reaching Tehuantepec. Further evidence for these routes exists in the form of the Zapotec "fort" of Guiengola which is on the west bank of the Tehuantepec River about four kilometers from the city and on a mountain side where mountains begin to constrict the valley. At several places spaced about the edge of the site are lookouts from which one can see for enormous distances up the river and even all the way to the Pacific coast (personal observation, H.G.B.). Burgoa (1934) states that the wall around Guiengola reached to Jalapa, doubtlessly an exaggeration but rather describing use of the natural terrain for preventing a flanking maneuver over the mountains along the sides of the river. It also would be possible to travel by boat down the Tehuantepec River from Jalapa, even in the dry season (personal communication, Thomas MacDougal). This route may have been used as early as 1000 B.C. for transporting marine shells into the Oaxaca Valley (Flannery et al. 1967: 451).

There are many other minor routes to Tehuantepec. Both the Mixe and Chontal came to Tehuantepec to get salt from works near Salina Cruz (Paso y Troncoso 1905, Vol. 4, p. 26). This still is a common Mixe practice.

The goods the Aztecs were carrying to these provinces included obsidian knives and lancets, needles and rattles, alum stone, grain, red ochre, and rabbit fur yarn (Sahagún 1969:

30–31). In return, they sought exotic textiles, gold dust, amber, a variety of precious and semi-precious stones, cacao, worked gold, and a great variety of feathers (Acosta Saignes 1945; Scholes and Roys 1968; Sahagún 1969; Barlow 1949; Chadwick 1966; Berlin 1947; Millon 1955).

The West Mexican-South Coast Combine Connection

The second great exchange network that operated in the fifteenth and early sixteenth century has been defined by Molloy and Ball (in prep.). Much less is known about this interaction sphere than about that of the Aztecs. The Combine is thought to have been characterized by the distribution of copper money axes (possibly an exchange tradition developed in Ecuador) and by a vigorous trade in other metal and tropical luxury goods. At present we can only outline briefly the interactions of this loosely allied economic conglomerate. The Combine included strong nation-states: the Tarascan Empire, the Yope state, the Tututepec mini-empire, the Tehuantepec kingdom, and the Chiapanec kingdom. It involved both direct and bridge-step exchange systems.

The Chiapanec carried out vigorous trade with linguistically related groups in Xoconusco and Nicaragua (Navarrete 1966: 5–7) and held in fief most of the Zoque towns on the Grijalva River (Scholes and Roys 1968: 33). In turn, the Zoque carried out extensive trade with the entrepôts of Anahuac Xicalango, Cimatan, Xicalango, and Acalan (Scholes and Roys 1968: 33). Burgoa discusses the friendship that existed between the Chiapanec and Tehuantepec (1934, Vol. 1, pp. 343–45). Navarrete details the trade in luxury goods between Tehuantepec and the Chiapanec (1966: 25–26).

Miahuatlan apparently participated in the Combine but presents an unusual situation because of having multiple alliances. Located in a large valley immediately south of the Valley of Oaxaca, it was a major market center and possible free port. Recent excavations there encountered a Postclassic shell-working station which suggests that Miahuatlan also

may have been engaging in manufacturing (Brockington 1973). It served as an exchange center for Teozapotlan, Tehuantepec, the Chiapanec, Suchixtepec, Guatulco, and Tututepec. Of these, Guatulco was a major port for long distance trade, presumably at least part of it by sea (Paso y Troncaso 1905, Vol. 4, pp. 213–52).

The Yope are said to share linguistic connections with peoples in Nicaragua (Radin 1933: 1; Harvey 1971). The Lienzo of Jucutacato, as interpreted by Jiménez Moreno (1947) and Chadwick (1971), depicts the presence of Oaxacan prospectors and metalsmiths who may have developed and later partially controlled the Tarascan copper trade. Furthermore, the Tarascans created a special organization for dealing with presumably foreign metal, feather, and precious stone traders (Craine and Reindorp 1970: 15). Molloy and Ball (n.d.) speculate, but cannot demonstrate, that coastal Oaxaca principalities, especially Tututepec, were implicated in long-distance sea trade with ports on the coasts of Guerrero, Colima, and Nayarit on one hand and Tehuantepec, Guatemala, and Central America on the other. Recent archaeological investigations on the western end of the Oaxaca coast encountered a distinctive early Postclassic polychrome pottery virtually identical to some found by Joseph Mountjoy on the Nayarit coast (personal observation, D.L.B.). In addition, at or near Amapa at the southern edge of the Nayarit coastal plain long distance trade must either have been transshipped overland into the interior or shipped by water around Colima to Guerrero, the south coast of Oaxaca, and points further south. Iconography from Amapa includes material that exhibits specific stylistic identities with iconography from Oaxaca (Bell 1971). This strongly suggests that direct sea trade between the Amapa decision node and coastal Oaxaca was present, possibly as early as the Late Classic (Molloy and Ball n.d.).

The principal goods involved in this system were products of bronze technology, utilitarian bronze and copper tools and especially copper money axes (West 1961; Mieghan 1969; Mountjoy 1969; Edwards 1969; and

Root 1946). Other probable luxury commodities handled by the Combine included scarlet macaws and feathers, quetzal birds and feathers, hallucinogenic drugs, and finished textiles. The Combine extended in various ways. For example, Tehuantepec was trading finished textiles to the Chiapanec and accepting cacao in exchange while the Chiapanec were shipping these textiles and others from the Zoque-Acalan region to Xoconusco for more cacao (Navarrete 1966a). This is discussed more completely in Molloy and Ball (n.d.).

Oaxaca Inland Highland-Lowland Symbiosis

A highland-lowland symbiosis was a crucial factor in the economy of Oaxaca. In Late Preclassic times ceramics apparently were traded from Bajos de Chila into Monte Alban (Brockington 1969: 35–36), probably up the valley of the Manialtepec River into its headwaters and then more or less following the present road between Oaxaca and Puerto Escondido. Judging from Late Preclassic and Early and Middle Classic similarities, there seems to have been another route connecting the coast around the Verde River and the central valley of Oaxaca, perhaps along the river canyon. By Late Classic times this system apparently collapsed, to be revived in modified form during the Late Postclassic (personal observation, D.L.B.).

Except for its eastern third, the coast was dominated and closely controlled by Tututepec during the Late Postclassic. Tututepec maintained active relations with highland Mixteco groups and was intruding into the valleys of Miahuatlan and Oaxaca (Davies 1968). This system was mediated in several ways. Caso documents a pattern of royal marriages linking Tututepec to mountain principalities in and around Tilantongo (1949). Also, Burgoa (1934) states that Achiutla, part of the Aztec-controlled Tlaxiaco tribute province, was required to take the "fruits" of their town to a fair at Putla where Tututepec took what was necessary for its needs. In addition, the distribution of the coast dialect of Mixteco is not only along the coast from about modern Río Grande to Guerrero but extends one arm inland to reach Putla. It appears possible that Tututepec was attempting to create a licensed trading center in the ecotome between Tlaxiaco and the coast. Also, it may have been attempting to initiate competition with Miahuatlan, an already highly organized port of trade that was mediating trade with some Aztec principalities. The Triple Alliance became the licensor of Miahuatlan's free port status under Montezuma Xocoyotzin. Miahuatlan also was trading regularly with Tlaxcala, Huezotzingo, and Teotitlan del Camino (Paso y Troncoso 1905, Vol. 4, pp. 127, 215). Tututepec apparently had conquered Miahuatlan and been driven out but was attempting a reconquest when Miahuatlan allied itself with the Aztecs (Barlow n.d.).

Tlaxiaco and Coixtlahuaca were caught in a curiously ambivalent position. On the one hand, they were squeezed between the contending empires of Tututepec and the Aztecs, and, on the other hand, they were able to function as trading ports handling commerce that flowed between the two. Both Tlaxiaco and Coixtlahuaca were required to give large amounts of quetzal feathers to the Aztecs, four hundred and eight hundred bundles respectively (Barlow 1949: 113, 117). The natural distribution of quetzal birds was limited to parts of Chiapas and Guatemala (Bowes 1969: 142), areas probably tied to the West Mexican-South Coast Combine. It seems probable that either Tututepec or Miahuatlan was supplying Tlaxiaco and Coixtlahuaca with this commodity. However, had Miahuatlan been the supplier, one would expect the Aztecs to have extracted tribute of feathers from Cuilapan, Miahuatlan's closest trading partner. Coixtlahuaca also could have been receiving feathers directly from its former dependency, Tuxtepec, or from Veracruz polities not within the Aztec or Tututepec political-exchange spheres. Therefore, we suggest that Tututepec held a monopoly on the quetzel feather market and directly supplied its subordinate trade partners.

A principal element in the highland-lowland symbiosis was cotton, which came from Tututepec, Tehuantepec, and the Port of Alvarado to numerous highland towns to be transformed into finished textiles. At least some highland towns, such as Teotitlan del Camino, Coixtlahuaca, and Tepeacac, were importing raw cotton as well as investing population in the lowland cotton growing market.

Finally, a route for highland-lowland communication probably was along the Copalita River canyon from the eastern Oaxaca coast into the Miahuatlan valley. Not only was this route used during early Colonial times as well as today, but it would have been the most convenient passage from Huatulco, an important center engaged in seaborne trade, to Miahuatlan and the Valley of Oaxaca. At modern San Miguel del Puerto is a large Late Classic and Early Postclassic site consisting of agricultural and habitation terraces on steep mountain slopes above the river canyon. The location in such a difficult place seems odd but would make sense if people were established there in order to control a trade route. Further, there is evidence of cultural and trade connections with western Tabasco (Brockington 1974).

Conclusion

We have hypothesized and superficially shown that there were three major exchange systems in late Postclassic Oaxaca. The first was operated by the Aztec states and linked the Meseta Central with southern Mesoamerica. The second was controlled by powerful nation-states in west Mexico and the southern Oaxaca coast and dealt in metal and luxury goods. The third mediated inland highland coastal-lowland symbiotic exchange and articulated the first two systems.

REFERENCES

Acosta 1940
Acosta Saignes 1945
Anonymous 1936, 1967
Barlow 1949, n.d.
Bell 1971
Berlin 1947
Borah 1954
Borah and Cook 1958
Bowes 1969
Brockington 1969, 1973, 1974
Brundage 1972
Burgoa 1934
Caso 1949
Chadwick 1966, 1971
Codex Nuttall 1902
Cortés 1971
Craine and Reindorp 1970
Dahlgren de Jordan 1954
Davies 1968
Díaz del Castillo 1956
Edwards 1969
Flannery et al. 1967
Gann 1918
Gibson 1971
Gillmor 1964
Harvey 1971
Jiménez Moreno 1947
McBryde 1947
Meighan 1969
Molloy and Ball n.d.
Millon 1955
Moorhead 1949
Mountjoy 1969
Navarrete 1966a
Paso y Troncoso 1905
Radin 1933
Root 1946
Roys 1943
Sahagún 1969
Sauer 1932
Scholes and Adams 1957
Scholes and Roys 1968
Stone 1972
Taylor 1972
Torquemada 1723
West 1961
Zorita 1942

10. CENTRAL MEXICO AS A PART OF THE GENERAL MESOAMERICAN COMMUNICATIONS SYSTEM
by
Jaime Litvak King

Mesoamerica, as does any other large area where diverse cultures have fused to shape a new, distinct whole, depended (and this aspect is vital for the explanation of its operating mechanisms) on the existence of a general trade network capable of being used to carry a constant, multidirectional, quantitatively great flow of people, merchandise, and ideas.

Indeed, the existence of such a web permits the area to be redefined as a territory where normal exchange occurs of articles, traits, and abstract items that are to be found anywhere regardless of the region of their provenance, having gotten there after being transported in ways congruent to the state of the network existing at the time of operation. Even occasional or catastrophic events like invasions or migrations occurred and were diffused along its lines.

For such a network to exist, it has to satisfy a number of requirements. Some of these are the presence of a series of markets, functioning at both intra- and interregional levels, that would permit the disposal of products in or out of their place of origin. These would fit within the network as distribution centers with values of their own that depended on their position along its lines. Also necessary are various sites for links and warehouses for the storage and retrieval of the trade items, some of them probably the same as those above, and several large stops or regional centers serving in the capacity of zonal accelerators for the flow of goods. Even the lines in the network have to comply with minimi, such as geographical conditions like slope, terrain, availability of water, and the presence of a hinterland capable of supporting services and maintenance of the route.

Historical conditions that permitted or curtailed the use of a route or made it preferable to or less convenient than others are, of course, important. Equally so are the economic, political, and military circumstances that affected a given route. Finally, the avail-

ability of alternative courses and their relative advantages also have to be considered. The general effect is that of a two-curve graph, similar to a supply and demand curve; it could very well be computed as the set of logarithmic curves that show the advantages and disadvantages of each possible course with confluence values for each one used.[1]

The former conditions define a situation whereby such a network, though permanent, cannot be said to be stable, since each link and line is affected by constantly changing circumstances, creating therefore a constantly dynamic, always different set of conditions that respond to impulses that modify the network's points of gravity, its inertia, the amount of flow through its components, and, therefore, its overall equilibrium. Local and regional responses to these alterations depend on conditions such as the area's position along the lines, its distance to the main links and foci, the competition from alternate routes, and, of course, other events, some of its own generation. These modifications of the network, when of a large enough magnitude, are part of the process that produced the great changes that affected the whole sequence for the superarea, and that are reflected in our periodification of the historical continuum.

One of the critical regions within Mesoamerica is the one known as Central Mexico. Geographically it is, as Wolf (1959) describes, a pyramid containing a series of chambers, each separated from its neighbours by mountain partitions. These chambers are tiered, from a higher level that comprises the Valleys of Mexico, Puebla, and Toluca, through a middle line formed by the Tenancingo region, the Valley of Morelos, the Atlixco zone, and

---

[1] This type of curve, normally applied to supply and demand in economics is also capable of representing other situations since its content is the showing of contrasting characteristics as opposed, inversely bent, hyperboloid curves with a meeting point that denotes optimum choice at given conditions.

the Jalapa-Orizaba area, as well as the Bajío to the north — not a part of cultural Mesoamerica but important for its development — to the coastlines of the Pacific and the Gulf of Mexico (Fig. 18).

The region is structured by its large mountain ranges, mainly the Sierras Madres and the Eje Volcánico as well as by smaller heights that, although part of the former, merit special mention, like the Ajusco and the North Guerrero mountains. Rivers divide the area into basins, rearranging it in an altogether different configuration whereby part of the Valley of Toluca is linked to the Bajío by the Lerma, and another with Tenencingo, Morelos, Atlixco, and a portion of Puebla are joined by the Balsas. The rest of Puebla and the Jalapa terrace drain into the Gulf via the Papaloapan. The basin of Mexico remains alone as an endorheic basin with a central lake system (Humboldt 1810).

Communication within Central Mexico is not unobstructed. Apart from differences in height and separation by non-navigable rivers, the mountain chains divide the components and offer only limited access from one compartment to the others. These passes have been important throughout Mesoamerican prehistory and were recorded in some instances by either Lienzo maps or chroniclers in the sixteenth century. Many colonial and even modern roads have used the same general routes of passage since the layout of the network would not have changed appreciably unless regional points of equilibrium changed in a considerable way, an event that hasn't occurred in colonial or modern Mexico.

Reviewing the possibilities of communication within different components, we shall start with the Valley of Mexico, where the presence of the great central Lake Tetzcoco has made authors think of it as a large, open, continuous system. Unfortunately, pretty as it is, this idea is erroneous and has led many to the wrong conclusions regarding historical developments in the zone. The lakes in the valley constituted a series of bodies of water, rather than one, with swampy areas, shallows, eddies, hidden rocks, zones overgrown with *tule*, etc., that made some places and courses

impassable and others preferable; this created a directed system, rather than an open one, with known, albeit changing routes, junctions, and limits well worth controlling for the inhabitants of the valley (Litvak King 1970a). Furthermore, the crossing of such a lake and the time it took to do it made islands in the center very important places and, from this, market and exchange locales. Thus the location of Tenochtitlan-Tlatelolco settlement could have been due to less than — or more than — divine orders. Other important centers, like Huitzilopochco, Coyohuacan, Tola, etc., can be shown to be related to junctions, landing spots, and other features of the navigable waterways.

Restricted to a given set of waterways, and because of its shape and zonification, the lake would serve most efficiently in east-west crossings while being relatively clumsy for north-south routes. These last would have been mostly overland, skirting the waterline, thus explaining the presence of chains of sites, from Tepexpam through Tetzcoco, Huexotla, Cuautlihchan, Culhuacan, and Itztapalapan to Xochimilco and Chalco, along the eastern shoreline, and from Ehecatepec to Atzcapotzalco, Tlacopan, Atlacuihuayan (Tacubaya), Mixcoac, Tizapan, and the Ajusco towns on the western shoreline. It is interesting to note that political divisions of the valley before the emergence of Mexico as a unifying power effectively carved up these routes into sections, each controlled by its main town, and that wars of conquest were carried on along them (Sanders and Price 1968, Chap. 1) in a north-south direction, extending Atzcapozalco's domain to include all except the southernmost part.

The northern portion of the valley lies within easy reach of the Tula region and, either directly or from there, communicated with the Mezquital and the general direction of the Otomí area. The northeastern part, in its turn, was open to the Valley of Puebla by its easiest access, through the low hills east of Tetzcoco; both were gates to the Tepeapulco-Apam zone that was also open to Puebla through Tlaxcala, although geographic and later cultural conditions made these routes not continuous in their use.

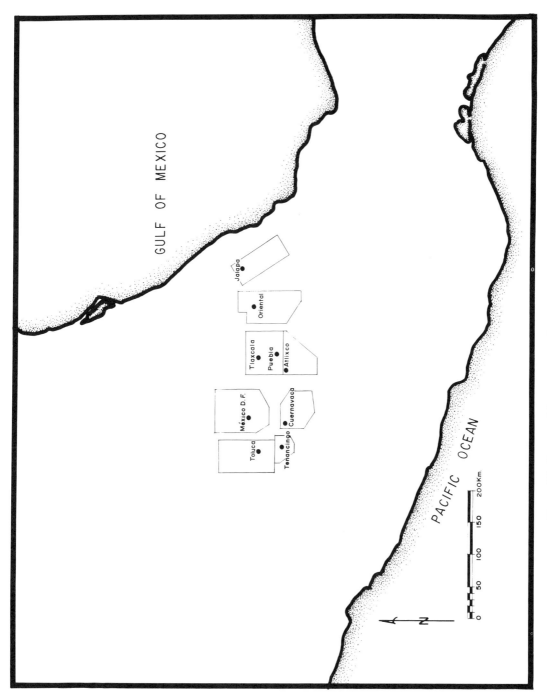

Figure 18. CENTRAL MEXICO AND ITS SEMI-INDEPENDENT REGIONS

Morelos, bordering the Valley of Mexico to the south and separated from it by the Ajusco comprises also several systems. The main one is formed by the Cuernavaca ravines, following a north-to-south direction, sometimes with bridges to ease passage where possible (Grove 1970). South of it, through Xochitepec, Alpuyeca, and Puente de Ixtla to Amacuzac, a plain, descending in height to less than 1,000 m. above sea level, links the region with North Guerrero. This route was used in historic times by the Aztecs and, as the Camino Real to Acapulco, was travelled over by explorers like Gemelli Carreri in the late seventeenth century and Humboldt in the nineteenth century.

West of this region and depending on it for communication with the rest of Morelos lies the valley of Xochicalco, open to the east and with limited passage to the west, north, and south, but close to the Iztapan-Tonatico area. Its communication with the latter would have been made via the Tetecala-Coatlan gap, with Chalma-Malinalco via Cuentepec, and with Cuernavaca by the alternate road through Tetlama as well as to North Guerrero through Coatetelco and the Tembembe River course (Litvak King 1970a).

The eastern part of the Valley of Morelos, the Cuautla region, is a flat plain also descending in height from north to south, and it is divided from the Cuernavaca zone by a smaller chain of mountains, perpendicular to the Ajusco, that have at least two passes, through Yautepec and the Cañón de Lobos, that have been in use historically both as borders and relays, especially the former (Sanders and Price 1968). Cuautla is connected to the Valley of Mexico by the Chalco-Amecameca-Nepantla route and is open to the south and the Balsas River via the Cuautla River basin (Grove 1970). A group of low hills divides it from Atlixco, forming the eastern slope of its basin and from there the terrain rises in height from Izúcar to the Valley of Puebla.

Puebla, to the east of Mexico and separated from it and from North Morelos by the Eje Volcánico in some of its most awesome heights, Popocatepetl and Iztaccihuatl, surrounds Malinche, a large mountain that has histori-

cally separated Puebla proper from Tlaxcala, giving the area two different lines of routes, both east–west. One joins the Valley of Mexico by the pass on the eastern low hills bordering the Valley of Mexico in the Tetzcoco-Tepetlaoztoc-Calpulalpam zone and ending in the high, dry lands near Oriental. The other one, west of Malinche, joined the Valley of Mexico by the precarious and high Paso de Cortés and joined Morelos via Atlixco; it joins Puebla with Tehuacán, where several routes, either by the Mixteca highway line or via the Teotitlan del Camino gap link it with Oaxaca. A route used up to the present, following the Papaloapan River through the Sierra Mazateca, crosses the Sierra Madre to the Gulf coastline.

The Jalapa terrace, after a rather precipitous drop from Puebla, has a general north–south orientation. It is connected to Puebla by the Papaloapan River, the Maltrata and Acultzingo drops and Oriental, through the pass used by Cortés on his way into the central valleys. Many possible ways are open for its connection with the wide, flat, swampy Gulf Coast plain and extensions north up to and beyond the Mesoamerican border, and south, toward the isthmus of Tehuantepec.

Another connection can be drawn from the northern part of the central Veracruz coastal plain into central Mexico: it follows the modern Tuxpan-Papantla-Tulancingo-Pachuca road and leads through practicable routes into the northern part of the valley or, skirting it, to To....

The Toluca region, structured around its greatest height, the Nevado de Toluca, can also be said to be crossed by two routes, both through Tenango and the Tenancingo regions, joining Morelos via the route historically documented and ethnographically still in use, that is, via Chalma[2] and ending just west of Cuernavaca at Tetlama, where it can link up with the Xochicalco Valley or, by a route similar to the one used by Aztec convoys, with

---

[2]This route has been traditionally used for Morelos-originating pilgrimages to Chalma and was used also for the retreat of the massive Huertista forces from Cuernavaca during the Mexican Revolution.

North Guerrero around the Mezcala-Iguala region. Historically this route ended, for political and military reasons, at the Tarascan border in Aztec times. A branch of it, though, continued southward to the Yopi frontier and, flanking it, to the Costa Grande on the Pacific (Litvak King 1971b).

Central Mexico came rather late to the position of an important focus of Mesoamerican culture. Evidence to this effect is present in the Preclassic, where connections with other parts of the superarea show the preeminence of Olmec, Olmecoid, or Olmec-related cultures centering in other regions. The area shows this evidence in sites like Tlatilco and others following the Cuautla River and North Guerrero to the Balsas.

Coe (1968) assigns these sites to a theoretical jade route that joined central Mexico with the southern Gulf Coast, probably through Oaxaca and from there to Puebla and Cuautla somewhere near Chalcatzingo where it would continue (although Coe does not say so explicitly) to the Balsas. It should be noted that the existence of such a route does not explain the presence of Tlatilcoid material in other parts of the area, specifically in West Morelos and Cacahuamilpa (cf. Cuernavaca Museum Exhibit) where it has been found, or, what is more important, in the Valley of Mexico. The former, of course, could be interpreted to be the products of side routes or short terminals of local connections, although this explanation could be too simplistic. More explanation is needed for finds in the Valley of Mexico, especially in view of the place it has been given in Mesoamerican archaeology. It is again possible to postulate the existence of a trade route linking southern Mesoamerica to Guerrero and points west, where jade was obtainable, following a route as proposed by Coe as the central explanation. It is even possible to propose, and this would not conflict with other explanations given (Litvak King 1972), a Morelos-Guerrero-Puebla-Oaxaca axis for the period as an exchange area centered on the Balsas basin, but neither of them clarifies to satisfaction the distribution of Tlatilco materials north of the proposed route.

One possible explanation, demeaning the importance of the Valley of Mexico in the Preclassic, would be the centering of the Tlatilco culture more to the south, somewhere in either East Morelos or West Puebla, with yet another route, linked to the former, going from Morelos to the Valley of Mexico and points north. A possibility for its object would be the obtention of obsidian, probably somewhere in the State of Mexico or Hidalgo. This hypothesis, of course, is even less well supported than the traditional one, but since it relegates Tlatilco to the position of a more or less important waystation rather than that of a principal culture focus, it is the author's opinion that it fits better within the trend pointed at by recent data in giving more emphasis to Morelos vis á vis Tlatilco.[3]

If this idea is found to be acceptable, the changes in settlement in the Late Preclassic and Early Classic show a pattern:

Starting from the probable bow-tie shape of pre-Olmec and early Olmec Mesoamerica, with the knot somewhere in South Veracruz and with wings toward the Balsas basin and Chiapas and Central America — Coe's (1968) jade and cacao routes — the extension of the area to the Valley of Mexico and the north had the effect of extending the exchange zone in that direction, thereby altering its focality by the modification of its central point, in effect making obsolete the geographical advantages of the Olmec metropolitan zone. Attention is called to the fact that the southernmost limits of Olmec, Olmecoid, and Olmec-related artifacts are not very different from the location of the Mesoamerican southern border at any time while, from Preclassic times onward, there seems to be an advance of the exchange area northwards bringing the superarea hub toward that direction. The opening of new regions, particularly northern Puebla, Hidalgo, and north central Veracruz in the east and their own contacts with regions as far as Guerrero in the west,

[3]Ever since Vaillant and Vaillant (1934) suggested that Morelos might have been the focal point for a Tlatilco-like culture this idea has been around and should be taken into account.

furthermore, would bring routes through eastern Morelos and western Puebla into obsolescence, replacing them with alternative routes
through the Valley of Mexico or, more pre-
cariously, through regions north of it and then
through Toluca.

This shift would help explain the rise in
importance of Central Mexico at the end of
the Preclassic, as well as the scarcity of sites
in the eastern Morelos-western Puebla region
for that time.

Another effect of the change in routes
would be the increase in importance of a Bal-
sas-to-Mexico route, and also of another one
from Mexcio to North Veracruz. This seems
to be evidenced by the presence of Gulf Coast
attributes in Teotihuacan, so important that
they led Jiménez Moreno (1958) to propose a
Totonac and Otomi settlement for this site,
and of the *yugo-hacha* finds at Xochicalco
(Saenz 1962) at early dates in the Classic. If
the whole equilibrium of the superarea swung
northward then the West Puebla-East Morelos
zone, linked with a more southern jade route,
would necessarily diminish in importance.

The consolidation of the Classic brings to
the whole of Mesoamerica a new form of focali-
zation that can be described as that of a system with one main focus, Teotihuacan, and
with regional centers oriented toward contact
with it. This situation affects the flow through
the central Mexican system. The Balsas route,
for example, probably increased in its importance through the flow of cacao from Guerrero
that would now be produced nearer the general system's hub and would be given further
emphasis by the existence of a large market,
relatively nearby, for North Guerrero and
Morelos cotton, previously too far away for
economical transport to the metropolis. This
would make control of this route and of the
central and western Valley of Morelos very
important business indeed. Xochicalco seems
to fulfill this role by sitting astride two of the
possible lines: Ixtapan-Tonatico to North
Guerrero and Cuernavaca to Amacuzae. Recent finding of sites related to Xochicalco in
more eastern parts of Morelos seems to indicate that the domain of the site extended fur-

ther than was thought, possibly even to the
control of the Atlixco-to-Morelos pass.

Communications between Teotihuacan and
Oaxaca, apart from the Chalco–East Morelos
route, through swampy areas while passing
through the Valley of Mexico, would probably rely on the Tlaxcala–Puebla–Teotitlan
route. The phenomenal growth of Cholula,
probably a regional center in the Classic,
along this route, is possible proof of this activity. The presence of a number of Oaxaca-
made materials in Teotihuacan also points in
that direction, or at least to the existence of
intense contact between the regions.

The end of the Classic, at least for Central
Mexico, could be ascribed to the overburden-
ing of the communications system. The central nucleus, Teotihuacan, lost control of its
approaches to the general network and, probably due to the growth of Xochicalco, Cholula,
a nascent Tula, and probably Tajin, would
have been reduced to its immediate domain,
thus clearly lacking the necessary elements to
support the great metropolis and finally suc-
cumbing (Litvak King 1970b).

The end of Teotihuacan brought about
what was probably the biggest change in the
Mesoamerican system throughout its whole
sequence. Regional systems, aligned to the
general network, had to be rearranged in completely new directions, both locally and with
relation to the newly important centers. Sites
that were too closely related to exchange with
Teotihuacan and its routes lost importance;
others, new or already existent, more in tune
with the state of the network, acquired it.

The situation, after the fall of Teotihuacan,
points to a complete severing of the web.
Many cuts, resulting from the regionalization
of the network are apparent. There does not
seem to be, for example, a general trade ware
for the period. Some more or less extended
networks remain in operation, like the one in
Toluca-Morelos-North Guerrero, where early
Matlatzinca Brown-on-Cream appears at
Xochicalco in late Phase 5. That the Valley of
Mexico maintained some contact with its
neighbours is shown by the occasional appearance of Coyotlatelco in other regions but

it certainly does not seem to be very solidly linked to the south. If Braniff's idea (Braniff 1966) is correct, it was related more with the north and west, probably through the Hidalgo–Bajío routes.

The severing of the network seems to have affected the West Coast at least as early as it did the central valleys. The Late Classic appearance of metal, not introduced into central Mexico until much later, leads to inferences in that direction; the non-diffusion of hollow, conical or cylindrical-hemispherical supports to the center that, although present in Guerrero at that time, have to wait until they are brought into the nodal area from either the Mixteca or the Toluca-Morelos-Puebla region, also points to the break.

The Gulf Coast seems somehow to have remained linked to the Morelos region, judging at least from architectural traits in Xochicalco at the time. These characteristics, however, need not be a result of constant contact and there does not seem to be any evidence for it in the form of materials present. Indeed, although Xochicalco Phase 5 seems to be the peak of the site's development, it could very well have been anticlimactic in the sense that although it may have dominated its immediate surrounding area and drawn much riches from it, it probably did not extend very much further because of the network gaps. This could have been one of the causes of the fall of Xochicalco. It never again shows up as an important part of the trade network until its valley is conquered by the Aztecs in the fifteenth century. A similar situation, caused by the same circumstances, could have occurred in the north central Veracruz area, with Tajin coming to a similar fate at about the same time.

The reestablishment of the network, in the Early Postclassic, shows a multifocal pattern for the superarea. Although a measure of dominance seems to be held by central Mexico, with its architectural and other traits present in other regions, where, by inference, a penetration is assumed that probably started earlier, general trade wares seem to come generally from the south and southeast rather than from the north or center. The presence of

Silho Fine Orange and Tohil Plumbate pottery in central Mexico shows not only that trade and contact had been reestablished but that its direction was now clearly multiple. One exception is the distribution of Mazapa ware that does show up outside the Valley of Mexico but extends more to the West and North, and reaches the middle Balsas, but does not come even to regions as close to the Valley of Mexico as Morelos in significant quantities. The logical assumption is that its penetration probably followed the Toluca–Balsas route rather than the Morelos channels. This is of course quite congruent with the fact that this ware's zone of concentration is not necessarily the whole Valley of Mexico but rather its northern part, but one cannot help but compare this with the wide distribution of wares like Thin Orange and Teotihuacan monochromes that can be found throughout Mesoamerica. Other regions, like the Toluca-Tenancingo-Morelos-North Guerrero axis are shown to be in operation as units, as witnessed by the Matlazinca-Tlahuica ware distribution. Puebla is apparently connected more with the Mixteca, as shown by the Cholulteca I phase and the Late Classic to Early Postclassic dates for the Mixtec codices. North and central Veracruz seem to be linked along the coastal plain with the south and from it to regions beyond the Isthmus, since Fine Orange and Plumbate are present and even a local imitation of the latter is distributed. There seems to be, indeed, a good possibility that this region, or some place to its immediate south, could be the production center for Thin Orange.

The Late Postclassic brought the restructuring of the general trade network, this time at a less than multifocal state. This was probably preceded by another, shorter breaking down of the system as shown by the lack of a general trade ware corresponding to the Aztec II time span and the limited distribution of this ware. The arrangement after this situation was overcome is bifocal. Its building up, certainly earlier than the Aztec expansion, probably corresponding to the unification of the Valley of Mexico under Tetzcoco and later Azcapotzalco, probably brought the earliest

Aztec III pottery to regions outside it, causing, for example, Tlahuica polychrome to imitate its and Cholula's forms. The Aztec conquest and influence finished the restoration, although it was never accomplished as extensively as in the Classic. Yucatán, for example, seems to be out of it or just marginally in. The other focus is constituted by Michoacán.

Some interesting aspects of the network are to be found for central Mexico at this time. They are probably similar to occurrences in earlier times but there is historical data for this occasion. The renaissance of the Mexico – Morelos – Puebla – Oaxaca – Veracruz route is one, this time due to the effective stopping of the Mexico–Puebla–through–Tlaxcala line by political and military conditions. Another one is the rerouting of contacts between southern and northern Puebla for the same reasons. Contacts between the Costa Grande and the Mixteca Baja, although known to exist, were probably detoured through a line north of the Sierra Madre del Sur or even further because of security.

Some other routes were either modified or strongly influenced by specific conditions. The Balsas route out of the Valley of Mexico seems to be definitely split. One branch, via the Toluca valley and into Malinalco and the region around Teloloapan was important not only economically but also militarily and it was defended by armed convoy and by a line of border forts between the Aztec and Tarascan empires. Another one, to central Guerrero, also affected by military pressures, was routed through central Morelos and Taxco, following the line of Itzcoatl's conquest and was used to

contain the Yopi. Yet another one, through the Cuautla area and into East Guerrero at the Olinala region divided the Yopi from the coastal Mixtec chiefdoms. Emphasis on each branch would be, of course, determined by the necessities of the moment but the presence of weighted options has to be considered as important for all times. The Aztec conquest itself would be affected by the choice.

One other possibility for this epoch is the surmisable development of a trifocal network, with Michoacan, Mexico, and Oaxaca as hubs. The first two would have been political units with factors that might or might not result in their union and the other one would be acting as a supplementary focus caused both by political happenings and by its distance from the nearest center point. This arrangement, very speculative of course, seems a reasonable end to the trend that was developing in Mesoamerica at the time of the Spanish conquest. If that was the case, the Oaxaca focus would have been in a good position to advance into the Maya area and restore the network to the size it was in the Classic period.

REFERENCES

Braniff 1966
M. D. Coe 1968
Grove 1970
Humboldt 1810
Jímenez Moreno 1958
Litvak King 1970a, 1970b, 1971b, 1972
Saenz 1962
Sanders and Price 1968
Vaillant and Vaillant 1934
Wolf 1959

11. TIMED TRAVELS IN TARASCAN TERRITORY: FRIAR ALONSO PONCE IN THE OLD TARASCAN DOMAINS 1586–1587

by
Lawrence H. Feldman

In the second half of the sixteenth century, Friar Alonso Ponce traveled through New Spain on a tour of inspection. Many Spanish officials made similar journeys in the sixteenth century. His travels are unusual only in the meticulously recorded details for otherwise obscure corners of Mesoamerica ("Dos Religiosos" 1873). This short paper focuses on two aspects of Ponce's data, the routes used by him in his travels and the time needed to traverse these routes. The areas under consideration are lands controlled by the Tarascan state in 1520 and the province of "Dávalos" (Fig. 19).

As the second most powerful political unit in pre-Hispanic Mexico, a special interest lies in Tarascan lines of communication. The Tarascan lands traversed by Ponce were, seventy years earlier, the core of that pre-Hispanic empire. The so-called province of Dávalos has no certain political affiliation in those same pre-Hispanic times (its name coming from the De Avalos whose family held it in *encomendero* for many decades). Authorities differ as to whether it was an integral part of the Tarascan hegemony (cf. Medinilla

Alvarado 1944: 283–84 and Brand 1971: 637–38 for conflicting views). However there can be no doubt of its, and the Tarascan land's mentioned above, potential as a link connecting Central Mexico with the peoples of the western borderlands of Mesoamerica. Also, Nayarit, Colima, and Jalisco sites exhibiting Central Mexican influences are known to the archaeologist (i.e., Meighan and Foote 1968; Furst 1965, 1966). One recent study of archaeological artifacts implies a movement of goods along what many centuries later was the route of Friar Ponce (Feldman 1974).

The Spanish friar, then, was traveling on what may have been a very old commercial route. Ponce was, of course, not a merchant; however, his schedule of departures and arrivals allows one to estimate what distance a pedestrian might travel per day, in an era when road conditions had not yet changed drastically from those encountered by the first European explorers. Settlements did change their location somewhat as a result of the dislocations produced by the Spanish Conquest, and at least to that extent the routes followed by Ponce differ from those of the

Table 7. Friar Ponce's Time Table: Citacuaro-Patzcuaro

Town	Arrival Time	Departure Time	Overnight Stop
1. Citacuaro		October 11, 1586	X
2. San Philipe	October 11	October 11	
3. Tuchpan	October 11	October 11	
4. San Marcos	October 11	October 11	
5. Tlaximaloya	October 11	October 14	X
6. Tzitzingareo	October 14	October 14	
7. Tarandacuau	October 14	October 15	X
8. Acambaro	October 15	October 19	X
9. Santa Clara	October 19	October 19	
10. Tzinapicuaro	October 19	October 20	X
11. Querendaro	October 20	October 20	
12. Hindaparapeo	October 20	October 21	X
13. Huruguetaro	October 21	October 21	
14. Tarimbaro	October 21	October 23	X
15. Guayangareo	October 23	October 27/3 A.M.	X
16. San Francisco	October 27	October 27	
17. Patzcuaro	October 27/11 A.M.		

LENGTH OF JOURNEY: 16 days   TIME SPENT ON ROAD: 8 days

earlier periods. The pre-Hispanic lines of communication can only be determined by a cross-checking and synthesis of *all* sources of information. The value of Ponce's timed route is as a basic model against which to test other data and thus is the first stage in the development of a broad synthesis of all available information. Toward this end a map (Fig. 19) is presented here delineating the routes of Friar Ponce and nine tables (Tables 7–15)

scheduling its usage in the years A.D. 1586 and 1587.

ACKNOWLEDGMENT

I would like to thank Dr. H. B. Nicholson for providing a copy of the Ponce material.

Table 8. FRIAR PONCE'S TIME TABLE: PATZCUARO–TARECUATO

Town	Arrival Time	Departure Time	Overnight Stop
1. Patzcuaro		October 31, 1586	X
2. Tacupan	October 31	October 31	
3. Tzintzuntzan	October 31	November 9	X
4. Santa Fe	November 9	November 9	
5. Purenchequaro	November 9	November 11	X
6. San Andrés	November 11	November 11	
7. Tzuptzeo	November 11	November 11	
8. San Francisco	November 11	November 11	
9. Tzacapo	November 11	November 13	X
10. Erongaricuaro*	November 13	November 15	X
11. Pechataro	November 15	November 17	X
12. Sibina	November 17	November 17	
13. Haranza	November 17	November 17	
14. San Pedro	November 17	November 17	
15. San Miguel	November 17	November 17	
16. Santa Clara	November 17	November 17	
17. San Philipe	November 17	November 17	
18. Charapa	November 17	November 18	X
19. Patamba	November 18	November 19	X
20. Tarecuato	November 19		

LENGTH OF JOURNEY: 20 days   TIME SPENT ON ROAD: 8 days

*Time spent at Erongaricuaro includes side trip to Xarequaro.

Table 9. FRIAR PONCE'S TIME TABLE: TARECUATO–CHAPALA

Town	Arrival Time	Departure Time	Overnight Stop
1. Tarecuato		November 26, 1586	X
2. Xaripu	November 26	November 26	
3. Xiquilpa	November 26	November 28	X
4. Matzamitlan	November 28	November 29	X
5. Teocuitlatlan	November 29	December 1	X
6. Xocotepec	December 1	December 2	X
7. Axixique	December 2	December 3	X
8. San Antonio	December 3	December 3	
9. San Buenaventura	December 3	December 3	
10. Chapala	December 3		

LENGTH OF JOURNEY: 8 days   TIME SPENT ON ROAD: 8 days

Table 10. FRIAR PONCE'S TIME TABLE: TLAXOMULCO–ETZATLAN

Town	Arrival Time	Departure Time	Overnight Stop
1. Tlaxomulco		January 7, 1587	X
2. Acatlan	January 7	January 7	
3. Titzapan	January 7	January 7	
4. Cocula	January 7	January 12	X
5. San Martín	January 12	January 13	X
6. Xalco	January 13	January 13	
7. Ayaualulco	January 13	January 13	
8. Etzatlan	January 13		

LENGTH OF JOURNEY: 6 days   TIME SPENT ON ROAD: 2 days

Table 11. FRIAR PONCE'S TIME TABLE: ETZATLAN–ZAPOTITLAN

Town	Arrival Time	Departure Time	Overnight Stop
1. Etzatlan		February 6, 1587	X
2. Ayaualulco	February 6	February 7	X
3. Cocula	February 7	February 9	X
4. Tecolutla	February 9	February 9	
5. Xuchitlan	February 9	February 9	
6. Itztlauac	February 9	February 10	X
7. Ayuquila	February 10	February 10	
8. Autlan	February 10	February 15	X
9. Zacapala	February 15	February 16	X
10. Tuchcacuexco	February 16		

LENGTH OF JOURNEY: 10 days   TIME SPENT ON ROAD: 6 days

Table 12. FRIAR PONCE'S TIME TABLE: COLIMA–TLAXOMULCO

Town	Arrival Time	Departure Time	Overnight Stop
1. Colima		February 20, 1587	X
2. Tonitlan	February 20	February 21	X
3. Tuchpan	February 21	February 26	X
4. Tamazula	February 26	February 27	X
5. Zapotlan	February 27	March 1	X
6. San Sebastián	March 1	March 1	
7. Axomaxac	March 1	March 1	
8. Tzayula	March 1	March 2	X
9. Amacueca	March 2	March 3	X
10. Atoyaque	March 3	March 4	X
11. Techalutla	March 4	March 5	X
12. Tzaqualco	March 5	March 6	X
13. Tlaxomulco	March 6		

LENGTH OF JOURNEY: 15 days   TIME SPENT ON ROAD: 10 days

Table 13. FRIAR PONCE'S TIME TABLE: TLAXOMULCO-ACAMBARO

Town	Arrival Time	Departure Time	Overnight Stop
1. Tlaxomulco		March 12, 1587	X
2. Acatlan	March 12	March 12	
3. Tzaqualco	March 12	March 12	
4. Cocalotlan	March 12	March 12	
5. Teocuitlatlan	March 12	March 14	X
6. Matzamitlan	March 14	March 15	X
7. Xiquilpa	March 15	March 16	X
8. Xaripu	March 16	March 16	
9. Tarequato	March 16	March 17	X
10. Patamba	March 17	March 17	
11. Ucumicho	March 17	March 17	
12. Zapitzirapo	March 17	March 17	
13. Tanaco	March 17	March 17	
14. Sivina	March 17	March 18	X
15. Pechataro	March 18	March 18	
16. Axuno	March 18	March 18	
17. Patzquaro	March 18	March 20	X
18. Guayangareo	March 20	March 21	X
19. Hindaparapeo	March 21	March 21	
20. Tzinapiquaro	March 21	March 21	
21. Santa Clara	March 21	March 21	
22. Acambaro	March 21	March 21	

LENGTH OF JOURNEY: 9 days   TIME SPENT ON ROAD: 8 days

Table 14. FRIAR PONCE'S TIME TABLE: PATZQUARO-URUAPAN

Town	Arrival Time	Departure Time	Overnight Stop
1. Patzquaro		April 6, 1587	X
2. Axuno	April 6	April 6	
3. Viramangaro	April 6	April 6	
4. Tingambato	April 6	April 6	
5. San Andrés	April 6	April 6	
6. Uruapan	April 6		

LENGTH OF JOURNEY: 1 day   TIME SPENT ON ROAD: 1 day

Table 15. FRIAR PONCE'S TIME TABLE: PATZQUARO-MARAUATIO

Town	Arrival Time	Departure Time	Overnight Stop
1. Patzquaro		May 1, 1587	X
2. Guayangareo	May 1	May 1	
3. Hindaparapeo	May 1	May 2	X
4. Tzinapicuaro	May 2	May 2	
5. Acambaro	May 2	May 2	
6. Marauatio	May 3/3.30 A.M.		

LENGTH OF JOURNEY: 2 days   TIME SPENT ON ROAD: 2 days

REFERENCES

Brand 1971
"Dos Religiosos" 1873
Feldman 1974

Furst 1965, 1966
Medinilla Alvarado 1944
Meighan and Foote 1968

12. PREHISPANIC CULTURAL CONTACT ON THE SOUTH-CENTRAL COAST OF NAYARIT, MEXICO

by
Joseph B. Mountjoy

When dealing with possible trade relations in pre-Hispanic West Mexico, one is faced with several dilemmas. Not the least of these is that trade in the sense of the act or business of exchanging commodities by barter or sale is extremely difficult to prove archaeologically because one must demonstrate that some system of exchange was in operation. Implicit in this is the elucidation of what was traded for what — often falling into the realm of "best guess" work in archaeology. Also, within the context of existent and emerging tribute states at the time of the Conquest, a one-way flow of goods could not fall within the definition of trade, yet this may have been the major vehicle for the flow of goods in some cases. Insofar as trade can be used to mean commerce, in the sense of the buying and selling of commodities on a large scale, the picture becomes even more complicated because it is quite difficult to infer large scale buying or selling from archaeological data. Items may travel through space for a variety of reasons other than trade or commerce. For example, raiding and looting, religious conversion, exogamy, and gift giving can all result in a significant geographical dispersion of material items. In sum, it is difficult to tell when items are *exchanged*, let alone the quantity involved or the mechanism in operation.

Given the above limitations, it would seem best, when dealing with pre-Hispanic West Mexican data, initially to limit the inquiry to evidence of contact, and proceed from there possibly to infer the nature of the contact. Unfortunately, archaeological deduction at this level faces several difficulties. So frequently the argument for or against contact is reduced to a professional judgment on the order of "how like is like," which often stimulates lengthy dialogues between colleagues on the relative merits or non-merits of the supposed "similarities." Some of this may be avoided by seeking relief in the haven of technological analysis which claims to trace such things as the probable source of obsidian used for tools or clay found in potsherds. But, to date, such methods have not yet seen wide enough application in Mesoamerica to test their full potential or illuminate all possible sources of error, and unfortunately such studies are really in their infancy in West Mexico.

There are of course other ways of approaching the problem of cultural contacts. One of these is to consider the possible "natural" geographical routes over which contact could, or most probably would, have occurred. This is not entirely satisfactory, as man may not always follow the route of least geographical resistance or the shortest distance between two points. We have difficulty, furthermore, in assessing the nature of cultural versus geographical barriers to certain types of interaction when working solely with archaeological data. Also, some contact, such as long-distance sea travel, may presuppose a certain level of technological development that may not be readily evidenced in archaeological remains. In sum, having a seemingly "natural" geographical route or barrier cannot be automatically taken as evidence for contact or non-contact.

Another approach is to look into the natural resource potential of a given area to find what sort of commodities might have been available for export, or missing and therefore necessarily imported. This is rather commonly done, and is usually reduced to some argument that a particular area had a lot of salt, or feathers, or copal, which could have been an important item for export, or that the people would have had to import metates, or obsidian, etc. In West Mexico it is often most difficult to prove that there was no local source, however small, of a given commodity, which would have forced its import. Nor does there seem to be much clear-cut evidence for tight monopolistic control over many rare resources on a regional basis. Besides this, such arguments have little real foundation unless export or import of goods can actually be proven. Again, such methods as neutron activation analysis have great potential value for tracing the source of certain raw materials. This, however, involves the extensive search and recording of the various sources which could have been exploited by the aboriginal population. Until this is carried out on a large scale in West Mexico, such source analysis will have limited application. And the mere location and recording of all possible sources of obsidian in the state of Jalisco alone would be no mean task.

As should be apparent from the above, much of what will be presented herein will involve elucidation of the many problems inherent in trying to study pre-Hispanic cultural contact in West Mexico, and specificially along the south-central coast of Nayarit. Many of the difficulties noted above are unavoidable in the following synthesis, but at least they have been duly noted and should be kept in mind.

The Nayarit coast can be divided into three major geographical zones: a northern part about 65 km. long with a complex system of small rivers, estuaries, and lagoons, part of the Marismas Nacionales; a central portion about 80 km. long which is of slightly higher general elevation and cut by two major rivers, the San Pedro and Santiago; and a southern portion of about 130 km. characterized by a very narrow coastal plain (or in many places, where mountainous relief extends down to the sea, no coastal plain at all) cut by small rivers which drop down from the highlands on a steep gradient to the sea. The principal area involved in this presentation is located along the south-central portion of the Nayarit coast, from a point just north of San Blas to the area of Santa Cruz to the south, a distance of about 20 km. (see Fig. 20). The area studied extends a maximum of 20 km. inland from the coast to the town of Navarrete. Research here in 1967–1968 involved the surface study of forty-six sites and excavations in three locations, yielding evidence of five major cultural complexes covering the period of approxi-

mately 2000 B.C. to A.D. 1500 (Mountjoy 1970a, 1970b). What I will attempt to do in the following is to present certain ideas relative to evidence for cultural contact during the five major periods of cultural development. In this discussion an attempt will be made to distinguish between intra-areal, intra-regional, and extra-regional contact and to interpret the nature of the apparent contact.

The earliest of the cultural complexes has been named the Matanchen complex. It is known from data salvaged from one shell midden about 90 m. long, 40 m. wide, and 4 m. deep, located on the eastern side of a low hill overlooking Matanchen beach some 3 km. southeast of San Blas. Three shell samples from the non-ceramic level (lower 3 m.) of the midden yielded radiocarbon dates of 2100± 100 B.C., 2000± 100 B.C., and 1810± 80 B.C. (U.C.L.A. 1652C, 1652A, and 1652E). The maximum correction of these results for possible error caused by upwelling would indicate dates no younger than about 1570 B.C. (Mountjoy, Taylor, and Feldman 1972).[1]*

The nearest pre-ceramic shell midden deposits of roughly comparable date are located some 640 km. in a straight line to the southeast at Acapulco, Guerrero, dated between 2940± 130 B.C. and 2440± 140 B.C. (Brush 1965), and some 1,300 km. in a straight line to the northwest at Punta Minitas on the northwestern coast of Baja California, where there are shell midden dates ranging from 5070 B.C. to A.D. 431 (Hubbs and Roden 1964).[2] In comparing the Matanchen complex with a shell midden such as Emeryville in California (Uhle 1907; Schenck 1926) one is impressed by the extreme paucity of manufactured artifacts in the Matanchen complex deposit — possibly only three notched rhyolite cobbles and perhaps a few obsidian flakes. It may be that the Matanchen people were involved in some sort of seasonal exploitation of shellfish resources, operating from a hunting and

*Note: numbers refer to comments at the end of this paper.

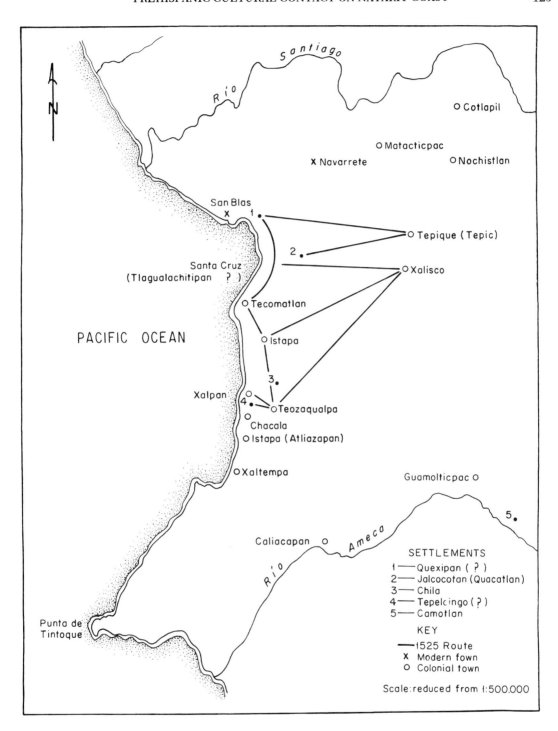

Figure 20. THE SOUTHERN NAYARIT COAST

gathering base. They may have been highly mobile, moving to the source of various subsistence resources for short-term exploitation. These small groups must have been intensively self sufficient within the framework of forced mobility, and population density quite low, with territorial control of exchangable commodities rather minimal. This adaptive picture could be changed significantly if the research by Scott and associates in the Marismas Nacionales in northern Nayarit (Shenkel 1971) reveals that some of the many shell middens there are contemporary with the Matanchen complex. However, at present, solid evidence of cultural contact of any kind (intra-areal, intra-regional, or extra-regional) is lacking. It is possible that such widely separate coastal adaptations were independent of one another. Certainly, it is doubtful, based on the data at hand, that there was any developed trade associated with the Matanchen complex.

The Matanchen complex is followed on the south-central Nayarit coast by the San Blas complex, dated ca. 700 B.C. to 450 B.C. on the basis of three radiocarbon dates (2,675± 85, 2,665±80, and 2,640±85 radiocarbon years; U.C.L.A. 1451A, 1652D, and 1451B, respectively).[3] The 450 B.C. minimum is based on a maximum correction of up to 240 radiocarbon years for the effects of upwelling. The San Blas complex is known from two sites (San Blas 16 and 17) located near the Estero de San Cristóbal on the northeastern outskirts of the town of San Blas. The artifacts associated with this complex, and its ecological orientation have been discussed in detail elsewhere (Mountjoy 1970c). It is readily apparent that the San Blas complex as an exploitative system represents a major adaptive advance over the earlier Matanchen complex. The total site area is approximately double that of the previous complex, and rather than such an overwhelmingly one-dimensional coastal-estuary shellfishing orientation, the San Blas people appear to have been using a greater number of nearby microenvironments, and more extensively. In addition to the intensive shellfish exploitation (with nearly double the number of genus-species utilized), there is increased dependence on turtles, along with crabs, waterfowl, estuary fish, dolphin, and perhaps dogs and humans. There is also some evidence of grinding meal, probably from nuts but perhaps from agricultural foodstuffs as well.

As has been pointed out elsewhere (Mountjoy 1970c), the ultimate origins of the San Blas complex would seem to be in early Preclassic developments along the coast of Guatemala and Chiapas. The hypothesis is that the adaptation based on efficient exploitation of concentrated microenvironments, which was so successful along the coast of Guatemala and Chiapas (Coe and Flannery 1964) eventually provided the impetus for a Preclassic adaptive radiation up the Pacific Coast. This radiation reached the San Blas area about 700 to 450 B.C., and may have expanded farther north, ultimately reaching the Southwest United States via the Gulf of California and involvement in Hohokam origins.[4] Such a radiation is assumed to have been a rather slow coastal expansion, with migration of groups northwestward seeking special ecological settings with the proper concentration of microenvironments, much as one would seek out oases in a desert. If one attempts to view the Pacific Coast of Mesoamerica from a maritime perspective rather than a purely land-riverine basis, perhaps some new understandings will become apparent.

It would follow that some of these settlements might be widely separated if the proper ecological conditions were not to be found along a considerable stretch of the coast. Although the overall process might have been slow, any newly established settlement could have represented quite a long-distance leap up the coast. Given the extensive coastal orientation of the San Blas complex, along with the considerable dependence on rather deep-water shellfish and sea turtles, it seems probable that at least some form of seacraft, perhaps the dugout canoe, was in use at that time, providing the mechanism for coastal movement. Furthermore, it is presently impossible to derive the San Blas complex from the preceding Matanchen complex, or from any nearby highland culture.

What remains here is to assess the situation of cultural contact during San Blas complex times. Regardless of the ultimate affiliations of the San Blas people, there seems to be little solid evidence of contact with other cultures once the settlement was established. There are some close ceramic similarities between the San Blas complex and Lower Morett from the Morett site in coastal Colima, especially in black-rim buff or orange pottery, and possibly some of the monochromes.[5] Because Lower Morett may date as early as 750 B.C. to 330 B.C. (Meighan, Foote, and Aiello 1968: 1073), there would seem to have been no reason why these two areas could not have been in contact at least on an occasional basis. There was probably at least one intermediary site at this date, somewhere in the Valle de Banderas area, and boatmen are known to take trips nowadays from San Blas to the Banderas area in nothing more than a dugout, keeping close to the coastline.[6] Nonetheless, it would be extremely difficult, at present, to prove the existence of any regular contact between San Blas and coastal settlements to the south. Judging from the cultural debris, it appears that the San Blas complex people were highly self-sufficient, with all they needed locally and little obvious need to engage in commerce with coastal cultures in similar ecological settings to the south.

On the other hand, it is possible that they needed to acquire obsidian from somewhere toward the interior. Obsidian tools are rather small and not really abundant, perhaps indicating that obsidian was in short supply. However, obsidian did find its way into domestic refuse deposits and not much is known yet about possible local sources. Ground or pecked stone items seem selected by type for different uses, but the different kinds of stone were probably available locally. There were two stones (one red and the other green) found in the San Blas complex deposit which may have been source material for pigment. Their origin is not known at present.

There is one problematical figurine fragment which should be mentioned here. It was said to have been found on the surface of the ground at the exact spot where we later ex-

cavated the trench which yielded most of the San Blas complex remains. The tenant of the land donated the figurine to the project. This figurine has a few stylistic ties with the Early Ixtlan complex, but none with any later occupation known from the area. On the basis of its apparent depositional position and stylistic affiliations, it should probably be assigned to the Early Ixtlan complex, but could have been mixed in from the San Blas complex. The figurine has a wasp waist, navel, extremely broad hips, two grooved hip bands, and legs which end in stubs instead of feet. It bears a marked resemblance to Type-D4 figurines of the Middle Preclassic at Tlatilco in Central Mexico (see M. D. Coe 1965: 71–73) which would be approximately contemporary with the San Blas complex. It is dissimilar to many of the D4 figurines in its impressive size; it is about 14 cm. wide at the hips.

Given the apparent situation of cultural contact in the Matanchen and San Blas complexes, the advent of the early Ixtlan complex is nothing short of spectacular. Prior to this time there is no really good evidence of even intra-areal interaction, but now the south-central coast appears to be incorporated into an extensive and intensive intra-areal interaction system as well as a close-knit intra-regional interaction sphere probably with some long-range extra-regional contacts.

In the San Blas area at San Blas 17, the Early Ixtlan complex debris lies directly upon the San Blas complex deposit, without any apparent depositional hiatus. This could mean a developmental continuity, with the Early Ixtlan then beginning perhaps as early as 450 B.C. and arising in part out of the earlier cultural development. In fact, there does seem to be some limited ceramic continuity between the two complexes (especially in the squash-form vessel). But in most every other way (ecology, settlement pattern, religious expression) they seem strongly dissimilar.

In the San Blas area, Early Ixtlan ceramics were recovered from twenty of the forty-six sites studied. One of the pure Early Ixtlan sites (San Blas 32) had ten surface structures and alone covered an area some five times that of the total known San Blas complex occupation. The sites studied seem to indicate a shift to a more inland orientation. Of the twenty sites at which Early Ixtlan ceramics have been found, only three are directly associated with an estuary environment. Two more are located on the coast, but are not associated with an estuary. One of these (San Blas 1) was tested with an exploratory (3 m. × 1 m.) trench (Trench 1). The lower 110 cm. seemed to pertain almost wholly to the Early Ixtlan complex. Although this site is right on the eroding coastline, and produced abundant pottery sherds (1,094 in the Early Ixtlan levels), only one shell fragment and one section of burned bone were found in the deposit. The sites in the area of San Blas which are primarily attributable to the Early Ixtlan complex are notable for their lack of shell (and such things as turtle bones or fish bones) whether or not this indicates an avoidance of such resources.[7]

Based on cross-correlation with other areas, one can assume that the Early Ixtlan complex dates at least within the range of 200 B.C. to A.D. 500. The evidence from the apparent domestic refuse deposits and burials indicates that these people were participating in the shaft-and-chamber tomb mortuary cult which was spread throughout a core area of southern Nayarit, western Jalisco, and Colima (also perhaps as far north as Sinaloa), at this time. There must have been a complex and sophisticated system of exchange operating in this region, the focus of which was accumulation of the proper goods to be deposited in the graves of the dead. This could have been an amazing system of goods distribution, perhaps rivalling such a complex system of exchange as the Kula Ring of Melanesia or a ritual amassing of goods such as the Northwest Coast Kwakiutl potlatch. In some respects (the accumulation of special scarce or exotic items for burial furnishings) it recalls the concept of interaction spheres as applied to the Hopewell development in the Midwest United States. On the other hand, it is impressive that even though it may be possible to correlate richness of offerings with elevation of social status of the deceased, the more common people apparently participated as

fully as possible in the rituals and offerings of the cult.

Some of the grave goods may have been manufactured intra-areally and so distributed, but others may have been accumulated on an intra-regional if not extra-regional basis. A good example of the latter would be the shaft tomb trumpets made from Caribbean snail shells which have been reported by Furst (1966) and Long (1966). It is also noteworthy here that Furst (1966: 240) thinks that there were pottery specialists and perhaps pottery workshops at this time, and Long (1966: 104) has proposed that the shaft-tomb people had a market economy.

In the San Blas area, there is some consistency in the style of the large hollow figurines deposited in the shaft tombs. They appear to depict women in mourning, with ashen tear-streaked faces, perhaps serving as containers for some liquid nourishment, intended to accompany the deceased spouse during his existence in the grave or into the afterworld, providing him with the comforts he enjoyed in life. This would tend to show some localization of shaft-tomb cult expression. On the other hand, there is some evidence of such exotic goods as pyrite mirrors, turquoise, greenstone (jadeite?), "redstone," and cream-colored rhyolite, which could indicate some rather long-distance contacts.[8] Strangely enough, in the San Blas area, informants do not report the presence of snail shells in the shaft tombs, although they are frequently reported from tombs in western Jalisco (Long 1967) and southeastern Nayarit (Furst 1966).

One of the most promising lines of investigation for determining cultural contact or interaction during this period would be extensive analysis of ceramic paste to determine if there were any major centers of pottery production. In the San Blas area, the paste of the Early Ixtlan polychrome pottery appears very distinctive, crosscutting various stylistic types, and different from the less ornate wares and the figurines. It may well be that the elaborate polychrome is involved in regional distribution, whereas other mortuary wares (bichromes and monochromes) were manufactured locally. It would seem that the figurines were made to order in accordance with certain local variations in religious expression of the shaft-tomb cult which may have arisen in instances from imperfect religious acculturation, a fascinating problem to unravel. It remains to be known to what extent the figurines were produced locally or were imported from craft centers; probably there was a little of both in some areas.

There are two possibilities for long-range extra-regional contacts at this time. The first is with Central Mexico. The figurine data from the San Blas area suggests some relationship between Early Ixtlan and Preclassic cultures of Central Mexico. With the recent early dates of around 1000 B.C. for the tombs at El Opeño, Michoacan, excavated by Arturo Oliveros, one may have the nearby dissemination point for such influences, but the relation between the early El Opeño tombs and the later shaft-tomb development is unclear at present. The collection of six hollow figurines from the San Blas 26 site (Mountjoy 1970a) seems to show some ties to Tlatilco. These figurines are the female mourners mentioned above. The seated (or sexual, or childbirth) foreward inclined position of the women, with the legs outstretched, arms entering the waist with no depictions of hands, and legs which end in stubs instead of feet, is reminiscent of the treatment of some Tlatilco figurines (see M. D. Coe 1965: 100, 101). Coe (*ibid.*: 112) also pictures one Olmecoid figurine from Tlapacoya which is comparable. There is also the aforementioned D4-like figurine from the San Blas 17 site, which may well pertain to the Early Ixtlan occupation.

Several authors have recently discussed the correspondences between West Mexican shaft tombs and the shaft tombs found in northwestern South America, mainly Colombia and Ecuador (Long 1966, 1967; Furst 1966, 1967; Meighan 1969). Although there is disagreement on the exact significance of the similarity, evidence seems to point toward some sort of contact between West Mexico and northwestern South America perhaps as early as 200 B.C. (Meighan 1969). Furst (1966) sees a whole complex of similarities involved, including marine snail shell trumpets, pyrite

mirrors, *claraboyas* (connecting ducts), the form of the shaft-and-chamber tombs, and tomb guardians. One could add to this a similarity between some of the early polychrome pottery from Manabí on the Ecuadorian coast and Early Ixtlan polychrome (Mountjoy 1970a).

If there was such contact, it would most probably have come through coastal movements, and Meighan (1969) believes present evidence best supports a diffusion of traits from south to north. Regardless of the direction of diffusion, there is not any present evidence that trade or commerce was involved. Rather, it would appear that most evidence for contact falls within the realm of the religious, perhaps diffusion of a complex of religious ideas or concepts which involved rather specific details of proper mortuary practices, belief systems, and necessary ritual accoutrements. Internal evidence from coastal Nayarit would suggest that there was little if any maritime orientation to the Early Ixtlan shaft-tomb culture, and it would seem to be a poor candidate for having initiated long-range contacts to the south. It would seem most likely that such ideas were primarily diffused out of northwestern South America and blended with local West Mexican cultural developments. They might have been passed along through contacts provided by coastal interaction, perhaps trade or commerce, but not enough is known of what was happening along the coast to the south at this time to evaluate properly the manner of contact.

Sometime about A.D. 500, the Los Cocos complex replaced Early Ixtlan in the San Blas area. This complex is represented at thirty sites, seven of which are wholly Los Cocos and nine more which are predominantly of that complex. The orientation of the occupation seems to emphasize small sites in a hilly upland environment. These sites average about 4,800 sq. m. and 2.2 mounds. They are frequently situated on the top of a low hill or on habitation terraces on the side. Most sites would seem to have had only a few families living there. Although the one Los Cocos deposit trenched was along the coastline, there is little evidence of exploitation of marine or estuary resources at most sites.[9] The emphasis seems to be on some system of small-scale slope agriculture and perhaps intensive utilization of the small nut from the oil-nut palm. Grinding and mashing tools are quite common on Los Cocos sites.

In regard to cultural contact, it would appear at this time that the Los Cocos complex abruptly displaces the shaft tomb culture on the southcentral coast. There is no good evidence at present to indicate any gradual transition between the two complexes. If there were long-distance contacts to the south, these appear to have been ended abruptly, and the focus of cultural contact turned toward the interior highlands of west-central and north-central Mexico.

There is some evidence of close intra-areal contact at this time. A comparison of Los Cocos pottery with ceramics from the Amapa site some 30 km. to the north on the Río Santiago (Grosscup 1964) yields direct correspondence with seven of the nine major Amapa phase types, some sherds being indistinguishable between the two areas. Slightly further afield, Los Cocos complex ceramics are nearly lacking in the Ixtlan del Río sequence of southeastern highland Nayarit (Gifford 1950). However, Gifford does illustrate one bowl and nine sherds which would be classified Los Cocos in the San Blas area.

In other parts of West Mexico, there are some close correspondences for the Los Cocos red-on-buff or red-on-brown pottery. Similar pottery has been reported by Bordaz (1964) from Peñitas in north-central coastal Nayarit and there is a close resemblance with Chapala Red-on-Brown and Chapala Red Rim at the Tizapan el Alto site in Jalisco (Meighan and Foote 1968), and in the red-on-buff and red-on-brown series from the Coralillo complex of southwestern Jalisco (Kelly 1949). However, some of the red-on-buff Los Cocos pottery has decoration identical to that found on sherds of San Miguel Rojo Sobre Bayo of the San Miguel and Tierra Blanca phases in Guanajuato (Braniff de Torres 1966, and personal inspection of collections in the National Museum of Anthropology in Mexico City, 1968). At present, the Guanajuato area seems to be

the most probable ultimate source of the red-on-buff ceramics which spread so widely over central and western Mexico during the Late Classic and Early Postclassic. Both the red-on-buff pottery and flat "gingerbread" figurines with applique features (instead of mold-made) tend to link the Los Cocos complex with Coyotlatelco and Mazapan developments in Central Mexico.

During Los Cocos times, it would appear that intra-regional contact was rather strong. The nature of the contact does not seem, from the archaeological data at San Blas to have been religious. It appears that most ceramic similarities resulted from a rather rapid expansion of a Central Mexican highland development westward. This might have involved the establishment of major regional centers or even colonies with sub-colonies set out on the periphery. Personal fieldwork in the Magdalena Lake Basin area of Jalisco in the summer of 1972 leads me to believe that this general expansion may be linked to exploitation of certain rare resources (Weigand 1971) and in some areas did involve definite religious reorientation. It may have been that the San Blas area was deemed rather unimportant for such exploitation or religious conversion.

It is really during the Santa Cruz complex (ca. A.D. 700–1500) that possibilities for trade and commerce on the south-central coast of Nayarit abound. There is evidence of the Santa Cruz complex at twenty-eight of the forty-six San Blas area sites, and it is the predominant complex at eighteen of these sites. The sites may be huge, averaging approximately 35,000 sq. m. and 14.8 mounds per site. In the immediate area of the modern settlement of Santa Cruz there are six sites which have a combined area of approximately 585,000 sq. m. and contain over 246 mounds (Mountjoy 1970a).[10]

Three of the large sites with extensive Santa Cruz complex debris (San Blas 1, 3, and 8) were mapped and sampled in detail. An attempt was made to obtain two collections from each of the mounds: a control collection of all artifacts which could be found in a 2-m. square located on the side of the mound, and a range collection of other artifacts from the mound which seemed to have potential temporal or functional significance. In addition to those collections, in some areas of the sites which had no surface features, 2-m. control squares were plotted every 50 m. and all artifacts collected within the square. Presently, this information has been coded and punched onto IBM cards for computer analysis of such factors as decorative pottery types, functional pottery types, functional stone tool types, mound height, mound area, etc. Analysis has just begun on the 24-mound San Blas 8 site, and it is hoped that this study will eventually yield some significant data for understanding inter-site specialization, or assessing the degree of apparent interaction or non-interaction between sites, and the dimensions involved.

There would seem to be two major phases of the Santa Cruz complex as defined in the San Blas area. The first seems to roughly correspond to the widespread northwest coast Aztatlan phenomenon, and may have lasted from about A.D. 700 or 900 to 1100. There are only three sites located in the San Blas area which could be pure early phase, but the pottery is found at other sites as well. It occurs in rather sparse quantities, except at the San Blas 8 site. There does seem to be some developmental continuity from Los Cocos times into this phase, seen both in the red-on-buff pottery and the incised pottery, both characterized by a band of geometric design elements usually around the interior of red-on-buff vessels and the exterior of the incised vessels. Other traits which have been associated with a late phase of the Aztatlan development, such as notched rim spindle whorls and copper artifacts (Kelley and Winters 1960) have not been found at this time period in the San Blas area, although Pendergast (1962: 370) states that metals were in use at the Amapa site near the beginning of the early portion of the Late Period there — comparable in time to this phase.

On the whole, it would seem that the San Blas area was somewhat influenced by the Aztatlan expansion, but lacks the fine polychromes, elaborate painted and incised wares, decorated spindle whorls, pottery masks, and pipes often suggested to be involved in the

Aztatlan complex. The only certain association of copper artifacts is with the latter part of the Santa Cruz complex. It would appear, however, that the Aztatlan development was involved in the initiation of eventual incorporation of many West Mexican areas into new spheres of influence emanating from Central Mexico, primarily having to do with systems of trade or commerce. Aztatlan may have been, in part, the commercial opening of the West Coast, perhaps through some sort of *pochteca*-like trade enterprises. The San Blas area apparently did not become fully involved this development until about A.D. 900–1100, during a later phase of the Santa Cruz complex. It might also be added that the Aztatlan influence from Central Mexico, supposedly from the Mixteca-Puebla area, might well have stemmed from contact with coastal Oaxaca via the Pacific. Personal inspection of Donald Brockington's ceramic collection from the Oaxaca coast has revealed some striking ceramic similarities with the San Blas area at this general time period.

During the later part of the Santa Cruz complex, there appears to have been quite a bit of intra-regional specialization, and perhaps even inter-site specialization. Bordaz (1964), for instance, argues for pottery craft specialization at Peñitas in north-central Nayarit at around A.D. 1100–1300. There are strong ties with Amapa at this time, several pottery types being indistinguishable, and some good ceramic correspondences with the Nayarit-Sinaloa border area, based on Scott's (1969) work there. However, there is also some local development of distinctive pottery types characteristic of and abundant in the San Blas area, whereas many of the finer wares from Amapa and sites northward are absent.

Ties with the Ixtlan del Río area are rather marked late in this period, particularly in the Ixtlan Late Period white-on-red pottery. This pottery, called Santiago White-on-Red at Amapa and Autlan White-on-Red in Jalisco (Kelly 1945), has a distinctive paste and crackled red paint with fugitive white overpaint decorations, and nearly always occurs as small jars. This type seems distinctive enough and uniform enough to have been manufactured in a limited geographical zone, and traded widely. Such a pottery type points up our general lack of effort in correlating very similar or indistinguishable pottery types toward an understanding of the relationships evident from such comparisons. For example, instead of always viewing vessels as commodities in and of themselves, it may be worthwhile to ask if something of value might not have been traded in pottery containers. The texture, form, size, and porosity of some of the Santiago White-on-Red ware leads one to suspect that it might have been used as containers for salt (see "Postscript to the Santa Cruz Complex" by L. H. Feldman, Paper 13 for further discussion). At least such an approach may lead to some hypotheses worthy of controlled testing, and is somewhat in contrast to the position that ". . . there was probably no extensive trade in pottery and that the archaeologists forced reliance on ceramics provide an inadequate record of communications in Mesoamerica in pre-conquest times" (Bordaz 1964: 2). Surely the possibilities for such analysis in West Mexico have yet to be exploited adequately.

It seems that coastal contacts with areas to the south, and perhaps to the north as well, regained prominence at this time. The possibility of contacts between northwestern South America and Nayarit, involving diffusion of metallurgy, has been discussed in detail elsewhere, with the strong possibility that copper metal-working was introduced into western Mexico sometime around A.D. 900 by seafaring traders associated with the cultures of the Guayas Basin of Ecuador, and perhaps also the central coast of Peru (Mountjoy 1969).

In addition to the correspondences which have been pointed out regarding metallurgy, there are some additional possibilities in ceramic comparisons. The evidence for contact would be strengthened by finding comparable pottery types in both areas at the appropriate time. Although comparative data are scanty for the Ecuadorian area, it seems there is a definite correspondence between Type 1 incised pottery from the San Blas area Santa Cruz complex and incised pottery from the Manteño period on the Manabi coast of Ecuador (Jijón y Caamaño 1930, Lám. 28).

From the limited illustrations of this incised Ecuadorian pottery which are available, the use of the same basic design elements in the same manner, with the same sort of two-zone format, makes the pottery very similar to Type 1 in the San Blas area (and comparable types, Tuxpan and Santiago Engraved, from Amapa). The people of the Manabi coast were among the seafaring Ecuadorians who could have been responsible for the introduction of copper metallurgy into West Mexico.

There is also the matter of the development of petroglyphs in the same area at about the same time. Elsewhere (Mountjoy 1971), it has been pointed out that at least the spiral motif has a rather continuous distribution from Central Mexico through West Mexico as far north as the Great Basin, at apparently about this time horizon. At least in West Mexico the spiral seems to represent a diffuse Quetzalcoatl concept related to water and probably crops, and may have been introduced into the Southwest United States with the "strong wave of ceremonialism and ceremonial art . . . [which] moved up the west coast of Mexico to the southern boundary of Sonora, almost face to face with the Hohokam, around A.D. 1100–1200" (Kelley 1966: 109).

Southward, there is a detailed and specific similarity of subject matter and style between the San Blas area petroglyphs and Colombian petroglyphs, especially those from the Boyaca, Cundinamarca, and Nariño regions (Mountjoy 1971). This includes the extensive use of the spiral and calls to mind the Quetzalcoatl-like tradition of the Chibcha in the central highlands of Colombia.

Assuming that such long-range extra-regional contacts did exist with northwestern South America, one still has the problem of assessing their nature and duration. First, it is rather doubtful that such contacts were frequent or continuous over any long time span. Such expeditions must have been an important but superficial luxury associated with a dynamic cultural development and a stable society. The fact that such contacts were not noted by the early Spanish conquerors may have been due to the east-to-west movement of the Conquest and the socio-economic disorganization which proceeded it, the land-based initial conquest of West Mexico, or even possibly the disruption caused by Aztec expansion.[11,12] It does seem quite likely, however, that if the base for maritime operations was coastal Ecuador, the conquest of Ecuador by the Incas, beginning somewhat prior to A.D. 1464 (Brundage 1963: 196), must have had serious consequences for the always somewhat tenuous long-range contacts.

As for the nature of the contact at this time, it would seem that it must have involved trade, but could have even included some colonization of coastal areas in West Mexico. There must have been certain highly desirable goods which were sought by the seafaring traders, but although peyote has been suggested as a possibility (Mountjoy 1969), concrete data are still lacking on definite commodities which were exported southward.

By the time of the Spanish Conquest, the data from the south-central coast of Nayarit would lead one to believe that the expanded population concentration in villages within the fertile lowland riverine areas may have been partially founded in an increased emphasis on certain agricultural products which could be exported. This was probably related to involvement in expanding systems of commerce emanating from the highland interior, ultimately as distant as Central Mexico. Some of the more notable changes during Santa Cruz complex times not yet mentioned are the introduction of prismatic obsidian blades and some comal-like vessels, along with manos and metates of a different form which are made of a specially selected hard basaltic rock, and black-on-orange pottery. It is possible that controlled analysis of the grinding stones for the source of the material might reveal trading patterns like those discussed by Rathje (1971b) for the Maya. The obsidian for the prismatic blades appears to be from several different sources, most probably located somewhere in the highlands to the southeast. There is no evidence that they were manufactured locally, as no cores or workshops have been found, and trace element analysis may ultimately reveal dispersal patterns similar to those found by Hammond

(1972c) in the Maya area. A sample of the prismatic obsidian blades has been submitted for neutron activation analysis of trace elements, but the results are not yet available.

Several of the coastal Santa Cruz sites show a selective exploitation of oysters. Many of these were evidently consumed locally, but oyster meat, as well as dried fish and other seafood, may have been incorporated into pre-Hispanic trade systems during Santa Cruz complex times.[13] Shell itself may have been traded into the interior. West coast shell has been reported from Cojumatlán, Michoacán, on Lake Chapala (Lister 1949: 78) at about A.D. 1100–1300.[14] Salt was another important commodity which could have been exploited locally. San Blas was a center of colonial salt manufacture, and salt is still produced there today.

In conclusion, the data presently available for the south-central coast of Nayarit show a changing picture of cultural contacts through the some 3,500 years of pre-Hispanic cultural development there. It is not at all easy to attempt to assess the probability of the supposed contacts, let alone their nature. In some cases trade and commerce were surely the main impetus for contact, but in other instances colonization or religious conversion may have been more important. Other than just needing much more archaeological investigation in West Mexico, the most crucial lines of research at this point would seem to be technical analysis of artifacts toward understanding sources of raw materials, plus the elucidation of possible models for dispersion of goods, based on ethnographic data from Mesoamerica, along with some idea of how a given mode of distribution might be recognized archaeologically.

COMMENTS
by
Lawrence H. Feldman

[1]Recent study of the geological history of the Nayarit coast has provided information on beach formation that is of value in the study of archaeological complexes. It was discovered that the Nayarit coastal transgression (rise of sea level) stopped at the mouth of the Río Grande at 4,750 years B.P., elsewhere in the

central to north central part of the area by 4,500 years B.P., except at the north and south edges of the area where it lasted into 3,600 years B.P (Curray, Emmel, and Crampton 1967: 89). The Matanchen Complex appears shortly after the termination of transgression and one wonders if it is somehow related to the changed coastal conditions.

[2]Shell middens on the Bahia de Los Angeles (Gulf of California coast of Lower California) have been radiocarbon dated at 4,138 years B.C (Feldman 1969: 167; Moriarty 1968: 11–38).

[3]A major change occurred in the area about 3,600 years B.P. The climate is thought to have become relatively cool and stormier. Also there may have been a drop in sea level for a few hundred years (Curray, Emmel, and Crampton 1967: 91).

[4]Sites on San José Island in the Gulf of California are similar to those of the San Blas Complex in that, like the San Blas middens, free-swimming pectens are very abundant and suggest the presence of a deep water fishing industry. Another point of relationship is a summer fishing industry (attested by the presence of shellfish available only in the summer months). Seasonal fishing is implied by a sixteenth century statement noting that on the Nayarit coast "those who have navigated say the sea and coast is very mild in the summer time and in the winter, which is from June to September, there are some disturbances although not very fierce" (Blanco 1947: 28).

[5]Many of the species utilized at the Morett site are very similar or identical to those found in the San Blas Complex (for a list of Morett species see Feldman 1972a).

[6]The very small samples from sites of unknown age in the Valle de Banderas support an acknowledgment of the similarity between molluscan species of these sites and those of both Morett and the San Blas Complex sites (data based upon inspection of unpublished UCLA collections by the author).

[7]The change to a relatively cool and stormier climate lasted to A.D. 500 when it again became warmer (Curray, Emmel, and Crampton 1967: 91). One is strongly tempted

to link the disappearance of the Early Ixtlan Complex to changes in atmospheric conditions. It does not, however, explain the shift *to* this complex from that of the San Blas.

[8]"Redstone" exotic goods might be identified as ground and polished portions of *Spondylus* shell. This mollusk has been collected live from Cabo Corrientes, Jalisco, by the southern shores of Banderas Bay (data based upon inspection of San Diego Natural History Museum Collections examined by the author).

[9]Accompanying a change to a general warming of the climate along the coast "was a realignment of the coastline which can be traced from one end of the area to the other. This particularly striking unconformity . . . produced some of the highest portions of the entire strand plain. . . . The middens lying on older ridges landward of this discontinuity are very rare, suggesting that this period of reorientation of the coastline, accompanied by a climatic change, marked the time of influx of a large population of Indians to the coastal region" (Curray, Emmel, and Crampton 1967: 91, 92).

[10]On March 7th of 1525 Spanish inspectors visited the town of Quexipan, near present-day San Blas. At that time Quexipan had 115 houses and 230 men. This town was located on some hills by which passed a stream of water. It had markets and in it they traded cotton of "which there was much." Its trade was with those of Tepique "who are their friends" and with a town called Tecomatlan "where there was cacao" (Coria 1937: 564). South of Quexipan, on flat land near the Santa Cruz River, was the independent town of Tlagualachitipan (today Santa Cruz?). It had a "ranch" called Quacatlan (today Jalcocotan?) subject to Tlagualachitipan. The said town and ranch had together 170 houses and 311 men. "They harvest in this town much cotton, and at the ranch some cacao, although little." Their trade was with those of Tepique and Xalisco (Coria 1937: 564).

[11]On coastal travel Blanco (1947: 30–31) notes in 1584 that to the southeast of the Punta de Tintoque were three small islands (today called the Islas Las Tres Marietas) where the

Indians "anciently" sacrificed and worshipped "The Devil."

[12]Another reason for the absence of reference to such contacts is a general lack of interest in all aspects of local culture by Spaniards who had just completed the conquest or annexation of the far more impressive Aztec and Tarascan states. In Nayarit disorganization caused by Tarascan expansion seems far more likely than that produced by the very distant Aztec Empire of the Triple Alliance.

[13]North of the Santiago River, near Acaponeta and Sentispac, Ponce notes (in 1587) the existence of "great fisheries" whose fishermen sent many loads of oysters to the Valley of Mexico "and other places." Their shells were made into a "very good" white lime that was used in the construction of buildings ("Dos Religiosos" 1873: 66).

[14]See Feldman (1968) for a discussion of these and other marine shells.

REFERENCES

Blanco 1947
Bordaz 1964
Braniff de Torres 1966
Brundage 1963
Brush 1965
Coe, M. D. 1965
Coe and Flannery 1964
Coria 1937
Curray, Emmel, and Crampton 1967
"Dos Religiosos" 1873
Feldman 1968, 1969, 1972a
Furst 1966, 1967
Gifford 1950
Grosscup 1964
Hammond 1972c
Hubbs and Roden 1964
Jijón y Caamaño 1930
Kelley 1966
Kelley and Winters 1960
Kelly 1945, 1949
Lister 1949
Long 1966, 1967
Meighan 1969
Meighan and Foote 1968
Meighan, Foote, and Aiello 1968
Moriarty 1968
Mountjoy 1969, 1970a, 1970b, 1970c, 1971
Mountjoy, Taylor, and Feldman 1972
Pendergast 1962
Rathje 1971b
Schenck 1926
Scott 1969
Shenkel 1971
Uhle 1907
Weigand 1971

13. POSTSCRIPT TO THE SANTA CRUZ COMPLEX: A TRIAL SURVEY OF SPECIALIZATION AND TRADE IN THE PERIOD OF INITIAL CONTACT

by

Lawrence H. Feldman

This is a report on the economy of Nayarit and Jalisco towns between the Santiago and Ameca Rivers during the first hundred years of European control in western Mexico. It is a preliminary report based on some of the major published documents of the period and is intended as an ethnohistoric supplement to the archaeological report of Mountjoy (preceding paper). A problem when utilizing archaeological data for economic analysis is the determination of points of origin of individual artifacts. Because the Spanish colonial administration was concerned with taxable resources it made special efforts to obtain precisely that data. Thus many documents, being a product of colonial administrative process, have valuable data on the localities of production of these resources. Less common, but also to be found in these same sources, are explicit statements on the nature of the movement of goods during the sixteenth century.

Ethnohistoric methods are not the answer to every problem of the archaeologist; for one thing they have very limited time depth, being a record only of contemporary colonial conditions and not those of earlier periods. Also, in western Mexico, to a degree greater than in most parts of Mesoamerica, sources are highly limited, being as yet restricted to only a very few documents (systematic archival research will undoubtedly expand the corpus of data, and for a critique of available information see Brand 1971). Nevertheless, for the purposes of this paper one report, giving a detailed picture of the economy and population at the very moment of initial European penetration, is of great value. It was a product of the Francisco Cortés expedition.

When Francisco Cortés was appointed by his cousin, Hernán Cortés, to be "Commandant and *alcalde mayor* of Colima" in 1524, he was given "instructions for a northern exploration ... for a distance of 130 leagues," (Sauer 1948: 19–20). When his expedition entered the lands between the Ameca and Santiago Rivers he found at least seven politically autonomous units: Aguacatlan, Tepique (Tepic), Quexipan, Tlagualachitipan, Tecomatlan, Teozaqualpan, and Etzatlan (Figures 20 and 21). The records of his expedition for the towns placed under Spanish control (Coria 1937) together with tax assessment papers dating from about twenty-five years later (Paso y Troncoso 1905), provide a glimpse of the specializations of these towns (cf. Table 16). Of special interest for the archaeologist is the severely limited number of towns manufacturing pottery.

Only Aguacatlan (with its dependency of Mexpan) and Matacticpan manufactured ceramics, with the second center apparently limited to *comals*. Archaeologists have argued for specialization in ceramic production in the temporally equivalent Santa Cruz complex; well, perhaps here one has an ethnohistoric confirmation of that hypothesis (see "Prehispanic Cultural Contact on the South-Central Coast of Nayarit, Mexico" by J. B. Mountjoy, Paper 11). Going one step further, it might be argued that a specific pottery type (i.e., Santiago White-on-Red) which is common in the Ixtlan area, could have been manufactured at Aguacatlan-Mexpan, being that the latter is a very close manufacturing center. If, as has also been suggested, this ware is of special value as a container for salt, there is then evidence for the production of ceramics purely for export, since salt was manufactured on the coast and not by the inhabitants of Aguacatlan-Mexpan.

Salt and pottery, then, are two commodities of potential trade importance. What were the means of exchange of these and other goods? In the Cortés papers (Coria 1937) there is reference to markets (*"tiangues"*) at Etzatlan, Ocotitlan, Aguacatlan, Mexpan,

Tetitlan, Tepique, Quexipan, Iztapa, and Tepelcingo. People of other settlements (e.g., Tecomatlan) brought their goods to these market towns for exchange with their own products (e.g., Tecomatlan maize for Iztapa salt). One of the items used for money may have been *cacao*. Certainly it had achieved the status of "the money of the Indians" by the 1580's (Blanco 1947: 26). If Central Mexican procedure can be any guide to West Mexican practices, one should be able to say that many markets were noted for certain specialties (e.g., as the slave market of Azcapotzalco or dog market of Acolman — Durán 1967: 218).

Existent information allows for some identifications. Quexipan was a trading center for cotton and cacao, Iztapa was noted for traffic in salt and fish, and Tepelcingo had a center for the exchange of maize (Coria 1937: 563–65). These markets each reflect their location in a particular zone of economic specialization. Five such zones may be identified for southern Nayarit: (1) a Maritime or Riverine zone that emphasized fishing or salt production, (2) a Lower Piedmont specializing in the raising of cotton, (3) a very humid Upper Piedmont where cacao was common, (4) Humid Highlands with very good maize crops, and (5) Dry Highlands characterized by maguey products (these zones are based upon the data in Table 16). Other goods depended upon deposits of raw material whose local distribution was restricted to particular localities rather than found in extensive zones (i.e., clay or

Table 16. THE SPECIALTIES OF SOUTHERN NAYARIT*

Township	Products
1. Aguacatlan	maize, beans, *ollas, comales*
2. Xala	maize, cotton, beans, turkeys, tomatoes, *"pepitas"*
3. Ixtlan ("Ixpan")	maize, maguey, cotton
4. Mexpan	maguey, cotton, *mantas*, honey, "platos", "ollas", maize, beans
5. Tetitlan	cotton, maguey, maize, beans, honey, *mantas*
6. Xalisco	maize, beans, "tablas de manteles," cotton "panizuelos"
7. Tepique (Tepic)	maize, *mantas*, beans, turkeys, honey
8. Quexipan	cotton, maize
9. Mecatlan (near Quacatlan)	maize, *cacao*, cotton
10. Tlagualachitipan	cotton
11. Quacatlan	*cacao*
12. Xalxocotlan	maize, *manteles*, "panizuelos," turkeys, honey, gourds
13. Tecomatlan	cotton, maize, cacao, fish
14. Teozaqualpa	fish, cotton, maize (in irrigated fields)
15. Istapa	cotton, salt, fish, turkeys, maize
16. Chila	cotton, maize (in irrigated fields)
17. Xalpan	cotton, chile peppers, maize, "naguas," *mantas*
18. Chacala	cotton, maize, *cacao*, fish, salt
19. Atliazapan (Istapa)	cotton
20. Xaltempa	maize, cotton
21. Cotlapil	maize, honey
22. Nochistlan	maize
23. Matacticpac	*mantas*, cotton, beans, maize, honey, "petates" (reed mats), *comales*, fish
24. Caliacapan	maize, fish
25. Guamolticpac	maize, "spin a little cotton"
26. Camotlan	*mantas*, "naguas," maize, beans, cotton, turkeys, fish
27. Tepezhuacan	*mantas*, cotton, beans, fish
28. Tepeguacan (near Camotlan)	*mantas*, honey, cotton
29. Tecpatitlan (by Camotlan)	*mantas*, "naguas," cotton, maize, beans, honey, chile peppers
30. Tecoxquines (by Camotlan?)	*mantas*, maize, beans, cotton
31. Zapotlan (by Camotlan?)	honey

*Based on Coria (1937) and Paso y Troncoso (1905). Data for Etzatlan, Ahualulco, Ocotitlan, and other adjacent Jaliscan towns will be presented separately at another time.

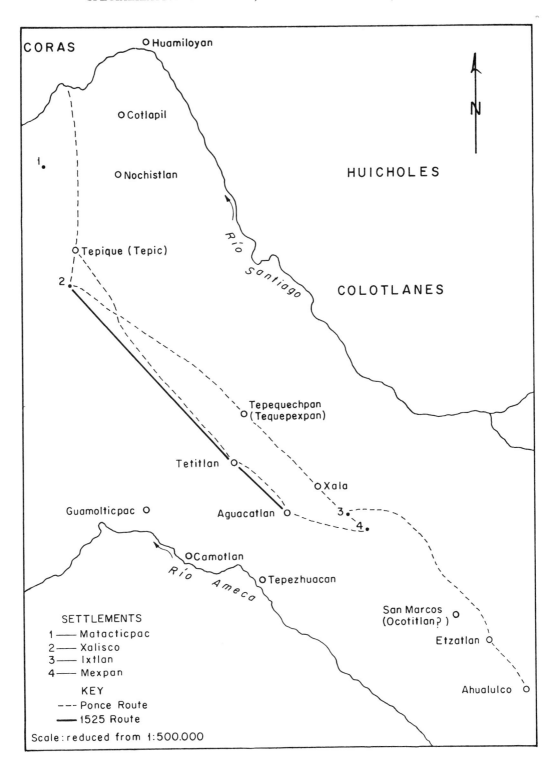

Figure 21. AREA BETWEEN THE AMECA AND SANTIAGO RIVERS, NAYARIT AND JALISCO

obsidian). Because no community possessed all necessary resources, trade was necessary between the different settlements.

The most international center for commerce was the market at Aguacatlan. To this center came merchants bringing silver from Cocula and Zapotitlan (these towns are said by Coria 1937 to be "in Michoacan;" for their location see "Timed Travels in Tarascan Territory" by the author elsewhere in this volume). From the other direction, the Pacific coast, came traders with cotton and salt (Coria 1937: 560). Routes in the 1520's were from the interior to Aguacatlan and thence either north or south along the coast from Iztapa. Another route went from the coast inland to Tepique (cf. Figures 20 and 21).

These routes are brought into sharper focus by the 1587 travels of Friar Ponce. Ponce left Cocula on Monday afternoon January 12, 1587, and arrived on the same day at San Martín for an overnight stop. It took him all day Tuesday to go, via Xalco and Ahualulco, to Etzatlan ("Dos Religious" 1873). Another day brought the friar to Ixtlan (by the way of San Andrés and Muchititic) and thence on the fifteenth (via Xala) to Tepequechpan and finally on the seventeenth to Xalisco (via Zapotlanejo and Analco). Xalisco was an important center in the second half of the sixteeth century, producing white honey for export to the Valley of Mexico and receiving fish from the Pacific coast ("Dos Religious" 1873: 58–59). One day's travel from Xalisco brought the friar through Tepique, across the Río Santiago and so beyond the area of concern here. Returning, Ponce went from Tepique (via Analco and Tetitlan) to Aguacatlan in one day, from Aguacatlan (via Tzoatlan and Mexpan) to Ixtlan in another, and then he retraced his steps back to Cocula.

The significance of Friar Ponce's travels is first that they place the local Nayarit routes in a larger Mesoamerican context, showing how this area was linked with other areas. Second, they tell how long travel took from one locality to another. Third, they add new routes to those known from the earlier source, and, finally, they describe some additional merchandise that was moved on these routes. In the Cortés papers it was noted that traders went to Aguacatlan from Cocula. Ponce by his travels shows precisely how traders could have gotten to Aguacatlan from Cocula. The days of travel needed to traverse the area, a factor that may be of significance to the archaeologist in learning how far perishable goods might have been exported by the local inhabitants, may be determined from this information. Ponce also demonstrates that it was physically possible to travel between the highland towns of the interior, without going to the coast, as was done in the trade noted in the Cortés papers. In this instance, pre-Hispanic trade (except for certain elite goods) directly between these inland towns seems very problematical, since these towns produced many of the same goods as all of these towns are in the same Humid Highlands zone of economic specialization. If one follows the movement of goods, the patterns of trade attest to the existence of at least three overlapping economic spheres, each composed of settlements whose populations depended upon others in the same sphere for the production of often utilized goods. These spheres are those of Tepic-Quexipan-Iztapa, Mexpan-Aguacatlan-Chila-Iztapa, and the towns near Etzatlan. In these spheres one has self sufficient economic units whose movements of goods should be reflected in the artifact distributions of the archaeologists. Thus in sixteenth century southern Nayarit (and adjacent portions of Jalisco), economic specialization was common but evidence for trade, with certain exceptions, is limited to within small geographical areas.

REFERENCES

Blanco 1947
Brand 1971
Coria 1937
"Dos Religiosos" 1873
Duràn 1967
Paso y Troncoso 1905
Sauer 1948

PART II
CULTURAL CONTACT THROUGH TRADE

14. TRADE MODELS AND ARCHAEOLOGICAL PROBLEMS: CLASSIC MAYA EXAMPLES[1]
by
William L. Rathje, David A. Gregory, and Frederick M. Wiseman

I. INTRODUCTION

An archaeologist's data consist of the debris of cultural systems. Archaeological problems arise from attempts to use this debris to describe and explain the way human behavioral systems develop and respond to changes in their environments.

1. *A Conceptual Scheme for Trade.*

Each complex cultural system[2] that has presented archaeologists with intriguing problems has been immeshed in large scale exchange networks. Trade is only one aspect of complex cultural systems, but trade as a phenomenon does have definite and measurable effects upon the system in which it functions and with which it develops. To participate in large complicated exchange networks a cultural system must develop certain organizational features. It is assumed here that the structure of the requisite trade organizations affected the internal structure of the cultural systems that maintained them and that changes in trade organizations created further modifications within supporting systems.

Trade models (as defined by this paper) provide descriptions and potential explanations of the processes through which cultural systems accommodate organizations requisite to long-distance exchange. Such models outline special types of organizational principles and components which lie behind the procurement and/or manufacture of local marketable resources and behind the transport and the exchange of these commodities in external markets. They also specify the dynamics of the sensitive feedback loop connecting trade organizations to their environments.

Archaeologists often attempt to solve their problems by employing trade model descriptions and explanations. The procedure involves two steps. A general model is related to specific ecological, social, and material culture components in order to predict the nature and spatial patterning of the material remains left in the archaeological record. Actural remains are then compared to the model as a test of its utility and to modify its form. As the links between trade models and material re-

[1]This paper is in large measure the result of papers and criticisms from the members of Anthro Seminar 316b, University of Arizona, Tucson, Spring Semester, 1972. The participants were David A. Gregory, Frederick M. Wiseman, Barney T. Burns, Jo Willie Rogge, Robert D. Cunningham, Mark E. Harlan, Peter J. Urban, Jr., Barbara W. Curran, and Hugh G. Ball. Honorable mention is also owed to T. P. Culbert who was a co-instructor for the seminar, and to Michael B. Schiffer and Barbara J. Price who weren't, but read the paper anyway. As always special thanks are owed to G. R. Willey, D. M. Pendergast, R. E. and A. L. Smith, and G. Tourtellot for their interest and for access to unpublished burial data. Parts of this paper were prepared through the aid of the Wenner-Gren Foundation for Anthropological Research, the Bowditch Exploration Fund, and the National Science Foundation. The restriction of E-Groups to the Core Zone and its immediate borders was noted by John P. Molloy. The figures were prepared by Charles Sternberg of the Arizona State Museum.

[2]A system is a set of component elements (interconnected by a series of feedback loops), the components' individual attributes, and the rules of structural organization and interaction between component elements. The component elements in archaeological systems are based on remnant pieces of material culture discarded by a specific system during its operation. The individual attributes of components include, not only shape, size, weight, locations, associations, and designs, but also all of the human behavior which was involved in the elements' procurement, preparation or manufacture, use or consumption, storage, transport, and discard (Schiffer 1972).

System boundaries are "artificial" constructs defined to analyse particular problems. The term "cultural system" will be used with two referents in this paper: 1. a system whose component elements are defined by the remnant materials of one archaeological site and its "sustaining area"; 2. in a collective sense as a construct which includes all of the common elements and interactions of the site systems in a specific geographic area.

mains are being forged by systematic examinations, the importance of trade in effecting and affecting the succession of complex civilizations through time can be evaluated. This paper does not apologize for using trade models to the exclusion of other types. Trade models will not answer all, or perhaps even most, questions about the past; however, it is only by pursuing mercantile models doggedly that their strengths and limitations can be diagnosed and efficiently exploited.

A useful model, as defined by this paper, is one which allows efficient testing by comparison against the archaeological record. Trade models, especially, fit this description. The end product of any exchange system is an artificially created distribution of goods. Many products imported by extinct cultural systems survive in refuse, burials, caches, and floor scatters as trace elements of exchange activities. Thus, many of the items that archaeologists excavate, whether because of material composition or stylistic elements, are immediately relevant to the evaluation of trade constructs.

Trade models and their tests need not, however, be limited to this obvious set of data. There are many direct, but subtle, linkages between trade models and archaeological data which allow expansion of the traditional role of each. These links are based upon the organization and technology which are needed to move commodities and upon the feedback interaction between demand structures, procurement organizations, and specific technologies of supply. This paper will use data from Classic and Postclassic Maya cultural systems in an attempt to illustrate briefly the potential utility of exploring new realms in which trade models can be applied.

2. The Mercantile Assumption.

From the most concrete archaeological fact that materials with extremely localized natural source areas are found throughout the Maya realm, to the tantalizing image of gods who carry time on their backs like cargo, the evidence strongly suggests that trade was a significant feature of the Maya civilization. Although the ancient Maya trade routes are now

lost to jungle growth and the ideology which supported and sanctioned trade survives only in motifs carved on stone and bone and shell, the effects of trade manifest themselves in material remains. They are therefore subject to examination by the archaeologist. Nevertheless, before deciding how much time to devote to trade models, it is useful to review some definitions and assumptions which such models employ.[3]

The first essential distinction made by these models is that between *retail* and *wholesale* trade. In retail trade one individual both produces and markets a commodity to consumers in a face to face situation. The consumers of his goods are, in turn, producers and sellers of other goods. Wholesale trade, on the other hand develops from a geographical separation of production and consumption. This situation creates a problem in exchange which is solved by the creation of an *agent-of-trade*, a middleman transport and marketing role between producer and consumer. Cultural systems engaged in wholesale trade are subject to pressures from internal and external agent-of-trade organizations which affect their structure.

As a starting point, trade or mercantile models require the *absence* of local self-sufficiency and the resultant demand for a wholesale organization (Vance 1971: 16, 155). Areas which are not self-sufficient and which have a strong *impulse-to-trade* are likely to be the most profitable for the application of trade models. Once these areas are identified, trade models can be expanded to describe the relationships between an area's internal development and its effect upon the development of external regions. Thus, defining the self-sufficiency of the study area is an efficient first step in applying trade models.

3. Classic Maya Ecology, Technology, and Self-Sufficiency.

Basic Resources are defined as those commodities found through time in every household participating in a given subsistence strat-

---

[3]The following definitions and assumptions were derived directly from Vance 1971.

egy (cf. Fried 1967, Leone 1968). Many such resources are rapidly consumed or debilitated through everyday use and must be replaced often (Netting, personal communication). They may be absolute (e.g., salt) or culturally defined (e.g., sinks, stoves, and indoor plumbing in the contemporary U.S.A.). These resources provide one avenue for descriptions of self-sufficiency because they represent the articulation between ecology, subsistence activities, and technology at the individual household level and because the procurement of basic resources is a prerequisite to the efficient functioning of many critical organizations in cultural systems (cf. Rathje 1971b, 1972).

For the Maya agriculturalists three basic resources were mineral salt, obsidian for razor-sharp cutting tools, and hard rocks for grinding implements[4] (for the rationale behind selecting these three resources see Rathje 1971b, 1972). All three commodities are exploitable throughout the Southern Maya Highlands. In the Central Maya Lowlands, however, there are few places where it is possible to procure these commodities efficiently[5] (Figure 22; Rathje 1971b, Fig. 1). The three resources were essential to the standard efficiency of slash and burn agriculture and/or silvaculture subsistence patterns to the degree that they were imported to all parts of the Maya Lowlands in all time periods (Rathje 1972). Specific site-level cultural systems within the lowlands were not self-sufficient. It is this fact which indicates the potential utility of trade models to describe and explain the development of ancient Maya civilization.

---

[4]Pottery temper, especially volcanic ash, may also have been a culturally defined basic resource. Volcanic ash is an excellent temper because it does not shrink or change in heat, it does not burn off and leave surfaces pitted, and it does bond clays well (Burns, personal communication). Volcanic ash, which does not occur naturally in the center of the Maya Lowlands, was used extensively at Tikal (Culbert, personal communication).

[5]For example, McBryde's (1947) map of modern exchange patterns in the Guatemalan highlands indicates that grinders are seldom moved more than 27 miles from their source and manufacture area. The Central Peten is over 90 km. from the Maya Mountains, the nearest source of hard stone for metates.

II. TRADE MODELS

For many years archaeologists have sought to understand the effect of trade upon the organization and development of cultural systems. They have usually looked to their own common sense constructs or to the work of other anthropologists. Both source areas have yielded interesting and useful models which are known and exploited by archaeologists (for example: Jacobs 1969; Sanders and Price 1968; Sanders 1962a, 1964; Parsons and Price 1971; Flannery 1968; M. Coe 1961a, 1965, 1968; Grove 1968; Renfrew 1967, 1969; Tourtellot and Sabloff 1971). There are, however, several other fertile fields that have produced formal trade-oriented models.

A theory of wholesaling with its strong dependence upon schedule and tradition and on the establishment of ties that persist in time and expand over distance, demands two qualities ... (1) an ability to deal with support and change induced from the outside, and (2) a dynamic quality, for the long and persistent ties found in wholesaling give evidence that history strongly influences the shaping of trade patterns (Vance 1971: 10).

The work of geographers and/or economists forms a largely untapped reservoir of basic dynamic models of trade with excellent historic documentation of referents. Adapting models from these sources adds new dimensions to archaeological interpretation and increases the communication between allied disciplines. The trade models outlined below are simplified segments of the mercantile model outlined by Vance (1971), a cultural geographer, and a general model of economic development summarized by Keeble (1967), an economist. The ability of these models to deal with the dynamic historical interrelationship of internal and external economic systems makes them extremely useful conceptual schemes for the study of ancient trade systems. The utility of both constructs will be illustrated by application to Maya archaeological problems.

4. *The Mercantile Model* (Vance 1971).

The establishment of trade between geographically separated areas depends in large part on the knowledge that the initiating area has of its own market and the distant market with which it ultimately develops trading relationships. This carefully guarded and restricted knowledge is the *intelligence complex* (Vance 1971: 148–49). Vance (1971: 149) suggests that "competition in wholesaling is as much organizational as it is geographical." Increases in speed of demand satisfaction are a constant objective of trade systems (Vance 1971: 156–57). The wholesaler whose organization is best able to meet such demands will win control of the market. This principle applies to production, transport, distribution, and to both internal and external markets. The importance of organizational variables in competition between merchant groups provides the rationale behind the restriction of access to intelligence complexes.

Points of initiation are those centers in an area which begin trade in distant markets, and these points have a definite advantage in trade not only because of their initial jump in the development of internal market for nonlocal commodities, but also because of their greater experience in external trade and a consequently more comprehensive intelligence complex. Wholesale organizations based in points of initiation invest large proportions of available capital in research and experimentation and in expanding and improving the organization of personnel and material culture. This is the merchant's *technology of supply*. The interaction between these and other activities makes points of initiation specially potent growth centers for complex cultural systems.

Points of attachment are the points in distant areas where the first connections are made through the efforts of the agents-of-trade from the initiating area, and may be "few or numerous largely in response to political and transportation conditions" (Vance 1971: 152). These points become *entrepôts*, developmental loci collecting and manufacturing exports and marketing imports from points of initiation.

The places that serve as receptacles along transportation routes for collection of goods within the external area are *depots of staple collection*. As the trading network grows, they too may become entrepôts of wholesaling as a result of the "knowledge related to the conditions of redistribution and demand in a broad region tributary to their depot" (Vance 1971: 152).

The *impulse to trade* which creates points of initiation is dependent upon two factors: the absolute mass of the potential market and the demand patterns that individuals practice (Vance 1971: 150). Two types of demand have been distinguished: *accumulated* and *continual*.

Accumulated demand is "the total demand for a good by one purchaser, either individual or institutional, over a relatively long period of time" (Vance 1971: 25). Often such a demand develops slowly before it reaches a threshold where fulfilling it is economically worth the effort. It can, however, be artificially induced to peak through advertising and other stimuli. Jade beads and similar status commodities which have no *direct* relevance to subsistence activities, are examples of accumulated demand items. These types of demands are subject to major fluctuations relative to the economic health of the system.

On the other hand, Vance (1971: 25) notes that "such demands as those for perishable foods, fuels, shelter, and other 'necessities of life' (basic resources) cannot normally be periodically satisfied and thus are not characterized by accumulation of demand." Satisfying the demand for basic resources entails little risk (except through competition) and opens up a massive and consistently exploitable market for the procurer. Many industries require a minimum market in order to operate economically, but once that critical threshold is reached economic development leaps forward (Keeble 1967). Basic resource demand is more likely than accumulated demand to cross critical thresholds early in exchange system development.

5. *The General Economic Development Model* (Keeble 1967).

In a recent review Keeble (1967) observed that economists have begun to devise spatial models of economic development in reaction to static equilibrium models which assumed that interregional variations in economic development would tend to equalize through time. Although the new dynamic models do not deal specifically with exchange systems, they are useful in providing a minimal context in which to consider trade.

In his summary Keeble discusses several spatial models designed to explain economic development on the sub-national, national, and supra-national level. The constructs outlined, for the purposes of this paper, are essentially variations of only one model which involves three basic concepts: cumulative causation, backwash, and spread.

The hypothesis of *cumulative causation* states that once growth begins it sets in motion a series of feedback loops resulting in accelerated development of economies which require a minimum demand in order to operate but which produce effects that stimulate further growth once past critical thresholds. Cumulative causation would apply to mercantile organizations which require minimum markets and threshold effects and certain levels of resource availability to get started. Once critical thresholds are crossed, often by a number of separate organizations, economic development crescendos due to cumulative feedback interactions.

The second concept, the *backwash*, involution, or polarization effect, holds that the growth center (i.e., the points of initiation in the mercantile model) will attract labor, capital, and commodities from the surrounding areas. The third concept is called the *spread*, expansive competition, or trickling-down effect. This process counteracts backwash effects because the growth center will also stimulate demand in surrounding areas (e.g., for agricultural products or minerals) and if the demand becomes strong enough to overcome backwash effects, a new center of growth (i.e., points of attachment and depots

turned entrepôts in the mercantile model) will be established.

6. *Summary Model.*

Centers of trade change function, drop and add products exchanged, and wax and wane. The importance of the mercantile and economic models is that they are dynamic and stress some of the critical variable components in three processes in the developmental cycle of exchange systems: (1) the role of wholesale trade in the economic geography of the area which initiated it; (2) a growth center's influence on the subsequent development of external areas; (3) the feedback between external development and the original growth center. Three related areas of variable interaction are relevant to this study: demand structure, competition based on organization and location, and the historical interaction between demand, competition, and technology of supply.

Wholesale systems develop in response to the nature of demand (i.e., impulse to trade, accumulated and continual demand, and threshold effects). Where there is a large demand, there will be a ready market for goods, and support for organizations capable of delivering desired commodities. The demand for basic resources, obtainable only from great distances, provides a potent impulse to trade. Determination of the structure of basic resource demand and associated growth centers is crucial to an application of the model.

Another critical variable identified by trade models is competition based upon organizational abilities and geographic location. A key process in the development of growth (i.e., initiation) centers is the exchange of products which satisfy external market demands for resources. It is important to note that in some cases growth center exports to external market centers are finished products made from resources imported from the same external centers (e.g., the British colonial policy). Meeting growth center resource demands requires and stimulates organizational developments in external areas. "Spread" (i.e., point of attachment or depot centers), if impelled above the same organizational thresholds as the original growth center, will have the potential to produce locally commodities to satisfy many of their own demands for initiation center imports. In addition, these commodities can be used to satisfy the demand in other trade markets for what had previously been growth center imports.

Spread centers can, therefore, become growth centers which compete for markets with the original growth center. Based upon combinations of technological and organizational innovations and differential proximity to resources this competition may lead to the elimination of an initiation role for one or the other center. The nature of demand, the nature of organizations stimulated by initiation centers, and the geographic distribution of resources are all crucial to defining when and how competition will affect the location, growth, and decline of initiation centers.

A third factor which the trade models emphasize is the intimate interaction between demand recognition, competition, technology of supply, and the specific historical events and processes through which procurement organizations evolved. Ancient Maya traders with steel axes and machetes would have been able to compete easily with merchants promoting stone tools. However, without all of the historically related technology and other material and behavioral systems associated with the industrial revolution, the production of steel in the Lowland Peten rain forests of A.D. 600 is unimaginable. Thus, the processes of development and competition must be analyzed in a context which emphasizes the historical interaction of demand and technology of supply.

III. APPLYING THE MODELS

The first procedure in relating trade models to archaeological problems is to develop meaningful units of analysis. The need to import goods into the Central Lowlands (Section 3) allows the use of ecological and geographical variables to attempt a relatively objective division of the Maya area into zones on the basis of criteria relevant to basic resource demand and to exchange potential.

7. Basic Resource Distribution.

The lack of basic resources is more severe in the middle of the Central Lowlands than in the periphery (Figure 22; Rathje 1971b, Fig. 1). The central area has none of the three critical commodities (mineral salt, obsidian, hard stone) locally available. In contrast, some sources are located in the periphery itself (mineral salt from the Chixoy River source and from the northern coast of Yucatan; hard stone from the Maya Mountains, [possibly] the Usumacinta drainage, and the Sierra de Yucatan — Rathje 1972); others (notably obsidian sources) are found in the highlands bordering the lowlands to the south.

Thus, on the basis of gross access to basic resources, three areas can be defined: 1. the highlands, where all three resources are clustered; 2. the periphery of the lowlands where the resources are found in scattered locations; 3. the center of the lowlands where none of these basic resources occur naturally.

8. Geographic Distance and Transport Potential.

The importance of basic resource distribution is clear when distance from specific areas to commodities is measured. In air miles the middle of the Central Lowlands is the farthest removed from resources (Figure 22; Rathje 1971b, Fig. 1). The Maya, however, did not travel by plane and had no beasts of burden other than themselves. Therefore, distances should be measured in a way that relates movement between two points to transportation realities faced by the Maya.

Water systems offer the only potential for relatively cheap bulk transportation available to the ancient Maya (cf. Fisk 1967; Adams, Paper 4; Lee, Paper 6; Edwards, Paper 17). The peripheral lowland areas contain viable river systems and/or border the Caribbean Sea. The Central Lowland zone is riverless and landlocked (Figure 22). Again, the middle of the lowlands clearly stands out as an entity separated from the lowland periphery.

9. Ecological Variety and Exchange Potential.

With a need to procure resources from other areas, the marketable natural products

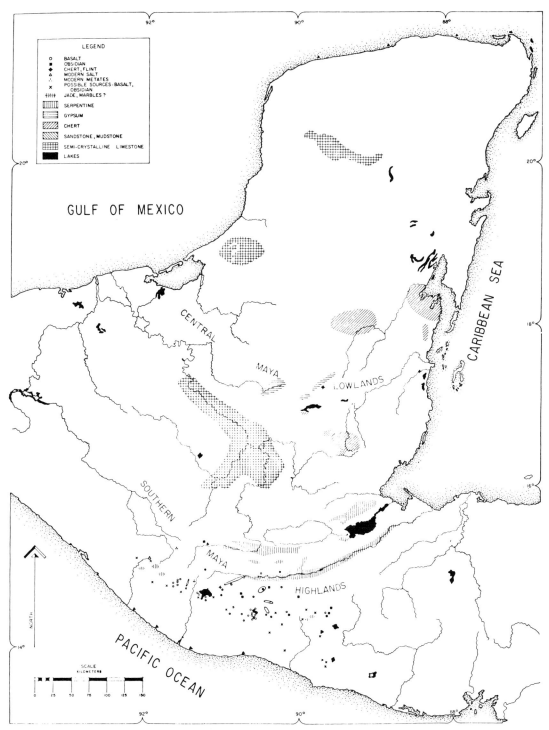

Figure 22. THE DISTRIBUTION OF SELECTED MINERAL RESOURCES IN THE MAYA AREA
This figure was constructed by Barney T. Burns on the basis of data from over 200 references. The bibliography can be obtained by writing to the Arizona State Museum Library, University of Arizona, Tucson, Arizona, 85721, U.S.A. Research to refine the maps is continuing; any relevant information would be appreciated and acknowledged.

of the lowlands are important variables in isolating areas useful to the study of trade. In 1938 Lundell identified sixty-six lowland plants which, based upon archaeological, ethnohistoric, and ethnographic data, were judged to have been useful to the ancient Maya. Forty-two plants were considered to have little immediate value to this trade analysis because they are generally available throughout the Central Maya Lowlands (or because the authors lack data on their distribution). Two maps (Figures 23 and 24)[6] were prepared which show the minimal distribution (based upon soil, rainfall, altitude and other requirements) of twenty-four plants which Lundell identified as potentially useful commodities, but which are differentially distributed within the Central Maya Lowlands (Table 17).

One lowland zone stands out as lacking almost all differentially distributed useful plants (Figure 25). The boundary of this zone is largely co-terminous with that of the basic resource deficient and low transport potential area in the middle of the Central Maya Lowlands.

10. *The Core, Buffer, and Highland Zones.*

The three areas created by describing basic resource distribution, transport potential, and ecological variety can be superimposed to give a tentative, but relatively objective, outline of zones useful to trade analyses. The

territory where all three outlined areas overlap in the center of the Maya Lowlands will be called the Core Zone (Figure 26). The area surrounding the Core Zone will be glossed as the Buffer Zone. These areas plus the Highland Zone, provide units of analysis relevant to the study of the diachronic interaction of ecological and behavioral-material systems through the use of trade models.

In brief the three areas are characterized as follows: 1. the Highland Zone is an area of great ecological diversity with close spacing of different resource zones (cf. Sanders and Price 1968); 2. the Buffer Zone borders and/or contains basic resource zones and borders and/or contains major bulk transport systems (rivers and the Caribbean Sea). The juxtaposition of tropical rainforest with several other ecozones creates general ecological variety throughout the Buffer Zone; 3. the Core Zone is landlocked and sequestered from basic resources by the Buffer Zone. Tropical rainforest is the only major ecozone in most of the Core and ecological variety is minimal.

IV. THREE ARCHAEOLOGICAL PROBLEMS

The next step of analysis is to use merchandising models to reconstruct specific Maya systems; to use these systems to predict their effect upon ancient Maya cultural systems as whole units; and to then compare these expectations with Maya archaeological data. Trade models will be used in this paper to: 1. reconstruct specific components of systems; 2. explicate the internal structure of, and interaction patterns between, specific systems; and 3. develop new useful viewpoints from which to analyze culture change.

11. *Specific Component Analysis: E-Groups.*

A complex of Lowland Maya structures with significant astronomical attributes was discovered at Uaxactun in the 1920's. The building complex was called Group E at Uaxactun and subsequent complexes with similar orientations have been called "E-Groups." Generally, E-Groups are composed of four structures. Three small structures are aligned north to south directly east of the fourth structure. The buildings are oriented so that solstices and equinoxes of the sun at horizon

---

[6]These maps were compiled by Frederick M. Wiseman from Roys (1931), Lundell (1934, 1937, 1938), and Steyermark (1950). Species lists and habitats were compared with soil, drainage, and topographic maps (i.e., Owen 1928) to determine possible regions of their occurrence on upland, rain forest and savannah sites. This may be considered a minimum distribution, since local factors outside the boundaries will allow a species to flourish. Plants characterizing humid mountain slopes may be found far below this region in valleys, due to the presence of moisture and cold air drainage. Riverine biomes will support localized communities of a great variety of plants which need a high water content in the soil (i.e., cacao and cedro). Plants adapted to drier, more Yucatecan environments may inhabit well drained uplands in the Peten. Until more detailed work has been done on the biogeography of the Maya area, such maps as these should be used with caution.

points fall at significant features of the three eastern structures when viewed from the center of the western mound (Ruppert 1940, Coggins 1967). Although E-Groups have long been recognized (Ricketson and Ricketson 1937) and have been identified at twenty-one sites, only a few explanations of their position within Classic Maya cultural systems have been offered.

It is generally assumed (and will be a given in this paper) that E-Groups functioned, at least in part, as observatories to conduct research to refine the Classic Maya calendar. Although the reason for this extremely detailed and accurate calendar is in doubt, determination of its function is crucial to understanding the development of Lowland Maya E-Groups. One explanation for the emphasis placed on a compulsively precise calendar is that it was essential to farmers. This proposition fails as a useful model for at least two reasons: 1. today Maya farmers depend upon climatic changes and crop growth cycles, not calendars, to cue the few activities which require accurate scheduling; 2. the restricted distribution and actual loci of calendrical research and development centers is not predicted or explained.

This section of the paper will attempt to use trade models as an alternative framework for understanding the position of E-Groups within Classic Maya cultural systems. As a test of the utility of the trade frame of reference, the geographic and temporal distribution of E-Groups will be predicted and compared to their identified occurrence on the ground. This procedure is a crucial application, as the analysis must state the linked relationship between trade models and Maya systems in terms of retrievable data.

12. *The Demand-Growth Center Link.*

The real linkage between trade models and cultural development begins by identifying the nature and locus of demand, the impulse to trade. A continual bulk demand (identified on the basis of archaeological materials which were actually utilized by the ancient Maya — Rathje 1972) existed for basic resources in all three Maya zones. In the Highland and Buffer Zones the commodities were often nearby, ecological diversity provided naturally occurring goods with trade potential, and water systems facilitated bulk transport. The demand could thus be satisfied by

Table 17. Useful Plants Differentially Distributed Throughout the Maya Lowlands
(after Lundell 1938)

Human Foods	Timbers	Thatching Materials	Fiber Plants	Dye Plants	Miscellaneous Useful Plants
Cereals and Vegetables	*cedro*	*ac* grass	*henequén*	logwood	calabash
ramón (breadnut)	(Spanish		cattail		pitch pine
Jatropha	Cedar)				Montain Pitch pine
cohune					
custard apple					
guayo					
mamey apple					
avocado					
sapote (sapodilla)					
yucca					
Wild Fruits					
nanze					
pasita					
mamey ciruela					
spondillas					
cashew					
Beverage Plants					
cacao					
balche					

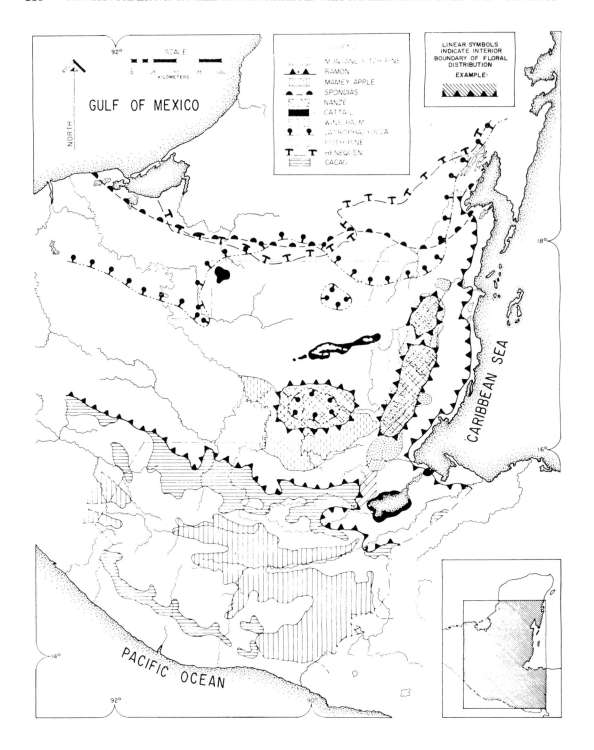

Figure 23. MINIMAL RANGE DISTRIBUTIONS OF USEFUL MAYA PLANTS — PART 1

Figures 23, 24, and 25 were constructed by Frederick M. Wiseman on the basis of data from over 40 references. The bibliography can be obtained by writing to the Arizona State Museum Library, University of Arizona, Tucson, Arizona, 85721, U.S.A. The maps are obviously crude and, for some areas, inaccurate. Research to refine the maps is continuing; any relevant information would be appreciated and acknowledged.

minimum time and effort expenditure in these areas.

In the Core Zone, however, where there were no local sources of basic commodities, the demand could only be satisfied effectively by a large-scale organization to procure, transport, and distribute the resources. This niche for large-scale organizations existed because of the distances and difficulties of transport. Another factor reinforcing the selective pressures favoring large-scale organizations in the Core Zone was the lack of exchange potential created by a lack of differentially distributed natural resources and a slash-and-burn settlement pattern that kept consumers relatively scattered (Rathje 1971b, 1972). The Core was settled, according to this construct, when (probably due to population pressure) the advantages of new and fertile[7] land outweighed the disadvantages of basic resource procurement. When there were few settlers, individuals personally had to donate time, travel, and resources to procure goods. Individual family or kin group scheduling of expeditions to acquire basic resources would necessarily have been structured around agricultural production cycles and other subsistence activities, and as population increased such scheduling would have become increasingly inefficient; as the number of settlers increased through birth and immigration, a potential developed for individuals to procure goods more cheaply by supporting a complex organization than by independent procurement efforts. Because of the continual demand for resources and their transport, this threshold would have been rapidly reached in the Core Zone.

In the Core the effects of continual demand as well as the effects of demand satisfaction were felt in every household. As a result capital would have been readily available from all household units to support efficient procurement efforts. The level of demand, in fact, created a major selective advantage and direct observable return (greater availability

of basic resources) toward efforts at establishing and maintaining complex procurement organizations. Given that "one of the basic characteristics of chiefdom social structure is the presence of a core lineage that enjoys privileged status and control of the distribution system" (Sanders and Price 1968: 131), then there is a logical continuity between the tribal groups which first contacted the highlands in trade and the development of ranked society. By providing the local populations with desired highland resources, the social groups involved in the conduct of trade would have had automatic status in relation to their control of these resources and their distribution.

It is assumed here (following Keeble 1967) that growth is related to the ability to export economically goods demanded in other regions. Few such goods were naturally available in the Core. The Core's potential exchange deficits were solved by a new accumulated demand threshold which developed along with complex, stratified, procurement organizations. Complex social organizations, especially those involved in collection, transport, marketing, and redistribution, are ideally fitted to develop a manufacturing branch, which could produce items for local status demands and for export. The accumulated demand threshold being crossed was not just local. In every area where Core growth centers stimulated the development of complex exchange organizations (depot and point of attachment centers), there emerged a ready market for the intelligence complex, the status items, and the organizational ideology of the Core. This market solved the Core's problem of the lack of a natural exportable commodity. The Core exported its organization and that organization's by-products (Rathje 1972).

In sum, because of a lack of basic resources, transport difficulties, and few marketable products, the Core Zone was not settled until some four hundred years after the Buffer Zone (Puleston and Puleston 1971; Culbert and Rathje 1971). However, once people moved into the Core Zone it rapidly reached a threshold which rewarded as selectively advan-

---

[7]Sanders (1973) and Price (personal communication) both stress that the soils of the Peten may be exceptionally fertile.

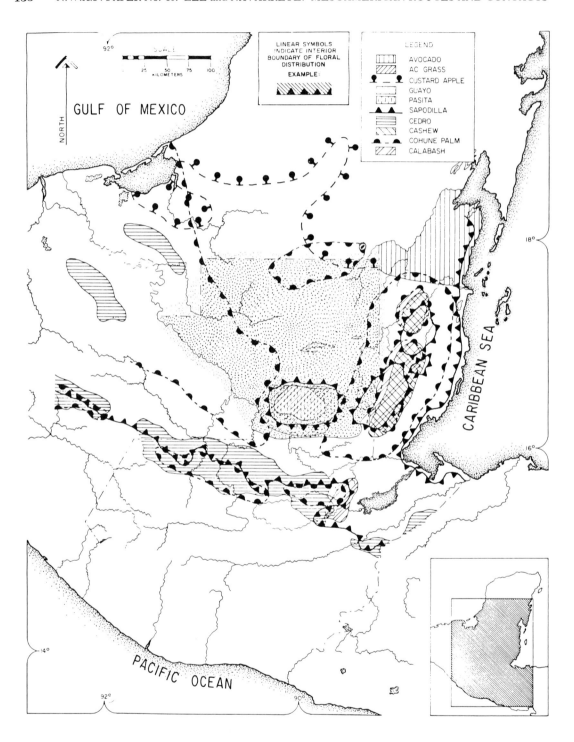

Figure 24. Minimal Range Distributions of Useful Maya Plants — Part 2
The area indicated for *sapodilla* also is the minimal area of distribution for *mamey, guava, manax, balche, sabal, botan,* and logwood in *bajos*.

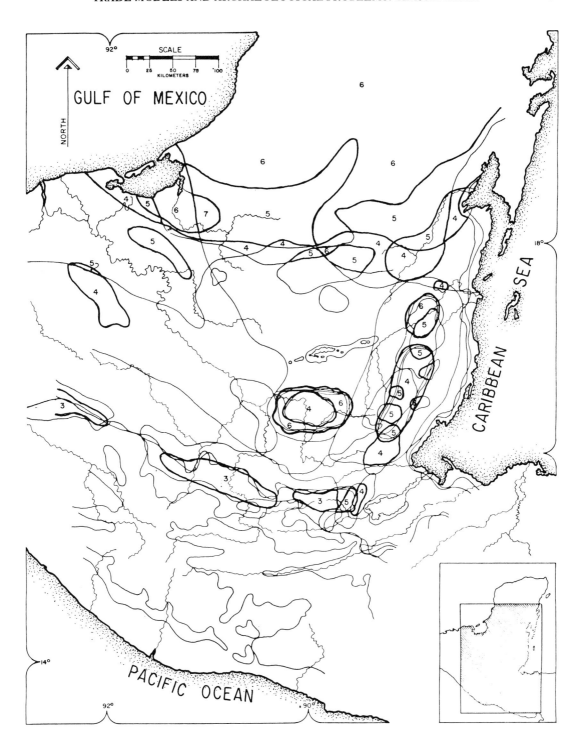

Figure 25. THE VARIETY OF USEFUL FLORA IN THE MAYA LOWLANDS

The number of flora for each outlined area is indicated. The pan-lowland distribution of *sapodilla et al.* is taken as given and is a great floral variety in riverine and lake shore environments.

tageous attempts at developing complex procurement organizations. In terms of trade development potential, the Core offered the most
easily exploitable Maya system available. In
the Core Zone the role of the agent-of-trade
would have become specialized early in time
as a central feature of exploitative patterns
and social organization.

13. *The E-Group Linkage.*

The above trade model-Maya system link
specifies that points of initiation should first
be apparent in the Maya Lowlands in the
Core Zone. The identification of points of
initiation should be apparent first in the Maya
Lowlands in the Core Zone. The identification of points of initiation can be based on
the material correlate of archaeological remains indicating heavy investment in a trade
intelligence complex and technology of
supply.

The technology of supply is crucially dependent upon the control of time variables.
Scheduling is the foundation of the ability to
collect and move men and material and the
ability to predict the spatial and temporal
occurrence of resource area markets and local
area demands.

> This was notably true in the past when
> much time and effort were required to
> carry goods even fairly modest distances.
> Then the trader had to solve a rather
> complex problem of cost of goods, cost of
> transport, places of sale today, and prob-
> ably changes in the price structure be-
> fore the goods could be delivered at the
> distant market.... Once the trading
> agent was created, men emerged who
> gave their full attention to commerce, ...
> and whose time could be broken down
> into segments that might be used for
> trade in distant places (Vance 1971: 50–
> 51).

To maintain supply in the face of increases in
the scale of demand due to population growth
and dissemination of information concerning
highland resources, trade groups would have
had to improve the technology of supply. This
required increasing precision in scheduling
so that greater numbers of people could de-

vote their time profitably to long-distance
trading activities.

The intricate divisions and precision of
the Maya calendar would have facilitated the
organization of trade activities effectively
with populations in areas which differed in
specific production cycles, market schedules,
or other temporal features affecting their trade
potential. Thus, the Core area should have
invested heavily and early in technology to
improve scheduling activities — for example,
in astronomical observatories to develop and
refine the calendar. This is not to suggest that
all Maya astronomical observations were
made to move salt. However, the economically
selective advantage these studies would have
given Core merchants would also have provided a base from which the Maya astronomical
exotica could have developed.

E-Groups are generally considered to be
astronomical observatories, built at great expense in material, manual labor, *and* research
time. If a mercantile model is used to predict
the time-space position of E-Groups in the
Maya Lowlands, the earliest E-Groups in the
lowlands should be found in the Core. In
addition, E-Group construction should reach
its maximum florescence in the Core.

E-Group complexes have been identified
at twenty-one different sites. Twelve are located within the defined limits of the Core
Zone; eight are on, or within forty kilometers
of, the Core/Buffer Zone border (Figure 27).
Of all the explored sites, only one E-Group
was found at an unequivocal Buffer Zone center and the identification of the E-Group at
that site (Uaxac Canal) is tentative (Ruppert
1940: Table 1). Thus, the distribution of E-
Groups coincides with the Core Zone and its
immediate borders (Molloy, personal communication). Although there is little available
information, the earliest known E-Group was
constructed at Uaxactun, almost at the center
of the Core. This is an important prediction
to watch as more E-Groups are dated. These
data provide a tentative confirmation of the
link between mercantile models and the
Core/Buffer Zone dichotomy. At the same
time they describe and partially explain one
element of Classic Maya cultural systems.

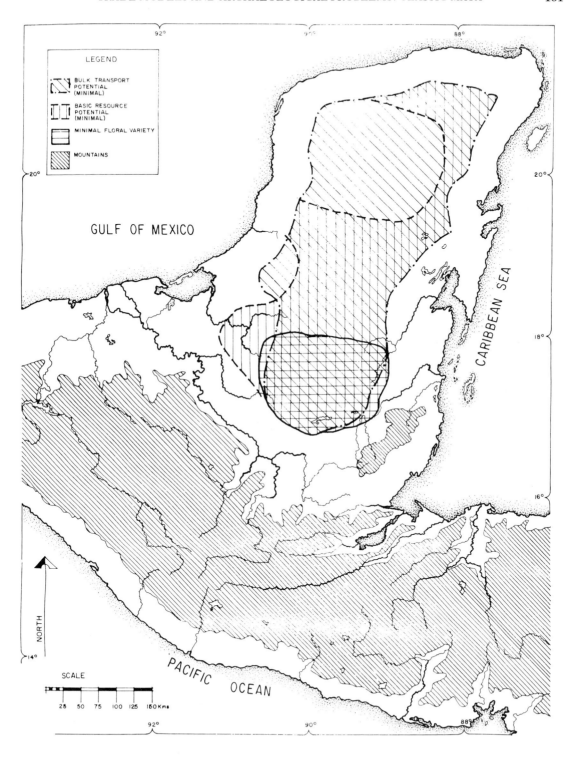

Figure 26. MAP OF CORE ZONE BASED ON A THREE-TRAIT DISTRIBUTION

Three areas defined on the basis of 1) over 50 km. distance (about one day's walk) to any one basic resource; 2) over 50 km. distance to any one bulk transport system, rivers, or the ocean; 3) lack of useful floral variety. The "Core" Zone is defined where the three regions overlap.

14. *System Development and Interaction: Grave Goods.*

The Classic Maya collapse and Classic/ Postclassic transition is a fascinating area for speculation and research. Following the trade perspective, major deviations in exchange systems should have affected and accompanied the Classic downfall and transition to the Postclassic. Although the "collapse" shook the whole Lowlands, the population drop was most dramatic and recovery most vestigial[8] in the Core (Thompson 1970, Sanders 1962, Rathje 1972). The Core Zone is, therefore, a likely place to begin an analysis of the Maya downfall.

The structural constraints on Core Zone systems required that to maintain population, basic resources had to be procured efficiently at a cost acceptable to the Core's subsistence base. In the Core Zone organization was especially important to that end. It was responsible for the efficient (minimized expenditures/maximized procurement) exchange, transport, and local redistribution of goods. Even more important, it managed production of scarce manufactured items (decorated textiles, carved wood, polychrome pottery, esoteric knowledge, etc.) (Rathje 1972). These commodities reinforced the necessary status structure of the procurement organizations while at the same time they were the scarce resources upon which Core Zone exchange transactions depended. From a trade perspective, the important developments just prior to and during the collapse are those which would have disrupted or undercut the ability of the Core's organization to fulfill its demand satisfaction functions.

15. *The Spread-Efficiency Linkage.*

The pre-collapse environment which the Core Zone faced can be drawn from economic development models. As Core systems grew they stimulated "backwash." This process seems to have reached a crescendo during the Early Classic (A.D. 300–600) when Palenque, Altar de Sacrificios, Seibal, and other south-

west Buffer Zone centers hit population basins (Smith, Tourtellot, Rands, personal communications). During the same time period Core sites continued to expand (cf. W. Coe 1963, 1965; Haviland 1968; Culbert, personal communication). By the Late Classic (A.D. 600–900), although Core centers continued to grow, a spread effect had filled the Buffer Zone with developing centers[9] (Rathje 1971b). For one example, between 9.3.0.0.0 (A.D. 495) and 9.18.0.0.0 (A.D. 790) the number of Core centers erecting stelae tripled from 4 to 11; during the same period the number of Buffer Zone sites erecting stelae increased to more than six times its original number, from 5 to 33 (Figure 28, data from Morley 1937–38). Obviously this contrast in growth is due in part to the size of the Core compared to the expanse of the Buffer Zone. Not only the number of sites was involved, however; the number of people integrated at Classic Maya sites increased differentially. "In this period (ca. A.D. 600–700) the frontier (Buffer Zone) towns assumed greater importance and developed into strong, independent centers" (Proskouriakoff 1950: 4). Sites like Palenque, Piedras Negras, Altar de Sacrificios, and others, in less than one hundred years boomed exponentially from minimum (Early Classic) to maximum (Tepeu 2 — A.D. 700) populations.

An analysis of the Core's role in the process of organizational and marketing development of Buffer Zone points of attachment and depots is relevant to a study of the Classic collapse. For this paper it will be assumed that when two systems are interacting, the closer their level of organization the more efficient that interaction becomes in exchanging materials and information (cf. Service 1955). This factor provided several economic reasons for Core systems to aid in the organizational development of Buffer and Highland systems.

The first reason for stimulating outside development was to minimize the size and complexity of the organizations which the Core needed to maintain. In resource areas commodities had to be collected and/or manufactured, packaged, and stored. In intermedi-

---

[8]This picture may change due to the comprehensive ethnohistoric project now being undertaken by Nicholas M. Hellmuth.

[9]For a detailed discussion of the transition from backwash to spread see Rathje (1973).

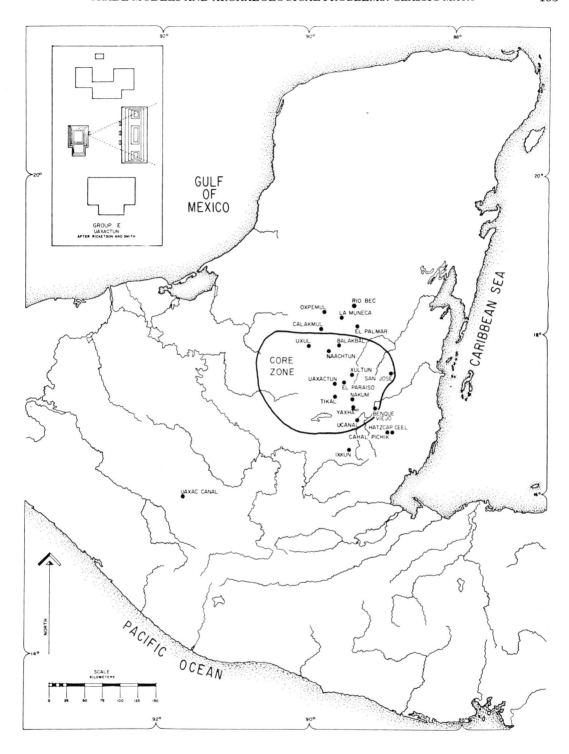

Figure 27. THE DISTRIBUTION OF CLASSIC MAYA SITES WITH IDENTIFIED E-GROUPS (AFTER RUPPERT 1940) AND THE "CORE" ZONE

ate areas expeditions had to be resupplied and the complex transfer from water to land transport had to be efficiently managed. The Core would have minimized its organizational complexity by developing locally based institutions which could fulfill these functions.

The second reason for Core stimulation of outside growth was related to the first. Systems developing status hierarchies require material representations of status differentials (Binford 1962). Since many Core Zone exports were manufactured status commodities, by supporting outside development the Core Zone was developing markets for its products.

Thus, for two sound economic reasons the Core underwrote "spread" into the Buffer Zone. The basic challenge to the Core in spread is summed up in the dictum that competition is as much organizational as geographical (Vance 1971: 149). Organizational superiority was especially crucial to the Core which suffered from marked ecological and geographical disadvantages. The Core was, nevertheless, forced to export its organization and both spawn and succor its own competition. This process would have eventually undermined the efficiency of the Core's procurement systems. Efficiency will be defined here as the ability to maximize procurement and minimize resource-labor-time costs.

One way to measure Core procurement efficiency, without quantifiable objective data of man-hours/commodity procured, is based upon an assumption about competition: the more competitors for a good at a given technological level, the more difficult it will become to minimize resource-labor-time costs to obtain the item. With the development of Buffer Zone systems in the Late Classic the number and the sheer mass of demand centers for highland resources increased exponentially. At the same time there was no noticeable increase in the number and size of highland extraction sites or in extraction technologies. In this situation, heightened competition for both constant and accumulated demand commodities would have been inevitable. One example of the result is provided by W. Coe who notes that "for some

reason or other Uaxactun's [Core] production of eccentric [obsidian] objects seems to have ceased at a time when Piedras Negras [Buffer Zone] artisans were making them in increasing quantities" (1959: 145).

A well-known concept borrowed from information theory provides another means of evaluating efficiency in demand satisfaction: other factors constant, the speed and volume of flow of goods is inversely related to the number of filters through which the goods must pass — the fewer the intermediate filters the more "efficient" the system. In the Late Classic the development of many Buffer Zone sites significantly restructured the whole highland/lowland exchange system. As Buffer Zone centers surrounding the Core evolved into major socio-political forces all imported or exported goods to or from the Core passed through more and/or stronger filters.

A final assumption can be used to view changes in efficiency: a trade item has exchange value to a specific group only so long as that group cannot produce the good locally at less cost than it can be brought from merchants. As long as Buffer and Highland Zone depot and attachment centers had poorly developed complex marketing and other organizations, it was efficient for them to import Core craft products. However, as spread created large complex organizations outside of the Core, these units had the specialization potential to meet many of their own accumulated demands through local production.

The use of this potential is evidenced by divergences between Buffer Zone and Core pottery art styles and manufacture loci during Tepeu 1 (A.D. 600–700) (cf. Rathje 1972). Proskouriakoff (1950: 109, 116) also provides many examples of the same process in stela carving and ceremonial construction, i.e., "along the Usumacinta monuments of early Cycle 9 do not differ essentially from those of the [Core] Peten, [but] at the inception of the Late Classic are already free of Peten traits and quickly develop original styles."

As Buffer Zone Centers imported fewer goods, the Core would have found its exchange potential diminished. This would have

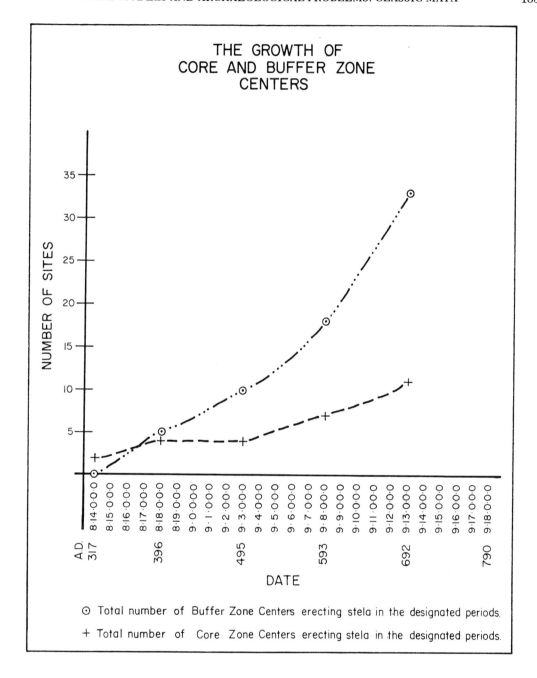

Figure 28. The Increase in the Number of Classic Maya Sites erecting Stelae in the Core
and Buffer Zones from the Early Classic through Tepeu 2
The data are taken from Morley (1937–39); all sites with stelae were counted regardless
of Morley's ranking.

created a change in the efficiency of Core procurement systems.

The specific links between "spread" models and the Classic Maya environment, therefore, clearly suggest that the efficiency of Core procurement systems should have dramatically diminished as the number of Buffer Zone centers increased. As a result, by Tepeu 2 Core center populations would have begun rapidly to outstrip the carrying capacity of withering long distance procurement systems. This hypothesis isolates one possible stress which might have contributed significantly to the Classic Maya collapse (for a more detailed explanation cf. Rathje, in press).

16. *The Burial Linkage.*

Because the Classic Maya so often took it with them, this prediction can be briefly tested by reference to a sample 1,009 burials from the Central Maya Lowlands (for the specific details of the sample see Rathje 1971a). The assumption must be made that the quantity and variety of goods placed in burials reflects local availability to a relatively significant degree. Goods placed in burials (and not robbed by the living) are effectively extracted from the economic, political, and social world of the living. Thus, it will be assumed that if goods can be easily replaced they will be more continually discarded than if goods are hard to obtain, in which case they will be more often recycled than allocated to gravelots. To add

confidence to the trade model, through time exotics in Core burials should decrease as they increase in Buffer Zone graves.

The burials to be analysed were first separated into Core sites (San José, Holmul, Uaxactun, Tikal) and Buffer Zone sites (Barton Ramie, Baking Pot, Altun Ha, Mountain Cow, Pomona, Copan, Altar de Sacrificios, Seibal, Piedras Negras, Palenque). Those burials which could be positively dated were placed into Preclassic, Early Classic, Tepeu 1, and Tepeu 2 categories. Next, these groups were divided into housemound burials (the definition of the excavator was used) and ceremonial center burials. Finally, for each group defined by time, site, and structure type, the percentage of imported objects in burials was calculated from the total number of grave goods. Imported items were those which could not be obtained within fifty kilometers of a burial locus. Each physically distinct object was counted, i.e., each bead in a necklace was counted separately. Although not statistically significant due to sampling and test methodology, the results of this exercise were interesting (see Table 18 and Figure 29).

The ceremonial center burial curves meet the model expectations (Figure 29b). The Buffer Zone curve is almost a mirror image of the core trajectory, except that the Buffer Zone rise is more dramatic than the Core fall. It is important to note that the Buffer Zone curve is representative of the changes at many

Table 18. PERCENTAGE OF IMPORTED GRAVE GOODS IN CORE/BUFFER ZONE BURIALS

Core					Buffer Zone				
Date	Structure Type	% of Goods Imported	Local/Imported Goods	No. of Burials	Date	Structure Type	% of Goods Imported	Local/Imported Goods	No. of Burials
PCL/ECL	HM	18	9/2	11	PCL	HM	54	90/74	32
					ECL	HM	37	109/185	99
T1	HM	24	20/6	8	T1	HM	30	107/251	114
T2	HM	6	32/2	20	T2	HM	41	165/241	101
PCL	CC	89	203/25	14	PCL	CC	10	623/66	56
ECL	CC	88	1611/209	41	ECL	CC	14	7312/1153	47
T1	CC	71	101/41	27	T1	CC	66	1319/695	51
T2	CC	75	218/70	39	T2	CC	89	1185/115	40

PCL = Preclassic (ca. 600 B.C.–A.D. 300)
ECL = Early Classic (ca. A.D. 300–600)
T1 = Tepeu 1, Late Classic (ca. A.D. 600–700)
T2 = Tepeu 2, Late Classic (ca. A.D. 700–800)

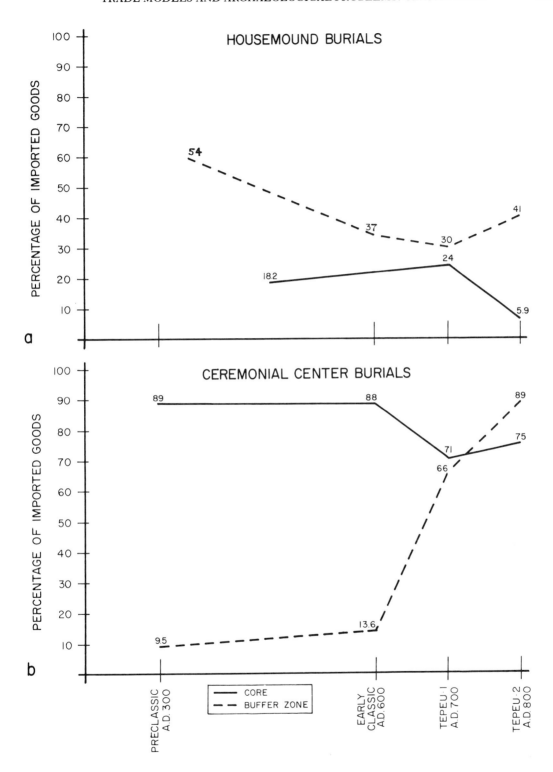

Figure 29. Trends in the Relative Quantities of Exotic Trade Goods deposited in Central Lowland Classic Maya Burials from the Preclassic through Tepeu 2

more sites than the Core curve, both in this graph and in real numbers of sites. Therefore, it is somewhat surprising that the percentage of imported goods goes up in the Core by four percent from Tepeu 1 to Tepeu 2. However, the answer to this puzzle is found in Figure 29a.

Individually, housemound burials have few goods to compare with ceremonial center graves; however, their actual number is many times that of ceremonial center burials. This paper will follow R. E. W. Adams' (personal communication) suggestion that ceremonial center elites made up no more than one to two percent of the population of a ceremonial center and its sustaining area's inhabitants. Since the model focuses on the relationship between mass demands and their satisfaction, data from housemounds provide a more significant context for a test of the model than burial data from ceremonial centers. Therefore, if these curves are representative of general burial trends, they are indicative of the distribution of more imported goods than symbolized by ceremonial center curves. It is clear that access to imported goods at the housemound level was, as hypothesized in the Core/Buffer Zone model, relatively easy in the Buffer Zone during the Preclassic. Through time as population increased and as backwash in the Early Classic added to the Core's procurement abilities, the percentage of imported goods decreased in the Buffer Zone as it increased in the Core. Then in the Late Classic, as spread developed, the trend reversed itself. The exceptionally dramatic *decrease* of imported goods in Core housemound burials in Tepeu 2 may explain the small increase in imported items in Core ceremonial center burials and represents attempts at concentrating imported goods to sustain previous ceremonial levels (perhaps to shore up faith in a failing procurement system through conspicuous consumption where it would be most easily seen). The paucity of imported grave goods in the Core in Tepeu 2 is evident from the fact that although the percentage of exotics dropped almost by 75% (24% to 6%) in 98% of Core burials, it only rose by about 6% in the other 2% where what resources were available seem to have been concentrated.

Due to population growth and exponential increases in investment in conspicuous consumption during the Late Classic, Tepeu 2 has always been considered the apogee of the Classic Maya culture. The burial curve results, however, indicate that already during the one hundred year period before the collapse the Core's ability to import goods may have declined drastically as the ability of Buffer Zone centers increased. Thus, Tepeu 2 may be viewed as the beginning of one important stress which could have contributed significantly to the nature of the Classic/Postclassic transition.[10]

It is obvious from the number of burials represented (i.e., lumping Preclassic and Early Classic Core housemound burials and still finding only eleven available for analysis) that the trends represented are not statistically significant. However, the developmental model predicted the general trends of imported resource distribution based on about 85% of all excavated Central Lowland Classic Maya burials (as of 1972). These results by no means substantiate the model, but they reaffirm the utility of the model for generating a research strategy and they provide a fresh insight into the Maya collapse.

17. Cultural Development: A Fine, Orange Example.

The depopulation of the Classic Maya sites in the Central Lowlands was the most spectacular event in a whole series of processes which made up the Classic/Postclassic transition on the Yucatan Peninsula. Other equally dramatic changes can be discovered by comparing Classic and Postclassic material culture and its distribution (Figure 30).

During their florescence the large inland Classic Maya centers were cultural foci of Mexico. Temples and palaces were carved laboriously from limestone. Intricate glyphs which still elude translation were etched onto

---

[10]A new model of subsistence intensification has recently been proposed (Culbert 1973) which also sees Tepeu 2 as leading disastrously toward the collapse. For a comprehensive study of the implications of the trade model for the Maya collapse see Rathje in Culbert (1973).

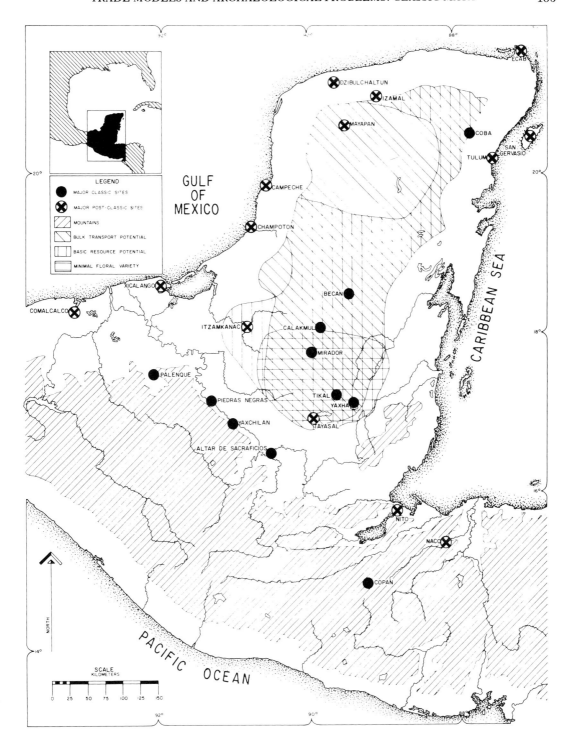

Figure 30. MAJOR CLASSIC AND POSTCLASSIC MAYA SITES
Although these sites were selected on a subjective basis, they represent the general shift of population centers from the center of the Yucatan Peninsula to its peripheries.

stone monuments beside solemn Maya lords. The finely crafted works of art in jade, shell, obsidian, pottery, and a myriad of other materials were the most fascinating in Mesoamerica.

The large Postclassic centers, most of which swelled along the coast of the peninsula, were of an entirely different sort. Structures were often built of rubble and covered with thick coats of plaster. Glyphs on stone and pottery were stylized and simple sets were reproduced repetitiously. The bulk of Classic astronomical esoterica was either forgotten or ignored. Much less interesting pottery and other craft items were produced in volume with simplified designs. From an aesthetic viewpoint Yucatan's culture had disastrously degenerated (cf. A. L. Smith 1962: 269).

It is clear that the drastic reorientation of the internal structure and geographic location of cultural systems was accompanied by major changes in trade patterns. Identifying these changes, from the perspective of this paper, will add important information to the description and explanation of this intriguing transition.

As the Late Classic closed most Buffer Zone systems were capable of local craft production of many status and non-status commodities. One of the most enigmatic attributes of the change from Classic to Postclassic systems on the Yucatan Peninsula is the far-flung occurrence of Fine Orange Pottery — from Veracruz-Tabasco, around the Yucatan Peninsula, to Honduras (R. E. Smith 1958, Hagaman and Longton 1972). In many sites it effectively replaced locally made decorated ceramics (cf. Altar de Sacrificios — Adams 1972, Seibal — Sabloff 1971). Its position in the transition, when acknowledged, is that of a marker of Mexican or Mexican-Maya groups which militarily invaded and conquered the Usumacinta Drainage and the northern coast of the Maya Lowlands (Jiménez Moreno 1966, Sabloff and Willey 1967, Sabloff 1971, Adams 1972, and others). From a trade perspective, however, Fine Orange pottery is indicative of far more than warrior groups pillaging with force of arms. Within Fine Orange lies a set of clues to the riddle of a major change in economic orientation in the Maya Lowlands.

18. The Competition-Technology of Supply Link.

A study of the Classic/Postclassic transition can profitably begin with two familiar mercantile maxims: 1. competition is as much organizational as geographic; 2. systems which are more efficient in satisfying a specific demand will replace less efficient systems. The processual factors outlined by the mercantile model emphasize that changes in competition and efficiency will be affected by: 1. the scale of the demand; 2. the technology of supply-manufacture; 3. the technology of supply-transportation/distribution. Major organizational reorientations will develop as a result of innovations in either the scale of demand, manufacture technology, or distribution technology (Vance 1971).

Following the organization-competition dictum, the Postclassic alternatives to the Classic system must have developed along with new merchandising methods for exploiting the energy resources of other systems. This new exploitative system must be based on an advance in technology and/or organization. The parameters of the characteristics of the advance probably included: 1. products with a low risk, high mass market; 2. products whose manufacture is dependent upon technical and organizational superiority; 3. products distributed by a new technology of supply. All these attributes are found in Fine Orange pottery.

19. The Fine Orange Linkage.

The above models may be used to suggest viable modes of research. The following section must be viewed, not as a finished description of the Maya Postclassic, but only as a set of preliminary hypotheses which are testable by direct reference to archaeological data.

In a pre-industrual, pre-metal society, pottery was an item which provided a low risk, high mass market. It was used for most everyday tasks and was often broken and replaced. Most demand was satisfied through local production because pottery is bulky and fragile and therefore difficult to transport and distribute over long distances. Even fineware was not widely traded in Mesoamerica due to its fragility, friability, soft slip, and easily marred and abraded paint (Shepard 1965: 352–54). A system that could produce and distribute pottery cheaply in bulk could have exploited the energy resources of many areas.

The requirements for widely distributed and marketed pottery can be abstracted from Roman amphorae and Wedgewood's "useful ware" (Callender 1965: XIX; Hillier 1965): 1. technically strong enough to withstand long trips; 2a. shaped to allow easy filling and emptying of a commodity and/or to allow nesting to maximize transport potential; 2b. standardized in form and substance so that pots could be stacked and not put uneven pressure on each other; 3. simplified in design and easy to manufacture in bulk.

Fine Orange and Fine Gray wares (specifically Z, Y, and X from the Classic/Postclassic transition) meet all of the above requirements for a widely-distributed, decorated, tradeware — one of only three in the history of Precolumbian Mesoamerica (Shepard 1965: 354). Fine Orange is strong, uniform in paste, standardized in form, shaped to facilitate transport, simply decorated with paint or caste in a mold, and widely traded. Neutron Activation studies indicate that almost all of Fine Orange pottery seems to have originated from a few closely spaced source areas in Tabasco (Sayre, Chan, and Sabloff 1971). To understand this ware further and the system involved in its production and distribution, *tentative* descriptions of its attributes will be covered separately.[11]

1. "Fine Orange is distinguished technically by a very dense, fine textured, hard paste. It attained high craftmanship but nevertheless is simple in style compared with many of the polychromes.... The wide distribution of [Fine Orange] points to the possibility of a general preference for pottery that is technologically superior" (Shepard 1965: 355). The paste is consistent throughout all specimens and is so fine that few inclusions have been identified, even under a microscope.

2. Fine Orange pots seem to be standardized in form. Many are made with molds (cf. R. E. Smith 1958). One of the most obvious characteristics of some standardized Fine Orange shapes is their stackability as compared to Classic forms. To illustrate this, arbitrarily selected pot shapes were reduplicated and nested (Figure 31). The typical flat-bottomed, outcurving-rim Classic bowls were unstable when stacked. The round-bottomed, incurving-rim Fine Orange pots with rounded feet settled neatly within one another. Evidence of manufacture to maximize compact packing comes from a burial at Seibal in which two Fine Orange bowls were tightly nested together as if ready for transport (Sabloff 1971, Figure 62). More work on these attributes is necessary, but the contrast between Fine Orange and preceding and coeval wares is at least an intriguing area of study.

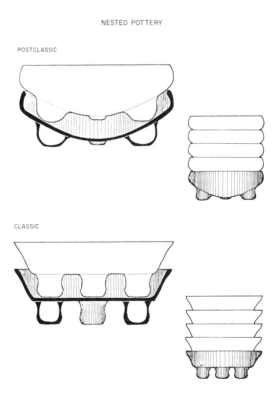

NESTED POTTERY

POSTCLASSIC

CLASSIC

Figure 31. POTENTIAL FINE ORANGE VERSUS TEPEU 2 POTTERY NESTS
(cf. Sabloff 1971 and R. E. Smith 1950).

---

[11]Methods of objectively measuring these attributes are now being devised and tested by Judith G. Conner (n.d.) as a part of the Cozumel Archaeological Project (cf. Connor and Rathje 1973).

3. Fine Orange pottery, although a decorated ware, was elaborated in a style that minimized individual time investment. Classic polychromes and other wares decorated with glyphs, figures and complex designs were the artistic progeny of ceramic masters. Relief pots were carved by hand. In fact, at Tikal, T. Patrick Culbert (personal communication) believes that in some burials stylistic features are distinct enough to suggest that the products of several different craftsmen are represented. This kind of analysis is not possible for Fine Orange ware. Painted design elements were simplified, often to just scallops and bands, and carving often to gradrooming. Molds were used to create some relief pottery with complex figural motifs. Even on relief pots glyphs were simplified to mere stylized patterns (see R. E. Smith 1958, 1971; Sabloff 1971; Adams 1972).

Paste is identical from one pot to another and must have been mined in huge quantities and prepared by a single formula shared by large numbers of people. Another aspect of minimizing effort was the fact that both Fine Gray and Fine Orange were made from the same basic potting clay; the color depended upon the way it was fired.

When all these features are pieced together a pattern emerges which may be called pre-industrial mass production. Its elements are technological superiority derived from uniformity of procedure and of materials and maximization of non-skilled labor through the use of molds, simplified designs, and standardized operations. This kind of system could have manufactured decorated pottery much more cheaply in bulk than the unit pottery batches of skilled craftsmen. The Fine Orange distribution system showed the same kind of concern for efficiency.

The transport system can be easily predicted. If the Fine Orange system stressed efficiency, it must have employed water transport to the exclusion of land transport. As Fisk (1967: 23) notes, "after 20 centuries of development, seaborne trade is still the cheapest method of transporting bulky, low-value goods over great distances" (cf. also Adams, Paper 4; Lee, Paper 6; Edwards, Paper 17). The

emphasis upon developing water transport technology may well have been stimulated by the development of Buffer Zone centers and the impediments they imposed on the movement of goods. As water traffic became heavy the technological skill to expand its advantages developed also. The result of the development is the wide distribution of Fine Orange.[12] From its hearth in Tabasco, it is found throughout the Yucatan Peninsula, from Seibal to Dzibilchaltun and from Benque Viejo to Palenque. Perhaps much of the importance of this fact has been missed due to the small quantities of Fine Orange which are found at each site, often less than one percent of the total sherds. It is, however, apparent that there is scarcely any site which has yielded terminal Classic/Postclassic remains which has not also included some Fine Orange pottery. If all of the thousands of sites occupied in early Postclassic Yucatan obtained Fine Orange pottery through a single distribution system, that system must have been truly impressive in scope.

Most ancient pottery was made for a comparatively short time period and then replaced by another type, usually through stylistic obsolescence. Although shapes and designs changed through time, basic Fine Orange pottery was manufactured for 750 years, until the Conquest when Spanish-controlled products replaced it. The whole Fine Orange system presents a new insight into the nature of the Classic/Postclassic transition.

Fine Orange pottery cannot be taken out of context. It is merely a symbol, a trace element, of the major trade organization which developed during the Classic/Postclassic transition. It is one piece of a new system, just as Wedgewood's ceramic mass production factories and transportation advances were just one minor piece of the industrial revolution (Hillier 1965).

It suggests that the Postclassic witnessed an increased emphasis on economic

---

[12]The efficiency of Postclassic transportation is substantiated by M. E. Harlan's tentative conclusion that, using a product-moment correlation (Pearsons r) test, distance from manufacture accounted for only 21% of the variability in distribution of Fine Orange pottery (Harlan n.d.).

efficiency and mass consumption. Production could have been geared to a rising standard of living rather than to the costly maintenance of deities, priests, and an elite minority. The high investment of labor and capital in the production of ceremonial-elite structures and paraphernalia during the Classic period brought little economic return to the non-elite population. The Postclassic system, however, could have effected a more even distribution of wealth through wide-scale population participation in commerce.

Some data already support this hypothesis. For example, Andrews (1965) noted an increased emphasis in the Postclassic upon the construction of administrative structures (palaces), and a building technique which employed mass produced component elements to form facades. A recent study of obsidian distribution patterns is also relevant. Although obsidian sources were located twice as far from selected Postclassic (average: 815 km.) as Classic (average: 420 km.) sites,[13] the ratio of obsidian to flint in Postclassic centers and housemounds (2.1:1) is usually double that in Classic centers (.9:1) (Urban n.d.).

Woodward's (1970: 278) comment about the relationship between mass production, efficient distribution, and demand satisfaction may be important in understanding the Postclassic:

> Standardization, specification, and simplification are the ideals on which modern manufacturing is based, and it is, of course, true that our [modern United States] increased standard of living depends upon standardized production.

Woodward further maintains that increases in standard of living produce increases in the demands for exotic and specialized craft production. The Fine Orange system did not, then, entirely replace the craft system, but to some extent served as an adjunct to stimulate it. Fine Orange production and distribution is related to a series of other new facets of production and distribution, just as Wedge-

wood was wedded to the industrial revolution.

Thus, given the rise of Buffer Zone growth centers, their development of local production potential to manufacture craft items, and their clogging effect upon overland trade channels, the outlines of the Postclassic production, distribution, and settlement patterns may be brought into a new focus by trade models. Technological superiority, standardization, efficiency of container shapes for filling and emptying procedures, stackability and other attributes relative to long-distance transport, time and skill expended upon forming, finishing and decorating, are all sets of variables which (especially for pottery) are potentially quantifiable and for which data are available. These variables, however, have received little or no attention. Trade models suggest that they might be extremely useful for elucidation of some important Late Classic/Postclassic developments.

V. SUMMARY AND CONCLUSIONS

A useful model, as defined by this paper, is one which allows efficient testing by comparison to the archaeological record. Three trade models which fit this description have been briefly presented.

In the first study demand estimation, objectively derived, led to a prediction that the earliest major lowland growth centers would be found in the Core Zone. Technology of supply furnished a bridge to the archaeological architectural remains of E-Groups, which were found to be restricted to the Core Zone. Technology of supply and intelligence complex constructs can be joined with archaeological data at many more loci to continue testing and refinement of this construct. For example, glyphic writing would have been a useful component in scheduling and other types of information storage at points of initiation and should develop earlier in growth centers than in depot and attachment centers.

Trade models propose that "backwash" and "spread" are two competing processes and that defining their relative importance is crucial to describing and understanding the history of Lowland Maya systems. The link with the specific Maya systems proposed that as Buffer Zone centers developed their own craft

---

[13]Classic sites: Altar de Sacrificios, Lubaantun, Piedras Negras, Uaxactun, Tikal, Barton Ramie, San José, Becan; Postclassic sites: Mayapan, Chichen Itza, Dzibilchaltun, Cozumel.

production systems, "backwash" would decrease and new points of initiation would develop outside the Core. This linkage led to the archaeological record through the prediction that as Buffer Zone systems increased in size and began to produce local craft commodities, Core systems would begin to discard fewer imported items and increased numbers of its own craft commodities in burials. Many more links can be developed between the model and quantifiable, retrievable data through Neutron Activation studies: stylistic comparisons of architecture, pottery, and other artifacts and computer analyses of the changes in the inter- and intra-site distribution of design elements and exotic items.

Demand, competition, and efficiency concepts were employed to present a new perspective on the nature of the Classic-Postclassic transition. This perspective is testable through objective measurement of the technological attributes of Fine Orange pottery and by analysing changes in availability and distribution patterns of exotic items; in the volume, technology and specific function of architectural construction; and in population densities and distributions.

No real solutions were presented by these tests — just more questions. To answer these questions archaeologists will need to broaden the parameters of description and explanation in their models. In this endeavor we will need all the help we can muster. This is not meant to suggest that archaeologists cannot develop their own models, but that as archaeologists build their own they should attempt to draw upon as much depth of research into relevant problems as they can grasp.

One aid in the development of mercantile models is the work of modern trade experts concerned with the economic, social and political effects of local and international exchange systems. Trading systems today face the same general problems as the Maya faced over one thousand years ago. The variables used in complex modern analyses and their interaction are applicable to all problems. For example, transport can always be broken down into resource-labor cost per bulk-weight units, whether a good is carried by cargador

through the Peten or by 747 over the Arctic Circle. If there are regularities in the development and change of trade systems, archaeologists can look for them as well as economists or modern merchants.

In fact, archaeologists, for all their problems of data retrieval and interpretation, have at least two advantages over scholars and businessmen studying modern systems. Archaeologists have fewer variables to control because their systems are usually simpler. Additionally, archaeologists have a temporal depth which few other disciplines can boast. Demand, schedules, production techniques, distribution methods, all change a little every day. This is the nature of a trading system. However, the important patterns of change can best be seen in the milieu of a long time perspective.

The work of most archaeologists (including this paper) has not settled to the task of testing and refining detailed multi-variate models of trade systems, perhaps due to the lack of a compatible data base. When archaeologists see complex formulae including variables like transport time, cargo space, packaging units, storability estimates, customs filters, and others, they often feel insecure and go back to their potsherds and bits of shell.

The stated goals of this volume, however, are an important step in the development of a set of data which can be used in complex descriptive and explanatory models. Use of existing, or development of new, models based upon the detailed analysis of the interaction of basic trade variables will lead to increased descriptive and explanatory potential, both for the problems of the past and for those of today.

In sum, this paper views archaeological problems as those of the description and explanation of cultural systems and their development through time. Trade models outline the organizational prerequisites and principles of change and development of long-distance exchange systems. The job of the archaeologist using trade models is to construct a link between the models and specific cultural and ecological systems and to test his bridge by predicting the material remains left by the interaction of exchange and other cultural and ecological systems. His tests along with those from allied disciplines can be used to evaluate the usefulness of trade models in general to describe and explain cultural development.

REFERENCES

Adams 1972
Andrews 1965
Binford 1962
Callender 1965
Coe, M. D. 1961a, 1965, 1968
Coe, W. R. 1959, 1963, 1965
Coggins 1967
Connor n.d.
Connor and Rathje 1973
Culbert 1973
Culbert and Rathje 1971
Fisk 1967
Flannery 1968
Fried 1967
Grove 1968
Hagaman and Longton 1972
Harlan n.d.
Haviland 1968
Hillier 1965
Jacobs 1969
Jiménez Moreno 1966
Keeble 1967

Leone 1968
Lundell 1934, 1937, 1938
McBryde 1947
Morley 1937–38
Owen 1928
Parsons and Price 1971
Proskouriakoff 1950
Puleston and Puleston 1971
Rathje 1971a, 1971b, 1972, 1973
Renfrew 1967, 1969
Ricketson and Ricketson 1937
Roys 1931
Ruppert 1940
Sabloff 1971
Sabloff and Willey 1967
Sanders 1962a, 1964, 1973
Sanders and Price 1968
Sayre, Chan, and Sabloff 1971
Schiffer 1972
Service 1955
Shepard 1965
Smith, A. L. 1962
Smith, R. E. 1958, 1971
Steyermark 1950
Thompson 1970
Tourtellot and Sabloff 1971
Urban n.d.
Vance 1971
Woodward 1970

15. PREHISPANIC TRADE IN CENTRAL CHIAPAS, MEXICO[1]
by
Donald E. McVicker

INTRODUCTION

Archaeological studies of trade in Meso-america have usually begun with objects and their distribution. In most cases these studies have concentrated upon a single class of objects, called luxury goods, and have presupposed the existence of a system of long distance commerce. In regard to this commerce, given the nature of the archaeological data, the reconstruction of the system has often relied more upon the interpretation of documents than upon actual artifacts encountered (Chapman 1957, Thompson 1970). Yet, available sources usually describe state-controlled commerce on a late horizon, dominated by professional merchants, and are difficult to use in the reconstruction of earlier systems. In regard to these luxury goods, given the problems of preservation in Mesoamerica, more attention has been paid to the distribution of trade pottery, a single subset of the class, than to the full range of goods traded. Yet, ethnohistoric sources indicate that long distance trade dealt mainly in raw materials and perishables, which are less often identified in the archaeological record. Nowhere in the extant lists does pottery figure prominently as an item of long distance trade or tribute. Cotton goods, feathers and skins; maize, beans and cacao; and precious metals and stones are the items commonly recorded (*Codex Mendoza*; Dibble and Anderson 1959).

In contrast to these considerations of far-flung commercial activities, are the studies of local exchange systems. Here again the archaeologist must often turn away from his excavated data, and draw upon the work of other anthropologists. However, in the best known ethnographic studies, for example those of Tax (1953) and Foster (1942), these local systems also deal mainly in raw materials and perishables. These products may be classified as subsistence goods, items which are necessary for survival, basic foodstuffs and essential household goods. The distribution of these products, carried out by producer-sellers, takes place within a system of community markets. This system, when compared to long distance trade supported by an expanding state or empire, appears closed or "corporate." Though such a system of local trade is admitted to be connected in a somewhat mechanical manner with others, the single network is still largely analyzed in isolation.

In recent studies the development of both long distance commerce and local exchange has been given an ecological base. However, reconstructions of the former have stressed the marked differences between hot country and cold country products, while studies of the latter have emphasized the microvariations around a lake or valley. In neither case has sufficient attention been paid to the variation in economic·potential of a single system relative to its articulation with other *exchange systems in operation*. In neither case have the contributions or consequent development of the local community been seen as much in terms of its location, market and manufacturing potential, as in terms of its ability to exploit available natural resources.

A typological dichotomy between the products, institutions and ecological potentials of long distance commerce and local exchange has obscured the importance of an intermediate type of trade, the regional network. This type of trade provides a framework for exchange neither as expansive as long distance commerce nor as corporate as local

[1]A preliminary version of this paper was presented at the American Anthropological Association meeting, Washington, D.C., 1967. The field research on which this paper was based was conducted in Mexico, 1961–62, and 1968. Support the author received from the National Science Foundation through the University of Chicago's Man in Nature project and from the Harvard University's Chiapas project is gratefully acknowledged.

market systems. It provides a place for itinerant merchants as well as full-time specialists and producer-sellers. It considers the contribution of all ecological zones, not only as the source of products, but also as points of exchange. It follows that it acknowledges the important role played by the midlands in the development of an effective regional symbiosis.

Such a regional network is characterized by the movement of utility items, which are desirable, but neither absolutely necessary nor unusually exotic. Though this class of utility items is difficult to delimit sharply, it includes many ceramic "trade wares" as well as other products of small industries (both manufacturing and extractive), and special foods which are consumed on festive occasions. In addition, it would probably include local goods which are defined as luxuries by provincial elites, and subsistence items which are not available within the confines of corporate exchange. However, despite these difficulties of definition, many members of this class of utility items appear to be more easily recovered from the archaeological record, or more easily inferred from specific ecological information, than are the members of the class of luxury items or subsistence items. Further, the initial identification of the regional network in terms of the distributional limits of culturally produced items is basic to the testing of propositions which assume the existence of natural regions defined in terms of ecological potential and ethnic unity.

THE REGION OF CENTRAL CHIAPAS

Central Chiapas offers a number of advantages for the study of regional trade (Fig. 32). The classic divisions of *tierra fría, tierra templada,* and *tierra caliente* are present in close proximity, and each major division contains substantial ecological variation (Wagner 1963). Yet, despite this internal ecological diversity and the presence of economically specialized communities, no locally limited exchange systems are recorded and solar system markets are lacking (Nash 1966). Instead, the traditional pattern of exchange is characterized by extensive interaction among all zones.

This development of a system of extensive regional exchange contrasts with the underdevelopment of long distance trade. Throughout most of its history, the isolation of Central Chiapas kept the export of its valuable resources to a minimum. Nonetheless, sufficient luxury goods were produced and traded to enable both historian and archaeologist to tie Central Chiapas to better known regions. Among these goods were special varieties of maize, cotton, dyes (cochineal, indigo, and *achiote* [annato]), and incense gums from tropical trees available along the Grijalva; amber, skins, and feathers obtained from the slopes; and numerous mineral resources extracted from the highlands (certainly flints and obsidian, and possibly jade, lime, volcanic tempers, pyrites, hematites, and iron oxide). Of importance to the highlands at the Conquest was an alabastar quarry controlled by Zinacantan. Though mentioned by Ximénez (1932), its exact location is unknown.

Not only were these goods of value in the network of inter-regional exchange, but they were undoubtedly exchanged intra-regionally as well. In fact it would appear that various regional centers, such as Zinacantan at Conquest, were gathering in these products and then serving as points of interchange between Central Chiapas and adjacent areas. However, at least in the case of Zinacantan, only a special type of indirect long distance trade was being carried on. It is obvious from Sahagún's account of the market at Zinacantan (Dibble and Anderson 1959: 21–22) that this highland center was not serving as a "port of trade," but as a major market in the regional network. Though the "disguised merchants," in addition to useful information, are there to obtain products of the highlands and slopes (amber, skins, and feathers), they are exchanging regional goods such as cochineal, red ochre, and rabbit fur, and items manufactured from locally available resources (obsidian blades and obsidian points). Thus, the flow of products in and out of Central Chiapas typically followed a number of indirect routes. For example, amber for the lip plugs of Yucatecan nobles (Thompson 1964) probably passed down the Grijalva through Cimitan to Acalan (Scholes and Roys 1948) before starting up the coast of the peninsula to the centers

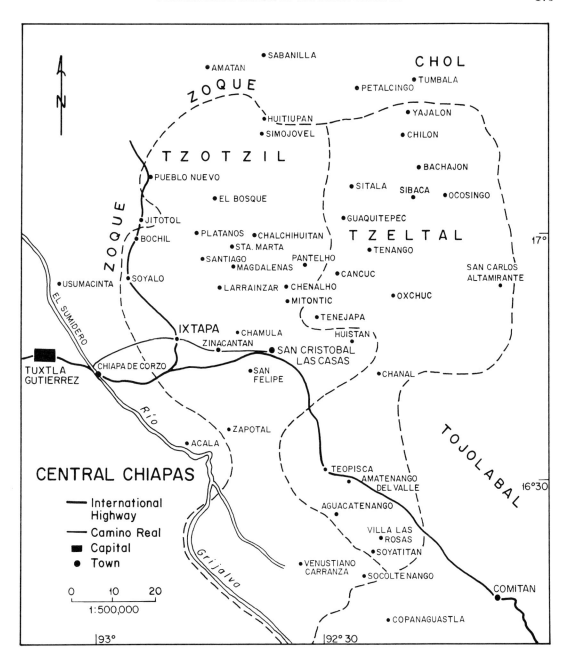

Figure 32. MAP OF CENTRAL CHIAPAS

of the north. In a similar fashion, after Conquest, *cacao* was obtained by Chiapa de Corzo through trade with the Soconusco, and from that point distributed throughout the highlands (Thompson 1958).

Only a few imports which indicate pre-Hispanic commercial ties with major trading centers have been recovered from Central Chiapas. When found, most of these imports can be assigned to a period marking the transition between Late Classic and early Postclassic cultures in the region. For example, scattered finds of Tepeu polychrome, Plumbate, and Fine Orange have been made. However, as Thompson (1964) suggests for Fine Orange and Plumbate, the presence of these widely distributed items in Central Chiapas may be as much an indication of major trade routes from the Pacific Coast and the Chiapas-Tabasco plains crossing the region as an indication of the importance of the import-export economy.

Contrasting with the rare occurrences of major Mesoamerican trade wares is the wide distribution of regional imitations. It is the presence of these ceramics in the archaeological record which will be used initially to trace the development and extent of the regional network of exchange.

Several well-known studies are particularly relevant to a discussion of this regional trade network in Central Chiapas. McBryde's (1947) description of the cultural geography of Southwest Guatemala provides data on an area historically and ecologically linked to Central Chiapas. In addition it places the "solar system markets" of Lake Atitlan and the Quetzaltenango-Totonicapan Valley in a regional context. Malinowski and de la Fuente's (1957) study of markets in the valley of Oaxaca is more than the description of the sun and planets of another "solar system." It is a regional analysis to the extent that it deals with trade routes extending out of the valley into the Sierras and down to the Isthmus. The participation of diverse ethnic and linguistic groups in the Oaxaca system (Zapotec, Mixtec, and Mixe), is similar to the modern Quiche, Cakchiquel, Zutuhil, and Mam involvement in southwestern Guatemala exchange. In the

past this was true in Central Chiapas as well, where Zoque, Tzeltal-Tzotzil, and Chiapanec were culturally divided but to a certain extent commercially united. Finally, Rands' (n.d., 1967) research on ceramic technology and trade in the Palenque region provides the best carefully documented archaeological example of the important place of pottery in a limited exchange system. Though Rands is dealing with a region which appears not to be as environmentally and ethnically diverse as the highlands, the extent to which local ceramic types are distributed, the presence of true imports and the appearance of regionally manufactured imitations appears to be comparable to ceramic events in Central Chiapas.

When the data from Central Chiapas were reviewed in the light of the above studies, the outlines of a regional trade network could be traced. Since no important local exchange systems are recorded for any one zone, and since the isolation of the area has reduced the significance of long distance trade, the dynamics of this regional network proved particularly useful in interpreting cultural developments in the area. However, available space limits the description of regional exchange in Central Chiapas to a single section, the southwest quadrant, and to the close examination of a single point of exchange, the valley of Ixtapa.

THE VALLEY OF IXTAPA

The valley of Ixtapa is located midway between the Grijalva lowlands and the summit of the Central Chiapas highlands (Fig. 33, McVicker 1969). The elevation of the valley floor is a bit above 1,100 m., placing most of its lands near the lower limits of *tierra templada*. In contrast to the temperate though somewhat dry climate of Ixtapa, the Grijalva trench below, with elevations near 500 m., is hot and semi-arid, while the plateau above, with elevations exceeding 2,000 m., is relatively cool and moist. The valley of Ixtapa is chosen for analysis not only because relatively little has been said of the role played by temperate lands in a regional symbiosis, but also because the pattern of progress and lag typical of the regions seems particularly marked in its culture history (McVicker 1970). In addition, the valley is a source of salt, an important regional trade product. The pre-Hispanic significance of the Ixtapa salt well is referred to by Ximénez (1929–31) and Remesal (1932), the archaeological evidence which supports this significance is reviewed in the next section.

Aside from salt, the major pre-Conquest resources of the valley are agricultural. Since the critical point for vegetation in this region is a bit below the plateau summit, around 2,000 m., in theory Ixtapa and the surrounding slope lands could supply the highlands not only with salt, but also desirable lowland products. However, despite the ecological

potential of these midland valleys, their agricultural products seem to have been of minor importance. For these valleys in contrast to the lowlands possess insufficient land for profitable crop specialization beyond local consumption.

Of more importance, perhaps, than the agricultural potential of the valley of Ixtapa is its location. For example, even today the merchants of highland Chamula prefer to travel to Ixtapa to trade with the merchants who travel up from the lowland Tuxtla. In fact, for the Chamulas Ixtapa is in hot country, and for the Tuxtlecos Ixtapa is in cold country. Ixtapa occupies not only the midpoint on the major

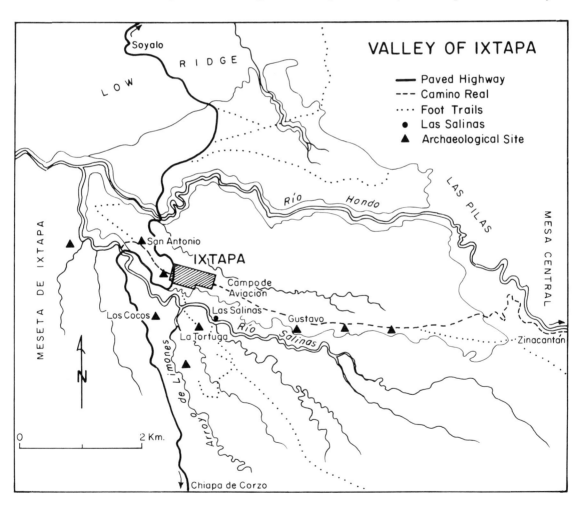

Figure 33. MAP OF THE VALLEY OF IXTAPA

route from the Grijalva to the Plateau, but also the juncture of this route with the main trail connecting the flank of the highland with the Chiapas-Tabasco plain. This locational factor must be considered, since at various times Ixtapa sustained ceremonial activities, distributed manufactured items, and shared in cultural developments to a greater extent than would be expected of an isolated intermontane valley located in a marginal region.

CULTURAL DEVELOPMENT AND TRADE

When the sites in the valley of Ixtapa are compared to others in the southwest quadrant of the Central highlands, several features are striking: first, the number and size of sites; and second, their location and occupational history. During the Late Preclassic at a time when the highlands seem to have been sparcely populated, a single large site was constructed on the edge of the open valley plain. This site, San Antonio, is comparable to major centers along the Grijalva. No evidence for extensive long distance or regional trade was recovered from San Antonio; however, the only other site to yield evidence for a Late Preclassic occupation was located above the salt well. Just prior to the explosive "Protoclassic" developments at lowland Chiapa de Corzo, ceremonial activity at San Antonio apparently ceased. Construction of public buildings was not resumed in the valley until late in the Early Classic, shortly after the decline of Chiapa de Corzo.

The Late Classic witnessed a time of rapid expansion of sites in the valley, on the plateau summit, and in the lowland region of the Frailesca adjacent to the Grijalva River. At that time in the valley the major center, La Tortuga, was defensively located on a finger ridge separated from the open valley by the canyon of the Salinas River. This site sits directly above the salt well. The plan of La Tortuga, the extent of its ceremonial precinct, and the surrounding concentration of low platforms, is more closely related to sites in the Frailesca and in the upper tributaries subregion of the Central Depression than to sites on the plateau. The distribution of Late Classic ceramics also ties this occupation to lowland manufacturing centers rather than to those located in the highlands.

In addition to La Tortuga, at least four other sites with mounds were occupied at the same time. All of these are strung along the open valley edge of the canyon of the Salinas River, and mark the most direct route between the Grijalva and plateau. The old Camino Real connecting Chiapa de Corzo and San Cristóbal still follows this same route.

Among the four open valley sites mentioned above, one, Campo de Aviación, is of particular interest. This relatively small site, just southeast of the present town of Ixtapa, located above the salt well across from La Tortuga, yielded the longest occupational sequence known from the valley. During all phases the ceramic samples yielded a remarkable percentage of jars, and running through the Classic-Postclassic transition, except for the Early Classic hiatus, the ceramics suggest a community involved in the transportation and/or storage of liquids. Today, as in the Colonial past, the Ixtapeños live on the open valley, and work the salt well on the river, carrying and keeping the saline waters in a variety of jars. Juan B. Sánchez, quoted in Mendizábal (1928: 163) describes the process of manufacture as follows:

> La sal de Iztapa se fabrica en ollas de barro, haciendo evaporar el agua saturada de sal que extraen los indios de unos pozos próximos al arroyo. El trabajo es laborioso y costoso por falta de combustible, pues solo usan leña y la vegetación es pobre en ese lugar.

In contrast to the contemporary Tsah phase settlements on the plateau, where the volume of ceremonial building is reported to be small in relation to the apparent size of the population (Adams 1961: 348), La Tortuga and its open valley of satellites appear committed to a Late Classic pattern of ceremonialism. Involvement in, if not control of, intraregional trade could have supplied the economic foundation for this commitment. Four ceramic types, two produced in Ixtapa, one in the Grijalva lowlands, and one probably manufactured along the Chiapas-Tabasco slopes, were used to test this possibility. They represent a tradition of regional imitations drawing its inspirations from Late Classic Fine Orange and Tepeu III polychromes. The history of the Fine Orange related ceramics of Ixtapa is considered first.

A fine-paste tradition can be identified in the valley at the beginning of the Late Classic. During this period white-slipping becomes common on vessels included in this tradition. The same technique is frequently encountered on Grijalva lowland types, where it develops into a double slipped ware including polychrome and resist decorated types (Warren 1961). At least one of these types, in turn, appears in the valley of Ixtapa, and is discussed below. The Ixtapa type itself, Ixtapa Fine: White-slipped Variety, is easily separated from examples of Grijalva types by its combination of hard, dense, orange, virtually temperless paste and often fugitive slip. Vessels of Ixtapa Fine have been recovered from Late Classic (Maravillas phase) tombs at the Grijalva site of Chiapa de Corzo and from the central highland site of Cerro Ecatepec (Lowe 1962, Culbert 1965).

About three-quarters of the material placed in the Ixtapa slipped group belongs to the Late Classic, and the bulk of it has been recovered from Ixtapa and the lowlands. However, the terminal Classic is marked by a rapid spread into the western highlands of late, either poorly slipped or possibly unslipped types related to this group. During this transition to the Postclassic, the Ixtapa slipped group retains its popularity in the valley and diminishes in importance along the Grijalva. Culbert (1965: 68–69) considers the highland peak to have occurred during the early Postclassic (Yash phase) with some imitations (e.g., "Cuchumton Variety") being produced into the late Postclassic (Lum phase). The shifting importance of Ixtapa Fine is probably an example of the merging and later separation of two traditions: 1. white-slipping, and 2. fine paste. The former was never typical of the highlands, and the latter never typical of the lowlands. The potters of Ixtapa combined both traditions, and during the Late Classic, when ties were strongest with the Grijalva, produced white-slipped wares, and during the early Post-classic, when ties became stronger with the plateau, continued to produce fine-paste wares.

In addition to Ixtapa Fine, a closely-related fine paste type, Ixtapa Red-on-Buff, was produced during the Late Classic. Though never as popular as the preceding type, and somewhat more limited in time and spatial distribution, it falls within the range of the Ixtapa fine paste tradition. Possibly exported for mortuary purposes, the only examples known outside of the valley have been recovered from the same tombs at Chiapa de Corzo and Cerro Ecatepec which yielded vessels of Ixtapa Fine.

The appearance and dynamic spread of a fine paste tradition during the Late Classic in the western Maya lowlands has been noted by Rands (n.d.: 13, 23). The importance and possible origin of this tradition in the adjacent Chiapas-Tabasco plains has long been suspected (Berlin 1952–1954: 113). Though this tradition by-and-large bypassed the dying centers of the central Peten, its later importance in the terminal complex at Altar de Sacrificios and Seibal on the rivers to the south has been discussed by Willey, Culbert, and Adams (1967: 302). The cultural implications of the spread of fine paste wares have been reviewed by Sabloff and Willey (1967).

Examples of trade pieces of true Fine Orange derived from the lowland fine paste tradition have been recovered from the highlands of Chiapas, particularly from the site of Moxviquil (Smith 1958), and from the Grijalva Valley (Lowe 1959). However, a related, and possibly locally manufactured carved type (or group of types) has been identified in the highlands (Culbert 1965: 69, Fig. 6a), Ixtapa (Orellana T. 1954), and the Central Depression (Lowe 1959: 25, 28, Fig. 32a). Though the intricate "model-carving" of this type is similar to Z-Fine Orange, when the paste and temper are examined, it clearly falls outside of the lowland Fine Orange groups as presently defined. The scanty distributional data available suggest that the center of production may have been located somewhere along the western slopes of the Chiapas highlands.

A fourth "regional imitation" probably manufactured in the Grijalva Valley, shares the same distributional pattern as the preceding types. This red-black-on-orange polychrome belongs to a group (Berriozábal double-slipped) most commonly encountered at the site of Berriozábal (Lowe 1959: 23, Fig. 39a; Navarrete and Martínez 1960–1961: 53–54, Fig. 2). It has been aptly described by Culbert (1965: 21) as combining "a sort of representation most common in the Early Classic of (the Tikal-Uaxactun area) with a vessel form that is typically Late Classic." Sherds of this polychrome proved to be useful markers of Late Classic deposits in the valley, and vessels have been found in highland, lowland, and midland tombs of the region. In fact, not only do the Tsah phase tombs from Ecatepec, Maravillas phase tombs from Chiapa de Corzo, and the Tortuga phase tombs from La Tortuga usually contain Berriozábal polychromes, but they also usually contain the other regional types as well.

If the distribution of these four types of pottery is used to locate communities participating in a network of exchange, and if it is assumed that other products traveled between these points, then the outline of a regional system begins to take shape. When the ecological potentials discussed above are reviewed, a productive symbiosis among the participant communities becomes a strong possibility. This system of exchange, in effect a microcosm of the macro-systems analyzed by Sanders (1962b), seems to have supported a small-scale regional prosperity and consequent elaboration of tradition analagous to the grand scale developments in nuclear Mesoamerica.

Central Chiapas seems to have experienced only a single period of fully developed regional prosperity. This occurred at a time when surrounding areas were disturbed and perhaps powerless to draw off local surplus through conquest, tribute and trade. The settlements and ceramics of the terminal Classic–Postclassic transition are marked by a series of closely related local cultural developments, which, though derivative, are nonetheless vigorous. In particular, the midlands seem to have benefited from the growth of regional exchange. Possessing small industries (both extractive and manufacturing), a wide range of raw materials, and an ideal marketing position, valleys such as Ixtapa boomed between the collapse of the major Classic ceremonial centers and the rise of the Postclassic military powers.

Though the Late Classic expansion in Central Chiapas continued without interruption into Postclassic times, by the early Postclassic a notable shift in settlement pattern and ceramics was already taking place. The remodeling of existing ceremonial structures continued at La Tortuga. However, the main building activity now centered at Arroyo de Limones, located on an adjoining finger ridge. The typical structures of this site are low platforms considerably larger than similar residential mounds encountered at La Tortuga and formally designed three-mound one-platform "plazas." These latter mounds are notably smaller and more complex in plan than the Tortuga "ceremonial" mounds. The site of Arroyo de Limones is more closely related to the early Postclassic highland sites (Yash phase) described by Adams (1961) than to the sites known from the Central Depression (Navarrete 1960). In particular, the pattern of ceremonial activities concentrated on one ridge (La Tortuga) and residential structures on another (Arroyo de Limones) is similar to that of the large Yash phase site of San Gregorio overlooking the Tzaconeja River (Culbert 1965: 17–18, Fig. 9).

The effect of the early Postclassic changes in settlement pattern on open valley sites is notable. The increase in residential concentration on the ridge of Arroyo de Limones is accompanied by a sharp decrease in building activity on the open valley. By the middle of the Postclassic, except for scattered ceramics at several sites, there is no evidence that communities on the plain continued to be of importance. However, at least during the earlier part of the Postclassic, the Tortuga-Limones complex is still larger than any comparable site from the highlands. This desertion of unprotected valley sites and growth of defensible hilltop sites is a common occurrence on the plateau summit, and has been compared to a similar phenomenon noted in the Guatemala highlands (Adams 1961: 347). Along the Grijalva a change in settlement pattern has also been suggested. In this area the shift was toward the foothills of the Sierras. During the early Postclassic, small defensible sites are also constructed on top of small hills scattered throughout this area. However, despite these changes, the Grijalva can still be characterized as an area of poorly defended sites when compared to the plateau. In fact, in the region of Central Chiapas a time gradient suggests itself in regard to settlement pattern. The characteristic Postclassic developments begin in the highlands during the transition, and are not fully present in the lowlands until the beginning of the early Postclassic.

During the Late Classic–Postclassic transition, ceramic evidence also indicates a shift in orientation toward the plateau. Lowland types disappear from Ixtapa, and the typical ware manufactured in the valley, Ixtapa Fine, increases in popularity throughout the western highlands. However, with the exception of Ixtapa Fine, reduction in the number of identified types and particularly the diminution of decorated types makes the ceramic evidence less useful in the identification of a Postclassic system of regional exchange. Even Ixtapa Fine appears to have been imitated rather than traded by the middle of the Postclassic. Whether exchange has truly decreased, or only appears to have decreased on the basis of available ceramic evidence, is an open question. However, when a few of the well-known highland types were searched for in the material from Ixtapa, they could not be found. Aside from ceramics, the only trade item which has been found distributed from the highlands to the Grijalva is the alabaster vase (Berlin 1946: 26–27). This item is as much an object of long distance commerce as one of regional trade.

If regional trade was decreasing in importance during the Postclassic, then it is possible that long distance commerce was increasing. However, the evidence to support this possibility is either lacking or confusing.

For example, vessels of Plumbate, the chief horizon marker for the early Postclassic and major indicator of long distance trade, though known from the Grijalva (Lowe 1959, Berlin 1946), are extremely rare in the highlands (Culbert 1965: 85) and in the valley of Ixtapa. Though this distributional pattern has been used as evidence for the increasing isolation of Central Chiapas during the Postclassic, the question may have to be reopened when, and if, early Postclassic tombs are finally discovered in the highlands and midlands. The same may be true in regard to X-Fine Orange, which is totally unrepresented in collections from the Central Highlands (Culbert 1965: 85) and the valley of Ixtapa.

By the mid-Postclassic, events become increasingly difficult to reconstruct. During the several hundred years before Conquest, a few major highland centers such as Chamula and Zinacantan formed petty "states" based on military and economic power. During this period, Ixtapa apparently fell under the domination of Zinacantan. When the early documents from Central Chiapas refer to the salt trade, they always place it under the control of the Zinacantecans. In fact, one legal document (Navarrete 1966) pictures Ixtapa as a pawn caught between the conflicting claims of highland and lowland centers. It would appear that the major occupation at both La Tortuga and Arroyo de Limones ended when control of the salt trade passed to Zinacantan and the Chiapanec-dominated lowlands withdrew from the postulated regional exchange system. The ethnohistoric sources make no mention of a major town in the valley, and only one late Postclassic settlement was identified there. Perhaps significant is the fact that this site, Gustavo, was located on the valley floor, near the salt well on the Camino Real.

Though the political units on the plateau were expanding at Conquest, the most powerful center in the region was located along the Grijalva. There, the then entrenched Chiapanecs were not only resisting Aztec pressures, but were in turn contesting highland control of sources of salt and alabaster. However, the Chiapanecs appear to have done more to disrupt trade than to promote it

(Navarrete 1966a). Unfortunately, in neither highlands nor lowlands have the major late Postclassic centers been excavated, and at least in the highlands, the late ceramic complexes have proved of little use in the reconstruction of these developments (Culbert 1965: 86–87).

The long-distance trade documented at Conquest may have gained slightly in importance over earlier periods. However, though amber, wild animal skins, and feathers recorded by Sahagún (Dibble and Anderson 1959: 21) were available in the market at Zinacantan and presumably were carried to the Valley of Mexico, the Aztecs were probably more interested in gaining control of the important trade routes which crossed the plateau than in exploiting its own products. In fact, as mentioned above, the Aztec "disguised merchants" were playing the role of regional traders, and as such, probably had little effect on the development of institutionalized long distance commerce in the societies of the Central Chiapas highlands.

Regardless of the growth of long distance commerce, it is obvious that the regional symbiosis established during the Late Classic, possibly encouraged by ethnic ties as well as by the isolation of the region, had been shattered by Postclassic internal disruptions and external demands. The boundaries of the Zoque were being pushed back toward the Isthmus by the Chiapanecs. The Maya-speaking highlands, already split into a Tzotzil-dominated west and a Tzeltal-dominated east, were being further fragmented by Chiapanec and Aztec pressures. The Midlands had lost whatever independence they may have at one time achieved.

To be sure, at Conquest Central Chiapas may be considered a "backward region," and "seems to have remained marginal to the nexus of interregional communication and trade" (Adams 1961: 359). However, at least on the basis of the data reviewed above, this marginality was limited in time. Actually, the components of the geographic region (Grijalva, intermontane valley and plateau) played various roles in a series of systems of inter-regional communication and trade. The mar-

ginal or central achievements of the region were determined by the organizational demands and economic requirements of competing and cooperating centers. Further, in the single recorded instance when intra-regional cooperation was maximized and extra-regional competition was at a minimum, cultural tradition and geographic region became one. At that time, Central Chiapas, though conservative, appeared prosperous and advanced relative to the disturbed adjacent areas. This response of the hinterlands to the decay of the center has been discussed at length by Wolf (1959) in his overview of Mesoamerican prehistory. The general theoretical implication of such regional progression and regression has been made clear by both Service (1960: 93–110) and Sahlins (1964: 132–146) in their consideration of "the law of evolutionary potential."

REFERENCES

Adams 1961
Berlin 1946, 1952–54
Chapman 1957
Codex Mendoza 1938
Culbert 1965
Dibble and Anderson 1959
Foster 1942
Lowe 1959, 1962
Malinowski and de la Fuente 1957
McBryde 1947
McVicker 1969, 1970
Mendizábal 1928
Nash 1966
Navarrete 1960, 1966a
Navarrete and Martínez 1960–61
Orellana Tapia 1954
Rands n.d., 1967
Remesal 1932
Sabloff and Willey 1967
Sahlins 1964
Sanders 1962b
Scholes and Roys 1948
Service 1960
Smith 1958
Tax 1953
Thompson 1964, 1970
Thompson, ed. 1958
Wagner 1963
Warren 1961
Willey, Culbert, and Adams 1967
Wolf, 1959
Ximénez 1929–31

16. PORTS OF TRADE IN MESOAMERICA: A REAPPRAISAL[1]
by
Frances Frei Berdan

As an outgrowth of Polanyi's project on economic aspects of institutional development, there have emerged several applications of the concept "ports of trade" to early empires (Polanyi 1966; Arnold 1957a; Revere 1957; Leeds 1962; Chapman 1957). The fullest theoretical exposition is given in his "Ports of Trade in Early Societies" (Polanyi 1963). "Ports of trade" are defined as intentionally neutral locales where representatives of political entities meet for the purpose of conducting commercial transactions.

Taken as a whole, these studies point toward a consideration of ports of trade as a predictable socio-economic structure under specified conditions: notably the presence of powerful neighboring state structures and the operation of non-industrial, non-market economies. Although there are certain features of these trading centers which do define this as a cross-cultural type, many other features serve to highlight the variation among them, and suggest further examination of the concept. It is the purpose of this paper to re-examine the concept "ports of trade" with special emphasis on variation. Late Postclassic Mesoamerica, exhibiting several examples of ports of trade (Chapman 1957), will provide the focus for this study.

ARCHAIC ECONOMIC SYSTEMS

Much of the basic conceptual work on archaic economic systems has been associated with Karl Polanyi and his colleagues. In *Trade and Market in the Early Empires* (1957), Polanyi and others presented a detailed statement of the substantivist position in economic

anthropology. For present purposes, this approach will be followed in principle. A brief resumé of the basic tenets of this orientation of economic anthropology follows, insofar as it bears on interpretations Polanyi and others have made regarding archaic economic systems in general and ports of trade in particular.

It is generally agreed that all societies have structured arrangements to provide the material means of individual and community life. It is these structured means that constitute the economic system. There are, indeed, important differences in the ways economic activities are institutionalized in societies, and the substantivist approach is designed to discover these ways. In Polanyi's (1957: 248) terms the economy is viewed as "instituted process": economic activity as embedded in institutions, such activity involving movements of material elements. This includes both the actual movements of goods and the structural features regulating and controlling these movements.

The importance of this institutionalized process is that it endows the economic process with stability and coherence with reference to the rest of the society. Such stability and coherence may be realized through certain forms of economic integration, and Polanyi (1957: 250) has isolated three generalized forms, or patterns, through which economies may be instituted. These are reciprocity, redistribution, and exchange (by which he means market exchange; all three of these forms are means of exchange):

> Reciprocity denotes movements between correlative points of symmetrical groupings; redistribution designates appropriational movements toward a center and out of it again; exchange refers to . . . movements taking place as between "hands" under a market system (Polanyi 1957: 250).

Certain social arrangements are associated with these different modes of transaction: sym-

[1]This paper was originally submitted to the IX International Congress of Anthropological and Ethnological Sciences, 1973, and is published in the *Cultural Continuity in Mesoamerica* volume edited by David L. Browman, *World Anthropology* series, Mouton Publishers, The Hague, 1975. Permission to reprint this article in its present form is gratefully acknowledged.

metrical groupings, centricity in group organization, or a price-regulated market system. The specific forms of transaction are embedded in these institutional arrangements, and only when these arrangements are present, claims Polanyi, will the particular modes of transaction effectively integrate the economy. For example, specific acts of exchange can produce a large-scale redistributive transactional sphere only when allocative centers have been established. In the case of archaic economic systems, generally characterized by a redistributive sphere, this necessitates some form of centralization of power regulating the movements of resources through the center. It is important to emphasize that Polanyi does not refer to these different forms of integration as entire economic systems, but rather as modes of transaction, in which two or all may be found in the same economic system. There are, he argues, emphases on particular modes of integration in different societies, but this does not *a priori* exclude the presence of other modes in the same society.

Within this framework, archaic economic systems are considered to form part of the complex organization of state-organized, nonindustrial societies. The early states are generally considered, economically, to be composed of an internal system of redistribution and a network of external, administered trade. There is also little doubt that patterns of reciprocity operated at a local level. In addition, there is historical evidence that forms of market exchange were also present and important in the circulation of goods in these societies.

It is important to note the social context of these economic networks. Economic arrangements are viewed in terms of a complex political unit: the non-industrial state or empire. It is characterized by centralization of power, and a formal organization of subordinate constituencies. Accordingly, the controlling powers of the center regulate the production and distribution of resources to some degree by imposing tribute and/or tax quotas on their constituencies (whether individuals, regions, or ethnic groups). As such, the center serves as a receiving and allocative center for the unit as a whole. This center is generally

considered to be urban in nature, both in terms of spatial-demographic configurations and as a point of concentration of functions and power for the society or region. The structure of this center, or non-industrial city, has been studied cross-culturally by Sjoberg (1960).

The social organization is also characterized by forms of social stratification, exhibiting generally a large social and economic gap between those who produce goods and those to whom goods are distributed. Social stratification can be defined in terms of differential control over strategic resources and is very likely a precondition for state organization (Fried 1960). Exclusive control over certain important resources (often as status symbols) is generally restricted to particular statuses in the society. The redistributive system serves to solidify and maintain a specific system of social stratification by controlling the distribution and accessability of important goods for particular, defined ends (frequently status-related) (Polanyi 1966: 193–94).

Eisenstadt (1963) discusses in depth the nature of social and political organization of the historic "bureaucratic empires" (his terminology for Polanyi's "archaic societies"). According to Eisenstadt, there is in such empires the presence of some relatively non-rigid (i.e., non-ascriptive) status hierarchies, and the presence of special elite positions not necessarily based on ascriptive criteria. The general stratigraphic type he describes is composed of a ruler and the upper echelons of the bureaucracy. Below these are various specialized urban groups and cultural elites, with far less political power at their disposal. The peasantry (and lowest urban classes) comprise the base of this type of society. Eisenstadt notes that many positions potentially and actually drew membership from all societal levels. This is apparent in the case of Mesoamerica. Aztec society, for example, allowed social mobility through non-ascriptive means, and there existed statuses by achievement (especially in the military realm, and perhaps to a lesser degree through success in commerce and religious activities). Although such channels were available for mobility, it should be emphasized that ascriptive criteria for societal position still predominated (see also Sjoberg 1960).

Relations with foreign political units are carried on through trading activities administered from the political center. Goods are allocated from the center for such trade, and the persons and groups conducting the transactions enjoy a special status endowed by the controlling political powers. Such professional merchants comprise the groups conducting commercial transactions in ports of trade. Their trade is generally considered to be in the service of the ruling powers and the elite, transactions usually involving status-related luxury goods.

Internally, markets appear to be present, but their exact nature and place in the economic system has not been adequately examined. Evidence points to extensive development of market places and marketplace activity, but rates of exchange appear to be regulated by administrative policy as well as by supply and demand factors. There appear to be markets at local, regional, and super-regional levels. The larger markets, at least, involve exchanges among a wide range of goods (both subsistence and luxury) as well as availability of services.[2] Persons conducting the transactions are the producers themselves, as well as professional, full-time merchants.

Features of reciprocity at the state level are evident, and seem to represent alliances or symbolize subjugation. Reciprocity no doubt was extensive in local communities, but the state-level orientation taken here does not lead to a discussion of such exchanges.

Economically, then, archaic societies exhibit forms of redistribution, "foreign" trade,[3] reciprocity, and a variant of market exchange. Each of these can be found with its social correlate: allocative centers, ports of trade, symmetrical political or kinship units, and market places with administrative policies. The rela-

tionships among these exchange sub-systems have been little explored. Arnold (1957b) and Polanyi (1966) suggest that market and foreign trade activities in the port of trade of Whydah (West Africa) were separate in both administrative organization and exchange activities. Chapman (1957) and Leeds (1962) follow the same premise for ports of trade in Mesoamerica and India. I have attempted to show elsewhere (Berdan 1973) that these exchange mechanisms may be linked through both actual exchange activities and social organizational features.

PORTS OF TRADE IN EARLY EMPIRES

Ports of trade have been discussed above as they relate to exchange through foreign trade, providing the focal institution for such trade in non-industrial states or empires. The general characteristics of these trading centers have been discussed by Polanyi (1963), Leeds (1962), and Belshaw (1965), and specific applications have been made by Arnold (1957a), Revere (1957), Leeds (1962), and Chapman (1957). These studies have been based primarily on historical materials, as is the present study. Such materials derive primarily from sources *external* to the trading centers. That is, they are predominately reports of foreign travelers or merchants to these locales. Some information is also available from nearby states, indicating their relationship and policies toward ports of trade. Information from the ports themselves, however, is sorely lacking.

The above writers on ports of trade have ennumerated a number of characteristics defining the nature of the origin and operation of these localities. Most of these characteristics have been considered to be applicable cross-culturally and through time under the "archaic" conditions discussed above. Variation undeniably exists, as both Polanyi (1963) and

---

[2]In the case of Colonial Mexico (ca. 1560), the Coyoacan market in the Valley of Mexico provided carpenters (Archivo General de la Nación, Tierras 1735). This very likely is a reflection of pre-Conquest patterns (Cortés 1928: 93).

[3]Polanyi (1957: 256) feels that foreign trade in archaic societies is based predominately on the "principle of reciprocity" (see also Sahlins 1965, for a discussion of types of reciprocity). I have used "foreign trade" here as separate from reciprocity as they appear to have very different correlative institutions and functions.

Belshaw (1965) agree, but the nature of this variation and its importance in describing this institution have been little explored.

The most frequently mentioned characteristic of ports of trade is that they are deliberately neutral, with guarantees of safety for foreign traders who transact business in that port (which need not be a seaport). According to Polanyi (1966: 100),

> Unless the government was both capable and willing to defend its neutrality and to enforce law and impartial justice, foreign merchants had to avoid places occupied by military power

Beyond neutrality, it is useful to discuss ports of trade in terms of, first, their relationships with nearby powers, and second, in terms of their characteristic internal organization.

It is often observed that ports of trade serve as points of transshipment between distinct ecological regions, and less frequently, that they serve as buffer zones. Politically and militarily, they are placed in positions of peripheral importance to nearby powers. Where powerful states confront one another, yet each controls the production of distinct and important resources, intermediate areas may develop a commercial importance beyond any military or political value. This will, of course, not be the case in each instance.

In terms of the structure of the port itself, it is considered as an autonomous town, city, or state intended to serve as a meeting place for various groups of foreign traders. Its autonomous character is undoubtedly linked to its neutrality, yet some ports seem to have been, at least to some degree, controlled by nearby states. Both 18th century Whydah (West Africa) and Xononochco (Mesoamerica) were overtly controlled by neighboring states. It would appear that the neutrality of the trading center could be seriously jeopardized under such a situation, yet guarantees for the safety of foreign traders apparently could be maintained (Polanyi 1963: 248–49).

Within the locale, there is evidence for a high development of transportation and communication facilities with an abundance of warehouses and other commercially-related structures and areas.

Strict administrative control is present in all foreign economic dealings, and prices are frequently fixed by treaty or other administrative arrangement. In addition, the activities of merchants are highly regulated while in the port, although it is often noted that groups of foreign merchants reside in the port itself.

The marketplace is generally considered to be geographically and economically separate from external trade; that is, if a market is present, it is an institution for the benefit of the local inhabitants and not used by foreign merchants. Polanyi, Arnold, Chapman, and others (in Polanyi et al. 1957) have emphasized the incompatibility of trade (foreign, administered trade) with markets. Arnold's observations on the port of trade of 18th century Whydah emphasize the exclusive nature of market and trade transactional spheres, the former involving exchanges of subsistence, utilitarian goods between local persons, the latter consisting of transactions between representatives of states dealing mainly in luxury goods. Both situations are conceived as being highly regulated, but through separate administrative channels. It is apparent, at least from the material available on Whydah, that the personnel, goods, and administration of the market and trade networks were institutionally separate and distinct, and served different ends. Similar information has not been adequately collected for other ports of trade. Nonetheless, the Whydah information has led students of archaic economic systems to consider these modes of transaction as exclusive and even incompatible in ports of trade. Although Chapman follows this premise, arguments for relationships between trade and markets in Mesoamerican ports of trade will be made here.

Two major features of ports of trade involve the range of control of resources by the local inhabitants, and the extent to which local groups engage in external commerce. It appears that the local persons are most commonly responsible for exchanges of goods with foreign traders; that is, they provide the link between the two trading states. For example, the Aztec merchants (*pochteca*) did not conduct commercial transactions directly with the Yucatecan Maya traders (*ppolom*), but rather with the Chontol of the Xicalango area, who traded Maya goods in return. Supposedly the same process held for transactions with the Maya *ppolom*.

Yet some groups appear to be involved in far-flung merchant ventures of their own, notably the Phoenicians (of Sidon and Tyre) and the Chontal of Acalan in Mesoamerica.[4] In a similar vein, these same two groups seem to have developed control over strategic resources, whether through means of production, through secondary manufacture, or through control of regional trade. While some areas are described as basically "empty" or a "no-man's land" (Revere 1957), others exhibit innovative and dynamic characteristics through control of resources: their production, manufacture, and/or distribution. These resources are valuable and strategic not only to the local group, but also to nearby powers. Eventual conquest of these areas by adjacent states appears as an inevitable course.

The historical development of these ports of trade will be, in some cases, a matter of conjecture. The general view has developed that neutral trading centers grew from the opposition of state societies, each requiring safety and neutrality for exchange of goods, without allowing emissaries of the other state into its territory. A different argument is made for parts of Mesoamerica, whereby it is conjectured that an already-existing trade network (perhaps pre-state organized) led to the preeminence of certain locales which controlled strategic resources. These locales, through control of these resources, became trading centers for long-distance merchants; not necessarily for the original strategic resource (cacao), but for other goods which had been attracted there by the abundance of this crop.

MESOAMERICAN PORTS OF TRADE

Chapman has discussed at some length locales in pre-Conquest Mesoamerica which she considers ports of trade according to the preceding characteristics. Preliminary to that discussion, she has detailed the role and activities of the Aztec and Maya merchants both in the ports of trade and in their homelands.[5] I do not intend here to duplicate Chapman's efforts in this regard, but would like to emphasize some of the more salient features of merchant organization, especially as it relates to activities in ports of trade.

At the time of the Spanish Conquest, Aztec society had emerged as a state organization, with social stratification, legally-sanctioned centralization of power, and complex economic specialization and networks. At that time, and probably for many centuries earlier, the professional merchant groups of Central Mexico (*pochteca* or *oztomeca*) enjoyed special privileges and a special status in relation to the state. The importance of merchants in entering enemy territory and transmitting information to the Aztec ruler is widely documented. In addition, they could declare and undertake wars (Katz 1966: 79) as well as conquer areas and found locales (Acosta Saignes 1971: 438). Their enormous military value to the state was complemented by an economic value: they provided the luxury items so necessary for the nobility. Outward symbols of status were prevalent in Aztec society, and rigidly defined.[6] Each rank in the society, whether ascribed or achieved, carried with it certain exclusive items of dress and ornamentation. Several manufactured items were provided through tribute, notably decorated cloth and warriors' costumes. Luxury raw materials were brought to the Basin of Mexico by the traveling merchants, as well as through tribute levies.

---

[4]Scholes and Roys (1968) present a particularly well documented study of this group.

[5]There are a number of these trading centers in Mesoamerica as discussed by Chapman: Xicalango and Cimatan on the Gulf Coast between the Maya and Aztec states, Xoconochco on the Pacific Coast near Guatemala, Nito and Naco on the Gulf of Honduras, and Acalan inland from the Xicalango area. Not only Xicalango, but the "Xicalango area," is considered as a port of trade "area," with numerous commercial communities.

[6]See Durán (1967, Vol. 2, pp. 211–14) for an enumeration of several laws relating to status.

The position of the merchant in Aztec society appears to be one of transition. Statuses traditionally were divided into two categories: nobility and commoner, and attainment of status was primarily by ascription.[7] Earmarks of status were not only access to and control over strategic resources (notably land and commoners to work that land), but also to specific luxury goods as outward displays of rank. The merchants emerge as a group intermediate between the commoners and the nobility. While they paid tribute (in goods only), they were at the same time greatly esteemed by the ruler, allowed to sacrifice slaves, and permitted to wear certain symbols of noble status at special annual festivals (Sahagún, Book 9). Although it is not clear whether they could own land,[8] this type of endowment does not appear as a regular occurrence as with the nobility. Rather than display their wealth (which was considerable in some cases), the merchants were constantly admonished by their elders to appear humble and dress simply (Sahagún, Book 9, p. 31). This was not necessarily a choice available to the merchants, as it appears that there were definite social obstacles to luxury consumption on their part (Katz 1972: 214). A possible conflict with the Otomi warriors is alluded to briefly in Sahagún (Book 9, p. 32), and may suggest broader social tensions. It should be noted that at the time of the Spanish Conquest, strains had been developing in Aztec society in terms of the definition of nobility status. Although there existed both nobility by achievement and nobility by ascription, the latter were placing pressures on the state to restrict the development of the former. In such a social climate, a group like the merchants would only provide additional tensions were they to attempt to also compete with the hereditary nobility. The secrecy of their dealings and concealment of their wealth,[9] then, are not difficult to understand.

Professional merchants are recorded for twelve Basin of Mexico cities,[10] and groups in each city were probably similarly organized. More important, there appears to have been an overall organization of *pochteca* from all these cities, and a system of internal ranking and laws applicable to all. This guild organization is characterized by exclusive residence, internal laws and codes, control over membership, rank in the organization and dispersal and allocation of tasks and rewards.

Most of the historical sources agree that merchants and artisans occupied exclusive sections (*calputin, barrios*) of the cities of Tlatelolco, Tenochtitlan, and Texcoco, and probably of other cities in the Basin of Mexico which contained organized merchant groups.[11] Zorita (1963: 112), however, mentions that each barrio contained its complement of merchants as well as agriculturalists. It is not entirely impossible (though undocumented) that merchants of a different order than those called pochteca or oztomeca were scattered about in other barrios or calpultin, and perhaps engaged exclusively in local or regional rather than international trading activities. On the other hand, trade in local markets was carried on by individuals who produced goods themselves, and Zorita may mean this when he lists "merchants" in this context.

The system of exclusive residence has been investigated in detail by Acosta Saignes (1971),[12] who suggests that the merchants occupied certain barrios in Tlatelolco, Tenochtitlan and adjacent areas: Axcotlan, Atlauhco, Auachtlan, Itzolco, Pochtlan, Tepetitlan, and Tzonmolco.[13] Van Zantwijk (1970: 5–6) offers the suggestion that Acxotlan and Pochtlan were dominant barrios, each with two lesser merchant barrios, while Tzonmolco was the major religious and educational center of the Tlatelolco-Tenochtitlan merchant guild

---

[7]High status in the society could be achieved primarily through success in warfare, but also through commercial and religious (priestly) activities.

[8]Katz (1972: 217) mentions this, the source apparently being Oviedo (1851–55, Vol. 3, p. 535).

[9]As Sahagún states (Book 9, p. 31), "And as to their goods, no one could see how much there was; perhaps they carefully hid — covered up — all the boats. Not at one's home did one arrive, (but) perhaps at the house of his uncle or his aunt . . . ."

[10]Tenochtitlan, Tlatelolco, Uitzilopochco, Azcapotzalco, Quauhtitlan, Mixcoac, Texcoco, Uexotla, Coatlichan, Otompan, Xochimilco, and Chalco.

[11]The notion of exclusive merchant barrios is emphasized by Sahagún, and supported by Ixtlilxochitl.

[12]Originally 1945.

as a whole. This hypothesis is consistent with other aspects of Aztec social organization, as *calpulli* (barrio) ranking was apparently the rule (Acosta Saignes 1971: 448). In any event, if the organized merchants did indeed occupy exclusive calpultin, and given the tendency toward calpulli endogamy (Carrasco 1971), this would tend to isolate them socially from the remainder of the urban population.

The strongest representation of merchants was found at Tlatelolco, which had undergone an extraordinary development of merchant activity. When Tlatelolco was conquered by Tenochtitlan in 1473, these merchants became closely related to the state organization at Tenochtitlan. It is a significant fact, and certainly no coincidence, that the great market of Tlatelolco was located at this center of pochteca activity and control.

The merchants, of all groups in Aztec society, were the ones allowed to create and enforce their own laws and codes, and the redistribution of private goods through the enactment of lavish feasts. Furthermore, merchants could extend their power to the marketplace, where they sat in judgment daily over the proceedings of the market of Tlatelolco, enforcing fair prices and proper conduct.

Little data exists on the extent to which the merchant guilds exercised control over membership.[14] Most secondary sources, however, agree that entry into commercial activities was through an hereditary path (Sanders and Price 1968: 152; Soustelle 1961: 61; Chapman 1957: 122). Membership into these guilds may indeed have been exclusive, based on kinship relations, and probably membership in a merchant calpulli as a prerequisite.

The manner in which the merchants obtained state goods for trade outside the empire is illustrative of their internal relations. According to Sahagún (Book 9, pp. 7–8), merchants from Tenochtitlan were given 1,600 *quachtli*[15] which belonged to the Aztec ruler. They carried these quachtli to Tlatelolco where the merchants of the two cities ex-

changed gifts and then divided the quachtli equally between them. With these, they purchased the goods (undoubtedly in the market of Tlatelolco) which they were to trade with the rulers in the ports of trade. The division of the quachtli is mystifying, although it may indicate some degree of equality in transactions involving state goods. The merchants of Tlatelolco and Tenochtitlan, along with those of Uitzilopochco, Azcapotzalco, and Quauhtitlan, were permitted to trade outside the empire, while those of seven other Basin of Mexico cities were required to remain within the empire for their commercial activities.[16]

State goods exported were the following (Sahagún, Book 9, pp. 8, 17):

    rulers' mantas, feathered in cup-shaped designs
    mantas of eagle face designs, and striped on the border with feathers
    rulers' breech clouts with long ends
    embroidered skirts and shifts

Of the actual transactions in these ports of trade, information is scanty. Sahagún (Book 9, p. 17) does state that the property of the Aztec ruler was traded with the rulers of Anahuac[17] (in this case, Xicalango, Cimatan, and Coatzacualco on the Gulf Coast) for quetzal feathers, green feathers, blue cotinga feathers, and trogonorus feathers. Elsewhere (Book 9, pp. 18–19), the same author adds other goods: jade (some cut), turquoise mosaic shields, shells of many kinds, tortoise shell cups, feathers of the red spoonbill, of the Troupial, the blue honeycreeper, and the yellow parrot, and skins of wild animals. Sahagún emphasizes that these goods, through all transactions, remained the property of the Aztec ruler.

---

[13]From Sahagún (Book 9, p. 12).

[14]The hereditary nature of merchant guilds is suggested both by Zorita (1963) and Sahagún (Book 9, passim).

[15]*quachtli*: large white cotton mantas, or pieces of cloth generally worn like capes. There is frequent mention of these quachtli in the sources as a form of money.

[16]Mixcoac, Texcoco, Uexotla, Coatlichan, Otompan, Xochimilco, and Chalco. That these merchants were prohibited from trading outside the empire is a sound indication that professional merchants traded within the empire. See page 190 for a further discussion of this point.

[17]Anahuac is the term used by Sahagún to refer to the two coastal trading areas on the Gulf and Pacific coasts.

Van Zantwijk (1970) presents a detailed outline of the complex hierarchy of ranks within the merchant organization. A series of "rites of passage" were necessary for an individual to become an esteemed or powerful member of the merchant guild. These rites included not only success in distant trading ventures, but also the accumulation of sufficient wealth to enter into a series of feasts. One of these feasts is described in detail by Sahagún (Book 9, Chapters 10–14). Briefly, such a ceremony involved the dispersal of goods "allowing one to become eligible" to sacrifice a slave at an annual festival. If he survived the feasts and exhibited the ability to supply sufficient goods (especially great quantities of food, drink, and mantas), the merchant was permitted to sacrifice the slave and enter into a higher category within the merchant organization. Merchants from other cities, as well as members of the hereditary nobility, were invited to these feasts. Apparently each rise in the ladder required similar outlays of goods, each probably more expensive than the last. It is clear that Sahagún is discussing the merchants of Tlatelolco, and possibly also of Tenochtitlan, but Acosta Saignes (1971: 447) feels that these ranks also applied to other towns with merchant populations.

As considerable personal wealth was involved in the performance of these feasts, the ability of the merchant to amass such wealth is an important consideration. While it is true that the merchants acted as emissaries for the state in carrying state goods to extra-empire trading centers,[18] it is clear from Sahagún that they also carried their own personal goods to these same areas.[19] The private property of the merchants on such expeditions was as follows (Sahagún, Book 9, pp. 8, 17–18):

> golden mountain-shaped mitres
> golden forehead rosettes
> golden necklaces of many kinds
> golden ear plugs
> golden covers used by the women of Anahuac
> finger rings
> rock crystal ear plugs

Additional private merchant goods are listed by Sahagún (Book 9, pp. 8, 18) as items for the commoners of these locales:

> obsidian ear plugs
> copper ear plugs
> obsidian razors with leather handles
> pointed obsidian blades
> rabbit fur
> sewing needles
> shells
> cochineal
> alum
> herbs of different kinds

Principal merchants and slave dealers also traded in these areas selling men, women, and children slaves.

In return for trading state goods in extra-empire ports of trade, the merchants received specific rewards from the ruler: a bundle of rabbit fur capes, and a boat load each of dried maize, beans, and *chía*. They also received decorated mantas and breech clouts of different designs (Sahagún, Book 9, pp. 5–6).

This list of goods should be compared, however, with that of the goods required by a merchant for the performance of a feast:

> 800 or 1,200 mantas
> 400 breech clouts of different types
> women's skirts and shifts of different designs[20]
> dried maize
> beans
> chía (wrinkled and small varieties)
> *atole* with squash seeds
> *chile*
> 40 or 60 jars of salt
> tomatoes (worth 20 small mantas)
> 80 or 100 turkeys
> 20 or 40 dogs
> 20 sacks of cacao beans
> 2,000 or 4,000 chocolate beaters
> sauce dishes

---

[18]Sahagún documents trips to Xicalango and Xoconochco, the Xicalango trip in greater detail.

[19]Sahagún clearly makes this distinction, although Chapman does not.

[20]These first three items mentioned were presented as gifts to distinguished warriors and nobles.

large baskets
earthen cups
merchants' plates
wood and charcoal
3 or 4 boats (loads) of water[21] (Sahagún
Book 9, pp. 47–48).

It is clear that the merchants could not have amassed sufficient wealth for feasts simply through gifts from the state. Therefore, the role of the merchant as entrepreneur must be considered as a source of this wealth.

There are numerous indications[22] that these merchants traded in markets within the empire, notwithstanding the hypothesis by Acosta-Saignes and Chapman that trade preceded tribute, and that once an area was conquered by the Aztecs, trade by professional merchants ceased there. It is not clear to what degree the professional merchants possessed a monopoly on such regional trade.

It has already been mentioned that the professional merchants traded both state and private goods. Although Sahagún describes transactions of state goods, he regretably fails to mention the nature of transactions involving the personal goods of the merchants. However, an unpublished document in the Archivo General de las Indias (Justicia 195) observes that Mexican Indian merchants in 1541 were trading in markets (*tiánguiz*) in these areas "as was their custom." In addition, contentions are made that these merchants regularly took advantage of local inhabitants in their dealings, a situation also noted by Durán (1967, Vol. 2, pp. 357–58). The suggestion is that this trade was a pre-Conquest pattern, and that the location for transactions involving the personal goods of the merchants were the markets in these port of trade areas. Local persons involved in such trade apparently were of both nobility and commoner status, given the types of goods carried by the merchants. The only commodity mentioned in trade is cacao, which the Mexican merchants obtained in these markets. This is consistent with the fact that the merchants are recorded in Sahagún (Book 9, pp. 27, 30)[23] as possessing cacao in their personal inventory after returning from trading ventures. Yet this valuable item is not mentioned specifically in trade with state goods. It is possible that cacao obtained in tribute was sufficient for the needs of the state, and that the Aztec merchants traded in these cacao-rich lands for other goods attracted there by the cacao.

Admittedly, there exists limited direct evidence for the trading of merchants' private goods in extra-empire centers. However, this evidence is substantiated by the indirect evidence of the great wealth of the merchants, and the suggestion that this wealth must have been accumulated primarily through success in personal trading activities. Combined, this makes a reasonable argument that merchants were engaged in activities from which the port of trade model normally excludes them.

Goods which the Aztec merchants found in the ports of trade would have been supplied locally or by the Maya merchants, especially from Yucatan, but also perhaps from Guatemala. Although there is little information on the activities of Maya merchants (*ppolom*), some conclusions can be drawn regarding the types of goods in which they dealt.

The merchant of Yucatan apparently operated more as an individual, in contrast to the Aztec merchant, who could only trade as a member of a guild. Again in contrast to the Aztec pochteca, the Maya ppolom could, and perhaps was required to be, of noble status. According to Roys (1943: 51):

Merchants ranged from the wealthy and noble wholesalers, who had their own factors, trading canoes, and slave carriers, to the petty itinerant who carried his own pack.

In an oft-mentioned statement, the son of the

---

[21]Goods required at other ceremonies and feasts are listed in Sahagún (Book 9, pp. 27, 28, 33).

[22]See especially Durán (1967, Vol. 2, pp. 185, 272, 327) and Note 15 above.

[23]The statements in Sahagún are not clear, and the possibility exists that the merchants could have obtained the cacao after their return to Tenochtitlan-Tlatelolco, or as disguised merchants.

ruler of Cocom is noted as engaging in trading activities in Honduras (Landa 1941: 39).

Details of such commercial relations are provided by Landa (1941: 94–96):

> The occupation to which they had the greatest inclination was trade, carrying salt and cloth and slaves to the lands of Ulua and Tabasco, exchanging all they had for cacao and stone beads, which were their money; and with this they were accustomed to buy slaves, or other beads, because they were fine and good, which their chiefs wore as jewels in their feasts . . . .

Other sources, notably the *Relaciones de Yucatan* (Vol. 11, pp. 71, 369, 370), indicate trading activities in 1579–80, generally suggesting pre-Conquest antecedents. In most cases, the merchants of Yucatan travel to Tabasco or Honduras for cacao, trading cotton mantas, salt, beeswax and honey. Torquemada (*Relaciones de Yucatan*, Vol. 11, p. 335) clearly notes that trade from Yucatan to Honduras was by canoe and, once again, for purposes of obtaining cacao. References to Yucatecan trade with "Mexico" are made in these same *Relaciones*,[24] but may refer to the Nahuatl speakers in Tabasco and perhaps Nito in Honduras.

In terms of movements of goods to and from these ports of trade, cacao played a dominant role for Yucatecan merchants, while feathers, jade, and salt[25] occupied a similar position among the Aztec merchants. Slaves were traded in ports of trade by both Aztec and Maya merchants and present a curious situation. Roys (1943: 68) suggests that the warfare common among the eighteen Yucatan provinces generated large quantities of slaves who were sold; and slaves from more distant areas were purchased for service in these provinces. Other slaves may have been required for work on cacao fields in the actual port of trade areas, and as laborers in the widespread commerce of the area (Scholes and Roys 1968: 29). It is suggested by Roys (1943: 54) that

Central Mexican goods of copper and rabbit fur were traded to Yucatan traders (probably through the Gulf Coast centers). These goods, brought to Xicalango by Aztec merchants (Sahagún, Book 9, pp. 8, 18), may have originated in Oaxaca and were common commercial items in Central Mexico. On the whole, it appears that the Aztec merchants traveled to these coastal areas primarily for goods available from more distant regions (Yucatan, Guatemala), while the Yucatan merchants traded mainly for goods actually produced in these port of trade areas (especially cacao) (see also Scholes and Roys 1968: 29).

Several of the Gulf Coastal towns are recorded with populations of Nahuatl-speakers, many of whom were probably merchants (Scholes and Roys 1968: 27). It was apparently not unusual for foreign merchants to reside in such towns, and in a similar type of locale in Honduras (Nito), Cortés (1928: 307) noted that an entire section of the town was occupied by merchants from Acalan.

Aspects of neutrality appear to pose problems in the port of trade model, as it is clear from Landa (1941: 32) that a garrison of Mexican soldiers was stationed at Xicalango and Tabasco. Although Tozzer observes that the event took place around A.D. 1200, this pattern no doubt continued through Aztec times. The *Relación de la Villa de Santa María de la Victoria* (*Relaciones de Yucatan*, Vol. 11, p. 364) indicates a fortress at Xicalango in Moctezuma's time. Díaz del Castillo (1964: 396) observes fortifications at one of these coastal communities. Furthermore, Scholes and Roys (1968: 34–36) infer that Aztec control was extensive in Xicalango, suggesting that a relative of Moctezuma was the leader of the resident Aztec merchants. These features would seem to indicate more control than usually considered appropriate for a neutral port of trade area.

The issue of neutrality again arises with Xoconochco. This province is described as a port of trade by Chapman, yet this was a province conquered by the Aztecs,[26] render-

---

[24]See Millon (1955: 153) for a listing of these *Relaciones*.

[25]Roys (1943: 53) observes that all the salt found in Tabasco was brought from Yucatan.

[26]Sahagún (Book 9, pp. 3–6) states that it was the merchants who conquered this province, an interesting possibility given their activities there as merchants in later times (Sahagún, Book 9, passim).

ing semi-annual tribute in, primarily, luxury raw materials.[27] Although it is reported that Aztec merchants traded there, little information exists on merchants from other areas trading at Xoconochco. A reference is made regarding merchants trading *huipiles* (blouses) from Teotitlan del Camino (allied to the Aztec Empire) for cacao in Xoconochco, Guatemala, Chiapas, and Suchitepeque, although the origin of these merchants is not made clear (*Relación de Teutitlan del Camino*, PNE, Vol. 4, pp. 215, 223). Brief mention is also made of cacao passing through this province from the Suchitepeques to New Spain in 1574, but it is inconclusive regarding actual exchanges in Xoconochco in pre-Conquest times (*Relación de la Provincia de Soconusco* 1961: 140).

Acalan poses quite a different problem. At the time of the Spanish Conquest, it was an independent state, and very likely neutral. Yet there is no direct information that Aztec merchants traded there, or were even allowed to do so. If this were the case, it would be difficult to include it among ports of trade.

Yet Acalan, with its capital of Itzamkanac, was a merchant center in itself, and provided traveling merchants for not only the Gulf Coastal region, but for Honduras and probably beyond as well. Speaking of this Chontal Maya province, Cortés (1928: 307) states:

> Many traders and natives carry their merchandise to every part, and they are rich in slaves and such articles as are commonly sold in the country ... from here they carry on a great trade by means of canoes with those of Xicalango and Tabasco ....

It is noteworthy that while merchants from other areas traveled to trading centers of Xicalango, Xoconochco, Nito, and perhaps Naco, there is no record of their entering the lands of Acalan. On the contrary, merchants from Acalan traveled to other areas, at times establishing themselves in sections of towns, as at Nito in Honduras:

> There was one quarter of the town peopled by his (the ruler of Acalan) agents, among whom was his own brother, who sold such goods of his as are most common in these parts ... cocoa, cotton cloths, colours for dyeing, another sort of paint which they use to protect their bodies against the heat and the cold, candlewood for lighting, pine resin for burning before their idols, slaves, and strings of coloured shells ... (Cortés (1928: 307).

In addition to controling extensive commercial networks, these same Chontal Maya of Acalan controlled the production of vast amounts of cacao, a strategic resource for the Aztec and Maya as well. These two latter areas controlled little of this crop, and obtained most of their supply from the coastal areas and Acalan.

From this brief overview, it is suggested that some Mesoamerican areas generally considered ports of trade tend to deviate from the characteristic model. Investigation has centered on the place of markets in these trading centers, the nature of neutrality, and the passive/dynamic nature of local involvement.

The first point of investigation would lead toward a broader definition of the role of professional merchants in ports of trade. It is entirely possible that their contacts in such locales were not limited strictly to administrative officials.

As the most diagnostic feature of ports of trade, neutrality stands out as a determining characteristic. That is, for example, Xoconochco was unquestionably integrated into the Aztec empire and its port of trade status should be reconsidered. Xicalango and other Gulf Coastal towns also exhibited features of Aztec control, as well as elements of defense. Although, as Polanyi has suggested, the safety of foreign merchants could be guaranteed under such conditions, further investigation is warranted in this area.

The last point considers the extent to which the locality is an innovative center in its own right, whether controlling resources in terms of production, distribution, or manufacturing. While Whydah, east coast India

---

[27]According to the *Matrícula de Tributos*, Xoconochco gave feathers, birds, cacao, jaguar skins, ambar, lip plugs, and pottery.

(Leeds 1962) and Al Mina/Ugarit (Revere 1957) appear to have been relatively passive points of transshipment of goods, the Phoenician cities and Mesoamerican Gulf towns either controlled the actual production of resources or were involved in the manufacture of highly desirable goods. In both cases, distribution was carried on by the local commercial group. Both Phoenecia and the Mesoamerican locales actively participated in interactions involving their own commercial groups. In these places, the strong economic-commercial organization seems to have had some impact on the structure of political power. In Mesoamerica this may have influenced the neutrality of these centers.

Although the port of trade model has served to define a particular structural type, important regular variations do exist among members of this type. In the case of Mesoamerica, the passive/dynamic role of local groups is especially noteworthy. Variations of this order should be recognized and incorporated into the port of trade model as alternative patterns of this general type.

REFERENCES

Acosta Saignes 1971
Archivo General de las Indias, *Justica legal* 195
Archivo General de la Nación, Tierras 1735, Exp. 2
Arnold 1957a, 1957b
Belshaw 1965
Berdan 1973
Carrasco 1971
Chapman 1957
Cortés 1928
Díaz del Castillo 1964
Durán 1967
Eisenstadt 1963
Fried 1960
Katz 1966, 1972
Landa 1941
Leeds 1962
Matrícula de Tributos
Millon 1955
Oviedo 1851–55
Polanyi 1957, 1963, 1966
Relación de la Provincia de Soconusco 1961
Relación de Teutitlan del Camino 1905–6
Relaciones de Yucatan 1898, 1900
Revere 1957
Roys 1943
Sahagún 1950–69
Sahlins 1965
Sanders and Price 1968
Scholes and Roys 1968
Sjoberg 1960
Soustelle 1961
Torquemada 1723
Van Zantwijk 1970
Zorita 1963

17. PRE-COLUMBIAN MARITIME TRADE IN MESOAMERICA[1]
by
Clinton R. Edwards

INTRODUCTION

The carriage of goods by water differs in a number of important respects from land carriage, especially where the latter lacks means of carrying burdens other than on men's backs. Watercraft can carry much larger and heavier cargoes in proportion to the human labor involved than can teams of porters. This is of special significance when the goods are of relatively low value, although the advantage is obvious for any type of merchandise to be transported. Water transport is generally faster, thus incurring less expense en route, such as sustenance of the labor force. Coastal routes can bypass regions where cultural hostilities may hinder or prevent travel, and the necessity of military conquest to assure safe passage to a desirable trading area is avoided.

The extent to which these principles operated in the pre-Columbian Mesoamerican context is still largely unknown, but it is reasonable to assume that they applied generally where economic considerations were paramount. However, cultural preferences and various non-economic factors may have intervened at different times and places.

The historical evidence for reconstruction of pre-Columbian maritime commerce is very sparse, probably because most seaborne trade was cut off quickly by the Conquest, as was much of the long distance land carriage. It its place grew a Spanish colonial pattern that, because of the great differences between Spanish and aboriginal nautical technology, cannot be referred by analogy to the pre-Columbian context. However, there are some historical records, ranging from casual remarks to fairly full descriptions, that allow partial reconstruction of the appearance of the vessels, trade routes, and other aspects of maritime activity. For the rest, archaeology has supplied data on the distribution of various artifacts and materials that can be identified with particular sources, and in some cases their distributions suggest strongly the possibility of carriage by sea rather than by land.

In the history of thought about trading patterns, until very recently it has been customary to assume land carriage unless there are very strong indications of sea carriage. However, when in the formulation of hypothesis one is persuaded by the most economical alternative, it appears to me that that of sea carriage is often preferable, especially when the mundane, practical aspects of moving merchandise from one place to another are taken into account. There is no reason to believe that the ancient Mesoamerican traders were any less practical-minded than those of modern times.

EARLY RECORD AT THE BAY ISLANDS

No later historical account containing evidence of pre-Columbian maritime commerce in Mesoamerica provides as much detail about watercraft, their crews, and their cargoes as the descriptions of the large trading canoes encountered at the Bay Islands during Columbus' fourth voyage (Fig. 34). The primary sources are the eyewitness records by Bartholomew and Ferdinand Columbus; an account attributed to Christopher Columbus, used by Peter Martyr and subsequently lost, that includes the observations of other partici-

[1]This paper is a sequel to my "Nautical Technology and Maritime Routes in Mesoamerica," to be published in the *Acts* of the 40th International Congress of Americanists, Rome, 1972. Both papers were prepared in connection with the symposium on *Routes of Communication and Cultural Contact in Mesoamerica* held during the ICA meetings and continued in this volume, and together they comprise my contribution to the theme. I am grateful to the following for support of the direct and related research incorporated in the papers: Graduate Research Committee and the Latin American Center, University of Wisconsin-Milwaukee; the Ford Foundation and National Endowment for the Humanities, through the American Council of Learned Societies; and the Fulbright-Hays Faculty Research/Study Program.

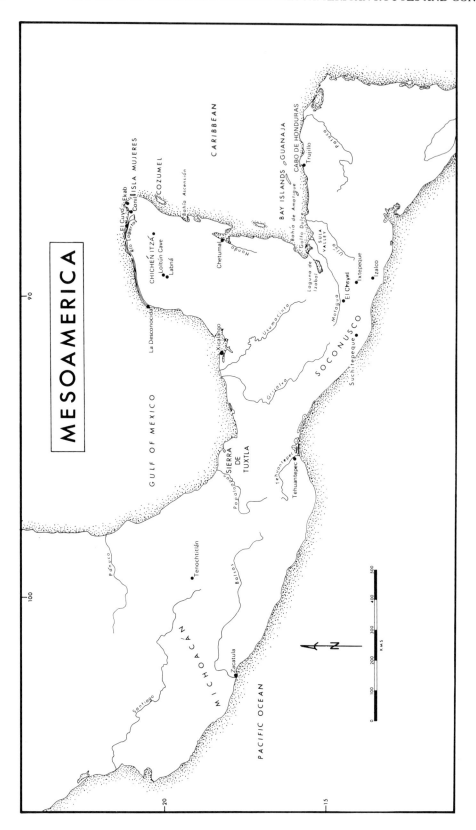

Figure 34. Map of Mesoamerica showing Selected Points Important to Maritime Communications

pants; and the testimony of various witnesses during the *pleitos* of Christopher's son, Diego.

Bartholomew's principal comment occurs in the *Informatiō di Bart° Colōbo della navicatiō di ponēte et garbī di Beragna nel mondo novo* (original in Biblioteca Nazionale Centrale di Firenze, *Banco Raro* 234, Folios 31–34v; for modernized transcriptions see Harrisse 1866: 471–74 and CDCR 1952: 72–74). The comment is brief, stating only that they captured a ship laden with fancy cloth goods that "they said came from a certain province called *Maiam*" (*In questo loco pigliorono una Nave* [*loro* inserted above the line] *carica di mercātia et merce la quale dicevō venia da una cierta pvintia chiamata* MAIAM [*vl Iuncatam* inserted above the line] *con molte veste di bābasio de le quale no erono il forcio di sede di divesi colori*). Earlier in this account the province is mentioned as "Maia." The *Informatiō* is a second- or third-hand record the validity of which has been questioned, but Sauer (1966: 143–46) defends it convincingly as "...the imperfectly recorded voice and hand of Bartholomew."

Peter Martyr's version of the lost account is roughly contemporaneous with the *Informatiō*. He implies that at least parts of it derive from a report written by Christopher Columbus. Thus the passages concerning the Bay Island canoes may include information supplied by the Admiral himself,[2] but since he did not observe the capture at first hand, part of the narrative was contributed by other participants, either through Columbus or directly to Peter Martyr. Bartholomew was sent ashore on one of the islands, and

> reconnoitering the beach, two dugout canoes (*Monoxylis*) of the country were encountered.... Naked and yoked slaves were drawing them along with ropes, as is usually done against the current on rivers. In the canoes were the

chief of the island with his wife and children, all naked. On the orders of their master the slaves indicated arrogantly to our men who had landed that they should make way when they approached, and made threats when they offered resistance. They are so simple that they neither feared nor marveled at the boats or the strength or number of our people. It appeared to them that our people should accord their master the same reverence as did they themselves. Columbus' men understood that he was a merchant returning from other lands. They have trade fairs, and were carrying trade goods: copper bells, blades, knives, and hatchets of transparent, shiny yellow stone hafted with a kind of hard wood; also utensils and vessels for cooking, marvelously made of clay and partly also of wood or of the same stone (*marmore*). But mostly they carried mantles and other cotton goods, woven in various colors. They captured the chief and his family and everything they carried, but the Admiral quickly ordered them freed and returned most of their things to gain their confidence. From them he gained information on the lands to the westward, and set his course thence.

The mainland was called Quiriquetana, with two regions called Taia and Maia (Mártyr 1966: Dec. 3, Cap. 4; 1944: 228).

Ferdinand Columbus did not see the capture of the canoes and their occupants, having stayed with his father aboard ship. He thus records only what was carried in one of the canoes, and what transpired after it was brought alongside the Admiral's flagship and the "chief" and his entourage came aboard. Although written many years later, Ferdinand's account provides the best description of the canoe and its contents:

> [The vessel was] as great as a galley, eight feet wide, all of a single trunk... Amidships it had a canopy of palm leaves, like that of gondolas in Venice, which protected what was underneath. ... The crew...were twenty-five.... [The cargo consisted of] cloths and

---

[2]Elsewhere in surviving writings by Columbus there is no mention of the canoes, and only very brief reference to the stay at the Bay Islands. While other participants called the island upon which Bartholomew landed *Guanasa* or *Guanaja* and a few noted that the Admiral named it *Isla de Pinos*, the only name that occurs in his extant writings is *Isla de las Bocas* (Columbus, C. 1961: 190).

sleeveless shirts of cotton that had been worked and dyed in different colors and designs, also pantaloons of the same workmanship with which they cover their private parts, also cloth in which the Indian women of the canoe were dressed, such as the Moorish women of Granada are accustomed to wear. Also long swords of wood with a groove along each edge, wherein stone knives were set by means of fiber and pitch, cutting like steel when used on naked people; also hatchets to cut wood, like those of stone used by other Indians, save for the fact that these were of good copper, of which metal they also had bells and crucibles for smelting. For food they carried roots and grain such as they eat in Española and a certain wine made of maize, like the beer of England, and they had many of those kernels which serve as money in New Spain, which it appeared that they valued highly (Sauer 1966: 128).

Ferdinand referred to Peter Martyr's "chief" as "an ancient named Yumbé, who seemed to be the wisest man among them and of greatest authority." On crossing to the mainland the Europeans found that the Indians "in the vicinity of Point Caxinas [Cabo de Honduras, near Trujillo] were dressed like those in the canoe, in dyed shirts and breechclouts" (Columbus, F. 1959: 232, 234.

In the *pleitos* of Diego Columbus several of the questions formulated by the contending sides and the testimony of a number of eyewitnesses corroborate and expand the foregoing record. In the first *probanza* the witnesses were asked if they knew that "the Admiral, on his last voyage, discovered a land called Maya, where there is a point that was named Caxinas, and some islands, one of which is called Guanasa..." (DIU VII: 92). The first witness was Ambrosio Sánchez, who had served as *maestre* in a ship owned by his father and chartered by Columbus. Sánchez responded that the names of the island and mainland were correct, except that it was "Guanaca" rather than "Guanasa" (*ibid.*, 96). In the compressed version of several *probanzas* his rendition becomes "Guacuaza" (DII, Vol.

39, p. 415). Pedro Mateos, a sailor, confirmed all points of the query, adding that he had recorded in a book "all the mountains and rivers in the province" (referring specifically to Veragua but probably meaning all lands seen on the voyage) but that the Admiral had taken it from him (DIU, Vol. 7, p. 152). Francisco de Estrada, a member of the third and fourth voyages, recorded the taking of possession on the mainland opposite a "small island that they called Guanasa" (DIU, Vol. 9, p. 165). Fourteen other eyewitnesses including Bartholomew Columbus offered corroboration, and four nonparticipants testified that they had heard such from members of the fourth voyage company.

During the *Fiscal's* response to this questioning no eyewitnesses responded, but in a later action by the *Fiscal* the same query was made, and this time several observers were on hand to testify. A sailor named Diego Cabezudo noted that before reaching Veragua they stopped at the "ysla de Pinos" (DIU, Vol. 9, p. 253). This is corroborated by the captain and pilot Vicente Yáñez Pinzón and by the ship's cooper, Juan de Noya, who said that the Admiral assigned the name (DIU, Vol. 9, pp. 257, 269). This testimony may have been the source for Las Casas' (1957, Vol. 2, p. 55) statement, which does not derive from Ferdinand's account, that Isla de Pinos was the name given by the Admiral to the island called Guanaja in later records. Other sailors, Diego Martín Barranco, Juan de Quexo, and Juan Quintero, called the island "Guanasa" (DIU, Vol. 7, pp. 255, 274, 280), as did Pedro de Ledesma, captain and pilot of the caravel *Vizcaína* of the fourth voyage fleet. Ledesma also noted Columbus' "ysla de Pinos," mentioned a ruler of the island named *Ynube,* and referred to the nearby mainland as *Uiuya* (DIU, Vol. 7, p. 264). Pending reference to the original we can prefer Fernández de Navarrete's (1964, Vol. 2, p. 327) rendition of the latter as *Maya*. Vicente Yáñez Pinzón heard the island's name as *Guanaxa* and the opposite mainland's as the "province of Ebuya [another mistranscription of "Maya"?] of the caçique Camarona, which is at the beginning of the sierra, and from there don Cristóbal turned toward the east..." (DIU, Vol. 7, p. 269).

As Diego continued to press his claims, other witnesses testified, corroborating further the toponyms with which we are concerned. The tailor Baltasar Calvo mentioned the island *Guana* and the mainland *Maya* (DIU, Vol. 7, p. 348). Another set of questions asked about the discovery of *Guanase*, where the Adelantado (Bartholomew) went ashore and "captured a canoe with many things and people of whom one called *Yunbera*, who was named Juan Pérez, was taken." Further inquiry also concerned the discovery of the province called *Maya* (DIU, Vol. 7, p. 397). The transcription of the next set of questions has *Guanasa, Junbe,* and *Maya* (DIU, Vol. 8, pp. 37–38). Bartolomé Colín, who knew Christopher Columbus well and had had many conversations with him, added the detail that the first two caravels to approach *Guanasa* went aground and mentioned the capture of "the Indian whom they afterwards called Juan Pérez" (DIU, Vol. 8, p. 51). Juan Moreno participated in the capture of the Indian *Junhera* at *Guanaja*, and described him as old and grey-haired. He also mentioned the province called *Maya* (DIU, Vol. 8, p. 76). Juan Rodríguez de Mafra heard *Guanasa* from Juan de Quexo, Diego Gómez, and other men of Palos who had accompanied Columbus (DIU, Vol. 8, p. 80).

Despite the imperfections of the transcriptions, and subject to corroboration through reference to the spelling in the original documents, it seems that the pronunciation heard and recorded most frequently among the participants and the litigants was *Guanasa*. Peter Martyr (1966, Dec. 3, Cap. 4; "Guanassa") also heard it thus, indicating that the part of his chronicle that deals with the capture of the canoes derives from the earliest descriptions before *Guanaja* replaced *Guanasa* completely in common speech and the written record. His is the closest to a detailed, eyewitness account that we have of the actual capture and the composition of the vessels' company, and it is free of the *ex post facto* ingredients introduced by Ferdinand, Las Casas, and others (see below).

It is clear that *Maiam, Maia,* and *Maya* referred to a stretch of the Honduran mainland opposite the Bay Islands and not to the Yucatan Peninsula, a fact once well established (Lothrop 1927) but since ignored occasionally in attempts to demonstrate a wider voyaging range for the Bay Island canoes. One source for the latter view is the statement in the Harrisse (1866: 471–74) transcription of Bartholomew's *Informatiõ* that the trader was said to have come from a province called *Maiam vel Iuncatam*. But as pointed out many years ago (Brinton 1969 [1882]: 10n.; see also Tozzer 1941: 7n.), in the original document *vl Iuncatam* is superscribed over Maiam in a different hand, most probably in a later gloss which is repeated in the left margin as *vl Iũcatã*, after the Yucatan Peninsula became known. Another widely quoted authority for the provenance of the canoes was Las Casas (1957 Vol. 2, p. 55), who, mentioning only one of them, glossed Ferdinand's account to the effect that it "must certainly have been from the land of Yucatan." Also, Ferdinand himself assumed that the canoe and its cargo represented the "great wealth, civilization, and industry of the peoples of the western part of New Spain" (Columbus, F. 1959: 233). Although this is a good literal translation of "... *los pueblos de las partes occidentales de la Nueva España,*" Ferdinand's original meaning was probably "the peoples to the west in New Spain." These opinions, of course, were set down well after the discovery and identification of Yucatan, the Indians called "Maya" by the Spaniards, and much of new Spain.

Attempts to incorporate this encounter into a pattern of lengthy coastwise voyaging for purposes of trade also ignore the specific evidence that the canoes were owned locally and had come only from the nearby mainland, not from Yucatan or farther lands. The presence of the "chief's" family also suggests a short voyage, although it is not impossible that affluent traders' families accompanied them on longer journeys. There is also the suggestion that his trading area did not extend very far to the east, because at about the Río Patuca his usefulness as interpreter ceased and he was set free to return home (Columbus, F. 1959: 232–33).

Thus far the first contact record. It is the only one sufficiently detailed for comparison with the mostly casual and fragmentary information from later sources.

OTHER EARLY RECORDS IN THE GULF OF HONDURAS

Near the end of Hernán Cortés' famous march to Honduras he sent Gonzalo de Sandoval ahead of the main party to reconnoiter the coast of the Bahía de Amatique. On arrival just north of the entrance to Golfo Dulce, Sandoval spotted a canoe under paddle and sail (*a remo y a vela*). That night, at a small bay that served as a "canoe port," he intercepted the canoe and found that it had been headed for Golfo Dulce with a cargo of salt and maize (Díaz del Castillo 1970: 476). Cortés corroborates that the canoemen were merchants and records the later capture of another canoe manned by a merchant and his three slaves. The merchant gave Cortés information on details of the local coastal route, having "passed through many times with merchandise," and pointed out a passage through an *estero* that was used when the sea outside was rough (Cortés 1971: 248, 250).

Spanish depredations in this region during the early 1520's may have affected seriously the seaborne as well as the land trade. Representatives from Xicalango, whom Cortés had interviewed in Coatzacoalcos about routes to their territory, complained that their trade with the east coast of the Yucatan Peninsula had been lost. It is not clear whether they were referring to a maritime route or to one across the base of the peninsula (Cortés 1971: 222). In any event, trade along the east coast itself continued. In 1533 as he retired southward from his disastrous attempt to settle at Chetumal, Alonso Dávila encountered trading canoes off the coast of British Honduras. Fernández de Oviedo, recording the eyewitness report of Alonso Luján, tells of traders from Yucatán who brought clothes and other merchandise to exchange for cacao on the Río Ulúa. Dávila met many of them and occasionally commandeered their canoes to continue

his voyage to Trujillo (Fernández de Oviedo 1959, Vol. 3, p. 422; see also DII, Vol. 14, pp. 118–20 for Dávila's briefer account).

FIRST-CONTACT EVIDENCE ON THE PACIFIC SIDE

The only substantive historical evidence for aboriginal maritime trade on the Pacific coast of Mesoamerica that has come to light so far is the brief mention garnered by Rodrigo de Albornoz in 1525 from Indians at Zacatula, at the mouth of the Río Balsas:

> . . . there are reports from the Indians who say that on the way there [the Spice Islands] are islands rich in pearls and precious stones, and being toward the south, there is reason to suppose that there is gold in abundance; and on being questioned how they know that there should be islands in that direction, the Indians of the Zacatula coast say that often they heard their fathers and grandfathers relate that from time to time Indians from certain islands toward the south, which they point to, would come to this coast in large canoes, and they brought there exquisite things which they would trade for local products; and sometimes when the sea grew rough, for there were much larger waves there than at any other part of the coast, those that had come would stay for five or six months until good weather occurred and the sea became calm, and then they would depart (translation by West 1961: 133; original in Archivo General de Indias (Sevilla), *Patronato* 184, ramo 2; transcription in DII, Vol. 13, pp. 63–64).

SUMMARY OF EARLY ACCOUNTS AND THE HISTORICAL EVIDENCE FOR TRADE ON THE EAST COAST

It will have been noted that there is no conclusive evidence in the foregoing first-contact accounts that canoes made lengthy trading voyages on the east side of Mesoamerica. The Bay Island canoes may have been locally owned and operated, voyaging between the islands and a port of trade on the Honduran mainland. Canoes with merchandise intercepted along the coast of British Honduras were not necessarily those of long distance traders. However, subsequent records, albeit for the most part secondary and rather casual, when taken collectively indicate the probability that at least some fairly lengthy point-to-point coastal carriage was occurring at the time of European contact.

Alonso Luján and others told Fernández de Oviedo of the great esteem in which cacao was held in Yucatan, and of the carriage of clothes and other merchandise to the Ulúa Valley in exchange for it (Fernández de Oviedo 1959, Vol. 3, p. 422). Antonio de Herrera (1952, Vol. 9, p. 108), using written sources for his description of Honduras, states that the Yucatecans came by sea in canoes with mantles, feathers, and other things and returned with cacao. Ciudad Real (1932: 325) was told by Indians in Yucatan of stone buildings near the Bahía de la Ascensión that were "temples of the gods and idols of the lords of *Chicheniza,* and when they went to *Honduras* for cacao and feathers, and other things, they passed by there going and coming to offer sacrifice to them, and there they embarked and disembarked." Taken together with inferences that can be derived from the nature of the trade goods and from archaeological evidence, these and other records support quite adequately the theory of substantial maritime trade significant to the economy of the Maya area and its margins (Tozzer 1941: 94–95 *et passim*; Scholes and Roys 1948: *passim*; Thompson 1970, Chap. 5; Roys 1972: 105–107, 113–20; 1965: 670–71).

A somewhat similar situation seems to have obtained on the west side of Yucatan, with canoe trade between salt-producing areas along the west and north coasts of the peninsula and Tabasco. Xicalango was the great entrepôt in this region, where traders from central Mexico exchanged goods with those who plied the southward routes (Chapman 1957: *passim*). There is much evidence of maritime trade along the coast of the peninsula, touching at various salt-producing points such as La Desconocida and the stretch between El Cuyo and Río Lagartos. Conil, Ekab, and other large towns on or near the

coast were active trading centers at contact time, as was the island of Cozumel. There is little doubt of frequent canoe traffic among these centers, but there remains the intriguing question as to whether the maritime trade was pursued by short range, point-to-point, and return voyaging, or by lengthy voyages in a kind of "tramp" trading in which parts of cargoes were exchanged for other goods at successive ports of call. The latter view is included by Thompson (1970, Chaps. 1 and 5) in his theory of the sea-oriented, trading Putun culture of Tabasco and its widespread influences, dispersed partly by an extensive maritime trading network that included voyages from Xicalango around the Yucatan Peninsula to Honduras and perhaps beyond. Although we have the evidence cited above that the "lords" of Chichen Itza embarked at Bahía de la Ascensión for Honduras, and that there was traffic from the Río Hondo to the Río Ulúa, as mentioned briefly by Alonso Dávila (DII, Vol. 14, p. 108), there is no mention of way ports. Some slight indication may be gained from the fact that Dávila's guides, whom he brought from Chetumal on his flight to Honduras, knew the coast well and when the party was in need of provisions they guided him to a number of Indian towns well upriver from the coast. Although the account is not explicit on this point, it may be that the guides knew of these towns through a trading pattern that included these stops along a lengthy route (DII, Vol. 14, pp. 119–20).

GOODS CARRIED BY SEA

1. Clothing and other cloth goods: The record of the encounter with trading canoes at the Bay Islands emphasizes these. There was "much clothing of bombazine without the silk *forcio* (interwoven decorative threads?), of various colors" (Bartholomew Columbus); "mantles and other cotton goods, woven in various colors" (Martyr); "cloths and sleeveless shirts of cotton that had been worked and dyed in different colors and designs, also pantaloons of the same workmanship ... also cloth in which the Indian women of the canoe were dressed" (Ferdinand Columbus). Bartholomew's account says that the

clothing was being brought from the mainland of Honduras, Martyr's that it came from "other lands," while Ferdinand noted that the occupants of the canoe that came alongside the flagship were dressed like the inhabitants of the mainland near Cabo de Honduras. Fernández de Oviedo, quoting Luján, and Herrera's sources give Yucatan as the source of cloth goods brought to Honduras. Modern writers are in agreement that the most probable source of the fancy clothing and other woven products was northern Yucatan (e.g., Roys 1972: 53).

2. Copper bells: These were mentioned by both Martyr and Ferdinand Columbus as part of the Bay Island cargo. The source for these was probably central Mexico (Thompson 1970: 127), or, more specifically, Michoacan (Sauer 1966: 129).

3. Copper axes: These were in the Bay Island canoe seen by Ferdinand. Thompson (1970: 127) ascribes these to central Mexico along with other copper items, Sauer (1966: 129) to Michoacan.

4. Hatchets and utensils of stone: If these items of the Bay Island cargo listed by Martyr were of the "marble or alabaster known as Mexican onyx," they came from central Mexico, as did those of yellowish obsidian (Sauer 1966: 129). If some were of yellow flint, as Thompson (1970: 127) suggests, they may have been from deposits in the *serranilla* of northern Yucatan. Martyr's description as "transparent" and "shiny" would seem to indicate the "onyx" and obsidian rather than flint.

5. Blades, knives, stone-edged swords: The great two-handed swords edged with many small, sharp obsidian "teeth" were all too well known to the Spanish invaders of Yucatan, and the ones in the Bay Island canoe seen by Ferdinand may have come from there. The obsidian for their manufacture, however, was from elsewhere (see below).

6. Cacao: There is general agreement that this was a significant import to Yucatan and the Valley of Mexico. If the Bay Island canoes were indeed headed for home port, as seems probable, the cacao aboard would have come from no farther away than the near-

by mainland, with the "chief" bringing a supply for local consumption. The nearest producing areas were the Sula Valley and the Izabal lowlands. The major cacao district closest to Tenochtitlan was in western Tabasco, but there was also importation from the Pacific-side sources in Soconusco (Chiapas-Guatemala), Suchitepeque (Guatemala), and Izalco (El Salvador), and perhaps from as far south as Nicaragua (Bergmann 1969).

7. Salt: The canoe seen by Sandoval near the Golfo Dulce entrance was carrying salt. This was a high bulk, relatively low cost cargo, probably not subject to frequent loading and unloading or passing through the hands of many traders. If this is correct, this record may yield important insight into one aspect of the maritime trade: there may have been a fairly large number of relatively modest entrepreneurs engaged in lengthy carriage of the less glamorous and costly cargoes. The Sandoval canoe had but three slaves as paddlers, whereas the "chief" at the Bay Islands, with his cargo of generally valuable items, had a crew of about twenty in one canoe and perhaps a like number in the other. The nearest source for the salt would have been Cozumel, where salt produced elsewhere was apparently stored for transshipment (Thompson 1970: 129), or Isla Mujeres. The major salt-pan operations, however, were on the north and west coasts of the peninsula. In any case, it was more than a brief coastal voyage to bring the salt to the Golfo Dulce.

8. Maize: The Sandoval canoe had maize aboard; the best guess is that it was picked up en route somewhere nearby for sale at one of the towns on the Golfo Dulce. In this particular instance the amount would have been small, and it seems doubtful that a modest-sized four-man canoe could have been employed profitably in long distance carriage of maize.

The foregoing are items listed specifically by eyewitnesses to actual cargoes or by those who obtained their information on actual cargoes directly from eyewitnesses. Many other goods, both manufactured and as raw materials, are mentioned in the literature by authors recording information at third hand. Some of these goods and yet other items have been discussed by archaeologists in the context of maritime trade because their distributions suggest that water rather than land transport is the better hypothesis. I have not searched the literature for an exhaustive list, but present the following as representative of the kinds of things that are particularly amenable to analysis as to source and route when found archaeologically.

9. Copper objects: There is general agreement that these were important in trade between central Mexico and the Maya area. A great variety of copper objects ranging from pins, awls, and needles to "hatchet money" and bells has been considered by Mountjoy (1969) in connection with the possibility that west Mexican metallurgy was introduced from northern South America. Meighan (1969: 15) suggests that the introduction "did not take the form of trade objects primarily, but was an introduction of a body of technical knowledge." Both Meighan and Mountjoy favor the hypothesis of transfer of the metallurgical technology by sea.

10. Pearls and precious stones: as related by Albornoz, these were brought formerly to Zacatula in canoes from the south. The pearls and "exquisite things" indicate possible connections with Panama or with the Manteño culture of coastal Ecuador (West 1961: 135–36).

11. Metates: Thompson (1970: 128–29) suggests that the heavy granite and lava metates found archaeologically at a number of sites in the Yucatan Peninsula must have been carried partly by coastal routes.

12. Obsidian: In addition to the Bay Island instance, obsidian has received attention because it is possible to identify the geologic sources of some types quite precisely. Hammond (1972c) has analysed the distribution in the Maya area of specific types from El Chayal and Ixtepeque in Guatemala and presented the hypothesis that for destinations in northern Yucatan the routes headed fairly directly to the sea. He points out that "the greater the proportion of the route covered by water, the further the obsidian is distributed, [suggesting that] canoe transport was more economical over long distances because of the larger load that could be carried."

Specific sites in northern Yucatan at which obsidian from Ixtepeque has been found are Chichen Itza, Loltun Cave, and Labna. The suggestion is that the sea routes began in the vicinity of the Río Motagua mouth and ended at Chetumal and Bahía de la Ascensión.

NAUTICAL CONSIDERATIONS

In two recent papers I attempted to summarize current information on nautical technology in Nuclear America and in Mesoamerica and to provide perspective from the practical seaman's point of view on the possibilities of long distance seaborne trade (Edwards 1969, n.d.). I shall only summarize here a few points; fuller documentation will be provided in a study in progress on aboriginal watercraft of Mexico.

The dugout canoe is mentioned consistently and exclusively as the bearer of maritime trade in Mesoamerica. It was also the principal watercraft on rivers, although rafts were also used, and in one instance rafts were probably used at sea, although not in trade. Stone was probably rafted from the Sierra de Tuxtla to Tabasco lowland sites for the creation of the monolithic scultpures found there. Of course, if Manteño traders from Ecuador ranged as far north as western Mexico, sailing rafts as well as dugout canoes might have been involved (West 1961: 135; Mountjoy 1968: 40; Edwards 1969: 8–9).

Dugout canoes are beached easily, even where moderate surf is running, and thus in canoe-borne trade there was no need for natural or artificial harbors or any kind of port facility. Indentations of the coast like the Bahía de la Ascensión figured in the maritime routes not because they offered shelter but simply because they were extensions of the sea allowing penetration farther toward inland destinations.

Wherever possible the canoemen probably took advantage of sheltered waters — lagoons behind offshore bars and sandpits and stretches protected by barrier reefs. This was not because the canoes were incapable of voyaging in the open sea, but simply because paddling was less strenuous in calmer water, especially when bucking a head sea and adverse wind. Substantial parts of all routes are so sheltered, and nowhere between Tabasco and Honduras, or between coastal Guatemala and Tehuantepec, would it have been necessary to voyage outside protected waters for more than a day or two at a time. Even on open sea segments canoes could be beached quickly to avoid a sudden squall.

QUESTIONS ON THE ORGANIZATION AND ECONOMIC SIGNIFICANCE OF MARITIME COMMERCE

The record yields little information on the organization of the maritime trade. We do know that slaves were used as paddlers in at least some instances, and it has been suggested that slaves were part of the merchandise in sea trade from Yucatan to Honduras and Tabasco and thus were carried in greater numbers than necessary just to propel the canoes. Presumably some were retained for the voyage back to home base. There is the evidence of the Bay Island incident and Ciudad Real's remark about the "lords" of Chichen Itza to support a theory that at least some of the maritime trade was pursued by persons analogous to the Aztec *pochteca* or Maya *ppolom* or *ah ppolom yoc* (Roys 1939: 61, as cited by Tozzer 1941: 94n.). Was "Yunbe" or "Yunbera" really the ruler of Guanaja and thus uniquely privileged in his use of many slaves as crewmen? He was certainly very affluent and held in awe by his crew. Or was he typical of a kind of sub-nobility like the richer *pochteca* of Mexico, translated from land to sea and with crewmen analogous to the slave bearers used on land routes?

On the other hand, the merchant captured by Sandoval seems to have been of much more modest estate, with only three slaves and a workaday cargo. Also, if the canoes encountered by Dávila between Chetumal and Honduras had been captained by nobility and carried goods of high value he would hardly have merely exchanged vessels with them. Even in their weakened condition his men surely would have attempted to obtain any desirable booty the canoes contained.

The land-traveling *pochteca* accompanied his goods for long distances. We know virtually nothing about the frequency of transfer, the method of keeping control over goods along sea routes, or control of the trade itself. The slight evidence cited above suggests that affluent merchants did indeed accompany their goods at sea, but that they did not control the trade to the extent of excluding smaller-scale operators from participation on lengthy segments of the routes.

That sea carriage was very important in the Maya area is attested by the locations of the "ports of trade" which were almost exclusively on or very near the seacoast (for elaboration see Chapman 1957). There is no question that the commerce handled by these centers was important to Maya economy. However, our present information yields little insight into the logistics of supporting the relatively dense populations of regions like northern Yucatan or, earlier, the southern Maya lowlands, with respect to basic foodstuffs. How significant was maritime commerce to the food supply of a people who otherwise depended mostly upon shifting field agriculture, a system presumed not sufficiently productive to support dense populations? Were there significant producers of surplus food — maize and the basic root crops — on the margins of the Maya population centers whose production made possible the concentrations in these centers?

Whether the maritime trade emphasized luxury goods or items basic to local economies, it is necessary in further study to consider it in direct and literal connection with riverine and land trade. Watercraft at sea and on rivers were the same; transshipment at river mouths was unnecessary. Goods originating well inland were brought to rivers and loaded aboard the canoes, perhaps not to be unloaded until the end of a very lengthy river and sea voyage.

PERSPECTIVES

The origins of the maritime trade and the length of time it has been pursued in Mesoamerica are questions that must be left to the archaeologists. However, we can note that the postulated introduction of copper and bronze metallurgy to the west coast of Mexico from South America occurred at least as early as A.D. 900, and the obsidian from Ixtepeque is found in Classic Period sites of northern Yucatan. We are thus not restricted in our hypotheses to the immediately pre-Conquest era, although most of the data, except archaeological, are from the observations of Europeans at the time of first contact or shortly thereafter. Further study of the watercraft, of trade items, of the ways in which the seaborne trade articulated with the overland carriage, and of the possibility that the routes were at times Mesoamerican segments of longer ones linking the "high cultures" of Nuclear America, will further our knowledge of the significance of human contacts to the development of the great New World civilizations.

REFERENCES

Bergmann 1969
Brinton 1969
CDCR 1952
Chapman 1957
Ciudad Real 1932
Columbus, Bartholomew ca. 1506
Columbus, C. 1961
Columbus, F. 1959
Cortés 1971
Dávila 1533
Díaz del Castillo 1970
DII 1864–84
DIU 1885–1932
Edwards 1969, n.d.
Fernández de Navarrete 1964
Fernández de Oviedo 1959
Hammond 1972c
Harrisse 1866
Herrera y Tordesillas 1934–58
Las Casas 1957
Lothrop 1927
Mártyr de Anglería 1944, 1966
Meighan 1969
Mountjoy 1969
Roys 1939, 1965, 1972
Sauer 1966
Scholes and Roys 1948
Thompson 1970
Tozzer 1941
West 1961

18. THE POCHTECA
by
Bente Bittman and Thelma D. Sullivan

Archaeological evidence indicates that organized groups of merchants were operating at a very early period in Mesoamerica. Bernal (1968: 140; see also Flannery 1968; Grove 1968), for example, basing his opinion on the incidence of import and export goods unearthed at Olmec sites on the Gulf Coast states:

> ... within the Olmec world the economic-military-commercial association of traits, which would later be characteristic of Mesoamerica had already been formed: the war-tribute-commerce complex that we find intimately bound together in the Aztec period.

The earliest information we have in a written source with respect to organized commerce refers to Tula, and is found in Ixtlilxochitl (1965, Vol. 1, p. 57). He relates the following:

> They also had fairs every twenty days — the number of days in a month — on the first day ... and even today this type of great fair is held in Tulantzinco, although in the cities and villages daily they sell all the necessaries in the market. However, when this great *tianquis* was held, there were many people from different provinces. They were not held in all cities but only in Tula, Tulantzinco, Teotihuacan, Cuauhnahuac, Tultitlan, Cholula, and five or six other cities or places.

Similar fairs were held during Aztec times and no doubt date from a time much prior to the Toltecs.

The Aztec merchants are the focus of this study, and for our sources we have relied primarily on written accounts such as codices and chronicles. We propose to show, in brief, how commerce developed among the Aztecs and with it a rich and privileged merchant class. Further, we shall offer a series of hypotheses regarding the position of the merchants in Aztec society and what might have happened to them as a group had the Conquest of Mexico not occurred.

DEVELOPMENT OF COMMERCE AMONG THE AZTECS

Tenochtitlan and Tlatelolco were founded on a swampy island during the first half of the fourteenth century. Ecologically it was far from ideal for human occupation, but this challenge was aptly met by the Aztecs, an ambitious, energetic, and enterprising people with a marked ability to learn from those more culturally advanced with whom they came in contact.

The aspirations of the Aztecs are well documented in such sources as Chimalpahin (1960: 43), the *Códice Matritense de la Academia de Historia* (Fols. 60r–61r), and Tezozomoc (1944: 36–42; 1949: 29–30; Sullivan 1971: 316), and the splendours they achieved in Tenochtitlan are vividly described by the conquerors. According to the results of a recent investigation, the urban area ultimately covered more than 12 sq. km. (Calnek 1972: 105). The number of inhabitants in the late pre-Hispanic period remains problematical, and estimates range between 60,000 and 300,000 (Calnek 1972: 103).

A major factor in the economic, socal, and political development of the Aztecs was commerce. The basic problems they had to face from the start were those of creating living space from the swamp lands and obtaining materials for construction. They initiated their trading activities with products available on the island and surrounding lake, bartering birds, fish, frogs, small worms, and certain edible aquatic plants in the markets of nearby towns for stone, wood, and lime (see Tezozomoc 1944: 16–17; Durán 1965: 31–42). Later, as the "empire" (the Triple Alliance of Tenochtitlan, Texcoco, and Tlacopan) expanded, they trafficked in goods from distant regions obtained via trade and tribute.

The texts of Sahagún (1956, Vol. 3, pp. 13–86; *Florentine Codex* 1959), the *Anales de Tlatelolco* (1948), and Tezozomoc (1944, 1949) and Durán (1965) contain considerable information on the *pochteca*. According to the

Florentine Codex (1959: 2) which is primarily a Tlatelolcan source, it was the Tlatelolcans who initiated commerce among the Aztecs during the reign of their first ruler Cuacuauhpitzahuac (1377–1405). It could be argued that this is an ethnocentric point of view. In any case, according to the text the only goods they sought in trade at that time were red *arará* feathers and red and blue parrot feathers. Under subsequent rulers new articles were added: jade, turquoise, precious feathers of all kinds, richly worked capes, breech cloths and *huipiles,* necklaces, nose ornaments and bracelets of gold, silver and precious stones, elaborate shields and war insignia, and the like (*Anales de Tlatelolco* 1948: 53–54, 57; *Florentine Codex* 1959: 2). In 1473, during the reign of Axayacatl, the Tenochcas went to war against the Tlatelolcans, and defeated and subjugated them (see Litvak 1971a for evidence of an earlier date for these events). During Ahuitzotl's rule, 1486–1502, the Tlatelolcan merchants opened up the route to Ayotlan Anahuac on the Pacific Coast (*Florentine Codex* 1959: 3; see also Tezozomoc 1944: 198–200; Durán 1965: 270).

By this time the *pochteca* in Tenochtitlan had become a highly esteemed and privileged group. They had their own courts of law, and in most respects they enjoyed the same status as the warriors and nobles. For example, a merchant who died on the road, like the warrior who died in battle, went to *Tonatiuh ichan,* the House of the Sun. For, as the *Florentine Codex* (1959: 23–25) states:

> ... they (the merchants) did not die; they went to heaven, they accompanied the Sun (on its course). Like those who died in battle, they say they accompanied the Sun, they went to heaven.[1]

Pochteca appears to have been the generic term for merchants. *Oztomeca* were merchants who went out on the road; they were also called *tecunenenque,* travelling lords, and *yaque,* travelers. *Nahualoztomecatl* was the term for the merchant-spy who was also a merchant-warrior, and also *teyahualoani,* "besieger," and *yaoc calaquini,* "enterer into battle." As Sahagún (1959: 20) states:

> The merchants of Tlatelolco were also called captains and soldiers, distinguished in merchant dress ... who lay siege and make war on provinces and towns.... These merchants were like knights already and had special insignia for their great deeds.

The Tenochca rulers not only used the merchants as spies and conquerors but apparently as agents of the state, also (see *Florentine Codex* 1959: 7–8, 17):

> ... the king, Ahuitzotl gave them 1,600 cloths (cloth-money), his own goods, to sell.... The Tenochcas took 800 and the Tlatelolcans 800, and with the cloths they bought royal capes with a design of cups in feathers, ones with golden eagle feathers, ones with striped feathered borders, royal breech cloths, and embroidered skirts and *huipiles.* These articles were the property, the goods, the possessions of Ahuitzotl.

By "Ahuitzotl's goods," is meant that these were the property of the state as represented by the king. However, the merchants carried on their own private business and bought and sold other goods, as the text enumerates (*Florentine Codex* 1959: 8, 18, 21–22):

> ... diadems of gold which were like crowns, gold rosettes for the forehead, necklaces of gold and jade with circular pendants, gold ear plugs, gold coverings which the women of Anahuac, the noblewomen, used to cover their bodies, gold finger rings ... and ear plugs of rock crystal. And (goods) that the commoners needed: obsidian ear plugs, tin (ear plugs), obsidian blades with leather (handles), sharp-pointed obsidian blades (for drawing blood), rabbit fur, needles and bells.

> All these were the goods, the merchandise, that the merchants, the traders, the traveling lords, the travelers, prepared for themselves.

---

[1] In this and subsequent texts from the *Florentine Codex,* the page references will refer to the Dibble and Anderson paleography but the translation will be that of Thelma D. Sullivan.

They also dealt in slaves, but slave-trading appears to have been reserved for the *teyacan-que, pochtecatlatoque,* "the leaders, the merchant-chiefs" (*Florentine Codex* 1959: 18).

All the *pochteca* would go as far as Tochtepec, but only the merchants from Tenochtitlan, Tlatelolco, Huitzilopochco, Azcapotzalco, and Cuauhtitlan, acting as agents of the king or state, were permitted to continue to the coastal regions of Anahuac Xicalanco and Anahuac Ayotlan, which were regarded as the exclusive "trading areas of Ahuitzotl" (*Florentine Codex* 1959: 17–18). And, as the text goes on to state:

> When the merchants reached Anahuac Xicalanco, they gave the rulers who governed the cities of Anahuac all (the things) that had been bought (with the 1,600 cloths) — the rich capes, rich skirts (and) rich *huipiles* — that were the property of Ahuitzotl.

The text then lists all the precious stones, feathers, shells, and animal hides, which the Anahuac rulers of Xicalanco, Cimatlan, and Coatzacoalcos gave in return (*Florentine Codex*: 18–19):

> ... All this that the merchants, the traveling merchants acquired in Xicalanco, that they brought back from there, belonged to Ahuitzotl.

As more regions were conquered and subjugated and more tribute was brought in, undoubtedly a surplus accumulated in the state warehouses. Many of the items of tribute were perishable, such as foodstuffs, or semi-perishable, such as cloths, capes, and feathers and these, perforce, had to be recirculated. Molins (1956: 73–77) has presented evidence that some of the tribute that came into Tenochtitlan-Tlatelolco was "reused" in commercial transactions (see also Litvak 1971b: 118). Who would be better equipped to handle these transactions than the merchants themselves? They knew the routes, the regions, the markets, the needs of the people as no one else did. They even knew the languages of the areas in which they traded. Furthermore, as Chapman (1959: 24) points out, in cases where commerce preceded conquest, once the conquest was effected and tribute began to flow

into the Axtec storehouses, trade with the area ceased. It was precisely these areas that the *pochteca,* as merchant-supies and merchant-warriors, had opened up to conquest. If their trading activities were curtailed as a result, did not the king, or state, owe them a favor? Surely, having the merchants act as the king's agents and giving them the opportunity to earn a commission would help compensate the merchants for their loss in markets, and it is entirely possible that the king appointed "royal merchants" as he did royal feather workers (see *Florentine Codex,* 1959: 90–91).

Living in their own *calpullis* and having their own temples and deities, the merchants were a closely-knit group. There were women *pochteca,* also, and the profession was handed down in the family from father or mother to son or daughter. There is no concrete evidence that Aztec women went out on the road, but apparently the women of Cholula did (Carrasco 1970: 180–81). The merchant profession was not open to anyone and only by special permission from the king could an outsider be admitted.

Outside the Valley of Mexico, the existence of various towns of free trade, great fairs, and important shrines where merchants of distinct ethnic affiliations has *barrios* and associated freely with each other suggests an international, or supranational association of merchants (see Chapman 1959; Thompson 1970: 126–58 for the Maya merchants — especially the Putun — and their contacts with the Aztecs; for the Maya see also Cardós 1959; for Guatemala, Feldman 1971).[2] According to Tezozomoc (1944: 132) and Durán (1965, Vol. 1, pp.

---

[2]In this connection it is interesting to note that Scholes and Roys (1948: 31) point out that the Aztec merchants had to cross enemy territory in order to reach Anahuac Xicalanco (i.e., the territory between Coatzacoalcos and Laguna de Términos). According to Sahagún (1956, Vol. 3, pp. 28–30), they sent word ahead and were met in the hostile territory by lords of Anahuac Xicalanco who conducted them to their towns. As water transport was common in Tabasco, the Aztec merchants were probably met by canoes (see Scholes and Roys 1948: 31). In Xicalanco, Cimatlán, and other towns, the Aztecs would sell their goods to local traders, who would handle further distribution (Scholes and Roys 1948: 31–33).

188–89) when Moctezuma I learned that a group of merchants from towns subject to the Triple Alliance had been killed in Coixtlahuaca, he sent off an expedition made up of warriors from tribute-paying towns, and also requested men from Cholula and Huexotzinco, traditional enemies of the Aztecs because, he said, "*tanto como a nosotros les pertenece la venganza.*"

While the position of the merchants in Aztec society was a privileged one, it appears that it also had its precarious aspects. Their operations were surrounded by the utmost secrecy. They always set out on their journeys and returned under cover of darkness, and when they returned the canoes transporting their wares were carefully covered so that no one could see their contents (*Florentine Codex*, 1959: 27, 31). Further, the merchant did not take his goods to his own home but hid them in the house of a trusted relative. It is entirely possible that they had become too rich and powerful and were now considered dangerous rivals to the nobles and rulers. Any ostentation on their part was frowned upon (*Florentine Codex* 1959: 31–32), as Sahagún (1956, Vol. 3, p. 37; *Florentine Codex* 1959: 32) states:

> And when they became proud and haughty and were corrupted by the favors and honors of (their) riches, the king was saddened and began to hate them. He sought false or trumped up reasons to oppress and kill them although they were guiltless, out of hatred for thur pride and arrogance, and he distributed their wealth to the old soldiers of his court called *cuachichictin*, Otomí, and *yautachcahuan* and thus maintained their pomp and ostenations.

At all costs a merchant had to be kept in his place. In the great banquet given by merchants in Panquetzaliztli, a *fiesta* which they celebrated on a par with the warriors, they lavished a considerable portion of their possessions on the nobles and warriors as gifts, an act that could be interpreted as a kind of payoff so that they would be left in peace.

The attitude of the ruler to the merchants appears to have contained a large element of ambivalence. That there were merchants who acted as agents for the king and that the king only allowed merchants from specific areas to trade for him and themselves in the rich coastal regions may signify that he entertained aspirations for the eventual creation of a state monopoly over trade, both domestic and foreign, as the Incas had in South America.

Cieza de León (1943, as recorded in Rostworowski 1970) tells us that merchant-spies were used by the Inca Yupanqui which indicates that a group of independent merchants were operating in Peru in pre-Inca times. Most modern writers agree that at the time of the Spanish Conquest the Inca state had taken over most of the economic activities of the nation which they had organised into a redistributive system: all surplus goods were collected by the state and doled out to the population according to its needs. In our opinion, there is evidence that Moctezuma II had visions of a similar state-controlled and regulated economy.

It is interesting to note, however, that in spite of state-controlled trade within the Inca Empire, or trade reduced to barter at the local level, a recently published document (Rostworowski 1970: 171) offers evidence that, at the time of Spanish Conquest there were organized merchants in the Chincha valley living in special *barrios*. These merchants were rich and highly esteemed by certain *caciques*. They carried on trade with the highlands as well as the coastal regions, but it is not known to what extent, if any, they might have been under Inca control.

In all probability there were direct and indirect contacts via trade between peoples within the region known as Nuclear America. That contact existed in the early Formative Period between Guatemala and Ecuador is supported by archaeological evidence (see Coe 1961b; Coe and Flannery 1967; Meggers and Evans 1964; Meggers, Evans, and Estrada 1965; Ford 1969). The extraordinary similarity of objects found in Occidental Mexico with those found on the Ecuadorian coast, the use of ax money, the construction of shaft tombs in both areas, and even architectural similarities (Lorenzo 1964) indicate that contact continued. The custom of flaying and stuffing the skin of a slain enemy and keeping it as a trophy, the preparation of small shrunken heads, and certain types of dental mutilation were practised by groups in Ecuador as well as Mesoamerica (see Acosta Saignes 1950: 37; Flores 1958: 95; Torquemada 1943, Vol. 2, p. 542; *Florentine Codex* 1961: 186; Leigh 1961; Motolinía 1967: 37; Broda de Casas 1970: 262-64). More recently there has been evidence that contact might have existed between Costa Rica and Ecuador (Paulsen 1971).[3]

In 1525, along the coast of Ecador the pilot Bartolomé Ruíz and his crew sighted a large balsa raft with some twenty men, women, and children aboard, loaded with rich goods and conch shells that may have served as money (*Relación Samano-Xerex* 1967: 65; see also Murra 1971, Paulsen 1972). The sailors in question may have been connected with the "league of seagoing merchants" which operated in coastal Ecuador according to Jijón y Caamaño (1941, Vol. 2, p. 92; see also Holm 1953). Then there was the famous large trading canoe seen by Columbus and his men off the coast of Honduras, the size of a galley, containing some twenty-five persons — men, women and children — and a cargo consisting of costly goods, *macanas*, copper objects, and *cacao* beans (i.e., currency) (see Colón 1947: 74-75; Las Casas 1965, Vol. 2, pp. 274-75). As Thompson (1970: 127) points out, the copper objects (and possibly the *macanas* too) had to be from Central Mexico, and in all probability the vessel had gone from the great trading center of Xicalanco, around the Yucatan Peninsula, with its destination the lower part of the Gulf of Honduras, and that "the merchants and crew were Putun (Chontal Maya), the Phoenicians of Middle America."

---

[3]To this should be added the results of recent investigations which point to northern South American influences not only in southern Mesoamerica and West Mexico but also in the central highlands at Tlatilco (apparently from the west). These data bring to mind the complex problem of the emergence and development of Mesoamerican civilization and the possibility that external stimuli (direct or indirect, through migration or trade) might have affected these processes.

Like the Incas, the Aztecs probably were not navigators and whether the Aztec merchants made journeys into distant lands is not known. However, there is little doubt that they traded and mingled with seagoing merchants of other nations in the great port of Xicalanco on the east coast and in the province of Xoconochco on the Pacific, and it is highly likely that the Mexican rulers via the *oztomeca* and *nahualoztomeca* obtained fairly detailed intelligence about conditions, not only within Middle America as far south as Panama, but also about Ecuador, and via Ecuador, directly or indirectly, about the Inca Empire. There were ample opportunities for contact and commerce as well as sharing of values between the two great powers of Nuclear America at the time of the Spanish Conquest, but the extent to which they availed themselves of these has not yet been determined.

CONQUEST, COLONIZATION, AND THE MERCHANTS

From all indications, commerce preceded conquest and the subsequent collection of tribute in the development of the Aztec Empire. Durán and Tezezomoc in particular give, as the principal pretexts for war and conquest refusal to trade, interference with free passage along the trade routes by the barricading of roads, injuring and/or killing traveling merchants, and stealing their goods. Several writers have insisted that the Triple Alliance and the *señoríos* and towns that paid tribute to it in no way corresponded to the political unit which in the modern occidental sense is called a state or empire. According to some sources the so-called Aztec Empire was an economic entity based solely on trade and tribute in order to insure an unimpeded flow of goods into Tenochtitlan and thus satisfy the ever growing needs of the Aztec rulers, their more privileged subjects, and their gods. Religious proselytism and interest in gaining true political control over conquered areas is generally believed to have been minimal.

However, there is a good deal of evidence in certain of the sources for an attempt at religious and political integration on the part of the Aztec ruler with respect to conquered areas.

In the realm of religion, Mendieta (1945, Vol. 1, p. 141; see also Motolinía 1967: 294) gives, along with other reasons the Aztecs had for declaring war, the slaying of envoys sent by the king to remote provinces demanding that they subjugate themselves to Mexico and that they accept the Mexican gods, place them in their temples, and worship them. Durán (1965, Vol. 1, p. 377), for example, mentions that conquests were made to further the glory of Huitzilopochtli. Foreign rulers were made to show reverence for the Tenochca gods and the "captured" gods of the conquered areas were "imprisoned" in the Coacalli, one of the buildings of the vast Great Temple complex in Tenochtitlan (*Florentine Codex* 1951: 168).

Political integration was implemented through a policy of colonization. As Tenochtitlan expanded and the population grew, the Aztecs were forced to reclaim land from the swamps by the construction of dikes, canals, and *chinampas,* man-made plots of land constructed on platforms and floated on the water, which were cultivated to provide food for the local population (see Calnek 1972: 105). This soon proved inadequate and by the time of the Conquest the city largely depended on external sources for its food which came in in trade or as tribute. The Aztecs also acquired additional land by the expropriation of conquered lands, which were distributed among the nobles and rulers, and the resettlement of the conquered people in other areas, as occurred in the case of Chalco, for example, during the reign of Moctezuma I (Tezozomoc 1944: 99; Durán 1965: 152; Torquemada 1943, Vol. 1, pp. 163–64).

More important, there was the establishment of colonies in distant regions, similar to the Inca *mitimaes,* an undertaking that was more commonly practised than is realized by students of Mexican history. Nigel Davies — in this symposium (Paper 20) has discussed in some detail the problem of colonies and the real meaning of the terms *"presidio"* and *"guarnición"* in early colonial sources. Suffice it to say, there are numerous references to the establishment of colonies and the resettlement of people. Thousands were involved,

and it is quite clear that few went voluntarily despite the gifts they were given and the facilities they were offered. The new towns were organized on the order of Tenochtitlan and the people settled in *barrios* according to their ethnic affiliations. The governors of these areas were always Mexicans, never Tezcocans or Tepanecs.

Undoubtedly the Mexican rulers, on occasion, resettled rebellious subjects, such as the Matlatzincas who, after being conquered by Axayacatl were sent to live in Xalatlauhco (i.e., Tlalatlauhco in the "province of Cuahuacan"; see Barlow 1949: 33–35) according to Torquemada (1943, Vol. 1, p. 181). In the main, however, they colonized strategic areas such as Oaxaca during the time of Moctezuma I, which they destroyed and decimated after a group of merchants was killed nearby. A cousin of Moctezuma was installed as "viceroy" (Tezozomoc 1944: 155–66; Durán 1965, Vol. 1, pp. 228–44; *Códice Ramírez* 1944: 183). In our opinion, proof that Oaxaca was a colony in the real sense of the word is contained in the glyph for this town (Huaxyacac) on page 1 of the *Matrícula de Tributos* and page 17r of the *Codex Mendoza* which is accompanied by two heads each with a *xiuhuitzolli,* the blue diadem which was the insignia of the ruler. One has the gloss *tlacatectli gobernador* and the other *tlacochtectli gobernador.* These functionaries, according to Sahagún (1956, Vol. 2, p. 140), assisted the king in the governing of the people.

Another example of the establishment of a colony took place in Ahuitzotl's time when the people of Teloloapan, Alahuiztlan, and Oztoman (Guerrero) closed their roads to the Mexican Oztomecas and as a consequence were destroyed by the Mexicans. It was decided to repopulate these towns "and imitate what Moctezuma did ... in the destruction of the land and people of Oaxaca ..." (Durán 1965: 360–67; Tezozomoc 1944: 155–66; *Códice Ramírez* 1944: 183). These colonies were established partially to secure the collection of trubute, partially for the purpose of keeping the roads open so that the tribute and merchandise for trade could get to the capital, and possibly even to raise certain products for the Aztecs in Tenochtitlan. What is most pertinent to this paper is that, according to the sources, these colonies in the main were a direct result of retaliatory wars touched off by aggressions against the merchants. This is one more example of the key role played by the merchants in the expansion of the Aztec Empire.

SUMMARY AND CONCLUSIONS

According to the historical sources, the Aztecs depended on trade for their survival from the time they settled on the inhospitable island of Tenochtitlan and, therefore, the merchants and their trading played an all-important part in the development of the Aztec culture. As a result, the merchants were granted privileges in proportion to the goods they traded in, not only in the material sense but also socially, politically, and ceremonially. After the defeat of Talatelolco, the Tenochca rulers took an ever-increasing interest in the commercial affairs of the nation and if routes of trade were interfered with or merchants molested, killed, or robbed while on trading expeditions, the Aztecs immediately made war on the offending parties and subjugated the area. What Bernal calls the "war-tribute-commerce" complex was actually commerce-war-tribute.

The *pochteca* were not only invaluable as traders but also as spies. The *nahualoztomeca* would supply the ruler with detailed information on given areas and based on this intelligence he would plan his wars of conquest. On certain occasions the *pochteca* acted as warriors too.

As conquest after conquest was effected and a surplus of tribute accumulated, the rulers traded with these goods, suing the merchants as agents of the state in this operation, for which they possibly paid them commission, perhaps in the same goods. Further, the role of the *pochteca* as instruments of contact between people of different cultures cannot be over-emphasized, nor that the values connected with certain objects, probably in particular exotic goods ("luxury goods," "status artifacts;" see Flannery 1968: 100) that contained some political, social, or religious sig-

nificance, may be shared. Cultural contact via trade occurred not only within Mesoamerica but probably within Nuclear America too through dealings between seagoing merchants of different nations.

Because they had become a rich, privileged and powerful group, the position of the *pochteca* in Aztec society eventually may have become precarious, particularly during the time of Moctezuma II, just prior to the Conquest. The increasing participation of the state in trade in order to redistribute the goods received as tribute may have led to more and more state control of trade and, had the Conquest not intervened, ultimately to the monopoly of trade by the state, most particularly foreign trade having to do with exotics. Had this occurred private enterprise in trade would have ceased to exist, commerce would have been nationalized and trade would have been reduced to barter at the local level, as happened in the Empire of the Incas.

Finally, in our opinion there is evidence that the Aztecs, like the Incas, were in the process of empire building. There are several references in the sources to religious proselytism and this, together with the establishment of colonies and the resettlement of people, points to the possibility of a move in the direction of eventual social and political integration. There is little doubt that these colonies were established for the purpose of gaining more direct control over conquered areas. The question that cannot, as yet, be answered with certainty is whether this control was strictly for economic reasons, that is, to make the trade and tribute routes safer, or whether political ambitions were involved also.

REFERENCES

Acosta Saignes 1950
Anales de Tlatelolco 1948
Barlow 1949
Bernal 1968
Broda de Casas 1970
Calnek 1972
Cardós de Méndez 1959
Carrasco 1970
Chapman 1959
Chimalpahin 1960

Cieza de León 1943
Codex Mendoza 1938
Códice Ramírez 1944
Coe 1961b
Coe and Flannery 1967
Colón 1947
Durán 1965
Feldman 1971
Flannery 1968
Florentine Codex 1950–69
Flores 1958
Ford 1969
Grove 1968
Holm 1953
Ixtlilxochitl 1965
Jijón y Caamaño 1941
Las Casas 1965
Leigh 1961

Litvak King 1971a, 1971b
Lorenzo 1964
Matrícula de Tributos
Meggers and Evans 1964
Meggers, Evans, and Estrada 1965
Mendieta 1945
Molins Fábrega 1956
Motolinía 1967
Murra 1971
Paulsen 1971, 1972
Relación Samano-Xerez 1967
Rostworowski de Diez Canseco 1970
Sahagún 1956
Scholes and Roys 1948
Sullivan 1971
Tezozomoc 1944, 1949
Thompson 1970
Torquemada 1943

19. INSIDE A MEXICA MARKET
by
Lawrence H. Feldman

The Market of Tlatelolco was one of the wonders of the ancient Mesoamerican world. Frequent detailed mention is made of its diverse and well ordered merchandise by the early Spanish chroniclers (Sahagún 1961 and 1954; Cortés 1962; Zorita 1909; Motolinía 1971; Anonymous Conqueror 1941; Díaz del Castillo 1963; Mártyr 1912; López de Gómara 1954; and Cervantes de Salazar 1936). Recently Durand-Forest (1971: 121) published a manuscript plan of a Tenochtitlan market in the "period of the conquest." It is an incomplete map of a market in the early years of the Spanish colony but nevertheless it is quite valuable. A blueprint is, in effect, provided for the organization of the pre-Hispanic market.

We see that the market (Fig. 35) is rectangular in outline, with a platform in its center and a small building in one corner. The entire area is further surrounded by other structures. Ninety-seven units are marked off, some being designated as the location of particular types of merchandise. By means of examination of the reports of people who actually saw this, or similar markets, in operation, it is possible to provide identifications for almost every unit and every structural feature in the plan. The method is to note all references in these sources to location, relative to other stalls and of types of merchandise in the market (sources used are cited above). As an example, there is the reference

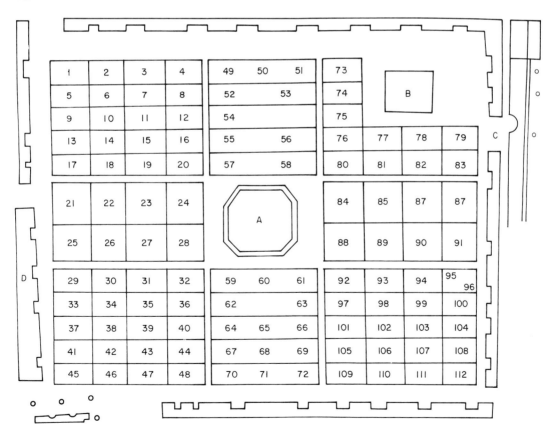

Figure 35. THE PARTS OF A MEXICA MARKET

219

in Díaz del Castillo (1963: 232) to dealers in gold, silver, precious stones, feathers, cloaks, embroidered goods, and slaves being adjacent to each other. They, in turn, adjoined those who sold coarser cloth and cotton goods. By using clues such as these, together with explicit notations on the base map, Figure 35, the Mexica market, has been reconstructed. The identification of stall activity is given in Table 19.

Figure 35 is, of course, not intended to be a perfectly accurate stall by stall delineation of the pre-Hispanic marketplace. But the broad outline it provides some clues as to its organization. Thus it was said that "each kind of merchandise is sold in its own particular street and no other kind may be sold there: this rule is very well enforced" (Cortés 1962: 89). A reflection of that order appears in Figure 35 where several areas seem restricted to one kind of goods. Stalls facing the center

stage almost all seem related to the clothing industry. Other areas are dominated by food serving, produce, high value, and other goods. The tentative market model provided here suggests what artifacts may be indicative of its archaeological presence. Other data inform us as to the nature of the vendors.

The most systematic listing of sellers in a Central Mexican market comes from Book 10 of the Florentine Codex (Sahagún 1961). This listing is of special interest because it goes beyond listing the merchandise of sellers. One learns also the nature of the seller; that is, whether he is a wholesaler (*tlaquixtiani*), retailer (*tlanecuilo*), importer (*pochteca* or *oztomecatl*), craftsman, producer, or more than one kind of seller. Plotting of the different types of vendors (Fig. 36) produces some interesting results. With a very few exceptions, all retailers are concentrated in the produce, food service, or cloth portions of the

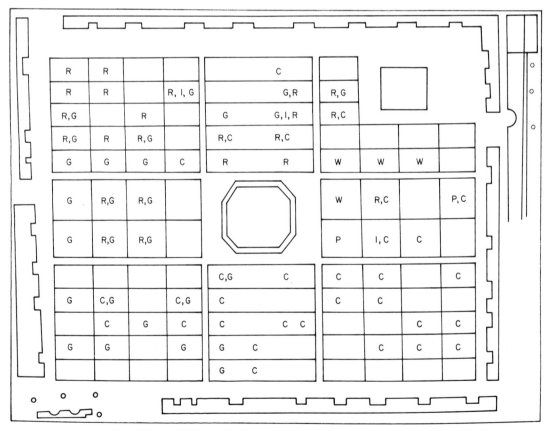

FIGURE 36. MEXICAN MARKET VENDOR TYPES
R, Retailers; W, Wholesalers; C, Craftsmen; G, Producer; I, Importer; P, Pochteca.

map. Wholesalers are limited to sellers of large cotton capes and importers to certain high value goods. Most of the market is made up of vendors who either make, kill, grow, catch, or cut their own goods. The few goods, other than those in the food service category, that are sold *only* by retailers deserve special mention. Amaranth, *chia*, and worked capes are the only items not also sold by their producers or craftsmen. In the sale of these articles, one sees the true beginnings of a new social class, an Aztec bourgeoisie.

Table 19. THE PARTS OF A MEXICA MARKET[1]

SECTION I: RESTAURANTS, PRODUCE, MEAT, AND FISH

1., 2. *Tlaxcalnamacac*: The Tortilla Seller
3. *Aioachnamacac*: The Seller of Gourd Seeds and cakes of gourd seeds
4. *Tlaquetzalnamacac*: One who provides people with the chocolate drink of the rulers, of the nobles
5., 6. *Tlaxcalnamacac*: see above No. 1
7. *Atolnamacac*: The Atole Seller, sells hot *atole* drink
8. *Cacaoanamac*: The Cacao Seller, sells *cacao* beans
9. *Totoltenamac*: The Egg Seller
10. *Picienamacac*: The Seller of Fine Tobacco
11. *Chiennamacac*: Teh *Chia* Seller; The Oil Seller (cf. *Chiamanamacac* of Molina 1944)
12. *Henamac*: The Bean Seller
13. *Totolnamacac*: The Turkey Seller
14. *Vauhnamacac*: The Amaranth Seed Seller
15. *Tlaolnamacac*: The Seller of Maize Grains
16. *Chiquippantlacatl*: The Displayer of Wares on a Large Basket, the seller of colors, of various colors, of dyes
17. *Nacanamacac*: The Meat Seller
18., 19. *Xoquilacanamacac*: The Stench Seller (Fish Seller)
20. *Tochominamacac*: The Seller of Rabbit Hair

SECTION II: MEAT AND PRODUCE

21. *Nacanamacac*: see above No. 17
22., 23. *Suchiqualpantlacatl*: The Man with Fruit; seller of maize stalks, green maize, tortillas, cooked gourds, tree fruit, cactus fruit, sweet potatoes, manioc
24. (thread)
25. *Nacanamacac*: see above No. 17
26., 27. *Suchiqualpantlacatl*: see above No. 22
28. (thread)

SECTION III: HARDWARE, HIDES, PHARMACY, AND WINE

29. *Ocnamacac*: Wine or Pulque Seller (Molina 1944)
30. *Amolnamacac*: Soap Seller (Molina 1944)
31. *Quinamaca Cuetlascactli*: Seller of Cured Leather Sandals
32. (rope)
33. *Quilnamac*: Herb Seller
34. *Hihujnamacac*: Feather Seller; the Spinner of Feathers into Thread
35. *Euanamacac*: Hide Seller (based upon Nahua rules of compound word construction)
36. *Siuhquilnamac*: Turquoise Herb Seller; sells black clay mixed with *uixachin* leaves for coloring things
37. *Panamacac*: The Medicine Seller; sells medicines of herbs, wood, stones, milk, alum, and things cooked in *ollas*
38. *Tzacunamacac*: The Glue Seller
39. *Suchiocutzonamacac*: The Seller of Liquidambar; sells pine resin, possessor of pine resin trees
40. *Acaquauhnamacac*: The Smoking Tube Seller
41. *Ocutzonamac*: The Seller of Pine Resin; sells pine and other resin, a woodsman, a collector of pine resin
42. *Poponamacac*: The Broom Seller
43. *Vitzmallonamac*: The Needle Seller; sells needles, awls, punches, bells, axes, adzes, fish hooks, chisels
44. *Olnamacac*: The Rubber Seller
45. (cochineal)
46. not known
47. *Pinolnamacac*: The *Pinole* Seller (based upon Durand-Forest 1971)
48. not known

SECTION IV: CLOTH, MINERALS, PRODUCE, AND SERVICES

49. *Tequixquinamacac*: The Seller of Saltpeter
50. *Tizanamacac*: The Chalk Seller
51. *Monamacac*: Self Seller (prostitute)
52. *Tomanamacac*: The Tomato Seller
53. *Chilnamacac*: The *Chile* Seller
54. *Chientzotzolnamacac*: Wrinkled *Chia* Seller
55., 56. *Iczotilmanamac*: The Seller of Palm Leaf Fiber Capes
57., 58. *Veicapantlacatl*: "The Principal Merchant;" sells worked capes, worked shifts, fine skirts

SECTION V: MAGUEY GOODS AND BUILDING MATERIAL

59. *Necunamacac*: The Maguey Syrup Seller
60. *Aianamacac*: The Seller of Coarse Maguey Fiber Capes
61. (hats)
62. *Cacnamacac*: The Sandal Seller; sells sandals of maguey fiber

63.   (hats)
64.   *Cacnamacac:* see above No. 62
65.   *Xiquipilnamacac:* The Bag Seller
66.   *Nelpilonamacac:* The Sash Seller; sells narrow strips of cloth
67.   *Quauhnanamaca:* The Wood Seller; sells lumber
68.   *Quauhxinqui:* "The Carpenter:" sells beams, wooden pillars, lintels, roofing, wooden columns, boards, planks
69.   *Tenexnamacac:* Seller of Lime; adjacent to seller of building stone
70.   *Quauhnanamaca:* see above No. 67
71.   *Quauhxinqui:* see above No. 68
72.   *Tenexnamacac:* see above No. 69

SECTION VI: PRODUCE, SALT, CLOTH, AND MONEY

73.   not known
74.   *Chilnamacac:* see above No. 53
75.   *Iztanamacac:* The Seller of Salt; sells salt balls and salt *ollas*
76.   (pieces of *cueitl* or skirt cloth sold — Durand-Forest 1971)
77.   (pieces of *tilmatli* or *manta* cloth sold — Durand-Forest 1971)
78.   (selling of gold filled quills)
79.   (*ocotl* torches sold — Durand-Forest 1971)
80.–82.   *Tilmapan Tlacatl, Quachnamacac:* The Man With the Capes, The Seller of Large Cotton Capes
83.   (seller of *tomitilmatli* or woolen *mantas* — Durand-Forest 1971)

SECTION VII: HIGH VALUE GOODS

84.   *Tilmapan Tlacatl, Quachnamacac:* see above No. 80
85.   *Xicalnamacac:* The Seller of Gourd Bowls
86.   *Tlapitzalnamacac:* The Seller of Cast Metal Objects; sells objects made out of precious metal, either gold or silver
87.   *Ihuinamacac:* The Feather Seller
88.   *Tecoani:* The Slave Dealer
89.   *Ámanamacac:* The Paper Seller
90.   *Chalchiuhnamacac:* The Seller of Green Stones
91.   (sellers of bees' honey)

SECTION VIII: WOVEN GOODS, POTS, TRINKETS, AND SERVICES

92., 93.   *Chiquiuhnamacac:* The Seller of Large Baskets
94.   *Cozcatetecpanqui:* The Displayer of Necklaces
95.   *Zoquichiuhqui:* The Clay Worker; sells all pottery except griddles

96.   *Comalnamacac:* The Comal Seller
97., 98.   *Chiquiuhnamacac:* see above No. 92
99.   not known
100.   *Tananamacac:* The Seller of Small Baskets
101.   (sellers of bird skins)
102.   (sellers of shells)
103.   *Tezcanamacac:* The Mirror-Stone Seller
104.   *Petlanamacac:* The Reed Mat Seller
105.   (barbers)
106.   *Itznamacac:* The Obsidian Seller; sells blades on demand
107.   *Otlachiquiuhnamacac:* The Seller of Stout Cane Carrying Baskets
108.   *Petlanamacac:* see above No. 104
109.–112.   not known

SECTION IX: STRUCTURAL FEATURES

A.   Stage: platform for public announcements pertaining to market and adjacent to it is the place for execution of thieves (Cortés 1962: 52)
B.   Court House: "A very fine building in the great square serves as a kind of audience chamber where ten or a dozen persons are always seated, as judges, who deliberate on all cases arising in the market and pass sentence on evildoers" (Cortés 1962: 89).
C.   Entrance to the Courts of the Great Temple (Díaz del Castillo 1963: 233).
D.   Arcades that "completely surrounded" Market (Cortés 1962: 87)

---

[1]Unless otherwise stated, all Nahua terms are from Sahagún (1961). Numbers refer to those in Figure 35.

ACKNOWLEDGMENT

I wish to thank Dr. Richard Deihl and the University of Missouri Archaeological Project at Tula, Hidalgo, Mexico, for the support that made this paper possible.

REFERENCES

Anonymous Conqueror 1941
Cervantes de Salazar 1936
Cortés 1962
Díaz del Castillo 1963
Durand-Forest 1971
López de Gómara 1954
Mártyr 1912
Molina 1944
Motolinía 1971
Sahagún 1954, 1961
Zorita 1909

20. THE MILITARY ORGANIZATION OF THE AZTEC EMPIRE
by
Nigel B. Davies

GENERAL PROBLEMS

We cannot understand the communications system of Mesoamerica unless we first ask ourselves for what purposes such routes were used, and why people travelled upon them.

Clearly Mesoamericans seldom journeyed simply to pay social calls, or in the guise of tourists, to see whose pyramid was tallest. As among other ancient peoples, travel, and therefore established land routes, were connected mainly with two activities, war and trade. In Mesoamerica, commerce often preceded conquest, and the old adage that trade follows the flag did not always apply.

I intend to take as my subject one of these two activities, and will permit myself to talk in general terms of the Aztec military organization, but with particular emphasis on a specific question: did they maintain provincial garrisons and the standing forces necessary to man them?

This point, often the subject of misunderstandings, is fundamental to the whole Aztec system of territorial domination. I am therefore grateful to be allowed to include in this symposium some remarks on a theme a little off the main topic but which at least considerably affects the whole problem of communications and routes.

For it is surely fair to say that only if we first determine what kind of provincial military organization the Aztecs possessed, can we then seek out the nature of any military communications system that would be required.

If the existence of real garrisons or colonies can be established, together with their location, we should then be able to identify the main imperial thoroughfares, involving perhaps even storehouses and staging posts, on the Inca model.

We must of course be clear about what is meant by the words "garrison" and "colony." "Garrison" should be taken to signify what it means today: a standing force of soldiers always available for the defence of a base, strongpoint, city, or region. The Concise Oxford Dictionary expresses this concept as follows: "Troops stationed in fortress, town, etc., to defend it." The soldiers who constitute such a defence force would obviously themselves not be native to the place; the word "stationed" implies clearly that they must be sent there from outside and presumably relieved from time to time. On the other hand, a colony is totally different; this would consist of people from outside who came to live in a certain palce. They might have been originally sent there for the purposes of defending the region, but they would not become a garrison, if they settled there.

THE CENTRAL MILITARY ORGANIZATION

We must first take a look at the central military organization of the Triple Alliance and ask: what kind of forces were deployed by Tenochtitlan, Texcoco, and Tacuba. Was there any standing force available for any task at any time, including garrison duty, or were the required levies simply raised for specific campaigns according to the needs of the moment?

Leaving aside deep religious motivations, and the need for sacrificial victims, war in Mesoamerica, as in Medieval Europe, was rather the sport of kings, and an occasion for members of the aristocracy to show their mettle. For this exercise, the bulk of the manpower came, as might be expected, from the lower ranks of society, rather than from the middle, or artisan class.

Most of our information comes from Tenochtitlan, and while we cannot discuss here every aspect of the complicated problem of social structure and land tenure, a few words are necessary on such aspects as affect military organization. In more precise terms, we must ask ourselves whether full-time soldiers existed among either patricians or plebeians, or whether the bearing of arms was more normally a part time calling.

As regards this ruling class or establishment, among otherwise contradictory accounts, a certain concensus of opinion is to be found as to the existence of two main categories of people; Katz has made this distinction very clear (Katz 1966: 29–32).

First we have the hereditary nobles, the "*pipiltzin por linaje*," or "*tlazopipiltzin*," and second, the "*tetecuhtzin*" or "*segundos señores*," as Zorita calls them (Zorita 1963: 142).

The land of the *pipiltzin*, many of whom were related to the *tlatoani*, was hereditary property and was cultivated by *mayeques*, serfs tied to the fields they tilled; the owners were thus freed from all tasks but those of general supervision, and were able to devote themselves to the service of the state.

The same is virtually true of the second category, the *tetecuhtzin*. They were perhaps more to be compared to English life peers, honoured for their own lifetime for their service to the community, but with the difference that they were also provided by the ruler with land, and with people to cultivate it (*Tecallec*). The *señor* virtually maintained them, and they even ate in the palace (Zorita 1963: 143).

Thus the two divisions of the lay ruling establishment had this in common: they were in a position to give the *tlatoani* virtually full-time service, but not necessarily of a military nature. Zorita makes it clear that they served the *señor* both in wars and in other public offices of a civil nature (Zorita 1963: 145).

When we turn to the lower classes, it becomes self-evident on the other hand that their everyday calling was the cultivation of the *calpulli* lands (the bulk of the armies was clearly recruited from these *macehuales* or freeholders; the *mayeques* on the other hand did not normally serve).

Pomar emphasises the dual role of the *macehual*: he explains that the common people sent their sons to the *telpochcalli*; they and their fathers were occupied with the cultivation of their land, which constituted their principal calling alongside the bearing of arms (Pomar 1941: 29). In other words, military service, while it perhaps offered greater

honour and glory, was not a full-time profession for the *macehual*.

It seems that the *macehuales* were organized for war on the basis of the land-holding unit, the *calpulli*. While great emphasis was placed on military valour, it would appear most unlikely that any of them were *permanently* under arms. The available evidence points the other way.

The Anonymous Conqueror, while insisting that Moctezuma had a "*guarnición*" of ten thousand men to guard his person, states that in the case of provincial uprisings: "*se reclutaba pronto en la ciudad y en sus confines.*" Before departing for war, the men all went to the Great Temple and collected their arms, not permanently in their possession and apparently stored above the main entrances (Conquistador Anónimo 1961: 65).

To take another instance: when preparations for war against Soconusco were afoot, the bulk of the forces had to be trained rapidly: "*Los mexicanos a gran prisa comenzaron a aderezar sus armas fuertes y cotaras y a prevenir los mancebos,*" (Tezozomoc 1944: 371). The recruits received daily training in the *telpochcalli* at the hands of the *achcauhtzin*.

The very nature of Mesoamerican warfare, with its emphasis on ritual exchanges before hostilities, rather than upon surprise attack, gave time for such preparations, and reduced the necessity to maintain forces constantly on the alert. Mobilization, when enforced, was thorough, and at times included the whole male population, except for elders and boys under the age of ten. All would presumably have received some previous military training in the *telpochcalli* prior to this last-minute "refresher course."

It is indeed hard to see what category of citizens could have manned the lower ranks of any standing army, without which such a force could hardly have existed.

Even the ruling classes, whose duties to the state were of a more full-time nature, appear to have given their service in a dual capacity, civil, and military. Again, as in the Middle Ages, such functions were more readily interchangeable than nowadays.

An exception may perhaps be made for those referred to as *tequihuaque* or *achcauhtzin*. Among the different categories of people who served, these might possibly be regarded as career officers, or even drill sergeants, according to the account of the Anonymous Conqueror. In addition, the possibility exists, but not any certainty, that the orders of knights, in particular the Eagles and Ocelots, like, say, the Knights Templar, might have constituted a kind of a full time *corps d'élite*.

But even if anything approaching a permanent *officer* class existed, this select band alone could not possibly have sufficed for garrison duty on a wide scale.

PROVINCIAL ORGANIZATION

The Aztecs normally left civil power in the conquered provinces in the hands of the existing *señores*, with the additional presence in key centers of their own *calpixques* as representatives of the central power, whose main duty was to supervise the payment of tribute to the Triple Alliance.

As to any more numerous standing or permanent presence, we possess in the first instance evidence of two major colonies, sent from the Valley of Mexico and nearby cities, rather after the pattern of the Inca *mitimaes*.

Oaxaca. During the reign of Moctezuma I, that indefatigable alter ego of the *tlatoani*, Tlacaelel, made the proposal that a colony should be settled in Oaxaca. As a result, six hundred married men, with their wives and children, were gathered together families from Texcoco, Chalco, Xochimilco and Cuernavaca were included. A cousin of Tlacaelel was put in charge of the new settlement (Durán 1967, Vol. 2, pp. 238–39).

During subsequent accounts of campaigns in that area, Durán and Tezozomoc refer on various occasions to these people who had been settled in Oaxaca. Once established, probably their military organization was not dissimilar to that of Tenochtitlan. Thus they would have provided levies for local wars, but the existence of any standing force among them must remain in doubt.

Equally, on various occasions, the *Relaciones Geográficas* of the sixteenth century

mention a Mexican force at Oaxaca, and write of contacts between its personnel and the local peoples (*Relación de Ixtepexi*: 16, *Relación de Amatlan*: 120–21; *Relación de Cuicatlan*: 185). It will be explained later what is the probable significance of the word "*guarnición*" in such contexts.

As to the route taken by Aztec forces going to Oaxaca, information is imprecise; *tezozomoc* and Durán merely imply that the armies passed by Izúcar and Chalco, which was indeed their most natural itinerary.

Oztoma and Alahuiztla. After Ahuitzotl had laid waste these two places, situated on the Tarascan border beyond Teloloapan, Guerrero, with even more than his wonted ruthlessness, putting most of the inhabitants to the sword, it was proposed that they should be repopulated with a colony from Central Mexico numbering nearly two thousand (*Relación de Alahuiztlan, Relación de Oztoma*). Four hundred people from each were to be sent from Tenochtitlan, Texcoco, and Tacuba and twenty each from thirty subject cities.

Nezahualpilli, who was apt to drag his feet where Anuitzotl's proposals were concerned, suggested that two hundred colonists from Texcoco would be sufficient, rather than the four hundred proposed. The net was certainly widely cast to obtain settlers, to include such places as Toluca and Jilotepec; probably however, bearing in mind the reduction of the Texcoco quota, the number fell short of the stipulated figure. When assembled, the people were given a consolatory talk; they were not particularly eager to set off into the wilds.

Some confirmation of the existence of such a colony also comes from the *Relaciones Geográficas*.

As to the route to reach this region, Ahuitzotl, on his return from Oztoma, passed Teloloapan, Zumpahuacan, Malinalco, Atlapulco, and Acaxochic (Tezozomoc 1944: 345–47). Even this account lacks precision; Zumpahuacan is only a few miles southwest of Malinalco, and from there to Teloloapan the route is not described.

The question of any additional permanent Aztec presence in the provinces of empire, apart from these two colonies, is much more problematical. In contrast to the relatively frequent mentions of the Oztoma and Oaxaca settlements, references do occur in isolation, and usually once only, to other places.

The *Relaciones Geográficas* do refer to other forces or garrisons in the provinces.

In connection with Tototepec Mexicans are mentioned: *"que quedaron allí por guarnición que solía tener Moctezuma"* (*La Suma de Visitas* 1905–6: 29).

Teozacualco, Oaxaca, is reported as being subject to Moctezuma, who maintained a *"guarnición"* there (*Descripción de Teozacualco*: 308).

Coixtlahuaca is reported as a place where Moctezuma: *"tenía puesta su frontera de gente de guerra"* (*Relación de Atlatlauhca y Malinaltepec* 1905–6: 165). However any standing force would probably have emanated from nearby Oaxaca.

Landa (1959) also incidentally mentions Mexican garrisons in Tabasco and Xicalango. But while armed pochteca might conceivably have made an appearance in this area, garrisons in the stricter sense of the word can hardly be sought outside the territory that paid tribute to the Triple Alliance.

In actual fact, all such mentions of garrisons, etc., lack precision, and it would seem more probable that any Aztec forces to be found in such places simply went there from time to time, as we will come to show in greater detail.

Two important centers, however, remain to be discussed as possible headquarters of some type of standing force:

Tuxtepec. The *Relación de Chinantla* (1905–6: 61) states: *"Los indios mexicanos que presidían en el pueblo de Tuchtepeque donde Moctezuma tenía una guarnición de gente muy grande."*

Now Tuxtepec, situated in the extreme northeast of Oaxaca, was of course the great merchant center par excellence and Sahagún tells how the traders of the principal cities of the Valley of Mexico maintained their own establishments there, where they could reside (*Florentine Codex*, Book 9, p. 48).

This fact in itself implies some kind of settlement or colony, provided by the pochteca, who were warriors as much as traders. They could scarcely have abandoned their property for part of the time to the depredations of the local inhabitants.

The Xiuhcoac region. While there is little actual evidence of a colony or garrison, ample testimony survives as to the primordial military importance of Xiuhcoac as the bastion of the northeast, situated between the Gulf Coast and the still independent principality of Metztitlan.

In this respect, it is significant that Bernal Díaz del Castillo (1969: 167) writes of a total of four *"guarniciones y capitanías"* in Mexico: one in Soconusco, one in Coatzacoalcos, one in Michoacan; the fourth was "Raya de Panuco." He describes the latter as lying between Tuzapan and Tuxpan, i.e., precisely where Xiuhcoac was probably located according to my own calculations.

Now any forces in the direction of Soconusco and Coatzacoalcos may well be regarded as offshoots of the colonists of Oaxaca and the pochteca of Tuxtepec, and Michoacan may well be taken to imply the Tarascan frontier, or Oztoma, thus conforming with our previous information.

It is most interesting that it is *only* on the presence of some permanent force in the Panuco area that Bernal Díaz del Castillo gives any precise information: he tells how the garrison stationed near Tuzapan exacted tribute and supplies from villages in the neighbourhood who were friendly with the Spaniards' allies of Cempoala. His information thus rests on solid foundations, since he was concerned with people who knew of this force from personal experience. The distance from Tuxpan to Cempoala is sufficient to account for the failure of such a contingent to put in an appearance on Cortés' landing.

FORTRESSES AND STRONGPOINTS

The function fulfilled by Oztoma, already mentioned, brings us to the general question of fortresses. Of their experience we have ample evidence, and in accounts of Aztec campaigns, the storming of bullwarks and barricades is often a prelude to victory.

Oztoma itself was one of a whole series of strongpoints on the Tarascan border, as part of a general defensive system.

To mention only two other fortified places, Cortés writes of Iztacimaxtitlan, near the Tlaxcalan border, as equal if not superior to Spanish fortresses (Cortés 1963: 39). Bernal Díaz del Castillo (1969: 65) describes Quiahuiztlan on the coast as a formidable strongpoint, difficult to attack.

But a fortress is one thing and a garrison another. The former appear usually to have been built and defended by *local* levies, perhaps reinforced by a contingent from the central power in times of emergency. If any defensive positions were permanently manned, this certainly did not apply to the famous wall on the Tlaxcalan border deserted by the Tlaxcalans when Cortés appeared.

In general, the Aztec Empire, a term we use for lack of an apter expression, was a mosaic of small *señoríos* which had been subdued and forced to pay tribute. It is striking that in numerous instances of border peoples, the *Relaciones Geográficas* relate that such tribute was paid, not in the conventional form but in contributions to the Triple Alliance of arms and actual military service.

And, quite apart from such frontier zones, people who lay on the line of march of the Aztec armies were expected to provide not only food and arms, but auxiliary forces. The main army set out well provided with supplies, but supplemented these by living off the land, and the people thus stood in great fear when they passed (Durán 1967, Vol. 2, p. 180).

The recruitment of manpower for the principal campaigns was certainly not confined to the three capitals of the Alliance, reinforced by tribes situated actually on the frontier. Not only did the Aztecs cast their net wide among nearby subject peoples, but exacted service also from those situated nearer to the proposed objective of the campaign. For instance, Ixmiquilpan and Atotonilco provided levies

for Tizoc's abortive attack on Metztitlan; Tehuantepec produced forces for Ahuitzotl's wars against Soconusco. The Empire in fact seems to have been held together, not only by the fear of massive retaliation from the center in case of rebellion, but also by a certain reliance on specific and selected allies in the provinces, such as those mentioned above. Once conquered, they could, on the whole, be relied upon to remain loyal.

WHAT THE CONQUERORS SAW

From accounts of purely native derivation, backed by one passage from Bernal Díaz del Castillo, we have been able to postulate the existence of three, and possibly four places where some permanent Aztec presence was to be found, probably in the form of established colonists, rather than of metropolitan troops.

It is now necessary to examine briefly what the conquerors themselves observed. Of these, the fullest and most precise accounts are of course those of Bernal Díaz del Castillo, on whom we shall mainly rely.

The key problem of the whole discussion lies in the question: supposing that the Triple Alliance maintained an elaborate system of local garrisons, just where were they when the Spaniards landed?

In the first place, the Spaniards encountered no kind of garrison, or, for that matter, any force at all on the whole stretch of coast between San Juan de Ulua and Quiahuiztlan, though the inhabitants were of doubtful loyalty.

Equally, on his march to Tlaxcala, Cortés met no Mexican soldiers; it was the local *señores* who, at Moctezuma's bidding, extended facilities to the Spaniards. Even if Moctezuma did not wish to oppose their march, surely any troops stationed near the route would have made an appearance.

The *calpixques* of Cataxtla and Tuxtepec had come to see Cortés on his first landing, but had apparently brought no military escort, notwithstanding reports already quoted of Aztec forces stationed in the latter place. They came accompanied merely by Indians bearing gifts (Díaz del Castillo 1969: 59).

An even more striking example is afforded by the five tax gatherers who arrived at Quiahuiztlan; they came surprisingly unprotected, and Cortés had absolutely no difficulty in arresting them. They appeared, "*muy acompañado de principales de otros pueblos de la lengua totonaca*" (Díaz del Castillo 1969: 73). Dressed in the height of fashion, their weapons consisted of bunches of flowers and fans. It is clear that they normally thought personal protection to be unnecessary, and relied for safety on the remorseless retaliatory power of the central authority. The local chiefs were horrorstruck at Cortés' audacity!

Equally, in Tenochtitlan itself, the position is most nebulous, as far as any standing forces are concerned. According to Bernal Díaz del Castillo, who was present, Cortés and only six other Spaniards, apart from the two interpreters, were sufficient to march Moctezuma off to their quarters. This occurred without the smallest show of resistance, notwithstanding various vague references to "*los de la guardia*," etc. The latter certainly made up by their appetites for whatever they lacked in military effectiveness, and are reported to have eaten a thousand dishes daily in the palace.

It is most probable that these were not really a fixed and permanent bodyguard, but a number of nobles and their sons, in attendance upon the ruler on a rotating basis; their duties would have been of a both civil and military nature, and no account is given of any arms that they might have carried.

It may also be worthy of note that the ability to kidnap rulers was not solely to be ascribed to Spanish guile or ruthlessness. Six of Moctezuma's captains were able to sequester an apparently unguarded Cacama, ruler of Texcoco, and bring him to Tenochtitlan (Díaz del Castillo 1969: 181).

GARRISONS AND GUARNICIONES

The real crux of the whole matter involves questions of semantics. Much confusion has been created by the use in conquerors' accounts and in *Relaciones Geográficas* of the word "*guarnición*." But one has only to read such reports carefully to realize by the sense of the text that garrisons, in the modern sense of the word, are not intended by such statements.

Shirley Gorenstein stresses this point most effectively, quoting a seventeenth century Spanish dictionary which defines a "*guarnición*" as simple "soldiers guarding or protecting a place where they were" (Gorenstein 1966: 56).

Now, quite apart from the older Spanish usage, if we examine the question from the Nahuatl point of view, the difference between old and new meanings becomes even more conclusive.

Molina does not list "*guarnición*" by itself, but translates "*guarnición de gente*" (a phrase often used by Bernal Díaz del Castillo) as "*centlamantin yaoquizque*," that is to say, "warriors gathered together;" no question is implied of a permanent force.

Now, if in Nahuatl there was no precise word for a standing garrison, and if equally in Spanish of that time, the only word, "*guarnición*," had a different sense, it is difficult to see how informants could possibly have reported the existence of an intensive network of fixed garrisons, if no word existed to denote what they meant. Surely they were mainly speaking simply of mobile warriors on military expeditions, and this was translated into Spanish as "*guarnición*," which had a different meaning in those times.

To conclude this argument, let us take a look at some of Bernal Díaz del Castillo's various mentions of this word, to see what he appears to mean.

a.) At Cingapacingo, a fortress two days' march inland from Cempoala, a force was reported of "*muchos indios de guerra de los culúas*" who had come to destroy their crops (Díaz del Castillo 1969: 77). But this same force is described in the chapter heading as "*guarniciones de mexicanos*." When the Spaniards arrived at the place the Mexicans had departed, but Bernal Díaz again refers to Mexicans who "*solían estar en guarnición en aquel pueblo*." It is surely clear that periodical visits rather than a standing force is intended by "*guarnición*."

b.) Various mentions are made of the word *"guarnición"* in connection with Cortés' forays from Tlaxcala when he had returned thither after the Noche Triste, but in the same context the word *"sent"* is invariably used or implied; that is to say, the Aztec force had been dispatched to the place in question to fulfill a particular task, and was not permanent. For instance, to Tepeaca Moctezuma *"mandaba ir muy grandes capitanías y guarniciones de gente de guerra para que mirasen no les entrasemos en sus tierras ..."* (Díaz del Castillo 1969: 249), or in the vicinity of Ixtapalapa *"los mexicanos siempre tenían velas y guarniciones contra nosotros, cuando sabían que íbamos a la guerra ..."* (Díaz del Castillo 1969: 268).

c.) If the matter is not by now abundantly clear, the siege of Tenochtitlan gives added confirmation. In the heading of Chapter CL, Bernal Díaz tells how Cortés *"mandó que fuesen tres guarniciones de soldados ... a poner cerco a la gran ciudad de México ..."*. By *"guarnición"* he clearly means simply a "force". Moreover, Cortés himself speaks of one of his three forces into which he divided his army as "la Guarnición de Coyoacán" (Cortés 1963: 52).

The *Relaciones Geográficas* on occasions use the same language: the *Relación de Coatlan* (Oaxaca) (1905–1906: 133) tells how Moctezuma sent to Miahuatlan captains and soldiers; it adds: *"y tenya quidado denbialles siempre gente de guarnycion."*

Teotitlan del Valle had wars with Mexican forces: *"que a este provincia ynbiava y tenia en guarnicion Moctezuma"* (*Relación de Teotitlan* 1905–1906: 106).

SOME CONCLUSIONS

It has often been taken for granted that the Aztecs maintained a network of imperial garrisons; such a view has been supported by vague mentions of *"guarniciones"* referred to above, but which in reality mean something quite different from the modern meaning of the word.

We are normally tempted to survey the Mesoamerican scene with minds attuned to Old World concepts; we think of Roman le-

gions maintaining eternal vigil against the perils of barbarian incursions; or we read of the valiant Sikhs and Ghurkas protecting the confines of the British Raj on the Northwest Frontier of India. We then automatically ask ourselves: but how could any empire possibly exist without numerous garrisons? How could the frontiers be protected and the conquered people be disciplined?

It is necessary to remind ourselves first that the Aztec domain was hardly an empire in the true sense of the word, but an area loosely dominated for the purpose of gathering tribute.

Second , there is ample evidence of a continual process of conquest, rebellion, and reconquest; that is to say, no proper control was maintained by local Aztec forces, and the people were apt to stage risings.

Nor when we come to examine the question, should it for one moment be assumed that all Old World empires were held together by standing forces. The Athenians' short-lived empire relied more on colonies. Perhaps the closest parallel to the Aztecs may be sought in the early Assyrian Empire. In the ninth and eighth centuries B.C. this was also a kind of tribute-gathering organization and the king annually made raids far and wide into provinces where he maintained no standing forces. It was only in the later empire, in the seventh century, that an imperial system complete with garrisons was set up.

Furthermore, it has to be realized, that, at the time of the Conquest, a standing army in Europe was something of a luxury. Charles V would have indeed maintained such a force, recruited from his Spanish, but not his Netherlands subjects. Over a century later, opposition to the sovereigns's determination to maintain a standing army added fuel to the flames which ignited the English Civil War.

In the early days of Colonial Mexico, the ex-conquerors, busy with their duties as *encomenderos* and with other remunerative tasks, could hardly have been defined as a force permanently under arms, even if they were available for emergencies. They maintained the country in subjection without established garrisons, which they would not have been able to man.

We conclude therefore by maintaining that in the Aztec Empire, any standing presence in the provinces, manned by personnel of the central power, was the exception rather than the rule; moreover, any such forces tended to be levied from colonists resident in the area.

Given the probable ubication of such settlements, the routes to Teleloapan — Oztoma, Oaxaca, Tuxtepec, and Tuxpan — Xiuhcoac would seemingly have constituted the main lifelines of empire. Many secondary routes would have branched out from these main ones, in order to give access to the territories of the far-flung and frequently insubordinate tributaries.

REFERENCES

Conquistador Anónino 1961
Cortés 1963

Díaz del Castillo 1969
Durán 1967
Florentine Codex 1950
Gorenstein 1966
Katz 1966
Landa 1959
Pomar 1941
Relaciones geográficas
  Descriptión de Teozacualco y Amoltepec
  Relación de Acapetlayuca 1905–1906
  Relación de Alahuiztlan 1905–1906
  Relación de Amantlan 1905–1906
  Relación de Atlatlauhca y Malinaltepec 1905–1906
  Relación de Coatlan 1905–1906
  Relación de Cuicatlan 1905–1906
  Relación de Chinantla 1905–1906
  Relación de Ixtepexi 1905–1906
  Relación de Oztoma 1905–1906
  Relación de Teotitlan del Valle 1905–1906
  La Suma de Visitas 1905–1906
Tezozomoc 1944
van Zantwijk 1969
Zorita 1963

21. COMMERCE AND CULTURAL PROCESS IN MESOAMERICA
by
Barbara J. Price

Trade, for the purposes of this paper, will be defined merely as the interchange of elements among cultural systems. Since this definition is perhaps too stark on the one hand, and too generalized on the other, an examination of its implications may be of value in mitigating both the austerity and the lack of specificity — and in emphasizing the inherent strengths of this sort of initial statement. A system is taken to be a number of elements in interaction. Some of these elements may themselves be organized as systems; we are dealing, in effect, with hierarchical and overlapping levels of complexity. What we as anthropologists call culture is a system; it is, however, a part of a much more inclusive ecosystem. It is furthermore composed of systemically organized institutions and functions — subsystems — such as the one that will be of primary concern to this discussion: the economy. This subsystem is in regular interaction with others: social organization, political organization, militarism. Economy, additionally, not only produces and distributes the entire energy content of the society, but in doing so acts as the most direct link between the cultural system (human behavior) as a whole, and the broader ecosystem of which the cultural system is one component.

Within a system the components, whether single elements or subsystems and however defined, are linked together by positive or negative feedback loops, where changes anywhere in the system bring about repercussive or compensatory changes elsewhere. It therefore follows that any ecological analysis is necessarily a systems one, since ecology is preeminently an interactive science. So too, similarly, is economics, where the components are, among others, capital (including goods and utilized resources), labor, and those institutions which constitute a flow chart of production, distribution, and consumption: an energy flow chart. Different empirical instances — specific ecosystems, specific economies — differ quite obviously among themselves, qualitatively and quantitatively. What is significant, however, is that the same analytical framework can, indeed must, be used to clarify and describe these differences. The same questions may be asked of different data, and in that the data really are different they will return different answers. This discussion is fundamentally little more than the restatement of the uniformitarian principle; it is the foundation of the comparative method.

Systems may be closed or open. Whenever we treat any system involving communities of living organisms, including their behavior, it becomes necessary to qualify this statement to read from relatively closed to relatively open along a continuum. No living system can ever be closed completely, for this would preclude the entry of new information; living systems are all to some extent amenable to the input of such new information. From the standpoint of economic systems in general, trade is a regular and patterned openness that is built in. No human group is ever entirely self-sufficient economically, though some are obviously more so than others. Trade — however it may be organized — functions in all instances to overcome closure. In that it does so, it has potential to enlarge the total size of an interacting system.

From the initial definition it follows that what has been defined as trade can be seen to encompass a number of processes and institutions that are formally quite disparate. Some scholars tend to accept them all as trade (this is the position of the present paper), while others accept some and reject some. The advantage of the present, extremely general statement is its inclusiveness capable of embracing a wide variety of forms while excluding none *a priori*. From at least the time of Mauss (cf. 1954) there has been a concerted effort to separate certain forms of exchange from the economy proper, and to consider them instead as aspects of kinship, religion, ritual, etc. If this is done assiduously, of course, quite a number of societies could be demonstrated to have no economy at all. Polanyi's (1957) concept of substantive economy was a major attempt to redress this situation; but as late as 1968 Flannery could still describe what is essentially a redistributive exchange system as follows:

> ... it seems that the upper echelon of each society often provides the entrepreneurs who facilitate the exchange. Second, the exchange is not "trade" in the sense that we use the term, but rather is set up through mechanisms of ritual and so on (Flannery 1968: 105).

In amplification of this example, Benedict (1946) analyzed the Northwest Coast redistributive economy not as an economy, but as one aspect of a highly competitive personality that worked itself out in this fashion. Rosman and Rubel (1971) take the same body of data as representing the manifestation of certain structuralist principles of mind.

From the present standpoint, rather, certain aspects of gift exchange, ritual exchanges, institutionalized raiding and piracy, certain aspects of taxation and tribute can quite legitimately be analyzed as economic instead. Insofar as the interchange of elements among systems results, they may all be treated as trade regardless of formal patterning. Our framework actually pushes us to analyze institutions as linked and interconnected, and forces us to treat an institution on the basis of what work it does, not on its form. This is not to deny the significance for evolutionary analysis of differences of form — only to point out the possibility that a given form might have several functions; and that the same functions could be carried out by forms that look quite different. It is thus important not to pre-judge. If we ask by what means institutions are interrelated, we ask that question on the bases of the observation of behavior and its systemic consequences. In sum, we are using an etic strategy (Harris 1968a). This contrasts with an emic strategy, which is actor-oriented, dependent for correctness upon the categorizations imposed by the people themselves. For our purposes, in other words, it

does not matter whether the Olmec, say, considered particular types of exchange to have been trade, or whether they had such a concept at all. However it was patterned (an interesting and valid question) we can observe the far-flung distribution, on the ground, of Olmec and Olmec-influenced objects. Obviously this is the result of human behavior, and obviously the requisite interchange of elements has taken place, even if the recipients stole them. It is suggested that all cultural institutions be defined — in a most untraditional but thoroughly pragmatic fashion — on the basis of the kind of work that institution performs. To the extent that kinship is responsible for the production and distribution of goods and services, it is proper to consider it economic. To the extent that a priest rides forth at the head of an army, to that extent one calls him, quite legitimately, a general. He is doing a general's work. While few of the papers in this symposium have used this sort of theoretical approach (that of Rathje *et al.* constitutes a partial exception, and so, less systematically and more by implication, does that of Litvak King), all are ultimately amenable to analysis and synthesis within this type of framework.

The data on trade in Mesoamerica span a wide range. Sources of data range from archaeological to ethnohistoric to ethnographic. Time periods considered include everything from the Formative to the Late Postclassic; the observed changes in level of complexity represented range from small, relatively egalitarian societies to large states/empires exhibiting a pervasive social stratification. Geographically Mesoamerican societies have occupied environments from wet to dry, from lowlands to highlands, with accompanying variability in productive and distributive systems, and in the size and distribution of population. For periods preceding the Late Postclassic, all components of cultural systems must be reconstructed and analyzed solely on the basis of archaeological evidence: artifacts and their associations (including distributions). Written records from the earlier periods — periods that are critical for the study of cultural evolution in the area — either do not exist or have not survived. Or —

a different sort of qualification — where they have survived, as in the Classic Maya inscriptions, they cannot yet be systematically read. By their nature, archaeological data demand an etic research strategy. Barring disturbance, the data are the observable result of human behavior, and permit thereby the reconstruction of that behavior, itself no longer directly observable.

Archaeological data may be analyzed, following Steward (1955) as core or as secondary features, depending upon the extent to which they are bound up with the production and flow of energy within a system. Core features are so linked. As such, it makes sense to apply concepts such as relative efficiency to their analysis. It is furthermore these features which are most subject to natural selection. Secondary features, those demonstrably less closely linked to an energy system, cannot reasonably be evaluated in terms of relative efficiency, can be in free variation because they are only tenuously subject to natural selection pressure (i.e., the variation makes little or no difference). Classes of data such as ceramic, architectural or sculptural style are generally considered secondary features.

Interestingly, it is upon these latter that archaeological attention has been largely focused. First of all, they are the data of primary observation. Second, because of their relative immunity from natural selection, they are preferable to use in culture-historical reconstruction. If, for example, the same pottery types are recovered from two widely separated areas, it is safe to postulate historical contact between them. If two agricultural systems from two separated areas resemble each other, however, it is illegitimate to assume contact; actually it is more parsimonious to assume that the resemblance is caused by the operation of similar causes in similar environments producing similar effects. That type of system is efficient in both areas, and can therefore be regarded as a product of selection; it is a core feature. Archaeological analysis of secondary features involves the traditional emphasis on stylistic features. It may also employ highly sophisticated

physico-chemical techniques for determining the sources of raw materials: ceramic clays and tempers, obsidian, turquoise.

Written records may offer different, and different classes, of both information and problem. Without such records, it is impossible to recover any emic data at all. This does not imply the absence of etic information from such sources; but any emic data at all must come from them. For Mesoamerica we have two classes of written evidence, each with its own kind of analytical caveat. Classic Maya inscriptions have recently been found to contain considerable historical information (Proskouriakoff 1960, Molloy and Rathje 1974). These are, of course, records left by the Maya themselves; as such, they presumably emphasize information deemed important by that society, or at least by its literate class. The selectivity of what is recorded and how — when this is not a mere function of differential recovery or preservation, or an as yet spotty ability to translate — reflects emic categories of Maya society. These may not reflect the questions we, as investigators, wish to ask. Ethnohistoric records, left not by native societies but by their 16th century conquerors, pose other interpretative problems. Since they are necessarily written largely from the outside looking in, they resemble ethnographies rather more than histories: they must be in part evaluated using criteria normally used in ethnographic work. In using such sources, we must allow for the biases and emic categories of the *conquistadores*, and for the fact of a colonial situation. However, it is these documents especially that provide economic data for the conquest period — one sphere of life in which a colonial power can logically be expected to take considerable interest. And because of this material, the impression of the Late Postclassic in most areas is one of a richness unparalleled in the rest of the archaeological record: we know much more about Tenochtitlan than about Teotihuacan.

Yet a third category of data drawn upon for this overview of trading patterns is ethnographic, obtained by the study of contemporary inhabitants of the areas. The approach through systematic ethnography has been used only sporadically by archaeologists, an observation generally reflected in these papers. One problem that has called it forth is the investigation of trade routes — which ones are used, and how long does it take to get from Ghent to Aix, so to speak. Part of this is actually an experimental archaeology — nothing more, really, than controlled ethnographic analogy. As an approach it is potentially very powerful, were it only used more often, and were some consistent methodology for employing it developed. While this is not the place for an extended discussion of the uses of ethnographic models in archaeology (cf. Price 1974), it is suggested that it might be productive, particularly on the explanatory level.

Influences upon current thinking on trade have come besides from fields at greater or lesser remove from anthropology proper. Input from geography, at various levels, has been applied to a number of problems. First, of course, is the question of production. Trade cannot be considered alone, without reference to primary production; it is still more illegitimate to use trade as a vehicle of explanation of cultural development without reference to the modes of production underwriting it. In an area so diverse physiographically and climatically as Mesoamerica it is a truism that what will grow well in one area will grow poorly if at all in an adjacent one. Some crops are relatively undemanding in their requirements — i.e., they will produce at least some yield in areas of very different characteristics. This may be because that species is per se relatively undemanding — manioc, for instance, is able to tolerate virtually anything except frost and prolonged submergence. Alternatively, it may be that varieties have been developed under cultivation that will produce in otherwise unprepossessing ecological niches — maize is the preeminent example. Still other species are more intolerant in their requirements — cacao is notorious in this respect. In some instances, some geographic or climatic limiting factors in the cultivation of a given species may be overcome through increased labor input on the part of the population. Terracing, irrigation, use of fertilizers and herbicides are all examples of

such techniques. This implies, of course, that a crop which in one zone can be grown relatively cheaply can be grown elsewhere only at the cost of more labor, i.e., much more expensively. This becomes not specifically a geographic problem, but an economic one as well: cost-benefit analysis could legitimately be applied to such situations.

Geography has also influenced the study of settlement patterns, the distribution of populations on a landscape, vis-a-vis physical features and vis-a-vis other populations. Not entirely unrelated to questions of production, the distribution of population is a major determinant of trade routes. Here, geographic variation acts on two levels. In the first of these, land forms and the location of navigable rivers help to render one route easier or more efficient than another; mapping and analyzing these features, as several papers have done, are basic and necessary tasks. However, geography alone cannot explain why these routes often shift from one time period to another, as Litvak King observes. The explanation may lie in this second level of input from geography: the geographic components affecting settlement patterns. Merchants, no matter how excellent the route, may nonetheless avoid it if it is too far from their markets: if it is not a route *to* anywhere. Shifts of trade routes are more likely to be effects, not causes, of demographic changes; there is a behavioral (= cultural) component, as well as the geographic one, in the analysis — or, perhaps, a system including interacting elements of both.

In the economic diversity of Mesoamerica, geography is one major permitting factor. What we have said of crops can be said equally of nonagricultural resources, the distribution of which is similarly spotty. Clays, obsidian, limestone, flint, salt, plant and animal species, precious stones, metals — all are restricted in occurrence and all were widely traded. The evidence for this fact is that the archaeological distribution does not correspond to the natural one of original sources. In the development of a body of empirical data that can be used to study trade, studies of individual polities — whether on the basis of archaeological or ethnohistoric evidence —

provide valuable building blocks. We know that even small polities were specialized in what they produced, what they sold, bought, or paid in taxes. That particular level of generalization, however, is not particularly informative. If the details of variation in local economies are not limned, we will have no consistent basis for processual study (cf. Piña Chan, Paper 4).

While this symposium does not deal specifically with demographic questions, the foregoing discussion has suggested the advisability of doing so, especially concerning questions of economic specialization. If the permissive conditions which engender specialization are frequently geographic, the forcing conditions are often demographic, based on increases of population size and density that lead to increasingly unfavorable man/resources ratios and thereby to increased competition. An initial small population can afford to maintain a generalized economy in its region: it is usually mobile, traveling to the resources it needs as it needs them and/or when they are available. Since the population is itself small, this exploitative system is efficient; if the entire population moves several times a year the overall total caloric expenditure remains low. Further, the small population implies lack of competition; the area has not filled in demographically, and if other groups are present, resources are present in quantities sufficient for all. This is an extremely extensive pattern of the use of space and the contents of that space.

As the population grows, hypothetically, groups bud off from the parent group — emigration as an economic solution to population pressure locally (Sanders and Price 1968). Eventually, the region is supporting a number of groups, each increasingly circumscribing the others. But the niches into which they move vary in what they can produce under any stated technological regime. This implies that — with each group still maintaining a generalized economy — some of these groups will grow relatively large, and others, in the less favorable environments, will remain small, or will migrate entirely out of the area or die out. The level of competition will continue to rise.

Specialization of economy may be an adaptive solution to some of these problems. Once it begins, it tends to be self-reinforcing, a positive-feedback loop. An area such as the Central Mexican Symbiotic region (Sanders 1956), the Southwest Highlands of Guatemala (McBryde 1947) in general and the Lake Atitlan region specifically (cf. Tax 1953) constitute examples representing the hypertrophy this set of processes; the Northwest Coast of the United States and Canada, at a lower level of sociocultural integration, is another. Geography is permitting; demography, forcing. A village, for instance, situated in a zone where maize grows poorly and insecurely will remain small and poor if it must produce what it consumes. If, however, it grows maguey well, and specializes in that crop, it will probably prosper. Life, however, is not so easy: man does not live by maguey alone. The specialization of our village in maguey cultivation presupposes that someone else is growing sufficient maize to sell, or to exchange for maguey products. There are two ifs buried here: not only is another village growing more than it consumes in order to exchange it (to that extent it too is specialized, or specializing), but regular institutions of exchange exist to keep the diverse production of different communities circulating. A market, in other words, or some institution of whatever form (possibly redistributive) that performs these functions.

The Southwest Guatemala Highlands constitute a clear ethnographic illustration of some of these principles. A number of populations in the Los Encuentros area raise sheep. The natural cover is a puna-like bunch grass, and the situation is too high and too cool for maize, or wheat, to be grown profitably if at all. Sheepherding permits an area that could otherwise support little, if any, population to support more people. They export wool and import staples. Interestingly, they do no wool-weaving — another village, lower down, Momostenango, does most of the wool weaving in the area and exports finished textiles — nor is there any evidence that lamb or mutton are eaten or exported to any significant extent. The market system is instrumental in expanding population in the Los Encuentros zone. Further, it permits the expansion of weaving activity in Momostenango, where labor need not be diverted to the raising of sheep. On a regional basis that involves a number of communities rather than just one, there seems to be an analog of Jane Jacobs' (1969) treatment of the expansion and specialization of work in single urban settlements.

Probably the clearest demonstration that the role of geography is more a permissive one comes from Lake Atitlan. Of the dozen or so villages that ring the lakeshore, nearly all have access to the same qualitative resource base. There are differences; while all are land-poor at their present demographic levels, some are more so than others. All have access to the lakeshore and to lake resources. Only one, however, does any fishing; these people, locally, are the ones from whom one buys fish. Only one weaves mats and baskets from shallow-water reeds, though all have access to the raw materials. Most communities retain boats, but only one runs what is in effect a ferry service across the lake. A number of villages do truck gardening of extremely labor-intensive nature; all such villages specialize in different crops. Significantly, none of these communities is even self-sufficient in maize. This entire economic sphere is dependent on regular market orbits for its security; were the institutions of exchange to disappear, one obvious result would be major population loss in the area as a whole.

The more generalized economy supports fewer people than the specialized one. Market size, in the broadest sense, is a function of population size; but this statement requires further qualification. If the components of the market are themselves specialists, producing little of what they consume, the same overall population will support a much larger market — larger in terms of criteria such as volume of business, diversity of goods bought and sold, numbers of transactions, frequency of meeting. Markets depend on customers, and specialized producers are better customers than generalized ones. This tends to explain why specialization and market expansion tend to be self-reinforcing, positive-feed-back, deviation-amplifying phenomena. Additional population growth tends also to result, and to exacerbate the pressure on and expansion of, the market system. This leads to still further specialization; a community becomes more specialized as its neighbors do. While this further expands the market, it has one additional ecosystemic effect that cannot be overlooked: specialization is a techno-economic device for reducing competition among communities for scarce resources. It does so by reducing total pressure on those resources (numbers of people competing for access thereto).

For both geographic and demographic reasons, trade in Mesoamerica from Classic times to the present has been most intense in highland zones (especially though not exclusively the Meseta Central). Such zones are internally more diverse in the numbers and types of ecological components in close proximity to each other, thus favoring the development of symbiotic networks at a fairly early time level (Sanders 1956). They are also natural demographic pressure cookers, at even a relatively low absolute population density (Sanders and Price 1968). The Meseta Central, further, contains an unusually large range of life zones within it, lacking only the humid and the tierra caliente components (an interesting observation if the expansionist behavior of the Classic and Postclassic Central Mexican empires is considered). This is also the zone where indigenous urbanism appears to be earliest, most persistent, and most hypertrophied. The relation of trade to cities will be considered briefly below.

A note, however, is in order concerning the nature of evidence and the means by which conclusions are drawn. It was not by accident that ethnographic instances were chosen to illustrate processes of specialization and exchange. But the present problems — some of them anyway — are archaeological; this raises the question of how direct observations can be reconstructed in another context with some reliability and validity. Of what lawyers would call the rules of evidence, archaeology has woefully few, and fewer still are explicit. Thus, for this paper at least, the following considerations should be taken into account. Take, for instance, the preceding statements on craft specialization. Ethnographically they are based on incontrovertible observation, some of which would be visible archaeologically, some not. Localized workshops dealing with nonperishable materials — ceramics, stone, etc. — can be directly observed whether patterned in separate villages or within large urban centers. Crafts such as featherwork, weaving, and woodwork would be less recognizable at all, depending on the quantity and distinctiveness of the tools used in those crafts and assuming those tools are of permanent materials. Such crafts can be reconstructed primarily — and note the lack of specificity here — on the basis that large numbers of known specializations tend to suggest the presence of others in some unstated proportion. The reconstruction of agricultural specialization can be more difficult still. Palynological studies might help to determine what was, or was not, being grown in a particular tract, but the degree of specialization, as opposed to say, crop rotation, would be difficult at the present state of the art to determine reliably. Other problems can be translated with comparative ease. Take the proposition that size and frequency of markets constitute an index of economic specialization. From the archaeological standpoint, frequency can no longer be observed — but some of its sequelae can. If an institution, such as a market (or a legislature, school, or whatever), meets often, it is going to require housing of its own. Today one may note in contemporary Mesoamerica numbers of communities where markets do not meet, or where small markets meet as often as weekly. Communities lacking markets may have one on the day of the community fiesta. These, like the small markets, meet in the plaza, and, if temporarily large, spill into adjacent streets. There is no reliable way to reconstruct them as markets archaeologically, even while noting that large open plazas were probably multipurpose. Communities that sustain a large weekly market, or a daily one, nearly always have a special market place. The etic definition follows, that an institution that is important in that system will be one which requires housing and which can divert

enough of the society's energy flow (equivalent to its GNP) to provide it. Relative importance can be gauged by the flow of energy, and the "freezing" of some part thereof into permanent form. If an institution is small and weak — or unimportant — this will not occur and it will leave at best ambiguous traces of its presence to the reconstruction process. Importance, in other words, is defined on the basis of position in an energy system. Data derived from informants (not a problem archaeologically) may contradict this; but these would represent emic categories which a priori cannot be dealt with archaeologically. Such elicited responses, further, may or may not answer certain kinds of questions that certain kinds of ethnographers ask either. What is advised is the selection of a research strategy most likely to be productive.

In sum, large, frequent markets tend to have a permanent address, proportional in size to the volume of business. They serve a larger, or more specialized, population of customers. Now if we compare the postulated but unexcavated market place at Tikal (Coe 1967) with that of the documented marketplace at Teotihuacan (Millon 1967) we find the latter to comprise some 55 times the surface area of the former (Parsons and Price 1971). It is difficult to consider this comparison meaningless.

A closely related problem also calling for an etic investigatory strategy is that of craft specialization. Both of the examples used at present derive from single settlements rather than the specialized-village-economy type. Craft specialists within a settlement have been taken — erroneously and oversimplistically — as an index of that settlement's urban status. Adams (1970) has amassed evidence for this economic pattern among the Classic Maya. At Teotihuacan, or at Tenochtitlan, however, the evidence fairly obtrudes itself wherever one looks. The Maya data are not nearly so obvious — a fact that suggests that the institution was less important. While it may sound odd to imply that a trait is important in proportion to the ease of its discovery, such a statement is true in the etic sense. Importance is derived from position within an energy system; if a trait or complex is in fact important, traces of its presence, direct and indirect, should be recoverable from a number of different contexts. The Classic Maya pattern, in fact, resembles the type of craft specialization found in Samoa — a ranked society not state-organized (Mead 1930). Here, hereditary guilds of specialized wood workers construct civic buildings (not residences) and seagoing canoes; they do so only for titled (chiefly) patrons, and are paid out of surplus amassed by that patron from his supporters (i.e., out of the redistributive network). The numbers of such specialists are clearly limited, cf. the limited number of patrons, and they seem to work only on commission. This pattern is obviously an old one in Mesoamerica, associated with chiefly/royal houses. But in some parts of Mesoamerica there is another kind of patterning, of specialization, if not several. Those systems are thus overall more complex, and show a strong tendency to be associated with markets and production for the market. One index of such production is the presence of tools indicating mass production —potter's wheel, for instance, or in Meso-america, potter's mold. Another might be distribution of types within a region, reflecting dependence on overlapping market orbits, each supplied by a somewhat different mix of producing communities. The specialists in question may be part- or full-time, may be part of a pattern of rural specialization by community, or of an urban pattern.

Markets in the technical sense, however, appear quite late in any sequence of the evolution of economy. When trade is defined as the interchange of elements among cultural systems, this definition presupposes no commitment to any single process responsible for that interchange. Rather, this is left open, as a separate group of problems — a solution that is preferable to building any single option directly into the definition. The processes of exchange constitute what Steward would term core features, immensely subject to the pressure of natural selection and therefore amenable to analysis in an evolutionay framework. Relative level of sociocultural integration is considered a major determinant of the patterning of trade, which in turn feeds back

into that level of integration itself. The preceding discussion of demography and specialization has been presented from this viewpoint. Diachronic material may now be presented, again from this perspective: evolution is itself a diachronic process, and thus well suited to reconstruction on the basis of archaeological data while providing in turn the most powerful theoretical integrative mechanism for such data.

Following Polanyi (1957) we may distinguish three overall types of pattern: the reciprocal, the redistributive, and the market. It is not necessary that each type exist in a "pure" state; in any given economy we might well find some transactions patterned in one, some in another way. One or another might nonetheless be clearly dominant in that quanitatively more energy is processed through that means; still, most empirically known economies do constitute mixtures. Furthermore, there are correlations between the dominance of one or another in the economy, and the level of complexity of the society as a whole.

Reciprocity tends to correlate with egalitarian societies of relatively small size, often though not exclusively of hunter-gatherers. Kinship ties, of consanguinity and affinity, plus partially overlapping ties of coresidence, act to pattern and direct the flow of exchanges. Some investigators might prefer to view these exchanges as simply an extension of kinship behavior, of which it empirically does constitute a regular part. Many of the participants in these transactions, the actors in the system, may well view their own behaviors in this fashion. It may, on the other hand, be more productive for us if we reversed this relationship, and regarded kinship as merely a serviceable way of patterning economic behavior. The first option is emic, the second, etic.

At the level of small, undifferentiated, egalitarian societies, reciprocity is a successful adaptive strategy in the face of problems regularly encountered by such societies. Within a group, it tends to equalize consumption in the context of a mode of production that has a high degree of randomness/luck built in. Second, between groups, reciprocal exchanges serve to help reduce economic inequities that may be regular and seasonal, or the result of catastrophe. Groups occupying different environments tend, qualitatively or quantitatively, to produce different commodities, or to produce them at different times. Reciprocity, like almost any form of exchange, helps to increase the security of each of the participants. Insofar as nearly everyone can claim some sort of relative, real or fictive, in nearly every local group with whom contact is maintained, distribution of goods and services tends to be efficient. As shall be seen below, however, this is the major limitation on the expansion of such systems.

The previous discussion of economic specialization treated the demographic causal nexus of this process: that under some circumstances specialization permitted the growth of larger populations than could be maintained if the economy of all groups remained generalized. At this, far simpler, economic level, reciprocity is a decided advance over local group self-sufficiency — if indeed any group ever practiced and maintained self-sufficiency through time. Efficiency is increased in that less total labor is required to procure resources from distant areas: you don't move your group to go after them, you trade for them with relatives who live in that area. The differential in efficiency may be small if the groups involved are small; as one or both grow demographically, the differential will necessarily increase correspondingly. So too will the degree of competitiveness, unless an institution like reciprocity exists to reduce it. Each group maintains a generalized subsistence base for the most part — but one in which efficiency in production is somewhat increased, as is security in resource procurement; competition, within and between groups, is correspondingly reduced. The overall result is an increase (quantitative extent unknown) in carrying capacity: the economic institution is analyzed in exactly the same way as though it were technology.

With additional population growth reciprocity unassisted by other institutions begins to break down; it becomes increasingly inefficient as a regular and reliable means of mov-

ing goods and services (= transmitting energy) around. This is simply a statistical function of greater numbers. The larger the individual groups in an area, and the greater their number, the lower the probability that a household will have a relative in each of all the other local groups that control necessary resources. One solution to this dilemma is the stabilization of population below this critical level. Most human populations do in fact possess the means for limiting their numbers — from emigration to infanticide — and/ or, the Malthusian Four Horsemen can take over to help restrict growth. If a population does, however, continue to grow, greater centralization of socioeconomic institutions becomes increasingly adaptive. The procurement of resources from areas inhabited by other local groups becomes the function not of the consumer, but of an individual occupying a nodal position, whose function it is to secure resources for a large number of consumers. This individual — a chief, or other titled position — engages in reciprocal exchanges with other such positions only; once he has done so he then redistributes what he has obtained in trade. These are the only ones to engage in systematic intergroup exchanges, and they do so on behalf of large numbers who lack direct access to the trade network. Some reciprocity is still maintained in the system, but its practice on any large scale is thus limited to a very few. The limitation of personnel is merely a way of stating what is meant by greater centralization. Second, the flow of good and services that in a reciprocal system is essentially horizontal becomes a part of a larger system including a diagnostic vertical movement as well. A redistributive economy has emerged.

The corresponding social order has been termed ranked (Fried 1967). This ranking can be relatively slight, as with the Melanesian Big Man, or very complex, with a large number of ranked positions at a number of hierarchical levels of inclusiveness, as in, say, Hawaii. Such nonegalitarian societies tend to be agricultural in mode of production, with the notable exception of the Northwest Coast hunter-gatherers. Redistributive exchanges have been characterized in the literature in various frameworks — potlatch-giving, title validation, competition for prestige, etc. — few of which have been essentially economic. This is a procedure which parallels precisely the reduction of reciprocity to simply another aspect of kin behavior. The same argument against it can be adduced here; the *raison d'être* of the entire rank pyramid is to assure the continuity of exchange. The positions do not create the exchange system, but are created by it.

Ranked/redistributive societies are relatively easy of recognition in the archaeological record. Their inherent nonegalitarian character will be amply manifest in the settlement pattern, which should show a distinctive site stratification hierarchy of settlements totally unlike anything obtaining in an egalitarian society. Certain sites should be larger, or contain types of buildings or artifacts not found in other sites of the same period and the same culture. Centers should contrast with hinterlands, on stated, observable grounds, some qualitative, others quantitative. Other types of artifacts and their contexts can be taken to strengthen this conclusion; "non-egalitarian" in a sense comes to refer also to commodities, as well as to the personnel using those commodities. As is generally not the case in a reciprocal economy, we find differences in the classes of goods exchanged. Some goods are passed back down the hierarchy once they are received in exchange; others are not — they are retained by the chief, and circulate only among chiefs. This latter class of commodities is termed sumptuary (cf. also the similar distinction drawn by Sabloff and Tourtellot [1969]). The shell armbands and necklaces of the Kula participants are sumptuaries (Malinowski 1961); turquoise in the American Southwest probably was. In Mesoamerica, items such as jade, gold, featherwork, precious feathers such as quetzal, jaguar, and perhaps other animal skins were sumptuary goods.

Sumptuary goods can be distinguished from other types of commodity on the basis of their differential behavior within the economic system. The archaeological test of this differential behavior is in context or associa-tion. Certain classes of goods are known almost exclusively from contexts that are clearly elite: burials recovered from chambers under pyramids, items found in residential structures which from their locations in the settlement, their size and degree of elaboration are obviously elite residences. Sumptuary goods tend not to be found, or to be found only occasionally and in small quantities, in what, from their size, location, and lack of decoration, are peasant houses; or from burials found under the floors thereof.

Probably because the preserved sumptuary goods recovered in Mesoamerica are so spectacular, archaeologists have tended to study them from a stylistic view rather than exploiting their potential in reconstructing an economic system. They are a clear indicator, initially, that we are dealing with a certain kind of sociopolitical organization. Further, these items tend to be those small items of high value and easy portability that can be imported and exported efficiently by populations having access only to foot transport for overland routes. In other words, they can be used to reconstruct the maximum extent of trade networks. Goods that are needed in large quantities and with regularity cannot be so used; the radii beyond which it becomes inefficient and unprofitable to import them are generally much shorter. The reconstruction of routes, in other words, depends on the commodity. Sumptuaries are good indicators, but the weight of explanation of systems lies elsewhere.

What we might term consumer commodities — those which in redistribution are passed back down by a chief to his supporters — receive overall rather less archaeological attention. Malinowski (1961) virtually ignored the followers haggling down on the beach in favor of august chiefly exchanges of armbands and necklaces. Benedict seemed to have lost track of the dried fish, the oil, and the blankets that circulated into areas that did not produce these commodities or the raw materials for their manufacture. In Mesoamerica, these are the goods which tend to be far more localized in their distribution, where trade networks would probably be reconstructed on the basis of the statistics of distributions of nonperishables like ceramics. Foodstuffs constitute a major component in this type of trade; they are as close to unrecognizable archaeologically as it is possible to imagine. Sanders and Price (1968) suggest a radius of 200 km. for the import of grain into Tenochtitlan; Feldman (Paper 2) gives the same figure for Guatemala — an indication that there may be a regularity in this figure. Some items might come from closer in, others from more distant points — again, depending on the commodity, and the restrictions of transport. Because such goods are needed in bulk and regularly, even could they be reliably identified in an archaeological context, it might be difficult to establish them as trade goods. The index, or marker, advantage of the sumptuaries is lacking.

However, from the point of view of evolutionary theory, this is where the action is. It is the circulation of these humble and unremarkable items that keeps the institution of redistributive exchange functioning, that renders the system efficient and causes it to grow. Jade beads do not expand carrying capacity; obsidian, maize, maguey, etc., when exchanged, do so. Etically, the sumptuary goods constitute the chief's recompense for managing the economy and for keeping the consumer goods coming. But it is the consumer goods which when traded act to raise local demographic ceilings by removing, or raising the value of, limiting factors. Unlike trade in exotica, basic energy flow is affected at the level of primary production and consumption at the household level. If trade in luxuries is a reliable indicator that a nonegalitarian society has evolved, it is not the trade in luxuries that is directly causally connected to that evolution (Parsons and Price 1971).

Market trade, where it occurs, does so in the context of societies that are state-organized — although not all such societies seem to have relied on this form of economic structure. The redistributive system does not atrophy, but its total context shifts. Taxation and tribute, however exploitative, are nonetheless redistributive in form and to a greater or lesser extent in function. Goods, of some types at least, are transferable between these spheres (Parsons and Price 1971). The state may or may not control the market system or

its personnel; etically, it would seem that there is probably a continuum of degrees of central control. Markets — as they grow large — may themselves show degrees of specialization, in some cases specialization in particular marketplaces. The contemporary pig market in Chichicastenango is an example; a parallel one is the Aztec period dog market in Acolman. More to the point, however, there is specialization of personnel, along several dimensions simultaneously. The emergence of a specialized merchant class is one very powerful instance, and an apt demonstration of correlation of specialization with the volume of business. Specialized merchants emerged as a class only in Central Mexico, not in the Maya area. In the latter, trade was the prerogative of the nobility, who ultimately consumed the goods in question. This suggests further that most Maya communities may have been basically self-sufficient in most consumer goods, and that Maya trade, unlike the Mexican, was primarily long-distance trade in luxuries.

Central Mexican merchants seem also to have functioned at various levels, and not all of them seem to have belonged to the merchants' guild. If, as Sahagún (1956) strongly implies, one could buy maize in any form from wholesale to prepared tortillas in the market, this indicates a corresponding differentiation of personnel dealing with it: that the seller of wholesale lots would not have been the same person who would sell by the *cuartillo*. Some vendors were themselves the producers; others were not, but were presumably middlemen for a number of producers. Finally, market systems imply increased specialization on the part of producers, on both an intra- and inter-community basis. In principle, the earlier discussion of this subject still holds, but with quantitative expansion. Again, geographic diversity tends to stimulate such development, geographic uniformity, to inherit it — holding constant at least in theory considerations of population size and density.

In all the social sciences the ultimate problems concern explanation; it is eventually necessary to ask what phenomena in cultural evolution and process can be explained with reference to trade. Steward (1955) for instance considered trade to have been perhaps as powerful a mechanism in the generation of Teotihuacan civilization as was irrigation (not then known for the site) — in other words, that the power relations engendered through the need for control of vital trade routes resulted in a political organization fully analogous to Wittfogel's (1957) Oriental Despotisms. Certainly the geography of Teotihuacan is capable of supporting this interpretation. The city is astride a major pass from the eastern Basin of Mexico to Puebla and then down to the Gulf Coast; this pass provides ready access to a major and productive ecological zone significantly not a component of the Basin ecosystem. The archaeological evidence is thoroughly consonant: a number of traits and complexes whose home is Teotihuacan constitute a major horizon style found all over Mesoamerica in the form of both direct imports and local copies. That something other than trade, or accompanying it, is indicated by the Teotihuacan site intrusion that erupts into Guatemala at Kaminaljuyu, in a context that is overtly mercantile (and perhaps also a militaristic one, however patterned; cf. Davies this volume, for Tenochtitlan). Conversely, the evidence at Teotihuacan itself is overwhelming, with Oaxacan, Maya, and other foreign goods recovered, some from what appear to be foreign *barrios* (Millon 1970, 1974). One would have to miss this evidence deliberately to do it at all. Trade is indubitably a core feature. This fact does not automatically imply what it is that trade explains, or how, or under what circumstances, or with what methodological strictures.

State formation as a process must first be distinguished from urbanization, a quite different process sometimes associated with state formation, sometimes not. Where urbanism occurs, state formation has also done so; the reverse, however, is not true, and there exist both the theoretical possibility and the empirical reality of nonurban states. State formation refers to the evolution of power; urbanization refers to quite specific conditions of population size, density, and economy. It is unfortunate that this distinction has not been made in Mesoamerican archaeology as systematically as its importance merits.

Social stratification — differential access to strategic resources — and the centralized control of internal and external force define the sociopolitical organization called a state (Fried 1967). As we have observed, the beginnings of this centralization occur apparently in ranked societies, in association with economic redistribution. In a sense, there is a continuum of development. While chiefs tend to lack differential access to land and water (the means of production), they do have differential access to trade goods. The energy implications of this fact rest once more on the distinction between sumptuary goods and consumer goods. Chiefs retain sumptuaries, which have little inherent utility and thus little effect on carrying capacity; they also, however, retain responsibility for passing the consumer goods back through the hierarchy. Depending on what these goods are in any one instance, and on the quantities involved, it would perhaps be debatable to conclude that no differential access accrued in all instances of ranking. Thus, in part at least, the differences between ranking and true stratification actually constitute a developmental continuum, with the only major discontinuity occurring instead in the division between egalitarian and nonegalitarian society.

This hypothesis is bolstered by the appearance of the archaeological remains of chiefdoms and states. Site stratification is common to both; the difference is more quantitative than qualitative, and a number of examples are difficult to classify (Sanders and Price 1968). Urban states are easy; but of course not all states are urban, cf. supra. The material evidence, in this case, is the foundation for an etic statement about the developmental processes involved.

A number of theories exist to explain state formation, none in itself perhaps entirely satisfactory as a nomothetic statement. Wittfogel (1957) emphasizes the control and managerial needs inherent in the functioning of large-scale irrigation systems. Carneiro (1970) stresses the role of warfare in stimulating changes in political organization; Adams (1966) appears to take changes in social organization and class structure as the independent variables. Steward (1955), while favoring reliance on irrigation as explanatory, had difficulty with the then apparent absence of evidence for irrigation at Teotihuacan, and fell back on trade to do the same explanatory work. Rathje's (1971)b position relies explicitly on trade to explain changes in sociopolitical organization either involving, or leading directly to, state formation.

This last-mentioned model states that populations living in the core area of a region (that lacking in certain or most basic resources) are forced to develop superior organization early in the sequence in order to assure systematic procurement of those resources from the buffer zones in which they are located. Thus, through the "technology" of organization they could exert some measure of control over adjacent areas. However, one might ask what all those people are doing in that core zone in the first place, if that area is so resource-poor. It would seem rather more like a refuge area, one into which people are pushed, not one in which they arrive early and watch their numbers swell. And if that zone is as poor as all that, the numbers would be held firmly and inexorably in check. One cannot escape asking what all those people were eating. Actually, Rathje's model, developed for the Maya area, seems to fit Mesopotamia rather better. The Mesopotamian states in fact traded for nearly all the resources they needed; their heartland lacked timber, building stone, stone for cutting tools, copper, tin, gems, etc. Beyond this, all the Fertile Crescent populations traded with pastoralists in the mountains for wool, cheese, meat, other animal products. Obviously a core area. All they had was irrigated grain, more irrigated grain than anybody else. This formed the basis of the symbiosis in consumer goods with the highlands. This was the primary production of those highly organized societies. Their control of the production of calories laid a foundation for not only their symbiosis with but their control of adjacent areas; it was the basis of their demographic superiority, and thus military edge, over other societies. Such a differential in agricultural potential has yet to be demonstrated for the Maya area; without it to underwrite the

demographic differences, the model based on trade lacks explanatory power.

It is not the purpose of this paper to provide an exhaustive review of the state formation debate. What must be emphasized, however, is that a satisfactory theory is going to have to accommodate all the factors mentioned, doubtless others, and state the kind of feedback relations obtaining among these superficially very different parameters. Causality, once more, is neither simple nor linear; and the more complex the problem, the more complex the epistemology becomes.

Turning to the problem of urbanism, we must consider a rather different complex of factors and their interrelations. As states are defined on the basis of differential power, cities are defined initially on the basis of their demography. Beyond basic descriptors of size, density, and economic composition, every other criterion is corollary and must be demonstrably linked to one or more of the primary factors. The selection of these parameters, furthermore, is nonarbitrary; all are intimately linked to the kinds of functions cities perform in an overall socioeconomic network. That they are also closely linked causally with each other will be seen from the discussion which follows.

We have earlier treated the question of the relation of population size to degree of specialization in economy. This argument holds, and is indeed strongly accentuated. Internal high density, or nucleation, is more difficult to explain. First, in cities, land values are usually too high to permit any land-use strategy other than maximization of density (why is there so little parking space in Manhattan?). Second, at least a large percentage of urban dwellers are not primary producers; they have occupations that require little land (cf. Jacobs 1969). Those who are farmers cultivate fields lying outside the settlement. The explanatory problem with nucleation (except for some people) lies in the fact that thoroughly rural communities may also show quite high densities in their settlement areas, implying again that fields cultivated lie outside the settlement area proper. A number of permitting conditions may be cited in explanation of a settlement pattern not generally considered efficient for farmers — conditions such as small land needs per cultivator, existence of bus transportation, etc. What has often not been cited is an apparent correlation, not perfect, of nucleated rural settlement with dependence on markets for basic subsistence goods: a testable, if untested, prediction.

The population composition in cities is as it is because the urban economy is distinctively as it is. Again, the previous discussion of specialization becomes relevant, but now the problem is not explaining the specialization of diverse rural communities, but the congregation of a diversity of different kinds of specialists into the same community. Cities are internally symbiotic. They may also be symbiotic with rural communities over quite a large area; in all probability they exert economic and political control over such rural communities. Only urban communities, however, are internally symbiotic; any community lacking this character, furthermore, is something other than urban. The degree of internal symbiosis is again, like the process of specialization itself, governed by positive-feedback loops, and thus self-reinforcing.

Given this internal economic base, the long-understood causal linkage between trade and urban development and growth becomes deductively obvious. Pirenne (1956) associates the revival of medieval cities with the revival of trade; he notes that those settlements on trade routes — especially those on navigable rivers — grew at the expense of those not so situated. Visual inspection alone of Teotihuacan — and the analyses of Millon (1970, 1974) and Cowgill (1974) reveal the confirmatory physical remains, remains which are remarkably consonant with Bernal Díaz del Castillo's and Sahagún's eyewitness descriptions of Tenochtitlan. The degree of internal symbiosis in both cases is extraordinary, in terms of class, occupational specialization, and the material evidence of both the import and export ends of the economic network and associated institutions and personnel.

Classic Maya once again seems to pose analytical problems; while this is not the time to review the enormous literature that attempts to prove them urban, it might be help-

ful to review some of the evidence. On the plus side, there is a site stratification hierarchy of considerable complexity, from which it may be safely inferred that the larger sites dominated, exerted some degree of economic and political control over, the smaller ones. Centers presumably drew upon the rural population for some or all of their supplies of food, and probably for their labor needs as well. Any number of settlement patterns that are hierarchical will exhibit these characteristics; they reflect processes common to any non-egalitarian society of some size and complexity. Were they in fact absent, we would have to reconstruct the society as egalitarian. The degree of nucleation stimulated by and at the centers appears to have been slight; in other words, the range of variation in density is only somewhat above that observed in tracts that seem to have been "countryside" where density differentials reflect, in all probability, microecological variations in characteristics affecting agriculture. The inhabitants of the centers proper appear to have been the nobility, their associated retainers and specialized craftsmen, and perhaps the rotating occupants of yearly positions in the center reserved for essentially rural dwellers (Price 1974).

Despite the posited need to import nearly all basic resources, the Classic Maya constitute a paradox here also. For, according to Chapman, writing on the Postclassic, Maya trade was in the hands of the nobility. She contrasts this with the Central Mexican situation, where trade was carried out by a large and diverse class of professionals, of whom only a minority were true *pochteca*. The difference in the degree of specialization involved in trading activities alone very strongly implies a difference in the volume of business. One may conclude legitimately that the size of the Maya market was insufficient to provide the economic basis for an entire social class, of whatever size. The nobility alone — a small fraction of the total population — were quite sufficient to handle all the business.

Chapman implies further that the nobility were the ultimate consumers of trade items — i.e., that the majority of Maya long-distance trade transactions involved sumptuaries.

Other commodities doubtless went along with these luxury goods, by analogy with the Kula situations; once more, it would have been these subsistence goods that in evolutionary terms can be considered responsible for keeping the trade network in the behavioral system. As in our prior discussion of redistribution we may note again that the subsistence goods will be passed back down the hierarchy, while the noble retains his share, plus all the sumptuaries. Granted, Chapman is writing about the Postclassic, where a certain amount of devolution of Maya culture seems to have taken place (not, however, in Central Mexico). Postclassic polities, in at least some areas, may well have been smaller and therefore somewhat simpler in their organizations than may have been the case during the Classic. However, the differences on even that late horizon are suggestive. From the point of view of the rural population, Lowland Classic Maya distributions would — if the previously suggested correlation between nucleation and dependence on markets holds — look quite thoroughly self-sufficient for most of their basic needs. Variations in their densities, as noted, seem rather to be the result of geographic variability, where some niches can support more, others fewer, people. Data, it must in fairness be pointed out, are as yet insufficient to prove this. In sum, we reconstruct a pattern whereby most trade was channeled through redistributive mechanisms; this reconstruction accounts for both the exclusive involvement of the nobility and the rural settlement pattern. Ultimately it feeds back on the urbanism question, and leads to a conclusion that will not be notably popular.

To sum up, several problems have been posed which seem to justify additional investigation. First, what sorts of feedback relations obtain between trade and the numbers of people an ecological niche can support through time? That such a relationship exists is probably incontrovertible; but the specifics vary widely between one technological regime and another, between one environment and another. Generalizations can be based only on certain empirical processes that must be evaluated and quantified for particular instances (cf. Steward's view that what is, or what is not, part of the culture core is a mat-

ter for empirical determination). Less obvious is the equally important point that the nomothetic statement itself may be used to generate those empirical data (Harris 1968b). A general paradigm such as the one sketched here can suggest both problems, and those parameters most likely to be productive in their solution.

Second, what are the relationships between trade on the one hand, and cultural evolution (including modification of local subsistence bases, augmentation of local and supralocal energy contents, enlargement of spheres of regular interaction and energy flow, and increase in level of complexity of sociocultural integration). For the present, it appears that changes in level of complexity can probably be related most powerfully to changes in the mode of production. Under some conditions trade may bring about such modifications, or accentuate them, under others, not. In the specific instance of urbanism, the relation to trade is more intimate; cities are a function of trade, a product of the mode of distribution.

REFERENCES

Adams, R. E. W. 1970
Adams, R. M. 1966
Benedict 1946
Carneiro 1970
Coe 1967
Cowgill 1974
Flannery 1968
Fried 1967
Harris 1968a, 1968b
Jacobs 1969
McBryde 1947
Malinowski 1961
Mauss 1954
Mead 1930
Millon 1967, 1970, 1974
Molloy and Rathje 1974
Parsons and Price 1971
Pirenne 1956
Polanyi 1957
Price 1974
Proskouriakoff 1960
Rathje 1971b
Rosman and Rubel 1971
Sabloff and Tourtellot 1969
Sahagún 1956
Sanders 1956
Sanders and Price 1968
Steward 1955
Tax 1953
Wittfogel 1957

REFERENCES

ACADEMIA DE GEOGRAFÍA E HISTORIA DE COSTA RICA
1952 *Cuarto y último viaje de Cristóbal Colón.* Imprenta y Librería Atenea, San Jose.

ACOSTA, JOSEPH DE
1940 *Historia natural y moral de las Indias.* Edmundo O'Gorman, ed., Mexico.

ACOSTA SAIGNES, MIGUEL
1945 Los pochteca; ubicación de los mercaderes en la estructura social Tenochca. *Acta Antropológica,* Vol. 1. Mexico.
1950 *Tlacaxipeualiztli: un complejo mesoamericano entre los Caribes.* Instituto de Antropología y Geografía, Facultad de Filosofía y Letras, Universidad Central de Venezuela, Caracas.
1971 Los Pochteca. In *De Teotihuacan a los Aztecas,* edited by Miguel León-Portilla, pp. 436-48. Universidad Nacional Autónoma de México, Mexico.

ADAMS, RICHARD E. W.
1970 Suggested Classic Period Occupational Specialization in the Southern Maya Lowlands. In "Monographs and Papers in Maya Archaeology," edited by William Bullard, pp. 487-502. *Papers of the Peabody Museum of Archaeology and Ethnology, Harvard University,* Vol. 61. Cambridge.
1971 The Ceramics of Altar de Sacrificios. *Papers of the Peabody Museum of Archaeology and Ethnology, Harvard University,* Vol. 63, No. 1. Cambridge.
1972 Maya Highland Prehistory; New Data and Implications. In "Studies in the Archaeology of Mexico and Guatemala," edited by John A. Graham. *Contributions of the University of California Archaeological Research Facility,* No. 16, pp. 1-21. Department of Anthropology, University of California, Berkeley.

ADAMS, ROBERT M.
1961 Changing Patterns of Territorial Organization in the Central Highlands of Chiapas, Mexico. *American Antiquity,* Vol. 26, No. 3, Pt. 1, pp. 341-60. Salt Lake City.
1966 *The Evolution of Urban Society.* Aldine, Chicago.

ADAMS, R. N.
1965 *Migraciones internas en Guatemala: expansión agraria de los indígenas Kekchis hacia el Petén.* Seminario de Integración Social Guatemalteca, Guatemala.

ALVARADO, PEDRO
1924 *An Account of the Conquest of Guatemala in 1524,* edited by Sedley J. Mackie. The Cortes Society, New York.

1934 Relación hecha por Pedro de Alvarado a Hernando Cortés. In "Libro viejo de la fundación de Guatemala y papeles relativos a D. Pedro de Alvarado. *Biblioteca "Goathemala,"* Vol. XII. Sociedad de Geografía y Historia, Guatemala.

ALVAREZ DEL TORO, MIGUEL
1961 Notas zoográficas de Chiapas. In *Los Mayas del sur y sus relaciones con los Nahuas meridionales, VII Mesa Redonda, Sociedad Mexicana de Antropología,* pp. 21-28. Mexico.

Anales de Tlatelolco
1948 *Anales de Tlatelolco y Códice de Tlatelolco.* Antigua Librería Robredo, de José Porrúa e Hijos, Mexico.

ANDONAIGUE, FR. JOSEPH
1936 Verapaz. *Boletín de Archivo General del Gobierno de Guatemala, C. A.,* Vol. 3, pp. 293-301. Guatemala.

ANDREWS, E. W.
1965 Archaeology and Prehistory in the Northern Maya Lowlands: An Introduction. *Handbook of Middle American Indians,* Vol. 2, pp. 288-330. University of Texas Press, Austin.

ANONYMOUS
1605 Juicio levantado contra cinco indígenas del pueblo de Chiapa de los Indios, por hechicerías e idolatrías, a requerimiento del Señor Obispo de Cudad Real. Año de 1605. Folder Cicerón Grajales, typescript of an original document. Archivo Histórico del Estado, Tuxtla Gutierrez.
1664 Comercio de plumas de Verapaz hacia Mirteca en Mexico. AGCA Al. 20/1030/fol. 272 vuelto.
1813a Cubulco; Padron. Archivo General de Centro América, A1.44/3020/2110. Guatemala.
1813b Rabinal; Padron. Archivo General de Centro América, A1.44/3019/29090. Guatemala.
1816a Coban; Padron. Archivo General de Centro América, A3.16/954/17780. Guatemala.
1816b Carcha; Padron. Archivo General de Centro América, A3.16/953/17776. Guatemala.
1820 Lanquin; Padron. Archivo General de Centro América, A1.44/3021/29111. Guatemala.
1821a Cahcoh; Padron. Archivo General de Centro América, A1.44/3021/29118. Guatemala.
1821b Cahabon; Padron. Archivo General de Centro América, A1.44/3021/29117. Guatemala.
1821c Tamahu; Padron. Archivo General de Centro América, A1.44/3021/29115. Guatemala.
1821d Tucuru; Padron. Archivo General de Centro

América, A1.44/3022/29137. Guatemala.

1825   Mapa correspondiente al dictámen de una comisión especial reunida de orden del Poder Ejecutivo de la República Federal de Centro América en el año 1825, con objeto de que se informase acerca de la legitimidad de la agregación de la Provincia, hoy Estado de Chiapas, a Mexico. Documento B 10-4, Expediente no. 3632, Legajo no. 171. Archivo General de Centro América, Guatemala.

1936   *Mexico, Air Navigation Map.* General Staff (G-2), United States of America, Washington, D. C.

1965   Nómina de nuestras minerales de Guatemala. *Dirección General de Minería e Hidrocarburos, Serie de Divulgación Técnica,* No. 4. Tiipografía Nacional, Guatemala.

1967   *Estados Unidos Mexicanos* (Geographical Sheets). Departamento Cartográfico Militar; Mexico.

?_   Noticia topográfica de la intendencia de Chiapas. Original manuscript in the library of the British Museum (Add. Ms. 17573, Folios 82-89). London.

`?   Sobre el estado que guardan algunos pueblos de indios zoques de la Provincia de Chiapas. Unsigned manuscript, Archivo Eclesiástico de la Catedral de San Cristóbal de las Casas. San Cristobal.

ANONYMOUS CONQUEROR (EL CONQUISTADOR ANÓNIMO)
1941   *Relación de algunas cosas de la Nueva España y de la gran ciudad de Temestitlán, México.* Mexico.

ARCHIVO GENERAL DE LAS INDIAS, SEVILLE
((cited as AGI)
1541- Son los de el Fiscal contra Alonso López,
1545   vecino de la villa de Santa María de la Victoria, sobre haverse titulado visitador, y exigido a los indios de la Provincia de Tabasco diferentes contribuciones. Justicia, Legajo 195.

ARCHIVO GENERAL DE LA NACIÓN, PALACIO NACIONAL, MEXICO CITY
(cited as AGN)
ca.   Juan Hidalgo Cortés Moctezuma y Guzmán,
1560   principal de esa villa, contra María, Petronila y Teresa Guzmán, por posesión del cacicazco que disfrutó Juan de Guzmán Ixtolinque. Tierras, Vol. 1735, Expediente 2.
1591   Ramo de Indias, Vol. 5, Expediente 942-43.
1816   Ramo de Infidencias, Vol. 100, Folio 15.

ARNOLD, ROSEMARY
1957a A Port of Trade: Whydah on the Guinea Coast. In *Trade and Market in the Early Empires,* edited by Karl Polanyi, C. Arensberg, and H. W. Pearson, pp. 154-76. The Free Press, New York.
1957b Separation of Trade and Market: Great Market of Whydah. In *Trade and Market in the*

Early Empires, edited by Karl Polanyi, C. Arensberg, and H. W. Pearson, pp. 117-87. The Free Press, Glencoe.

BALLINAS, JUAN
1951   *El desierto de los lacandones. Memorias 1876-1877.* Ateneo, Tuxtla Gutiérrez.

BARLOW, ROBERT H.
1949   The Extent of the Empire of the Culhua Mexica. *Ibero-Americana,* Vol. 28. University of California Press, Berkeley and Los Angeles.
n.d.   Tututepec. Unpublished and incomplete typescript. University of the Americas Library, Cholula.

BARRERA VÁSQUEZ, ALFREDO
1957   Códice de Calkini. *Biblioteca Campechana,* No. 4. Campeche.

BEALS, RALPH L.
1971   Estudios de poblados en la Sierra Zapoteca de Oaxaca, Mexico. *American Indígena,* Vol. XXXI, No. 3, pp. 671-91. Mexico.

BECERRA, MARCOS E.
1930   *Nombres geográficos indígenas del Estado de Chiapas.* Imprenta del Gobierno, Tuxtla Gutierrez.

BELL, BETTY
1971   Archaeology of Nayarit, Jalisco and Colima. In *Handbook of Middle American Indians,* Vol. 2, pp. 694-753. University of Texas Press, Austin.

BELSHAW, CYRIL S.
1965   *Traditional Exchange and Modern Markets.* Prentice-Hall, Englewood Cliffs.

BENEDICT, RUTH F.
1946   *Patterns of Culture.* New American Library, New York.

BENZONI, GIROLAMO
1970   *History of the New World,* translated by W. H. Smith. Lenox Hill Publisher, New York.

BERDAN, F. F.
1973   Interrelations among Economic Exchange Spheres in the Aztec Empire. Paper presented at the annual meeting of the Southwestern Anthropological Association, San Francisco.

BERGMANN, JOHN F.
1961   The Distribution of Cacao Cultivation in Pre-Columbian America. *Annals of the Association of American Geographers,* Vol. 59, No. 1. Lawrence, Kansas.

BERLIN, HEINRICH
1946   Archaeological Excavation in Chiapas. *American Antiquity,* Vol. 12, pp. 19-28. Salt Lake City.
1947   *Fragmentos desconocidos del Códice de Yanhuitlan y otras investigaciones Mixtecas.* José Porrúa e Hijos, Mexico.
1952   Archaeological Reconnaissance in Tabasco.
-54   *Carnegie Institution of Washington, Depart-*

ment of Anthropology, Current Reports 1. Washington, D. C.

BERNAL, IGNACIO
1968   Views of Olmec Culture. In *Dumbarton Oaks Conference on the Olmec*, edited by Elizabeth P. Benson, pp. 135–42. Dumbarton Oaks Research Library and Collection, Trustees for Harvard University, Washington, D. C.
1969   *El mundo Olmeca*. Editorial Porrúa, Mexico. (In English: *The Olmec World*. University of California Press, Berkeley and Los Angeles.)

BINFORD, L. R.
1962   Archaeology as Anthropology. *American Antiquity*, Vol. 28, No. 2, pp. 217–25. Salt Lake City.

BLANCO, LÁZARO
1947   Relación de Compostela. *Papeles de Nueva España*, Segunda Serie, Vol. 8, pp. 11–32. Collected by Francisco del Paso y Troncoso, edited by Vargas Rea. Biblioteca Aportación Historia, Mexico.

BLOM, FRANS
1932   Commerce, Trade and Monetary Units of the Maya. *Middle American Research Series, Publication* no. 4, pp. 531–56. Tulane University, New Orleans.
1956   La gran laguna de los Lacandones. *Tlatoani*, No. 10. Sociedad de Alumnos de la Escuela Nacional de Antropología e Historia, Mexico.
1959   Historical Notes relating to the Precolumbian Amber Trade from Chiapas. *Amerikanistische Miszellen* (Termer Festband). Mitteilungen des Museums für Völkerkunde zu Hamburg, Vol. 25, pp. 24–27. Hamburg.

BLOM, FRANS, AND GERTRUDE DUBY
1957   *La Selva Lacandona; Part 2: Andanzas arqueológicas*. Editorial Cultura, Mexico.

BORAH, W. W.
1954   Early Colonial Trade and Navigation between Mexico and Peru. *Ibero-Americana*, Vol. 38, University of California Press, Berkeley and Los Angeles.

BORAH W. W., AND SHERBURNE F. COOK
1958   Price Trends of Some Basic Comodities in Central Mexico, 1531–1570. *Ibero-Americana*, Vol. 40. University of California Press, Berkeley and Los Angeles.

BORDAZ, JACQUES
1964   Pre-Columbian Ceramic Kilns at Peñitas, a Post-Classic Site in Coastal Nayarit, Mexico. Ph.D. dissertation, Columbia University, New York.

BOWES, ANNE LABASTILLE
1969   The Quetzal, Fabulous Bird of Mayaland. *National Geographic Magazine*, Vol. 135, No. 1, Washington, D. C.

BRAND, DONALD D.
1971   Ethnohistoric Synthesis of Western Mexico.

In *Handbook of Middle American Indians*, Vol. 11, pp. 632–56. University of Texas Press, Austin.

BRANIFF DE TORRES, BEATRIZ
1966   Secuencias arqueológicas en Guanajuato y la cuenca de México: intento de correlación. Mimeo., Museo Nacional de Antropología, Mexico.

BRASSEUR DE BOURBOURG, CHARLES
1858   *Histoire des Nationes Civilisées du Mexique et du l'Amérique Central*. Paris.

BRINTON, DANIEL G.
1969   *The Maya Chronicles*. AMS Press, New York. [Reprint of 1882 edition, Philadelphia].

BROCKINGTON, DONALD L.
1969   Investigaciones arqueológicas en la costa de Oaxaca. *Boletín INAH*, No. 38. Instituto Nacional de Antropología e Historia, Mexico.
1973   Archaeological Investigations at Miahuatlan, Oaxaca. *Vanderbilt University Publications in Anthropology*, No. 7. Nashville.
1974   Reconnaissance from the Rio Tonameca to Salina Cruz. In "The Oaxaca Coast Project Reports, Part 2." *Vanderbilt University Publications in Anthropology*, Nashville. (In press).

BRODA DE CASAS, JOHANNA
1970   Tlacaxipeualiztli: a Reconstruction of an Aztec Calendar Festival from 16th Century Sources. *Revista Española de Antropología Americana*, Vol. 5, pp. 197–273. Madrid.

BRUNDAGE, BURR CARTWRIGHT
1963   *Empire of the Inca*. University of Oklahoma Press, Norman.
1972   *A Rain of Darts; The Mexica Aztecs*. University of Texas Press, Austin.

BRUSH, CHARLES F.
1965   Pox Pottery; Earliest Identified Mexican Ceramic. *Science*, Vol. 149, pp. 194–95. Washington, D. C.

BUNZEL, RUTH
1959   *Chichicastenango, a Guatemalan Village*. University of Washington Press, Seattle.

BURGOA, FRANCISCO DE
1934   Geografía descripción de la parte septentrional y sitio astronómico de esta provincia de predicadores de Antequera, Valle de Oaxaca. *Publicaciones del Archivo General de la Nación*, Nos. 25 and 26. Mexico.

BUTLER, MARY
1940   A Pottery Sequence from the Alta Verapaz, Guatemala. In *The Maya and Their Neighbors*, edited by Clarence L. Hay et al., pp. 250–67. D. Appleton-Century, Inc., New York.

CALLENDER, M. H.
1965   *Roman Amphorae; With Index of Stamps*. Oxford University Press, London.

CALNEK, EDWARD E.
1970   Los pueblos indígenas de las tierras altas. Ensayos de Antropología en la zona central de Chiapas, estudios recopilados por Norman A. McQuown y Julian Pitt-Rivers. *Instituto Nacional Indigenista, Collección de Antropología Social,* No. 8, pp. 105–33. Mexico.
1972   Settlement Pattern and Chinampa Agriculture in Tenochtitlan. *American Antquity,* Vol. 37, No. 1, pp. 104–15. Salt Lake City.

CARDÓS DE MÉNDEZ, AMALIA
1959   El comercio de los Mayas antiguos. *Acta Antropológica,* Epoca 2, Vol. 2, No. 1. Escuela Nacional de Antropología e Historia, Mexico.

CARNEIRO, ROBERT L.
1970   A Theory of the Origin of the State. *Science,* Vol. 169, pp. 733–38. Washington.

CARRASCO, PEDRO
1964   Los nombres de persona en la Guatemala antigua. *Estudios de Cultura Maya,* Vol. 4, pp. 323–34. Seminario de Cultura Maya, Universidad Nacional Autónoma de México, Mexico.
1970   Carta al rey sobre Cholula. *Tlalocan,* Vol. 6, No. 2, pp. 176–92. Mexico.
1971   Social Organization of Ancient Mexico. In *Handbook of Middle American Indians,* Vol. 10, pp. 349–75. University of Texas Press, Austin.

CASO, ALFONSO
1949   El mapa de Teozacoalco. *Cuadernos Americanos,* Vol. 8, pp. 145–81.

CASTAÑÓN GAMBOA, FERNANDO
1951   Panorama histórico de las comunicaciones en Chiapas. *Ateneo,* Año 1, Vol. 1, No. 1, pp. 75–127. Tuxtla Gutiérrez.
1953   Diario de viaje del Alcalde Mayor de Tuxtla, 1783-1789. *Documentos Históricos de Chiapas,* No. 2. Archivo Histórico del Estado, Tuxtla Gutierrez.
1954   Exploración del río Usumacinta o de la Pasión, año de 1822. *Documentos Históricos de Chiapas,* No. 3, pp. 73–120. Archivo Histórico de Chiapas, Tuxtla Gutierrez.
1956   Apertura de un camino entre Bachajón y Palenque, año 1821, y establecimiento de una bodega en playas de Catazajá. *Documentos Históricos de Chiapas,* No. 6. Archivo Histórico de Chiapas, Tuxtla Gutierrez.
1957   El Capitán Diego de Mazariegos ordena correr información contra Pedro de Guzmán, Alcalde de la villa de Coatzacoalcos, por las depredaciones que cometió en 1528 en varias pueblos de la Provincia de Chiapas. *Documentos Históricos de Chiapas,* No. 7. Archivo Histórico de Chiapas, Tuxtla Gutierrez.

CAY, JOSÉ (TRANSLATOR?)
1785   Testamento y título de los antecesores de los señores de Cahcoh, San Cristóbal, Verapaz. Archivo General de Centro América, A1.18/6074/54885. Guatemala.

CDCR
1952   *Colección de Documentos para la Historia de Costa Rica relativos al Cuarto y Ultimo Viaje de Cristóbal Colón.* Academia de Geografia e Historia de Costa Rica, San José.

CERRATO, ALONSO DE, *et al.*
1549   Tasaciones de los naturales de las provincias de Guatemala. Archivo General de Indias, Legajo no. 128. Seville.

CHADWICK, ROBERT
1966   The "Olmeca-Xicalanca" of Teotihuacan; A Preliminary Study. *Mesoamerican Notes,* Nos. 7–8. University of the Americas, Mexico.
1971   Archaeological Synthesis of Michoacan and Adjacent Regions. *Handbook of Middle American Indians,* Vol. 11, pp. 657–93. University of Texas Press, Austin.

CHAPMAN, ANNE M.
1957   Port of Trade Enclaves in Aztec and Maya Civilization. In *Trade and Market in the Early Empires,* edited by Karl Polanyi, Conrad M. Arensberg, and Harry W. Pearson, pp. 114–53. The Free Press, Glencoe.
1959   Puertos de intercambio en Mesoamérica prehispánica. *Instituto Nacional de Antropología e Historia, Serie de Historia,* No. 3. Mexico.
1971   Commentary on: Mesoamerican Trade and its role in the Emergence of Civilization. In "Observations on the Emergence of Civilization in Mesoamerica," edited by Robert F. Heizer and John A. Graham. *Contributions of the University of California Archaeological Research Facility,* No. 11, pp. 196–211. Berkeley.

CHECA Y QUESADA, FERNANDO DE
1936   Atitan y Tepanatitan. *Boletín del Archivo General del Gobierno, C. A.* Vol. 3, pp. 279–87. Guatemala.

CHÍ, GASPAR ANTONIO
1941   *Relación.* Appendix in Landa 1941.

CHIMALPAHIN CUAUHTLEHUANITZIN, FRANCISCO DE SAN ANTONIO MUÑON
1960   Das Geschichtswerk des Domingo de Muñon Chimalpahin Quauhtlehuanitzin von Günther Zimmermann. *Berträge zur Mittelamerikanisches Völkerkunde,* Vol. 5. Hamburg.

CIEZA DE LEÓN, PEDRO
1943   *Del señorio de los Incas.* Ediciones Argentinas Solar, Buenos Aires.

CIUDAD REAL, ANTONIO DE
1873   *Relación breve y verdadera de algunas cosas*

de las muchas que sucedieron al Padre Fray Alonso Ponce en las provincias de la Nueva España . . . . Madrid.

1932 Fray Alonso Ponce in Yucatán 1588. Translated and annotated by Ernest Noyes. *Middle American Research Series, Publication* No. 4. Department of Middle American Research, Tulane University. New Orleans.

COBO, BERNABÉ

1944 Cartas del P. Bernabé Cobo, de la Compañía de Jesús, escritas a un campañero suyo residente en el Perú. In *Descripción de la Nueva España en el siglo XVI, por el Padre Fray Antonio Vásquez de Espinosa y otros documentos del siglo XVI.* Editorial Patria, S. A., Mexico.

Codex Mendoza or *Códice Mendocino*

1925 Mexican document of the 16th century in the Bodleian Library, Oxford, England. Photocopy made available by Don Francisco del Paso y Troncoso, notes and commentary by Jesús Galindo y Villa, Mexico.

1938 The Mexican manuscript known as the Collection of Mendoza, Bodleian Library, Oxford, England. Edited and translated by James Cooper-Clark. Waterlow and Sons, London.

Codex Nuttall

1902 Peabody Museum of Harvard University, Cambridge.

Códice Ramírez

1944 *Relación del origen de los indios que habitan esta Nueva España según sus historias.* Editorial Leyenda, S.A., Mexico.

COE, MICHAEL D.

1961a Social Typology and the Tropical Forest Civilizations. *Comparative Studies in Society and History,* Vol. 4, No. 1, pp. 65-85.

1961b La Victoria; An Early Site on the Pacific Coast of Guatemala. *Papers of the Peabody Museum of Archaeology and Ethnology, Harvard University,* Vol. 53. Cambridge.

1965 *The Jaguar's Children: Pre-Classic Central Mexico.* The Museum of Primitive Art, New York.

1968 *America's First Civilization.* American Heritage, New York.

1970 The Archaeological Sequence at San Lorenzo Tenochtitlan, Veracruz, Mexico. *Contributions of the University of California Archaeological Research Facility,* No. 8, pp. 21-34. Berkeley.

COE, MICHAEL D. AND KENT V. FLANNERY

1964 Microenvironments and Mesoamerican Prehistory. *Science,* Vol. 143, pp. 650-54. Washington, D. C.

1967 Early Cultures and Human Ecology in South Central Guatemala. *Smithsonian Contribu-tions to Anthropology,* Vol. 3. Washington, D. C.

COE, WILLIAM R.

1959 Piedras Negras Archaeology; Artifacts, Caches, and Burials. *Museum Monographs.* University of Pennsylvania, Philadelphia.

1963 A Summary of Excavation and Research at Tikal, Guatemala, 1962. *Estudios de Cultura Maya,* Vol. 3, pp. 41-64. Seminario de Estudios Mayas, Universidad Nacional Autónoma de México, Mexico.

1965 Tikal, Guatemala, and Emergent Maya Civilization. *Science,* Vol. 147, No. 3664, pp. 1401-419. Washington, D. C.

1967 *Tikal: A Handbook of the Ancient Maya Ruins.* The University Museum, Philadelphia.

COGGINS, CLEMENCY

n.d. Palaces and the Planning of Ceremonial Centers in the Southern Maya Lowlands. Ms. (1967), Peabody Museum Library, Harvard University, Cambridge.

COLÓN, HERNANDO

1947 *Vida del Almirante don Cristóbal Colón.* Fondo de Cultura Económica, Mexico.

COLUMBUS, BARTHOLOMEW

ca. Informatiō de Bart° Colōbo della navicatiō
1506 di ponēte et garbī di Beragna nel mondo novo. Ms. in Biblioteca Nazionale Centrale di Firenze, *Banco Raro* 234, fols. 31-34v.

COLUMBUS, CHRISTOPHER

1961 *Four Voyages to the New World. Letters and Selected Documents.* Translated and edited by R. H. Major. Bi-lingual Edition. Introduction by John E. Fagg. Citadel Press, New York.

COLUMBUS, FERDINAND

1959 *The Life of the Admiral Christopher Columbus by his Son Ferdinand.* Translated and annotated by Benjamin Keen. Rutgers University Press, New Brunswick. (Completed ca. 1539, first published [Italian] Venice, 1571).

CONNOR, J. G.

n.d. Technological Implications in Prehistoric Ceramics: Strategy for testing a Hypothesis. Ms., Arizona State Museum.

CONNOR, J. G., AND W. L. RATHJE

n.d. Mass Production and the Ancient Maya: Experiments in Cracking Maya Pots. Paper read at the annual meeting of the Society for American Archaeology, San Francisco, 1973.

CORIA, DIEGO DE ("scribe of the said *visitación*")

1937 Visitación que se hizo en la conquista, donde fué por Capitán Francisco Cortés. In "Nuño de Guzmán contra Hernán Cortés, sobre los descubrimientos y conquistas en Jalisco y Tepic, 1531." *Boletín, Archivo General de la Nación,* Vol. 8, pp. 556-72. Mexico.

CORONADO, J. ADRIAN
1953   *Monografía del Departamento de Sacate-péquez.* Editorial del Ministerio de Educación Pública, Guatemala.

CORTÉS, HERNÁN(DO)
1928   *Five Letters of Cortes to the Emperor,*
and   *(1519-1526)*, translated by J. B. Morris. W.
1962   W. Norton and Company, Inc., New York.
1960   Cartas de relacion. *Colección "Sepan Cuantos,"* No. 7. Editorial Porrúa, Mexico.
1963   Cartas y Documentos. *Biblioteca Porrúa,* No. 2. Editorial Porrúa, Mexico.
1971a   *Hernan Cortes, Letters from Mexico,* translated and edited by A. R. Pagden. Grossman Publishers, New York.
1971b   *Cartas de Relación.* Editorial Porrúa, México.

CORTÉS Y LARRAZ, PEDRO
1958   *Descripción geográfico-moral de la Dióesis de "Goathemala,"* Guatemala. Biblioteca "Goathemala," Guatemala.

COTO, PEDRO
1608   Testamento. Archivo General de Centro América, A1.20/54 892/6074. Guatemala.

COWGILL, GEORGE
1974   Quantitative Studies of Urbanization at Teotihuacan. In *Mesoamerican Archaeology: New Approaches,* edited by Norman Hammond, pp. 363-96. Duckworth, London.

CRAINE, EUGENE R. AND REGINALD C. REINDORP
1970   *The Chronicles of Michoacan.* University of Oklahoma Press, Norman.

CULBERT, T. PATRICK
1965   The Ceramic History of the Central Highlands of Chiapas, Mexico. *Papers of the New World Archaeological Foundation,* No. 19. Provo.

CULBERT, T. PATRICK, EDITOR
1973   *The Classic Maya Collapse.* University of New Mexico Press, Santa Fe.

CULBERT, T. PATRICK AND WILLIAM L. RATHJE
n.d.   Procurement Prerequisites and Critical Commodities. Paper read at the annual meeting of the American Anthropological Association, New York, 1971.

CURRAY, J. R., F. J. EMMEL, AND P. J. S. CRAMPTON
1967   Holocene History of a Strand Plain, Lagoonal Coast, Nayarit, Mexico. In *Lagunas Costeras, Un Simposio: Memoria del Simposio Internacional sobre Lagunas Costeras,* edited by A. Ayala Castanares and F. B. Phleger, pp. 63-100. Universidad Nacional Autónoma de México, Mexico.

DAHLGREN DE JORDAN, BARBRO
1954   *La Mixteca.* Imprenta Universitaria, Mexico.

DAVIES, CLAUDE NIGEL BYAM
1968   Los señorios independientes del imperio azteca. Instituto Nacional de Antropología e Historia, Mexico.

DÁVILA, ALONSO
        (See DII, Vol. XIV) Relación de lo Sucedido á Alonso Dávila, Contador de su Magestad en Yucatán, en el Viaje que Hizo para Pacificar y Poblar Aquella Provincia (Junio de 1533).

DÍAZ (DEL CASTILLO), BERNAL
1947   Veradera historia de los sucesos de la conquista de la Nueva-España. *Biblioteca de Autores Españoles, Historiadores Primitivos de Indias,* Vol. 2, pp. 1-317. Madrid.
1956   *The Discovery and Conquest of Mexico, 1517-1521,* translated and annotated by A. P. Maudslay. Straus and Cudahy, New York.
1960   *Historia verdadera de la conquista de la Nueva España.* Editorial Porrúa, Mexico.
1963   *The Conquest of New Spain,* translated with an introduction by J. M. Cohen. Penguin Books, Baltimore.
1964   *Historia de la Conquista de la Nueva España.* Editorial Porrúa, Mexico.

DÍAZ DEL CASTILLO, BERNAL
1970   *Historia Verdadera de la Conquista de la Nueva España.* 8a. edición. Introducción y notas de Joaquin Ramírez Cabañas. Editorial Porrúa, México. [First published in Madrid, 1632].

DIBBLE C. E., AND A. J. O. ANDERSON
1959   Florentine Codex: General History of the Things of New Spain; Book 9, The Merchants, by Fray Bernardino de Sahagún. *Monographs of the School of American Research,* No. 14, Pt. X. University of Utah Press, Salt Lake City.

DIESELDORFF, E. P.
1926-1933 *Kunst und Religion der Mayavölker.* Berlin.
1873   *Relación breve y verdadera de algunas cosas de las muchas que sucedieron al Padre Fray Alonso Ponce en las provincias de la Nueva España, siendo Comisario General de aquellas partes.* Imprenta de la Viuda de Calero, Madrid.

DII
1864-   *Colección de Documentos Inéditos, rela-*
1884   *tivos al descubrimiento, conquista y organización de las antiguas posesiones españolas de América y Oceanía, sacados de los archivos del reino, y muy especialmente del de Indias.* 42 vols. Madrid.

DIU
1885-   *Colección de Documentos Inéditos rela-*
1932   *tivos al descubrimiento, conquista y organización de las antiguas posesiones españoles de ultramar.* 25 vols. Madrid.

DRUCKER, PHILIP
1948   Preliminary notes on an Archaeological Survey of the Chiapas Coast. *Middle American Research Records,* Vol. 1, No. 11, pp. 151-69. Tulane University, New Orleans.

DURÁN, (FR.) DIEGO
1951   *Historia de las Indias de la Nueva España.*
        Editora Nacional, Mexico.
1965   *Historia de las Indias de Nueva España y*
and   *islas de tierra firme.* Editora Nacional,
1967   Mexico.
1967   *Historia de las Indias de Nueva España e*
        islas de tierra firme. Editorial Porrúa,
        Mexico.

ECHAEGARAY BABLOT, LUIS
1957   *Lo que ha sido y lo que puede ser el*
        sureste. Secretaría de Recursos Hidráulicos,
        Mexico.

EDWARDS, CLINTON
1969   Possibilities of Pre-Columbian Maritime Con-
        tacts among New World Civilizations. In
        "Pre-Columbian Contact within Nuclear
        America," edited by Charles Kelley and
        Carrol L. Riley, *Mesoamerican Studies*, No.
        4. University Museum, Southern Illinois
        University, Carbondale.
n.d.   Nautical Technology and Maritime Routes
        in Mesoamerica. *Acts* of the XL Congresso
        Internazionale degli Americanisti, Rome,
        1972. (in press)

EISENSTADT, S. N.
1963   *The Political Systems of Empires.* The
        Free Press, Glencoe.

EKHOLM-MILLER, SUSANNA
1973   The Olmec Rock Carving at Xoc, Chiapas,
        Mexico. *Papers of the New World Archaeo-*
        logical Foundation, No. 32. Provo.

ESTRADA, JUAN DE AND FERNANDO DE NIEBLA
1955   Descripción de la provincia de Zapotitlán
        y Suchitepéquez. *Anales de la Sociedad de*
        Geografía e Historia de Guatemala, Vol. 28,
        pp. 68-84. Guatemala.

FALCÓN DE GYVES, ZAÍDA
1965   *Análisis de los mapas de distribución de la*
        población del estado de Tabasco. Instituto
        de Geografía, Universidad Nacional Autó-
        noma de México, Mexico.

FELDMAN, LAWRENCE H.
1968   Some West Mexican Archaeological Mol-
        lusks. In *Excavations at Tizapan El Alto,*
        Jalisco, by C. W. Meighan and L. J. Foote,
        pp. 165-73. Editorial Sucre, Caracas.
1969   Panamic Sites and Archaeological Mollusks
        of Lower California. *Veliger*, Vol. 12, pp.
        165-68. Berkeley.
1971   A Tumpline Economy: Production and Dis-
        tribution Systems of Early Central-East
        Guatemala. Ph.D. dissertation, Pennsylvania
        State University, Pittsburgh.
1972a   Coliman Archaeological Mollusks: Comments
        and Species Lists. In "The Archaeology of
        the Morett Site, Colima," by C. W. Meighan.
        University of California Publications in
        Anthropology, No. 7. University of Cali-
        fornia, Los Angeles.

1972b   Moving Merchandise in Prohistoric Quauh-
        temallan. Paper read at XL Congresso In-
        ternazionale degli Americanisti, Rome, 1972.
1974   Shells from Afar; "Panamic" Mollusks in
        Mayan Sites. In *Mesoamerican Archaeology;*
        New Approaches, edited by Norman Ham-
        mond. University of Texas Press, Austin.

FERNÁNDEZ DE NAVARRETE, MARTÍN
1964   Colección de los Viajes que Hicieron por
        Mar los Españoles desde Fines del Siglo
        XV. 3 vols. [Biblioteca de Autores
        Españoles, Vols. 75-77]. Ediciones Atlas,
        Madrid.

FERNÁNDEZ DE OVIEDO, GONZALO
1959   *Historia General y Natural de las Indias.*
        Edición y estudio preliminar de Juan Pérez
        de Tudela Bueso. 5 vols. [Biblioteca de
        Autores Españoles, Vols. 117-121].
        Ediciones Atlas, Madrid.

FISK, G.
1967   *Marketing Systems; An Introductory An-*
        alysis. Harper and Row, New York.

FLANNERY, KENT V.
1968   The Olmec and the Valley of Oaxaca: A
        Model for Interregional Interaction in For-
        mative Times. In *Dumbarton Oaks Confer-*
        ence on the Olmecs, edited by Elizabeth P.
        Benson, pp. 79-110. Dumbarton Oaks Re-
        search Library and Collection, Trustees for
        Harvard University, Washington, D. C.

FLANNERY, KENT V., T. KIRKBY, M. J. KIRKBY, AND
A. V. WILLIAMS, JR.
1967   Farming Systems and Political Growth in
        Ancient Oaxaca. *Science*, Vol. 158, pp. 445-
        54. Washington, D. C.

Florentine Codex
1950   General History of the Things of New Spain,
-69   translated from the Nahuatl with notes by
        A. J. O. Anderson and C. E. Dibble. *Mono-*
        graphs of the School of American Research,
        No. 14. University of Utah Press, Salt Lake
        City.

FLORES, G.
1958   Relación de Tuspa, Tamazula y Zapotlán.
        In *Relaciones Geográficas de la Diócesis de*
        Michoacán, 1579-1580, edited by J.
        Corona Núñez, pp. 83-107. Colección
        "Siglo XVI", Guadalajara.

FORD, JAMES A.
1969   A Comparison of Formative Cultures in the
        Americas; Diffusion or the Psychic Unity of
        Man. *Smothsonian Contributions to Anthro-*
        pology, Vol. II. Washington, D. C.

FOSHAG, WILLIAM F.
1954   Estudios minerológicos sobre el jade de
        Guatemala. *Antropología e Historia de*
        Guatemala, Vol. 6, No. 1, pp. 3-48. Guate-
        mala.

FOSTER, GEORGE M.
1942   A Primitive Mexican Economy. *Monographs of the American Ethnological Society,* Vol 5. New York.

FRIED, MORTON H.
1960   On the Evolution of Social Stratification and the State. In *Culture in History,* edited by Diamond, pp. 713-31. Columbia University Press, New York.
1967   *The Evolution of Political Society: An Essay in Political Anthropology.* Random House, New York.

FUENTES Y GUZMÁN, FRANCISCO ANTONIO
1932   *Historia de Guatemala o recordación flor-*
-34   *ida.* Biblioteca "Goathemala," Guatemala. Guatemala.

FURST, PETER T.
1965   Radiocarbon Dates from a Tomb in Mexico. *Science,* Vol. 147, pp. 612-13. Washington, D. C.
1966   Shaft Tombs, Shell Trumpets and Shamanism: A Culture-Historical Approach to Problems in West Mexican Archaeology. Ph.D. dissertation, University of California, Los Angeles.
1967   Tumbas de tiro y cámara: un posible eslabón entre México y los Andes. *Eco,* Vol. 26, pp. 1-6. Instituto Jaliscience de Antropología e Historia. Guadalajara.

GAGE, TOMÁS
1946   Nueva relación que contiene los viajes de Tomás Gage en la Nueva España. *Biblioteca "Goathemala,"* Vol. XVIII. Sociedad de Geografía e Historia de Guatemala, Guatemala.

GALL, FRANCIS
1963   Título del Ajpop Hutizilzil Tzunun y Probanza de Méritos de los de León y Cardona. *Colección Documentos,* No. 25, Centro Editorial "José de Pineda Ibarra," Ministerio de Educación Pública, Guatemala.

GANN, T. W. F.
1918   The Maya Indians of Southern Mexico and Northern British Honduras. *Smithsonian Institution, Bureau of American Ethnology, Bulletin* 64. Washington, D. C.

GARCÍA DE BARGAS Y RIVERA, JUAN MANUEL
1774   Relación de los pueblos que comprende el Obispado de Chiapas, número de gente que tiene cada uno de todas edades y castas, su carácter e inclinaciones; remitido por el Obispo Juan Manuel García de Bargas y Rivera, mercedario. Biblioteca del Palacio, Ms. 2840 (Misc. de Ayala XXVI, f. 282-322). Madrid.

GARCÍA DE LEÓN, ANTONIO
1969   Pajapan: una variante del Nahua del este. Professional thesis, Escuela Nacional de Antropología e Historia, Mexico.
1970   Etnografía antigua del area olmeca (siglos

XVI-XIX). Ms. Centro de Estudios Mayas, Universidad Nacional Autónoma de México. Mexico.

GARCÍA PELAEZ, FRANCISCO DE PAULA
1968   *Memorias para la historia del antiguo reino de Guatemala.* Biblioteca "Goathemala," Guatemala.

GIBSON, CHARLES
1971   Structure of the Aztec Empire. In *Handbook of Middle American Indians,* Vol. 10, pp. 376-94. University of Texas Press, Austin.

GIFFORD, E. W.
1950   Surface Archaeology of Ixtlan del Rio, Nayarit. *University of California Publications in Archaeology and Ethnology,* Vol. 43, No. 2, pp. 183-239. Berkeley.

GILLMOR, FRANCES
1964   *The King Danced in the Marketplace.* University of Arizona Press, Tucson.

GODOY, DIEGO DE
1852   Relación hecha por Diego Godoy a Hernando Cortés, en que trata del descubrimiento de diversas cuidades y provincias, y guerra que tuvo con los indios, y su modo de pelear; de la provincia de Chamula, de los caminos difíciles y peligrosos, y repartimiento que hizo de los pueblos. *Historiadores Primitivos de Indias,* Vol. I, pp. 465-70. Madrid.

GÓMARA, FRANCISCO LÓPEZ DE
1954   *Historia general de las Indias.* Editorial Iberia, Barcelona.

GONGORA, FR. EUGENIO
1725   Vocabulario de lengua Kekchi. Archivo General de Centro América, A1.1/6074/54906. Guatemala.

GONZÁLEZ, PEDRO A.
1946   Los ríos de Tabasco. *Contribuciones de Tabasco a la Cultura Nacional,* No. 8. Gobierno Constitucional de Tabasco, Mexico.

GREEN, DEE F., AND GARETH W. LOWE
1967   Altamira and Padre Piedra, Early Preclassic Sites in Chiapas, Mexico. *Papers of the New World Archaeological Foundation,* No. 20. Provo.

GROSSCUP, GORDON L.
1964   The Ceramics of West Mexico. Ph.D. dissertation, University of California, Los Angeles.

GROVE, DAVID C.
1968   The Pre-Classic Olmecs in Central Mexico; Site Distribution and Inferences. In *Dumbarton Oaks Conference on the Olmecs,* edited by Elizabeth P. Benson, pp. 179-85. Dumbarton Oaks Research Library and Collection, Trustees for Harvard University, Washington, D. C.

1970   The San Pablo Pantheon Mound: A Middle

Preclassic Site in Morelos, Mexico. *American Antiquity*, Vol. 35, No. 1, pp. 62–73. Salt Lake City.

GRUNING, E. L.
1930   Report on the British Museum Expedition to British Honduras, 1930. *Journal of the Royal Anthropological Institute*, Vol. 60, pp. 477–82. London.

HAGAMAN, R. M., AND T. M. LONGTON
        Fine Orange Pottery. Ms., 1972, Arizona State Museum.

HAMMOND, NORMAN
1972a   Locational Models and the Site of Lubaantún: A Classic Maya Center. In *Models in Archaeology*, edited by D. L. Clarke, pp. 757–800. London.

1972b   Lubaantun 1926–70: The British Museum in British Honduras. Ms., London.

1972c   Obsidian Trade in the Mayan Area. *Science*, Vol. 178, pp. 1092–93. Washington, D. C.

Handbook of Middle American Indians
1965   Vol. 2: *Archaeology of Southern Mesoamerica*, Pt. 1, Gordon R. Willey, volume editor. University of Texas Press, Austin.

HARLAN, M. E.
n.d.   Maya Wholesalers and Their Wares. Ms., Arizona State Museum.

HARRIS, MARVIN
1968a   Comments. In *New Perspectives in Archaeology*, edited by Sally R. Binford and Lewis R. Binford, pp. 359–61. Aldine, Chicago.

1968b   *The Rise of Anthropological Theory*. Thomas Y. Crowell Co., New York.

HARRISSE, HENRY
1866   *Bibliotheca Americana Vetustissima: A Description of Works Relating to America Published between the Years 1492 and 1551*. New York.

HARVEY, HERBERT R.
1971   Ethnohistory of Guerrero. In *Handbook of Middle American Indians*, Vol. 11, pp. 603–18. University of Texas Press, Austin.

HAVILAND, W. A.
1968   Ancient Lowland Maya Social Organization. *Tulane Middle American Research Series, Publication 26*. New Orleans.

HELBIG, KARL M.
1964   *La cuenca superior del Río Grijalva*. Instituto de Ciencias y Artes de Chiapas, Tuxtla Gutierrez.

HELLMUTH, NICHOLAS M.
1970   Preliminary Bibliography of the Chol, Lacandon, Yucatec Lacandon, Itza, Mopan and Quejache of the Southern Maya Lowlamds, 1524–1969. *"Katunob," Occasional Publications in Mesoamerican Anthropology*, No. 4. Museum of Anthropology, University of Northern Colorado, Greeley.

1971   Some Notes on the Ytza, Quejache, Verapaz Chol, and Toquegua Maya: A Progress Report on Ethnohistory Research Conducted in Seville, Spain (June–August, 1971). Mimeo.

HERRERA, ANTONIO DE
1728   *Historia general de las Indias Occidentales*. Antwerp.

HERRERA Y TORDESILLAS, ANTONIO DE
1934   *Historia general de los hechos de los cas-
-36   tellanos en las islas i tierra firme del mar océano*. Ediciones Atlas, Madrid.

HILLIER, B.
1965   *Master Potters of the Industrial Revolution: The Turners of Lane End*. Cory, Adams and Mackay, London.

Historia de los Reynos de Colhuacán y de México
        see Lehmann, Walter (editor)

HOCKETT, C. F.
1958   *A Course in Modern Linguistics*. The Macmillan Company, New York.

HOLM, OLAF
1953   El tatuaje entre los aborigenes prepizarrianos de la costa ecuatoriana. *Cuadernos de Historia y Arqueología*, Año III, Vol. 3, Nos. 7–8, pp. 56–92. Guayaquil.

HORCASITAS, FERNANDO, translator and editor
1972   *Life and Death in Milpa Alta*. University of Oklahoma Press, Norman.

HUBBS, CARL L. AND G. I. RODEN
1964   Oceanography and Marine Life along the Pacific Coast of Middle America. In *Handbook of Middle American Indians*, Vol. 1, pp. 143–86. University of Texas Press, Austin.

HUMBOLDT, ALEJANDRO VON
1810   *Vues de Cordilleres et Monuments de Peuples Indigenes de l'Amerique*. Paris.

IXTLILXOCHITL, F. DE ALVA
1965   *Obras históricas*. Editora Nacional, Mexico.

JACOBS, JANE
1969   *The Economy of Cities*. Random House, New York.

JIJÓN Y CAAMAÑO, JACINTO
1930   Una gran marea cultural en el noroeste de Sudamérica. *Journal de la Société des Américanistes de Paris*, Vol. 22, pp. 107–197. Paris.

1941   *El Ecuador interandino y occidental antes de la conquista*. Quito.

JIMÉNEZ MORENO, WIGBERTO
1947   Historia antigua de la zona Tarasca. In *El Occidente de Mexico: IV Reunión de Mesa Redonda*. Sociedad Mexicana de Antropología, Mexico.

JIMÉNEZ MORENO, WIGBERTO
1958   *Apuntes para la clase de historia antigua de México*. Sociedad de Alumnos, Escuela Nacional de Antropología y Historia, Mexico.

1966   Mesoamerica before the Toltecs. In *Ancient Oaxaca*, edited by J. Paddock. Stanford University Press.

JOYCE, T. A.
1929   Report on the British Museum Expedition to British Honduras, 1929. *Journal of the Royal Anthropological Institute*, Vol. 59, pp. 439-59. London.
1933   The Pottery Whistle-figurines of Lubaantun. *Journal of the Royal Anthropological Institute*, Vol. 63, pp. 15-25. London.

JOYCE, T. A., J. COOPER CLARK, AND J. E. S. THOMPSON
1927   Report on the British Museum Expedition to British Honduras, 1927. *Journal of the Royal Anthropological Institute*, Vol. 57, pp. 295-323. London.

JOYCE, T. A., T. GANN, E. L. GRUNING, AND R. C. E. LONG
1928   Report on the British Museum Expedition to British Honduras 1928. *Journal of the Royal Anthropological Institute*, Vol. 58, pp. 323-50. London.

JUARROS, D. DOMINGO
1936   *Compendio de la historia de la Ciudad de Guatemala*. Tipografía Nacional, Guatemala.

KATZ, FRIEDRICH
1966   *Situación social y económica de los Aztecas durante los siglos XV y XVI*. Universidad Nacional Autónoma de México, Mexico.
1972   *The Ancient American Civilizations*. Praeger, New York.

KEEBLE, D. E.
1967   Models of Economic Development. In *Models in Geography*, edited by R. J. Chorley and P. Haggett. Methuen & Co., Ltd., London.

KELLEY, J. CHARLES
1966   Mesoamerica and the Southwestern United States. In *Handbook of Middle American Indians*, Vol. 4, pp. 95-110. University of Texas Press, Austin.

KELLEY, J. CHARLES AND H. WINTERS
1960   A Revision of the Archaeological Sequence in Sinaloa, Mexico. *American Antiquity*, Vol. 25, No. 4, pp. 547-61. Salt Lake City.

KELLY, ISABEL T.
1945   The Archaeology of the Autlán-Tuxcacuesco Area of Jalisco, I: The Autlán Zone. *Ibero-Americana 26*. Berkeley and Los Angeles.
1949   Archaeology of the Autlán-Tuxcacuesco Area of Jalisco, II: The Tuxcacuesco-Zapotitlán Zone. *Ibero-Americana 27*. Berkeley and Los Angeles.

KINGSBOROUGH, LORD
1831   *Antiquities of Mexico: Comprising Facsimiles of Ancient Mexican Paintings and Hieroglyphics*. London.

LANDA, FRAY DIEGO DE
1938   *Relación de las cosas de Yucatan*. Edición Yucateca, Merida.
1941   Landa's Relacion de las cosas de Yucatan, edited and translated by A. M. Tozzer. *Papers of the Peabody Museum of American Archaeology and Ethnology, Harvard University*, Vol. 18. Cambridge.

LAS CASAS, BARTOLOMÉ DE
1909   *Apologética historia de las Indias*. Serrano y Ganz, Madrid.
1957   *Historia de las Indias*. Estudio preliminar y edición por Juan Pérez de Tudela Bueso. 2 vols. [Biblioteca de Autores Españoles, Vols. 95-96]. Ediciones Atlas, Madrid.

LEE, THOMAS A., JR.
1965   San Pablo Cave, El Cayo, Usumacinta River, Chiapas. Ms., Comitan.
1966   Una exploración del Cañón del Sumidero. *Edición de la Sección XXXVII, Sindicato Nacional de Trabajadores de la Educación*, No. 8. Tuxtla Guiérrez.
1970   Fiesta del niño florero. *Renovación, Hebdomadario, Comentarista y Crítico, Epoca III*, No. 1. Tuxtla Gutiérrez.
n.d.   The Historic Routes of Tabasco and Northern Chiapas: Hypothesis and their Effect on Cultural Contact. Ms., Comitan.

LEEDS, A.
1962   The Port of Trade in Pre-European India as an Ecological and Evolutionary Type. In *Proceedings of the 1961 annual Spring Meeting of the American Ethnological Society*. University of Washington Press, Seattle.

LEHMANN, WALTER, editor
1938   Die Geschichte der Königreiche von Colhuacan und Mexico. *Quellenwerke zur Alten Geschichte Amerikas*, Vol. 1. Stuttgart-Berlin.

LEIGH, HOWARD
1961   Head Shrinking in Ancient Mexico. *Science of Man*, Vol. 2, No. 1, pp. 4-7.

LEÓN-PORTILLA, MIGUEL
1962   La institución cultural del comercio prehispánico. *Estudios de Cultura Nahuatl*, Vol. 3, pp. 23-54. Mexico.

LEONE, MARK P.
1968   Economic Autonomy and Social Distance: Archaeological Evidences. Doctoral dissertation, University of Arizona, Tucson.

LISTER, ROBERT H.
1949   Excavations at Cojumatlán, Michoacán, México. *University of New Mexico Publications in Anthropology*, No. 5. Tucson.

LITVAK KING, JAIME
1970a   El valle de Xochicalco. Doctoral dissertation, Universidad Nacional Autónoma de México, Mexico.
1970b   Xochicalco en la caída del clásico, una hipótesis. *Anales de Antropología*, Vol. 7, pp. 131-44. Universidad Nacional Autónoma de México, Mexico.

1971a Las relaciones entre México y Tlatelolco antes de la conquista de Axayacatl. Problemática de la expansión Mexica. *Estudios de Cultura Nahuatl*, Vol. 9, pp. 17-20.

1971b Cihuatlán y Tepecoacuilco: provincias tributaries de México en el siglo XVI. Instituto de Investigaciones Históricas, Universidad Nacional Autónoma de México, Mexico.

1972 Las relaciones externas de Xochicalco; una evaluación de su significado. *Anales de Antropología*, Vol. 9, pp. 53-76. Universidad Nacional Autónoma de México, Mexico.

LONG, STANLEY V.

1966 Archaeology of the Municipio of Etzatlan, Jalisco. Doctoral dissertation, University of California, Los Angeles.

1967 Form and Distribution of Shaft-and-Chamber Tombs. *Revista Universidad de Los Andes*, No. 1. Bogota.

LÓPEZ, ROBERT S. AND IRVING W. RAYMOND

1954 *Medieval Trade in the Mediterranean World*. W. W. Norton and Company, New York.

LÓPEZ DE COGOLLUDO, DIEGO FR.

1957 *Historia de Yucatán*. Mexico.

LÓPEZ DE GÓMARA, FRANCISCO DE

1941 *Historia General de las Indias*. Espasa-Calpe, Madrid.

1943 *Historia de la Conquista de México*, Introduction and notes by J. Ramírez Cabanas. Mexico.

LORENZO, JOSÉ LUIS

1955 Los Concheros de la Costa de Chiapas. *Anales del Instituto Nacional de Antropología e Historia*, Vol. 7, No. 36, pp. 41-50. Mexico.

1961 Un buril de la cultura precerámica de Teopisca, Chiapas. In *Homenaje a Pablo Martínez del Río*, pp. 75-90. Instituto Nacional de Antropología e Historia, Mexico.

1964 Primer informe sobre los trabajos arqueológicos de rescate efectuados en el vaso de la presa de "el Infiernillo," Guerrero y Michoacán. *Boletín INAH*, No. 17, pp. 24-31. Instituto Nacional de Antropología e Historia, Mexico.

LOTHROP, SAMUEL K.

1927 The Word "Maya" and the Fourth Voyage of Columbus. *Indian Notes*, Vol. IV. Museum of the American Indian, Heye Foundation, New York.

1961 Archaeology, Then and Now. In *Essays in Pre-Columbian Art and Archaeology*, by S. K. Lothrop and others. Harvard University Press, Cambridge.

LOWE, GARETH W.

1959 Archeological Exploration of the Upper Grijalva River, Chiapas, Mexico. *Papers of the New World Archaeological Foundation*, No. 2. Orinda.

1962 Mound 5 and Minor Excavations, Chiapa de Corzo, Chiapas, Mexico. *Papers of the New World Archaeological Foundation* No. 12. Orinda.

1969 The Olmec Horizon Occupation of Mound 20 at San Isidro in the Middle Grijalva Region of Chiapas. Unpublished Master's thesis, University of the Americas, Cholula.

1971 The Civilizational Consequences of Varying Degrees of Agricultural and Ceramic Dependency within the Basic Ecosystems of Mesoamerica. In *Contributions of the University of California Archaeological Research Facility*, No. 11, Chapter 11, Chapter 15, pp. 212-48. Berkeley.

LUNDELL, C. L.

1934 Preliminary Sketch of the Phytogeography of the Yucatan Peninsula. *Carnegie Institution of Washington, Publication* 436 (*Contribution* 12). Washington.

1937 The Vegetation on Peten. *Carnegie Institution of Washington, Publication* 478. Washington.

1938 Plants Probably Utilized by the Old Empire Maya of Peten and Adjacent Lowlands. *Papers of the Michigan Academy of Science*, Part 1. Ann Arbor.

McBRYDE, FELIX WEBSTER

1947 Cultural and Historical Geography of Southwest Guatemala. *Smithsonian Institute, Institute of Social Anthropology, Publication* 4. Washington, D. C.

McDONALD, ANDREW

n.d. Tzutzuculi, a Preclassic Site of Coastal Chiapas. Unpublished Master's thesis, 1972. University of the Americas, Cholula.

MacNEISH, RICHARD S. AND FREDRICK A. PETERSON

1962 The Santa Marta Rock Shelter, Ocozocoautla, Chiapas, Mexico. *Papers of the New World Archaeological Foundation*, No. 14. Provo.

McQUOWN, NORMAN

1964 Los orígenes y la diferenciación de los mayas según se infiere del estudio comparativo de las lenguas mayanas. *Desarrollo Cultural de los Mayas*, edited by Evon Z. Vogt and Alberto Ruz L., pp. 49-80. Seminario de Cultura Maya, Universidad Nacional Autónoma de México, Mexico.

McVICKER, DONALD E.

n.d. The Place of the Salt: Archaeological Survey and Excavation in the Valley of Ixtapa, Chiapas, Mexico. Unpublished doctoral dissertation, University of Chicago, Chicago, 1969.

1970 Cambio cultural y ecología en el Chiapas central prehispánico. In *Ensayos de*

Antropología en la Zona Central de Chiapas, edited by N. McQuown and J. Pitt-Rivers, pp. 77-103. Instituto Nacional Indigenista, Mexico.

MALINOWSKI, BRONISLAW
1961   *Argonauts of the Western Pacific*. E. P. Dutton and Co., New York.

MALINOWSKI, BRONISLAW AND JULIO DE LA FUENTE
1957   La economía de un sistema de mercados en México. *Acta Antropológica*, Epoca 2, Vol. 1, No. 2. Escuela Nacional de Antropología e Historia, Mexico.

MARTÍNEZ MARÍN, CARLOS
1972   Santuarios y peregrinaciones en el México prehispánico. In *Religión en Mesoamérica, XII Mesa Redonda*, pp. 161-78. Sociedad Mexicana de Antropología Mexico.

MÁRTYR DE ANGELERÍA, PEDRO [PETRUS]
1892   *Fuentes históricas sobre Colón y América*. Madrid.
1912   *De Orbe Novo, the Eight Decades of Peter Martyr d'Anghiera*, edited by F. A. MacNutt. New York.
1944   *Décadas del Nuevo Mundo*. Editorial Bajel, Buenos Aires.
1966   *Opera. Legatio Babylonica, De Orbe Novo Decades Octo, Opus Epistolarum*. Akademische Druck- u. Verlagsanstalt, Graz, Austria.

MATRÍCULA DE TRIBUTOS
?   Manuscript in the Museo Nacional de Antropología, Mexico.

MAUSS, MARCEL
1954   *The Gift*. The Free Press, Glencoe.

MEAD, MARGARET
1930   Social Organization of Manu'a. *Bernice P. Bishop Museum, Bulletin* 76. Honolulu.

MEDINILLA ALVARADO, FRANCISCO DE
1944   Relación de Xiquilpan y su partido: 1579, edited by Robert H. Barlow. *Tlalocan*, Vol. 1, pp. 278-306. Mexico.

MEGGERS, BETTY, AND EVANS, CLIFFORD
1964   Especulaciones sobre rutas tempranas de difusión de la cerámica entre sur-y Mesoamerica, *Hombre y Cultura*, Vol. I, No. 3, pp. 1-15. Panama.

MEGGERS, BETTY J., CLIFFORD EVANS AND EMILIO ESTRADA
1965   Early Formative Period of Coastal Ecuador: the Valdivia and Machalilla Phases. *Smithsonian Contributions to Anthropology*, Vol. 1. Washington.

MEIGHAN, CLEMENT W.
1969   Cultural Similarities Between Western Mexico and Andean Regions. In "Pre-Columbian Contact Within Nuclear America," *Mesoamerican Studies*, No. 4, edited by J. Charles Kelley and Carrol L. Riley,

pp. 11-25. Southern Illinois University, University Museum, Carbondale.

MEIGHAN, CLEMENT W. AND LEONARD J. FOOTE
1968   Excavations at Tizapan El Alto, Jalisco. *Latin American Studies*, Vol. 11. University of California, Los Angeles, and Editorial Sucre, Caracas.

MEIGHAN, CLEMENT W., L. FOOTE AND P. AIELLO
1968   Obsidian Dating in West Mexican Archaeology. *Science*, Vol. 160, No. 3832, pp. 1069-1075. Washington.

MENDIETA, FR. GERÓNIMO DE
1945   *Historia eclesiástica indiana*. Editorial Salvador Chavez Hayhoe, Mexico.

MENDIZÁBAL, M. O.
1928   *Influencia de la sal en la distribucion geográfica de los grupos indígenes de México*. Mexico.

MILLON, RENÉ F.
1955   When Money Grew on Trees: A Study of Cacao in Ancient Mesoamerica. *Doctoral Dissertations Series, Publication* No. 12,454. University Microfilms, Ann Arbor.
1967   Teotihuacan. *Scientific American*, Vol. 216, No. 6, pp. 38-48.
1970   Teotihuacan: Completion of Map of Giant Ancient City in the Valley of Mexico. *Science*, Vol. 170, pp. 1077-82.
1974   The Study of Urbanism at Teotihuacan, Mexico. In *Mesoamerican Archaeology: New Approaches*, edited by Norman Hammond, pp. 313-34. Duckworth, London.

MOLINA FÁBREGA, N.
1956   El Códice Mendocino y la economía de Tenochtitlán. *Ediciones "Libro Mex", Biblioteca Mínima Mexicana*, 30. Mexico.

MOLLOY, JOHN P. AND HUGH G. BALL
n.d.   The Tarascan Connection. In preparation.

MOLLOY, JOHN P., AND WILLIAM L. RATHJE
1972   Sexploitation among the Late Classic Maya. In *Mesoamerican Archaeology: New Approaches*, edited by Norman Hammond. University of Texas Press, Austin.

MONTERO DE MIRANDA, FR. FRANCISCO
1954   Descripción de la provincia de la Verapaz. *Anales*, Vol. 27, pp. 342-58. Sociedad de geografia e historia de Guatemala, Guatemala.

MOORHEAD, MAX L.
1949   Hernan Cortes and the Tehuantepec Passage. *The Hispanic American Review*, Vol. 29, pp. 370-79.

MORÁN, PEDRO
1935   *Arte y diccionario en lengua Choltí de 1625*. The Maya Society, Baltimore.

MORELET, ARTHUR
1872   Reisen in Central Amerika. In *Deutscher Bearbeitung von H. Hertz*. Jena.

MORIARTY, JAMES R.
1968 Climatologic, ecologic and temporal inferences from radiocarbon dates on archaeological sites, Baja California, Mexico. *Pacific Coast Archaeological Quarterly*, Vol. 4, No. 1, pp. 11–38.

MORLEY, SYLVANUS G.
1937– The Inscriptions of Peten. *Carnegie Institu-*
1938 *tion of Washington, Publication 437*. Washington.

MOTOLINÍA, FR. T. DE B.
1967 *Memoriales*. Edición facsímile. Guadalajara.

MOUNTJOY, JOSEPH B.
1969 On the Origin of West Mexican Metallurgy. In "Pre-Columbian Contact within Nuclear America," edited by J. Charles Kelley and Carrol L. Riley, pp. 26–42. *Mesoamerican Studies*, Vol. 4. Southern Illinois University Museum, Carbondale.
1970a Prehispanic Culture History and Cultural Contact on the Southern Coast of Nayarit, Mexico. Doctoral dissertation, Southern Illinois University, Carbondale.
1970b La sucesión cultural en San Blas. *Boletín INAH*, Vol. 39, pp. 41–48. Instituto Nacional de Antropología e Historia, Mexico.
1970c San Blas Complex Ecology. Paper presented at the thirty-fifth annual meeting of the Society for American Archaeology, Mexico City. Mimeographed. Revised edition accepted for publication in *The Archaeology of the Occident of Mexico*, edited by B. Bell, Guadalajara.

MOUNTJOY, JOSEPH B., R. E. TAYLOR AND L. H. FELDMAN
1972 Matanchén Complex: New Radiocarbon Dates on Early Coastal Adaptation in West Mexico, *Science*, Vol. 175, pp. 1242–43.

MURRA, JOHN V.
1971 El tráfico de *mullo* en la costa del Pacífico. Paper presented at Primer simpsio de correlaciones antropológicas Andino-Mesoamericano. Salinas, Ecuador.

NASH, MANNING
1966 *Primitive and Peasant Economic Systems*. Chandler Press, San Francisco.

NATIONAL GEOGRAPHIC INSTITUTE OF GUATEMALA
1965 *Mapa oficial preliminar de la república de Guatemala, Hipsométrico; 1:5,000,000.* Guatemala City.

NAVARRETE, CARLOS
1960 Archaeological Exploration in the Region of the Frailesca, Chiapas, Mexico. *Papers of the New World Archaeological Foundation*, No. 7. Orinda.
1966a The Chiapanec, History and Culture. *Papers of the New World Archaeological Foundation*, No. 21. Provo.
1966b Excavaciones en la presa Netzahualcoyotl,

Mal Paso, Chis. *Boletin INAH*, No. 24. Instituto Nacional de Antropología, Mexico.
1968a La relación de Ocozocoautla, Chiapas; *Tlalocan*, Vol. V, No. 4. La Casa de Tlaloc, Mexico.
1968b La cerámica postclásica de Tuxtla Gutiérrez, Chis. *Anales, 1966*, Vol. XIX. Instituto Nacional de Antropología e Historia, Mexico.
1969 Los relieves Olmecas de Pijijiapan, Chiapas. *Anales de Antropología*, Vol. VI, pp. 183–95. Universidad Nacional Autónoma de México, Mexico.
1971 Piezas Olmecas de *Chiapas y Guatemala*, *Anales de Antropología*, Vol. 8, pp. 69–82. Universidad Nacional Autónoma de México, Mexico.

NAVARRETE, CARLOS AND THOMAS A. LEE, JR.
1969 Apuntes sobre el trabajo del ámbar en Simojovel, Chiapas. *Boletín INAH*, No. 35, pp. 13–19. Instituto Nacional de Antropología e Historia, Mexico.

NAVARRETE, CARLOS AND EDUARDO MARTÍNEZ E.
1960 Investigaciones arqueológicas en el Río Sabi-
–61 nal, Chiapas, Mexico. *ICACH*, No. 5. Instituto de Ciencias y Artes de Chiapas, Tuxtla Gutierrez.

NOYERS, ERNEST
1932 Fray Alonso Ponce in Yucatan. *Middle American Research Series, Publication 4.* New Orleans.

Nuttall, Codex
n.d. Facsimile edition, with commentary by C. A. Burland, Akademische Druck-u, Verlagsanstalt. Graz.

ORELLANA TAPÍA, RAFAEL
1954 El vaso de Ixtapa, Chiapas. *Yan*, Vol. III. Centro de Investigaciones Antropológicas de México, Mexico.

OTHÓN DE MENDIZÁBAL, MIGUEL
1946 Influencia de la sal en la distribución geográfica de los grupos indígenas de México. *Obras Completas*, Vol. 2, pp. 177–340. Mexico.

OVIEDO Y VALDÉS, GONZALO FERNÁNDEZ DE
1851 *Historia general y natural de las Indias.*
–55 *Islas y tierra-firme del mar océano.* Madrid.

OWEN, L. H.
1928 Geology of British Honduras. *Journal of Geology*, Vol. 36, pp. 494–509.

PAEZ BETANCOR, ALONSO AND FR. PEDRO DE ARBOLEDA
1964 Relación de Santiago Atitlán. *Anales*, Vol. 37, pp. 87–106; Vol. 38, pp. 265–76. Sociedad de Geografía e Historia de Guatemala, Guatemala.

PALACIO, DIEGO GARCÍA DE
1860 *Carta dirijida al rey de España, 1576.* Translated and published by E. G. Squier. Charles Norton, New York.

PANIAGUA, FLAVIO ANTONIO
1876 *Catecismo elemental de historia y estadística*

de Chiapas. Imprenta El Porvenir, San Cristóbal de Las Casas.

PARSONS, LEE A. AND P. S. JENSON
1965   Boulder Sculpture on the Pacific Coast of Guatemala. *Archaeology,* Vol. 18, No. 2, pp. 132–44. New York.

PARSONS, LEE A. AND BARBARA J. PRICE
1971   Mesoamerican Trade and Its Role in the Emergence of Civilization. In "Observations on the Emergence of Civilization in Mesoamerica," edited by Robert F. Heizer and John A. Graham. *Contributions of the University of California Archaeological Research Facility,* No. 11, pp. 196–95. Berkeley.

PASO Y TRONCOSO, FRANCISCO DEL, EDITOR
1905   Suma de visitas de pueblos por orden alfabético. *Papeles de Nueva España, Segunda Serie 1. Geografía y Estadística.* Sucesores de Rivadeneyra, Madrid.
1905   *Papeles de Nueva Espana.* Sucesores de Rivadeneyra, Madrid.
1905–6 Relación de Teutitlán del Camino, 1581. In *Papeles de Nueva Espana,* Vol. 4, pp. 213–31. Madrid.

PAULSEN, A. C.
1971   La secuencia de la cerámica de Guangala de la península de Santa Elena y sus implicaciones para un contacto prehistórico entre el Ecuador y América Central. Paper presented at Primer simposio de correlaciones antropologicas Andino-Mesoamericano. Salinas, Ecuador.
1972   The Thorny Oyster and the Voice of the Gods: *Spondylus* and *Strombus* in Andean Prehistory. Paper presented at meeting of Society for American Archaeology, Miami.

PENDERGAST, DAVID M.
1962   Metal Artifacts from Amapa, Nayarit, Mexico. *American Antiquity,* Vol. 27, No. 3, pp. 370–79. Salt Lake City.

PERALTA, M. M. DE
1883   *Costa Rica, Nicaragua, y Panamá en el siglo XVI: su historia y sus límites.*

PIÑA CHAN, ROMÁN
1970   Campeche antes de la Conquista. *Gobierno del Estado de Campeche, Publication* 12, Campeche.

PINEDA, JUAN DE
1925   Descripción de la Provincia de Guatemala. *Anales,* Vol. 1, No. 4, pp. 327–63. Sociedad de Geografía e Historia de Guatemala, Guatemala.
1952   Descripción de la Provincia de Guatemala, año de 1594. *Anales del Museo Nacional "David J. Guzman,"* Vol. 3, No. 11. San Salvador.

PIRENNE, HENRI
1956   *Medieval Cities.* Doubleday Anchor Books, New York.

POLANYI, KARL
1957   The Economy as Instituted Process. In *Trade and Market in the Early Empires,* edited by K. Polanyi, C. Arensberg, and H. W. Pearson, pp. 243–69. The Free Press, Glencoe.
1963   Ports of Trade in Early Societies. *The Journal of Economic History,* Vol. 23, No. 1, pp. 30–45.
1966   *Dahomey and the Slave Trade.* University of Washington Press, Seattle.

POLANYI, KARL, CONRAD M. ARENSBERG, HARRY W. PEARSON, EDITOR
1957   *Trade and Market in the Early Empires.* The Free Press, Glencoe.

PONCE, FRAY ALONSO
1873   *Relación breve y verdadera de algunas cosas de las muchas que sucedieron al Padre Fray Alonso Ponce en las provincias de la Nueva España, siendo Comisario General de aquellas partes.* Madrid.

PONCE DE LEÓN, LUIS
1961   Relación de la Provincia de Soconusco. In *La Victoria: an Early Site on the Pacific Coast of Guatemala,* by M. D. Coe. *Papers of the Peabody Museum of Archaeology and Ethnology, Harvard University,* Vol. 53, pp. 139–40. Cambridge.

PRICE, BARBARA J.
1974   The Burden of the Cargo: Ethnographic Models and Archaeological Inference. In *Mesoamerican Archaeology: New Approaches,* edited by Norman Hammond, pp. 445–65. Duckworth, London.

PROSKOURIAKOFF, TATIANA
1950   A Study of Classic Maya Sculpture. *Carnegie Institution of Washington, Publication* 593. Washington.
1960   Historical Implications of a Pattern of Dates at Piedras Negras. *American Antiquity,* Vol. 23, pp. 454–75. Salt Lake City.

PULESTON, D. E. AND O. S. PULESTON
1971   An Ecological Approach to the Origins of Maya Civilization. *Archaeology,* Vol. 24, No. 4, pp. 330–37.

RADIN, PAUL
1933   Notes on the Tlapanecan language of Guerrero. *International Journal of American Linguistics,* Vol. 8, pp. 45–72.

RANDS, ROBERT L.
1967   Ceramic Technology and Trade in the Palenque Region, Mexico. In *American Historical Anthropology, Essays in Honor of Leslie Spier,* edited by Carroll L. Riley and Walter W. Taylor, pp. 137–51. Southern Illinois University Press, Carbondale.
1969   Maya Ecology and Trade, 1967-1968. In "Mesoamerican Studies," *Research Records,* Series 69-M-2-A. Carbondale.
n.d.   Pottery of the Greater Palenque Region,

Mexico. Progress Report on investigations conducted in 1964-1965 by the Research Laboratories of Anthropology, University of North Carolina.

RATHJE, WILLIAM L.
1971a   Lowland Classic Maya Socio-Political Organization: Degree and Form in Time and Space. Doctoral dissertation, Harvard University, Cambridge.
1971b   The Origin and Development of Lowland Classic Maya Civilization. *American Antiquity*, Vol. 36, No. 3, pp. 275-85. Washington.
1972   Praise the Gods and Pass the Metates: An Hypothesis of the Rise and Fall of Lowland Rainforest Civilizations in Mesoamerica. In *Contemporary Archaeology*, edited by M. P. Leone. Southern Illinois University Press.
1973   Classic Maya Development and Denouement: A Research Design. In *The Classic Maya Collapse*, edited by T. Patrick Culbert, pp. 405-54. Albuquerque.

Relación Samano-Xerez
1967   Original in the Library of Vienna. In *Las relaciones primitivas de la conquista del Perú*, edited by Raúl Porras Barrenedica, pp. 63-72. Lima.

Relaciones de Yucatan
1872   *Colección de documentos inéditos relativos al descubrimiento, conquista y organización de las provincias Españolas de Ultramar*, Vols. 11 and 13. Imprenta del Hospicio, Seville.

Relaciones de Yucatan
1898-   In *Colección de documentos inéditos relativos al descubrimiento, conquista y organización de las antiguas posesiones españolas de Ultramar*, 2nd series, Vols. 11-13. Real Academia de la Historia, Madrid.
1900

REMESAL, A. DE
1932   *Historia general de las Indias occidentales y particular de la gobernación de Chiapa y Guatemala*, Vols. 4 and 5. Biblioteca "Goathemala," Sociedad de Geografía e Historia, Guatemala.

RENFREW, COLIN
1967   Colonialism and Megalithismos. *Antiquity*, Vol. 41, No. 164, pp. 276-88.
1969   Trade and Culture Process in European Prehistory. *Current Antropology*, Vol. 10, No. 2-3, pp. 151-69. Chicago.

REVERE, ROBERT B.
1957   No Man's Coast: Ports of Trade in the Eastern Mediterranean. In *Trade and Market in the Early Empires*, edited by Karl Poanyi, C. Arensberg and H. W. Pearson, pp. 38-63. The Free Press, Glencoe.

RICKETSON, O. G., JR. AND E. B. RICKETSON
1937   Uaxactun, Guatemala, Group E, 1926-1931.

Carnegie Institution of Washington, Publication 477. Washington.

ROOT, WILLIAM C.
1946   Metallurgy. In *Handbook of South American Indians. Bureau of American Ethnology, Bulletin* 143, Vol. 5. Washington.

ROSMAN, ABRAHAM AND PAULA RUBEL
1971   *Feasting with Mine Enemy*. Columbia University Press, New York.

ROSTWOROWSKI DE DIEZ CANSECO, M.
1970   Mercaderes del Valle de Chincha i en la época prehispánica: un documento y unos comentarios. *Revista Española de Antropología Americana*, Vol. 5, pp. 135-77. Madrid.

ROYS, RALPH L.
1931   Ethnobotany of the Maya. *Papers of the Middle American Research Institute*. Tulane University, New Orleans.
1939   The Titles of Ebtún. *Carnegie Institution of Washington, Publication* 505. Washington, D.C.
1943   The Indian Background of Colonial Yucatan. *Carnegie Institution of Washington, Publication* 548. Washington.
1957   The Political Geography of the Yucatan Maya. *Carnegie Institution of Washington, Publication* 613. Washington.
1965   Lowland Maya Native Society at Spanish Contact. In Archaeology of Southern Mesoamerica, Part Two, edited by Gordon R. Willey. *Handbook of Middle American Indians*, Vol. 3. University of Texas Press, Austin.
1972   *The Indian Background of Colonial Yucatan*. University of Oklahoma Press, Norman.

RUBIO SÁNCHEZ, MANUEL
1956   Puertón de Iztapa o de la Independencia (primera parte). *Antropología e Historia de Guatemala*, Vol. 7, No. 2, pp. 24-49. Guatemala.

RUPPERT, KARL
1940   A Special Assemblage of Maya Structures. In *The Maya and Their Neighbors*. Harvard University Press, Cambridge.

SABLOFF, JEREMY A.
1971   Type Descriptions of the Fine Paste Ceramics of the Bayal Boca Complex, Seibal, Peten, Guatemala. *Papers of the Peabody Museum of Archaeology and Ethnology, Harvard University*, Vol. 61, Part 4, No. 2. Cambridge.

SABLOFF, JEREMY A. AND GAIR TOURTELLOT
1969   Systems of Exchange among the Ancient Maya. Paper presented at the 68th annual meeting of the American Antropological Association, New Orleans.

SABLOFF, JEREMY A. AND GORDON R. WILLEY
1967   The Collapse of Maya Civilization in the

Southern Lowlands: A Consideration of History and Process. *Southwestern Journal of Anthropology*, Vol. 23, pp. 311-36. Albuquerque.

SAENZ (DE SANTA MARÍA), CARMELO
1940 *Diccionario Cakchiquel-Español of Fr. Francisco Barela (1600)*. Tipografía Nacional, Guatemala.

SAENZ, CESAR A.
1962 Xochicalco, Temporada 1960. *Departamento de Monumentos Prehispánicos, Informes* 11. Instituto Nacional de Antropología, Mexico.

SAHAGÚN, FRAY BERNADINO DE
1946 *Historia general de las cosas de la Nueva España*. Editorial Nueva España, S. A., Mexico.
1950 *Florentine Codex*, translated by J. O. Anderson and C. E. Dibble. University of Utah Press, Salt Lake City.
-69
1952 Gliederung des alt-azrekischen Volks in Familie, Stand und Beruf. Übersetzt und erlautert von Leonhard Schiltze Jena. *Quellenwerke zur alten Geschicte Amerikas*, Bd. 5. Stuttgart.
1956 *Historia general de las cosas de Nueva España*. Editorial Porrúa, S.A., Mexico.
1969 *Historia general de las cosas de Nueva España*. New edition with numeration, notes, and appendices by Angel María Garibay K. Biblioteca Porrúa, Mexico.

SAHLINS, MARSHALL D.
1964 Culture and Environment: the Study of Cultural Ecology. In *Horizons of Anthropology*, edited by Sol Tax, pp. 132-47. Aldine-Atherton Publishing Company, Chicago.
1965 On the Sociology of Primitive Exchange. In *The Relevance of Models for Social Anthropology*, edited by M. Banton, pp. 139-86. Praeger, New York.

SÁNCHEZ, JESÚS B.
1915 *Elementos de la historia de Chiapas*. Mexico.

SÁNCHEZ DE AGUILAR, PEDRO
1937 *Informe contra idolorum cultores del obispado de Yucatan* ... Merida. Published originally in 1639. Madrid.

SANDERS, WILLIAM T.
1956 The Central Mexican Symbiotic Region. In "Prehistoric Settlement Patterns in the New World," edited by Gordon R. Willey, pp. 115-27. *Viking Fund Publications in Anthropology*, No. 23.
1962a Cultural Ecology of the Maya Lowlands, Part 1. *Estudios de Cultura Maya*, Vol. 2, pp. 79-121. Seminario de Estudios Mayas, Universidad Nacional Autónoma de México, Mexico.
1962b Cultural Ecology of Nuclear Mesoamerica.

American Anthropologist, Vol. 64, pp. 34-44. Menasha.
1964 Cultural Ecology of the Maya Lowlands, Part 2. *Estudios de Cultura Maya*, Vol. 4, pp. 203-241. Seminario de Estudios Mayas, Universidad Nacional Autónoma de México, Mexico.
1965 The Central Mexican Symbiotic Region: A Study in Prehistoric Settlement Patterns. In "Prehistoric Settlement Patterns in the New World," edited by Gordon R. Willey. *Viking Fund Publications in Anthropology*, No. 23, pp. 115-27. New York.
1973 A Re-evaluation of the Cultural Ecology of the Maya Lowlands. In *The Collapse of Ancient Maya Civilization: A New Assessment*, edited by T. P. Culbert. American School of Research, Santa Fe.

SANDERS, WILLIAM T. AND BARBARA J. PRICE
1968 *Mesoamerica: The Evolution of a Civilization*. Random House, New York.

SANTIBÁÑEZ, ENRIQUE
1908 Lenguas indígenas de Chiapas. *Boletín de la Sociedad Mexicana de Geografía y Estadística*, 5a. épcoa, Vol. 3, pp. 65-74. Mexico.

SAPPER, KARL
1904 Título del Barrio de Santa Ana, Agosto 14 de 1565. *International Congress of Americanists, Proceedings*, pp. 373-97.

SAUER, CARL O.
1932 The Road to Cibola. *Ibero-Americana* 3. University of California Press, Berkeley and Los Angeles.
1948 Colima of New Spain in the Sixteenth Century. *Ibero-Americana* 29. University of California Press, Berkeley and Los Angeles.
1966 *The Early Spanish Main*. University of California Press, Berkeley and Los Angeles.

SAYRE, E. V., L. CHAN, AND J. A. SABLOFF
1971 High-Resolution Gamma Ray Spectroscopic Analyses of Fine Orange Pottery. In *Science and Archaeology*, pp. 165-81, edited by R. H. Brill. MIT Press, Cambridge.

SCHENCK, W. EGBERT
1926 The Emeryville Shellmound Final Report. *University of California Publications in American Archaeology and Ethnology*, Vol. 23, No. 3, pp. 147-282. Berkeley and London.

SCHIFFER, M. B.
1972 Archaeological Context and Systemic Context. *American Antiquity*, Vol. 37, No. 2, pp. 156-65. Salt Lake City.

SCHOLES, FRANCES V., AND ELEANOR B. ADAMS
1957 *Información sobre los tributos que los indios pagaban a Moctezuma, Año de 1554*. José Porrúa e Hijos, Mexico.

SCHOLES, FRANCES V. AND RALPH L. ROYS
1948 The Maya Chontal Indians of Acalan-

Tixchel. *Carnegie Insitution of Washington, Publication* 560. Washington.

1968   *The Maya Chontal Indians of Acalan-Tixchel.* University of Oklahoma Press, Norman.

SCOTT, STUART D.
1969   Archaeological Reconnaissance and Excavations in the Marismas Nacionales, Sinaloa and Nayarit, Mexico. *West Mexican Prehistory* 3. State University of New York, Buffalo.

SEDAT, DAVID W. AND ROBERT J. SHARER
1972   Archaeological Investigations in the Northern Maya Highlands: New Data on the Maya Preclassic. *Contributions of the University of California Archaeological Research Facility,* No. 16. Berkeley.

SERVICE, E. R.
1955   Indo-European Relations in Colonial Latin America. *American Anthropologist,* Vol. 57, No. 3, Part 1, pp. 411-25. Menasha.

1960   The Law of Evolutionary Potential. In *Evolution and Culture,* edited by M. D. Sahlins and E. R. Service, pp. 93-110. University of Michigan Press, Ann Arbor.

SHENKEL, J. RICHARD
1971   Quantitative Analysis and Population Estimates of the Shell-Mounds of the Marismas Nacionales, West Mexico. Paper presented at the 36th annual meeting of the Society for American Archaeology, Norman.

SHEPARD, ANNA O.
1965   Ceramics for the Archaeologist. *Carnegie Institution of Washington, Publication* 609. Washington.

SISSON, EDWARD B.
1970   Settlement Pattern and Land Use in the Northwestern Chontalpa, Tabasco, Mexico: A Progress Report. *Ceramica de Cultura Maya et al.,* No. 6, pp. 41-54. Temple University, Philadelphia.

SJOBERG, GIDEON
1960   *The Preindustrial City: Past and Present.* The Free Press, Glencoe.

SMITH, A. L.
1962   Residential and Associated Structures at Mayapan. *Carnegie Institution of Washington, Publication* 619, Part 3, pp. 165-320. Washington.

SMITH, R. E.
1958   The Place of Fine Orange Pottery in American Archaeology. *American Antiquity,* Vol. 24, No. 2, pp. 151-60. Salt Lake City.

1971   The Pottery of Mayapan. *Papers of the Peabody Museum of Archaeology and Ethnology, Harvard University,* Vol. 66. Cambridge.

DE SOLÍS, JOSEPH
1945   Estado en que se hallaba la provincia de Coatzacoalcos en el año de 1599. *Boletín*

del Archivo General de la Nación, Volume 16, No. 2, pp. 195-246; No. 3, pp. 429-79. Mexico.

SOUSTELLE, JACQUES
1937   La Famille Otomi-Pame du Mexique Central *Travaux et Mémoires de l'Institut d'Ethnologie,* Vol. 26. University of Paris, Paris.

1961   *The Daily Life of the Aztecs on the Eve of the Spanish Conquest.* Stanford University Press, Stanford.

STEWARD, JULIAN H.
1955   *Theory of Culture Change.* University of Illinois Press, Urbana.

STEYERMARK, J. A.
1950   Flora of Guatemala. *Ecology,* Vol. 31, pp. 368-72.

STONE, DORIS Z.
1932   Some Spanish Entradas (1524-1695). *Middle American Research Series, Publication* No. 4. Tulane University, New Orleans.

1972   *Pre-Columbian Man Finds Central America; the Archaeological Bridge.* Peabody Museum Press, Cambridge.

SULLIVAN, THELMA D.
1971   The Finding and Founding of Tenochtitlan. *Tlalocan,* Vol. 6, No. 4, pp. 312-36.

TAX, SOL
1953   Penny Capitalism, A Guatemalan Indian Economy. *Institute of Social Anthropology, Smithsonian Institution, Publication* 16. Washington.

TAYLOR, WILLIAM B.
1972   *Landlord and Peasant in Colonial Oaxaca.* Stanford University Press, Stanford.

TEZOZOMOC, HERNANDO ALVARADO
1944   *Crónica mexicana.* Editorial Leyenda, S. A., Mexico.

1949   *Crónica mexicayotl.* Imprenta Universitaria, Mexico.

THOMPSON, J. ERIC S.
1927   See Joyce, Cooper Clark, and Thompson 1927.

1929   Comunicaciones y comercio de los antiguos Mayas. *Anales, Sociedad de Geografía e Historia de Guatemala,* Vol. 2. Guatemala.

1964   Trade Relations between the Maya Highlands and Lowlands. *Estudios de Cultura Maya,* Vol. 4, pp. 13-49. Seminario de Estudios Mayas, Universidad Nacional Autónoma de México, Mexico.

1970   *Maya History and Religion.* University of Oklahoma Press, Norman.

THOMPSON, J. ERIC S., EDITOR
1958   *Thomas Gages' Travels in the New World.* University of Oklahoma Press, Norman.

TORQUEMADA, FR. JUAN DE
1723   *Primera, segunda, tercera parte de los viente i un libros rituales i monarchía indiana, con el origen y guerras, de los indios occiden-*

tales, de sus poblaciones, descubrimiento, conquista, conversión, y otras cosas maravillosas de la misma tierra. Madrid.

1943   Monarquía indiana. Editorial S. Chávez Hayhoe, Mexico.

1969   Monarquía indiana. Fourth edition. Introduction by Miguel León-Portilla. Biblioteca Porrúa, Mexico.

TORRE, FRAY TOMAS DE LA

1944   Desde Salamanca, España, hasta Ciudad
-45   Real, Chiapas. Diario de viaje: 1544-1545. Notes and Appendices by Frans Blom. Editora Central, Mexico.

TORRES, TOMÁS

        Relación de la visita a diversos pueblos y conventos de la Provincia de Chiapas hecha por el Fraile Visitador Tomás Torres, por mandato del Obispo de la dicha provincia. Ms. in the Hemeroteca "Fernando Castañón," Instituto de Ciencias y Artes de Chiapas, Tuxtla Gutierrez.

TOURTELLOT, G. AND J. A. SABLOFF

1971   Exchange Systems Among the Ancient Maya. American Antiquity, Vol. 37, No. 1. Salt Lake City.

TOVILLA, MARTÍN ALFONSO

1960   Historia descriptiva de las provincias de la Verapaz y de la Manche. Editorial Universitaria, Guatemala.

TOZZER, ALFRED M., EDITOR

1941   See Landa.

TRAVEN, B.

19   Rebelión de los colgados. Mexico.

TRENS, MANUEL B.

1957   Historia de Chiapas. Desde los tiempos mas remotos hasta la caída del Segundo Imperio. Second Edition. Mexico.

TSCHOHL, PETER

1964   Kritische Untersuchungen zur spätindianischen Geschichte Südost-Mexikos. Teil I: Die aztekische Ausdehnung nach den aztekischen Wuellen und die Probleme ihrer Bearbeitung. Doctoral dissertation, Hamburg.

UHLE, MAX

1907   The Emeryville Shellmound. University of California Publications in American Archaeology and Ethnology, Vol. 7, No. 1, pp. 1-104. Berkeley.

URBAN, P. J., JR.

n.d.   A Proposed Method to Measure the Efficiency of Long Distance Trade of the Maya. Ms., Arizona State Museum.

VAILLANT, SUZANNAH B. AND GEORGE C. VAILLANT

1934   Excavations at Gualupita. Anthropological Papers of the American Museum of Natural History, Vol. 35, Part 1. New York.

VANCE, J.

1971   The Merchant's World. Prentice-Hall.

VÁSQUEZ, FR. FRANCISCO

1937   Crónica de la Provincia del Santísimo Nom-

-1944   bre de Jesús de Guatemala. Biblioteca Goathemala," Guatemala.

VÁZQUEZ DE ESPINOSA, ANTONIO

1948   Compendio y descripción de las Indias Occidentales. Smithsonian Institution, Miscellaneous Collection, Vol. 108. Washington.

VEDIA, DON ENRIQUE DE, EDITOR

1946   Historiadores primitivos de Indias. In Biblioteca de Autores Españoles, Vol. 1. Contains the "Relación hecha por Diego Godoy a Hernando Cortés." Madrid.

VIANA, F. DE, L. GALLEGO, AND G. CADENA

1955   Relación de la Provincia de la Verapaz hecha por los religiosos de Santo Domingo de Coban, 1754. Anales, Vol. 28, pp. 18-31. Sociedad de Geográfia e Historia, Guatemala.

VILLAGUTIERRE Y SOTO-MAYOR, J. DE

1933   Historia de la conquista de la provincia de el Itza, reducción y progresos de la de el Lacandon. Biblioteca "Goathemala," Vol. 9. Sociedad de Geografía e Historia, Guatemala.

VOGT, EVON Z.

1969   Zinacantan: A Maya Community in the Highlands of Chiapas. Belknap Press, Cambridge.

WAGNER, PHILLIP

1963   Indian Economic Life in Chiapas. Economic Geography, Vol. 34, pp. 156-64.

WAIBEL, LEO

1933   Die Sierra Madre de Chiapas. Mitteilungen der Geographischen Gesell-schaft in Hamburg, Vol. 43, pp. 12-162. Hamburg.

1946   La Sierra Madre de Chiapas. Sociedad de Geografia y Estadística de Mexico.

WALLRATH, MATTHEW

1967   Excavations in the Tehuantepec Region, Mexico. Transactions of the American Philosophical Society, New Series, Vol. 57, Part 2. Philadelphia.

WARNER, JOHN AND LYNN ELLEN DIXON

1969   An Ethnographic Survey in Central-East Guatemala. Ms.

WARREN, BRUCE W.

1961   The Archaeological Sequence at Chiapa de Corzo. In Los Mayas del sur y sus relaciones con Nahuas meridionales. Sociedad Mexicana de Antropología, Mexico.

1964   A Hypothetical Reconstruction of Mayan Origins. In Proceedings of the 25th International Congress of Americanists, pp. 289-305. Mexico.

WEIGAND, PHIL C.

1971   The Ahualulco Site and the Shaft Tomb Complex of the Etzatlán Area. Paper presented at the 36th annual meeting of the Society for American Archaeology, Norman.

WEST, ROBERT C.

1961   Aboriginal Sea Navigation between Middle

and South America. *American Anthropologist*, Vol. 63, No. 1, pp. 133–35. Menasha.

1964 Surface Configuration and associated geology of Middle America. *Handbook of Middle American Indians*, Vol. 1, pp. 33–83. University of Texas Press, Austin.

WILLEY, GORDON R, T. PATRICK CULBERT AND R. E. W. ADAMS, EDITORS
1967 Maya Lowland Ceramics: A Report from the 1965 Guatemala City Conference. *American Antiquity*, Vol. 32, pp. 289–315.

WITTFOGEL, KARL A.
1957 *Oriental Despotism: A Study in Total Power.* Yale University Press, New Haven.

WOLF, ERIC
1959 *Sons of the Shaking Earth.* The University of Chicago Press, Chicago.

WOODBURY, RICHARD B. AND AUBREY S. TRIK
1953 *The Ruins of Zaculeu, Guatemala.* The William Byrd Press, Richmond.

WOODWARD, J.
1970 Technology and Organization. In *The Sociology of Organizations: Basic Studies,* edited by O. Grusky and G. A. Miller. The Free Press, Glencoe.

WOOLRICH B., MANUEL A.
1948 *Enciclopedia Chiapaneca, Parte III: Hidrología,* pp. 169–280. Sociedad Mexicana de Geografía y Estadística (reprint). Mexico.

WRIGHT, A. C. S.
1970 A Classification of the Soils of the South Toledo District, Belize, in Terms of their Utility to the Classic Maya. Ms.

XIMÉNEZ, FRAY FRANCISCO
1929–
1931 *Historia de la provincia de San Vicente de Chiapa y Guatemala de la orden de predicadores.* Biblioteca "Goathemala," Sociedad de Geografía e Historia. Guatemala.

VAN ZANTWIJK, RUDOLF
1963 Los últimos reductos de la lengua Nahuatl en los altos de Chiapas. *Tlalocan,* Vol. 4, No. 2, pp. 179–84. Mexico.

1970 Las organizaciones social-económica y religiosa de los mercaderes gremiales Aztecas. *Boletín de Estudios Latino-Americanos,* Vol. 10, pp. 1–20.

ZIMMERMAN, GUNTER
1955 Das Cotogue. Die Maya-Sprache von Chicomucelo. *Zeitschrift für Ethnologie,* Vol. 80, pp. 59–87. Braunschweig.

ZORITA, ALONSO DE
1942 *Breve y sumaria relación de los señores de la Nueva España,* translated with an introduction by Benjamin Keen. Phoeniz House, London.

1963 *Breve y sumaria relación de los señores de la Nueva España.* Universidad Nacional Autónoma de México, Mexico.

ZÚÑIGA, FR. DIEGO DE
1608 *Diccionario Pocomchi-Castellano y Pocomchi de San Cristóbal Cahcol.* Copy in Peabody Museum Library, Harvard University.